Revisiting the Question of Imputation in Corporate Criminal Law

Revisiting the Question of Imputation in Corporate Criminal Law

By

Constantine N. Nana

CAMBRIDGE SCHOLARS

PUBLISHING

Revisiting the Question of Imputation in Corporate Criminal Law,
by Constantine N. Nana

This book first published 2010

Cambridge Scholars Publishing

12 Back Chapman Street, Newcastle upon Tyne, NE6 2XX, UK

British Library Cataloguing in Publication Data
A catalogue record for this book is available from the British Library

ISBN (10): 1-4438-1919-0, ISBN (13): 978-1-4438-1919-0

In loving memory of my father and mentor, Dr M.F. Nana Nukechap

TABLE OF CONTENTS

Preface ix
Acknowledgements xi
Table of Cases xii
Table of Statutes xx

Chapter One 1
The Lack of Coherence and Integrity
Source of the problem

Chapter Two 15
Circumscribing the Nature of the Corporation within Criminal Law Discourse
2.1 Introduction
2.2 Ascertaining the corporation as an entity in esse
2.3 Ascertaining the corporate entity in esse as a legal person
2.4 Ascertaining the corporate entity in esse as a responsible legal person
2.5 Conclusion

Chapter Three 61
The Adaptability of the Criminal Law in Dealing with the Corporate Person
3.1 Introduction
3.2 Direct (non-derivative) liability
3.3 Secondary (derivative) liability
3.4 Conclusion

Chapter Four 99
Generating Parameters for Determining an Appropriate Mechanism of Imputation
4.1 Introduction
4.2 From rule of attribution to mechanism of imputation
4.3 Parameters for determining the appropriate mechanism
4.4 Conclusion

Chapter Five **143**
Substantive Evaluation of the Applicable Mechanisms of Imputation
5.1 Introduction
5.2 The identification doctrine
5.3 Evaluating the senior management failure test
5.4 Conclusion

Chapter Six **177**
Substantive Evaluation of Alternative Mechanisms of Imputation
6.1 Introduction
6.2 The vicarious liability doctrine
6.3 The aggregation doctrine
6.4 The corporate culture mechanism
6.5 Conclusion

Chapter Seven **225**
Evaluating the Mechanisms with Reference to the Rules of Adjudication
7.1 Introduction
7.2 Rules governing the prosecutorial decision-making process
7.3 Sanctioning the corporate offender
7.4 Conclusion

Chapter Eight **275**
Conclusion
8.1 Introduction
8.2 Determining the least inadequate mechanism
8.3 Modifying the least inadequate mechanism
8.4 The modified aggregation mechanism as the appropriate mechanism
8.5 Concluding Thoughts

References 311

Index 337

PREFACE

The debate on the validity and effectiveness of the use of the criminal law to regulate the activities of corporations is ongoing and may continue for the next centenary. This debate is particularly fuelled by the inconsistency in the way courts impose criminal liability on corporations. The inconsistency persists because of the quandary of imputing acts and intents (or causal relationships) of agents to corporations in order to hold the latter liable. A choice is required between conventionalised principles that extend a corporation's liability to all offences perpetrated by all of its agents within the scope of their authority and principles that restrict the corporation's liability to the offences perpetrated by only a few agents that are often remote from routine management. As such, legislators in many countries have heeded the advice of some commentators that the process for adjudicating claims that a corporation has violated the criminal law should be improved by sacrificing procedural justice on the altar of speed, simplicity and cost effectiveness.

However, this book argues that facilitating the prosecution and conviction of corporations undermines fundamental principles of the criminal law and flouts the rule of law by disregarding the rights of the (corporate) defendant. It maintains that the legitimacy and efficacy of the system geared towards regulating corporate behaviour depends on the coherence and consistency in the way courts impute acts and intents of agents to corporations. This book therefore revisits the question of imputation because it is the linchpin that prevents the concept of corporate criminal liability from sliding off the axles of the criminal law and the rule of law. My objective is to demonstrate that the string of contradictions and impediments stretching across substantive and procedural corporate criminal law may be avoided if courts refer to an ascertained way of imputing acts and intents of agents to corporations. This ascertained way of imputation is referred to as a 'mechanism of imputation' and it is submitted that the more appropriate the mechanism the higher the chances of overcoming impediments and eliminating contradictions in corporate criminal law.

A three-step process will be adopted to achieve the objective. The first step involves elaborating on the lack of coherence and integrity in the imputation of acts and intents (or causal relationships) to corporations caused by the disjunction of rules invoked by courts. The second step involves establishing parameters by which mechanisms of imputation may be evaluated in order to determine whether they are appropriate or not. The third step involves evaluating a number of samples with reference to the established parameters. Five mechanisms of imputation applicable in the United Kingdom and in some jurisdictions that may trace their legal heritage to the United Kingdom will be evaluated.

I will then submit that although none of the mechanisms evaluated may be deemed to be fully appropriate, the aggregation doctrine is the least inadequate. This is because it can best be aligned with propositions of how the criminal liability of corporations may be established on a coherent and consistent basis. As such, if criminal law courts and agencies employ the aggregation doctrine as modified in this book, acts and intents of agents would be attributed to corporations on a consistent basis and the criminal law would be used to regulate the activities of corporations in a more coherent and justifiable manner.

This book discusses the law as ordained and specified in the sources available to me as at 30 June 2009.

ACKNOWLEDGEMENTS

I would like to express my gratitude to Professor Celia Wells, Dr Sam Middlemisss, Professor Rebecca Wallace and Dr Sarah Christie who examined this study as a doctoral thesis. I acknowledge the benefit of their criticisms and guidance. My kindest regards also extend to Professor Louis De Koker, with whom I worked as a research student and had very fruitful discussions about the prosecution and sanctioning of corporations.

I am grateful to my friends and colleagues whose pertinent interest in my work has been a strong motivation for excellence. I am especially grateful to Afolabi, Sathia, Abih, Bee Ching, Kofi, Crispen, Lucy, Jerry, Owusu, Joy, Esse, Besi, Diego, Omo, Daniel, Maggie and Patrice.

It is not possible to name all those who contributed in one way or the other, especially when it is difficult to recall names such as those of the courteous lady at the Institute of Advanced Legal Studies and the particularly punctual gentleman of the Law Commission who sent me soft copies of old reports.

Most important are the love of God and the moral support of my family and family-in-law. I would like to thank my mother and father (who was with us for two of the three years) and my brothers and sisters.

Finally, I am very grateful to my wife, for her love, commendable proofreading skills and celebrated perseverance.

TABLE OF CASES

UNITED KINGDOM

-A-

Admiralty v Owners of the Steamship Divina (The Truculent) [1951] 2 All ER 968
Alphacell Ltd v Woodward [1972] AC 824
Armstrong v Strain [1952] 1 KB 232
Attorney-General of Hong Kong v Lee Kwong-Kut [1993] AC 951
Attorney General's Reference (No 2 of 1982) [1984] QB 624
Attorney-General's Reference (No 2) [2000] 3 All ER 182 CA
Attorney-General's Reference (No 3 of 1994) [1997] 3 All ER 936
Austin Reed Ltd v Royal Assurance Co Ltd [1956] 3 All ER 490

-B-

B v DPP [2000] 1 All ER 833
Baden v Société Générale Pour Favoriser le Développement du Commerce et de l'Industrie en France [1993] 1 WLR 509
Baldwin v Casella (1872) LR 7 Exc 325
Bank of India v Morris [2005] EWCA Civ 693
Banque Internationale de Commerce de Petrograd v Goukassov [1923] 2 KB 682
Barwick v English Joint Stock Bank (1867) LR 2 Ex 259
Bater v Bater [1950] 2 All ER 458
Baxter v H.M. Advocate 1998 SLT 414
Belmont Finance Corporation Ltd v Williams Furniture Ltd and Others [1979] Ch 250

-C-

Canadian Pacific Railway v Lockhart (1942) AC 591
Cartesio Oktató és Szolgáltató bt [2008] BCC 745
Compania Maritima San Basilio SA v Oceanus Mutual
Underwriting Association (Bermuda) Ltd [1977] QB 49
Co. Inst., Pt. III, ch.7
Coppen v Moore (No 2) (1898) 2 QB 306
Chuter v Freeth and Pocock Ltd [1911] 2 KB 832
Citizen's Life Assurance Co Ltd v Brown [1904] AC 423

-D-

Dean v John Menzies (Holdings) Ltd 1981 JC 23
Director of Public Prosecution v Kent and Sussex Contractors Ltd [1944] 1 KB 146
Docherty v Brown 1996 SLT 355
Donoghue v Stevenson [1932] AC 562
DPP of Northern Ireland v Lynch [1975] AC 653
DPP of Northern Ireland v Maxwell [1978] 1 WLR 1350
Dubai Aluminium Co Ltd v Salaam and Others [2003] 2 AC 366
Duchy of Lancaster Case (1561) 75 ER 325

-E-

Edwards v Brooks (Milk Ltd) [1963] 3 All ER 62
El Ajou v Dollar Land Holdings Plc [1993] 3 All ER 717
El Ajou v Dollar Land Holdings Plc [1994] 2 All ER 685
Eley v Positive Government Life Security Assurance Co 1876 1 ExD 88
Espin v Pemberton (1859) 3 De G & J 547
Eyston v Studd (1574) 75 ER 688

-F-

Fanton v Denville [1932] 2 KB 309
Foss v Harbottle (1843) 2 Hare 461

-G-

Gammon (Hong Kong) Ltd v Attorney-General of Hong Kong [1985] AC 1
Gencor v Dalby [2000] 2 BCLC 734
Gilford Motor Company Ltd v Horne [1933] Ch 935
Glinski v McIver [1962] AC 726

-H-

Hamlyn v Houston & Co [1903] 1 KB 81
Harrow London Borough Council v Shah [1999] 3 All ER 302
Hedley Byrne & Co Ltd v Heller & Partners Ltd [1964] AC 465
Hickman v Kent or Romney Marsh Sheep-Breeders' Association Ltd [1915] 1 Ch 881
HL Bolton (Engineering) Ltd v TJ Graham & Sons Ltd [1957] 1 QB 159
HM Advocate v Camerons 1911 2 SLT 108
HM Advocate v Tannahill and Neilson 1943 JC
Huzzey v Field (1835) 2 CM & R 432

-I-

Irving and Irving v Post Office [1987] IRLR 289

-J-

J C Houghton & Co v Nothard, Lowe & Wills Ltd [1928] AC 1
John Henshall (Quarries) Ltd v Harvey [1965] 2 QB 233

-K-

Kennedy v Green (1834) 3 My & K 699
Kirkheaton District Local Board v *Ainley Sons & Co* (1892) 2 QB 274

-L-

Lee v Lee Air's Farming [1961] AC 12
Lennard's Carrying Co Ltd v Asiatic Petroleum Co Ltd (1915) AC 705
Leicester University v A [1999] ICR 701
Lewis v Buckpool Golf Club [1993] SLT 43
Leyland Shipping Co v *Norwich Union Fire Insurance Society* [1918] AC 350
Lister and Others v Hesley Hall Ltd [2002] 1 AC 215

-M-

M v Vincent [1998] ICR 17
Majrowski v Guy's and St Thomas' NHS Trust [2007] 1 AC 224
Maxwell and Others v HM Advocate 1980 JC 40
Meridian Global Financial Management Asia Ltd v Securities Commission [1995] 2 AC 500
Moore v I Bresler [1944] 2 KBD 515
Morris v CW Martin & Sons Ltd [1966] 1 QB 716
Morse v Slue (1674) 1 Vent 190
Moses v *Midland Railway Co* (1915) 113 LT 451
Mousell Bros v London and North Western Rail Co [1916-17] All ER Rep 1101
Myers v DPP [1965] AC 1001

-N-

National Coal Board v Gamble (1959) 1 QB 11
National Rivers Authority v Alfred McAlpine East Homes Ltd [1994] 4 All ER 286
Nelson v Larholt [1948] 1 KB 339
Nisbett v Dixon and Company (1852) 14 D 973

-O-

OLL Ltd v Secretary of State for Transport [1997] 3 All ER 897

-P-

Paton v HM Advocate 1936 JC 19
Pearks, Gunston and Tee, Ltd v Ward [1902] 2 KB 1
Pharmaceutical Society v London & Provincial Supply Association (1880) 5 App Cas 857
Priestly v Fowler (1837) 1 M and W 1 (Ex Ch)
Purcell Meats (Scotland) Ltd v McLeod 1986 SCCR 672

-Q-

Quinn v Cunningham 1956 JC 22

-R-

R v Adomako [1995] 1 AC 171
R v Alan Mark, Nationwide Heating Services Ltd [2004] EWCA Crim 2490
R v Andrews-Weatherfoil Ltd [1972] 1 All ER 65
R v Associated Octel Co Ltd [1996] 4 All ER 826
R v Bateman (1925) 19 Cr App R 8
R v Birmingham and Gloucester Railway Company 3 QB 224
R v Blamires Transport Services Ltd (1963) 3 WLR 496
R v British Steel [1995] 1 WLR 1356
R v Buck and Buck (1960) 44 Cr App R 213
R v Caldwell [1982] AC 341
R v Corporation of Stanford upon Avon (1811) 14 East 348
R v Cory Bros [1927] 1 KB 810
R v Creamer [1965] 3 All ER 257
R v Crown Prosecution Service, Ex parte Waterworth [1996] COD 277
R v Dennis Clothier and Sons Ltd (Bristol Crown Court, 23 October 2002, Unreported)
R v English Brothers Ltd & Melvyn Hubbard (Northampton Crown Court, 30 July 2001, Unreported)
R v Forman and Ford [1988] Crim LR 677
R v Gateway Foodmarkets [1997] 3 All ER 78
R v Great Western Trains Co Ltd [2000] QB 796
R v Hertfordshire County Council ex parte Green Environmental Industries Ltd and another [2000] 1 All ER 773
R v Hinggis (1730) 2 Ld Raym 1574
R v HM Coroner for East Kent, Ex parte Spooner and Others (1989) 88 Cr App R 10
R v HM Coroner for Reading ex parte West Berkshire Housing Consortium Ltd. Unreported, 11 July 1995 CO/2994/94

R v Holbrook (1878) 4 QBD 42
R v Howe and Sons (Engineers) Ltd [1999] 2 All ER 249
R v ICR Haulage [1944] 1 KB 551
R v Inhabitants of Dorset (1825) 77 ER 1442
R v Jackson Transport (Osett) Ltd 1996 (Unreported) 18 *Health and Safety at Work*, November 1999
R v JF Alford Transport Ltd [1997] CLR 745
R v London (North) Industrial Tribunal, ex Parte Associated Newspapers [1998] ICR 1212
R v McDonnell [1966] 1 QB 233
R v Muhamad (2003) QB 1031
R v Northern Strip Mining Construction Co Ltd (1 February1965, Unreported)
R v OLL Ltd and Kite [1996] 2 Cr App R 295
R v Prentice [1993] 4 All ER 935
R v P & O European Ferries (Dover) Ltd (1991) 93 Cr App R 72
R v Rayment and Others Central Criminal Court, 24 March 2005 (Unreported)
R v Robert Millar (Contractors) Ltd and Robert Millar (1970) 1 All ER 577
R v Seymour [1983] 2 AC 493
R v Scartlett [1993] Crim LR 288
R v Steven and Wye Railway Co (1819) 2 B & Ald 645
R v Summers [1952] 1 All ER 1059
R v Telggaard Hardwood (UK) Ltd (Hull Crown Court, 24 February 2004 – Unreported)
R v The Great North of England Railway Company (1846) 115 ER 1294
R v Wacker [2003] 1 Cr App R 329
R v Walker (1992) 13 Cr App R (S) 474
RC Hammet Ltd v London County Council (1933) 97 JP 105
Re A (Children) Conjoined Twins: Surgical Separation [2004] 4 All ER 961
Re European Bank (1870) LR 5 Ch App 358
Re Hampshire Land Co [1896] 2 Ch 743
Re Sevenoaks Stationers (Retail) Ltd [1990] BCC 765
Re Supply of Ready Mixed Concrete [1995] 1 AC 456
Reader's Digest Association Ltd v Pirie 1973 JC 42
Real Estate Opportunities Ltd v Aberdeen Asset Managers Jersey Ltd and others [2007] Bus LR 971
Richmand v Russell Mcnee and Company (1849) 11 D 1035

Rio Tinto Zinc Corporation v Westinghouse Electric Corporation [1978] 1 All ER 434
Roberts v Woodward (1890) 25 QBD 412
Rose v Plenty [1976] 1 WLR 141
Rubie v Faulkner [1946] 1 KB 571
Rudd v Elder Dempster & Co [1933] 1 KB 566
Russell v Men of Devon 100 ER 359 (1788)
Rylands v Fletcher [1868] UKHL 1

-S-

Salmon v Quin and Axtens Limited [1909] AC 442
Salomon v Salomon and Co Ltd [1897] AC 22
Standard Chartered Bank v Pakistan National Shipping Corporation [2002] 3 WLR 1547
Stanley Tenant v Stanley [1906] 1 Ch 131
Stone v Dobinson [1977] QB 354
Stoneleigh Finance Ltd v Phillips [1965] 2 QB 537
Stone & Rolls Ltd (in liquidation) v Moore Stephens (a firm) and another [2008] 3 WLR 1146
Sutton's Hospital Case [1558-1774] All ER 11
Sweet v *Parsley* [1970] AC 132

-T-

Tate Access Floors Inc v Boswell [1990] 3 All ER 303
Tesco Supermarkets Ltd v Nattrass [1972] AC 153
Tesco Stores Ltd v Brent London Borough Council [1993] 2 All ER 718
The Lady Gwendolen [1965] 2 All ER 283
Transco Plc v HM Advocate (No 2) 2004 SCCR 553
Tremblay v Daigle [1989] 2 SCR 530
Triplex Safety Glass Co Ltd v Lancegaye Safety Glass Ltd [1939] 2 KB 395
Tuberville v Stampe (1697) 1 Ld Ray 264

-W-

W v HM Advocate 1982 SLT 420
Walkers Snack Foods Ltd v Coventry City Council [1998] 3 All ER 164
Whitfield v South Eastern Railway Co (1858) 120 ER 451
Williams v A&W Hemphill Ltd 1986 SC (HL) 31
Williams v Natural Life Health Foods Ltd [1998] 1 WLR 830
Willion v Berkley (1561) 75 ER 345
Wills v Tozer (1904) 53 WR 74

Wilson and Clyde Coal Company Ltd v English (1937) 53 TLR 944
Woodhead v Gartness Mineral Company (1877) 4 R 469

-Y-
Yorkshire Dale Steamship Co Ltd v *Minister of War Transport, The Coxwold* [1942] AC 691

EUROPEAN COURTS

Agrotexim Hellas SA and Others v Greece (1996) 21 EHRR 250
Autronic AG v Switzerland (1990) 12 EHRR
Belgium v Spain ICJ Rep (1970) 3
Demuth v Switzerland (2001) 31 EHRR 772
Pudas v Sweden (1998) 10 EHRR 30
Saunders v United Kingdom [1997] 23 EHRR 313
Uberseering BV v Nordic Construction Company Baumanagement GmbH (NCC) C-208/00 ECJ 2002

AUSTRALIA

Brambles Holdings Ltd v Carey (1976) 15 SASR 270
Fightvision Pty Ltd v Onisforou (1999) 47 NSWLR 473
S and Y Investments (No 2) Pty Ltd v Commercial Union Assurance Co of Australia Ltd (1986) 82 FLR 130

CANADA

Bazley v Curry (1999) 174 DLR (4th) 45
Blackwater v Plint 2005 SCC 58
Jacobi v Griffiths (1999)174 DLR (4th) 71
R v Canadian Dredge & Dock Ltd (1985) 19 CCC (3d) 1
R v Safety Kleen Canada Inc (1997), 145 DLR (4th) 276
"Rhone" (The) v "Peter BB Widener" (The), [1993] 1 SCR 497
Tremblay v Daigle [1989] 2 SCR 530

NETHERLANDS

IJzerdraad Hoge Raad, February 23, 1954 NJ 378

NEW ZEALAND

Baby P (An Unborn Child) [1995] NZFLR 577
Gifford v Police [1965] NZLR 484
Harvey v Whitehead (1911) 30 NZLR 795
Natural Life Health Foods and *Trevor Ivory Ltd v Anderson* [1992] 2 NZLR 517

SOUTH AFRICA

N K v Ministry of Safety and Security [2005] JOL 14864 (CC)

UNITED STATES

Commonwealth v Pulaski County Agric & Mech Association 17 SW 442 (1891)
Dartmouth College v Woodward, 4 Wheat 518 (1819)
Liverpool and London Life and Fire Insurance Company v Commonwealth of Massachusetts 77 US 10 Wallace 566 (1870)
New York Central and Hudson River Railroad v United States 212 US 481 (1909)
Riggs v Palmer 115 NY 506 (1889)
United States v Bank of New England 821 F 2nd 844 Court of Appeals (First Circuit) 1987
United States v TIME-DC, Inc 381 F Supp 730 (1974)
United States v Twentieth Century Fox Film Corp 882 F2d 656 (2d Cir. 1989)

TABLE OF STATUTES

ACTS OF PARLIAMENT

UNITED KINGDOM

Criminal Law Act 1827
Railway Clauses Consolidation Act 1845
Accessories and Abettors Act 1861
Offences Against the Person Act 1861
Salmon Fishery Act 1861
Sale of Food and Drugs Act 1875
Rivers Pollution Prevention Act 1876
Merchant Shipping Act 1894
Interpretation Act 1899
Sale of Food and Drugs Act 1899
Finance (No. 2) Act 1940
Law Reform (Personal Injuries) Act 1948
Occupiers' Liability Act 1957
Occupier's Liability (Scotland) Act 1960
Carriage of Air Act 1961
Criminal Evidence Act 1965
Trade Descriptions Act 1968
Unsolicited Goods and Services Act 1971
Fair Trading Act 1973
Defective Premises Act 1972
Control of Pollution Act 1974
Health and Safety at Work etc Act 1974
Criminal Procedure (Scotland) Act 1975
Criminal Law Act 1977
Civil Liability (Contribution) Act 1978
Magistrate's Court Act 1980
Criminal Attempts Act 1981
Occupiers' Liability Act 1984
Companies Act 1985
Prosecution of Offences Act 1985
Company Directors Disqualification Act 1986
Income and Corporations Taxes Act 1988

Environmental Protection Act 1990
Criminal Justice and Public Order Act 1994
Criminal Justice (Scotland) Act 1995
Criminal Procedure (Scotland) Act 1995
Merchant Shipping Act 1995
Competition Act 1998
Scotland Act of 1998
Financial Services and Markets Act 2000
Insolvency Act 2000
Enterprise Act 2002
Criminal Justice Act 2003,
Companies Act 2006
Fraud Act 2006
Legislative and Regulatory Reform Act 2006
Corporate Manslaughter and Corporate Homicide Act 2007

AUSTRALIA
Australian Courts Act 1828
Interpretation Act 1918
Interpretation Act 1919
Australia Act 1986
Australian Criminal Code 1995

CANADA
Canadian Criminal Code 1985 as amended by Bill C-45

FRANCE
Code Pénal 1992

NEW ZEALAND
New Zealand Securities Amendment Act 1988

SOUTH AFRICA
South African Criminal Procedure Act 1977

UNITED STATES
Currency Transaction Report Act 1982

STATUTORY AND PREROGATIVE INSTRUMENTS

UNITED KINGDOM

Defence (General) Regulations 1939
Motor Fuel Rationing (No. 3) Order 1941
Convention on the Limitation of Liability for
Maritime Claims 1976
Companies (Northern Ireland) Order 1986
Treaty Establishing the European Community (Consolidated Version 2001)
Prosecution Code, 2001
Code for Crown Prosecutors, 2004
Control of Asbestos Regulation 2006
Asbestos License Assessment Guide 2007
Regulators' Compliance Code 2008

DRAFT CODES

UNITED KINGDOM

Corporate Manslaughter: The Government's Draft Bill for Reform Cm 6497, March 2005
Draft Corporate Manslaughter Bill Cm 6755, March 2006
Corporate Manslaughter and Corporate Homicide Bill 220, July 2006 220
Fraud (Trial Without a Jury) Bill 31 HL 2006/2007

UNITED STATES

Model Penal Code 1956 (Proposed Official Draft)

CHAPTER ONE

THE LACK OF COHERENCE AND INTEGRITY

There is some degree of consensus that a corporation[1] is a distinct person and criminal liability may be imposed upon it for offences committed *qua* corporation.[2] Nonetheless, this logic has not always guided courts in the United Kingdom. They have imposed criminal liability on corporations due to the entreaty of the equity or spirit of the relevant statute or to further public interests and this seriously compromises efforts at assembling related rules of corporate criminal liability within a rational whole. The first thing a researcher notes while going through cases in corporate criminal law is a sequence of contradictions and lack of integrity. Some commentators contend that this is because corporate criminal liability evolved around the notion of individualism[3] and without a cogent theoretical base.[4] However, the contention that criminal law principles were established only with individuals in mind may hardly be justified. Mestre[5] and Valeur[6] have shown that criminal sanctions were imposed on collective entities as far back as the Roman era and Schlegel[7]

---

[1] The term 'corporation' is used in this book as a synonym of 'company.' Both forms of association have a common origin (See Hickson and Turner, 2005: 3) and have been used interchangeably to refer to business undertakings that have attributes such as legal personality, limited liability and perpetuity. See also Png, 2001: 4. However, Gower (1956: 1371-1372) intimated that many American legislators prefer the term 'corporation' while British legislators often use 'company.' See also Nicholls (2005: 6-7) on the use of both terms (as well as 'body corporate') for a single taxon by Canadian legislators.

[2] See Ragozino, 1995: 424 and 441-443; Png, 2001: 1; and Wells, 2001: 3.

[3] See Schlegel, 1990: ix; Fisse and Braithwaite, 1993: 19; Wells, 2001: 1; and Gobert and Punch, 2003: 3 and 46. Some commentators have employed this argument to buttress their opposition to the use of the criminal law to regulate the activities of corporations. See Wolf, 1985; and Khanna, 1995.

[4] See Schlegel, 1990: 5, 14; Fisse and Braithwaite, 1993: 101; and Wells, 1993: 551. *Cf* Png, 2001: 1.

[5] 1899: 34.

[6] 1931: 9-10.

[7] 1990: ix.

asserts that corporations have violated criminal law standards since their inception.[8] Also, if it is accepted that the criminal law has always targeted criminal behaviour then all 'persons' capable of conducting themselves in such a manner as to breach criminal law standards may be said to have always been the concern of the criminal law.[9] Thus, one may contend that the lack of coherence and integrity manifested in corporate criminal law is due to the lack of a cogent theoretical base. However, the search for such a base may undermine the practical utility of the subject especially where theoretical legal scholarship (as opposed to doctrinal analysis) is conceived of as the study of the law from an 'external' standpoint.[10] This is because leaving the door open to the use of external knowledge may be as good as opening the floodgate to a plethora of contradictions.[11] Hence, it may be important to first of all avoid contradiction and incoherence internally or within the legal frame before delineating instances where external knowledge may be sought.[12]

In other words, building the theoretical framework of corporate criminal law involves achieving internal coherence[13] and integrity[14] in the

---

[8] It is generally agreed for example that the principle of vengeance was the earliest source of criminal liability. See Holmes, 1938: 39-40; Binavince, 1964: 1-2; and McVisk, 1978: 75. However, vengeance does not relate only to the actions of individuals since collective actions by groups may equally be incited by a collective feeling of vindictiveness.

[9] We may therefore agree with Tur (1987: 123) that there is no general law that applies to persons but rather sets of rules governing relationships and determining liabilities.

[10] 'External' here refers to non-legal. This follows from Hart's (1994: 102-103) distinction between external and internal points of view. See also Cheffins' (1999: 197-198) definition of theoretical legal scholarship. See also Green (2005: 565) who contends that a theory of law is an explanation of cosmopolitan import.

[11] If judges are allowed to import knowledge from the wide varieties of non-legal categories that may have relevance in a case the number of contradictions would certainly increase exponentially.

[12] It may be important to avoid instances where judges give regard to ideas "plucked literally from the air." See Harris, 2001: 226.

[13] Coherence here is held to mean that rules and their interpretations by courts are logically connected in a rational whole. See MacCormick, 2005: 189, 190 and 206. See also Siems, 2008: 149. In other words, the assortment of propositions that judges and legislators introduce ought to be consistent with each other within a rationale whole, which is the criminal law.

[14] Integrity may be understood here to imply that the interpretation of statutes and precedent by judges is governed by principles such as fairness and good conscience (see Dworkin, 1986: 225). However, these principles ought to conform

different ways in which courts impose criminal liability and sanctions on corporations. This will in turn delimit instances where external viewpoints may be imported into corporate criminal law discourse. However, owing to the fact that corporations invariably act through the agency of natural persons, coherence and integrity may actually be achieved only if the disparate ways in which courts impute acts and intents (or causal relationships) to corporations for the purposes of imposing criminal liability and sanctions on the latter are harmonised. Such harmonisation in turn requires establishing common ways of interpreting rules of statutes and precedent through mechanisms designed to collate relevant rules. It will be shown here that each jurisdiction has at least one of such mechanisms because it is the logical consequence of the endeavour by courts and Parliament to ascertain a measure of determining when the act or knowledge of an agent will be imputed to the corporation under defined circumstances. Equally, it will be shown that each mechanism comprises a number of rules that indicate the requisite pattern of attributing acts and intents to corporations for the purposes of imposing criminal liability and sanctions on them. As such, the proposition I am putting forward is that where courts are guided by an appropriate mechanism of imputing acts and intents (or causal relationships) to corporations the probability of achieving coherence and integrity in the ways in which criminal liability and sanctions are imposed on corporations will be higher.

Source of the Problem

Early judgements that affirmed the separate personality of corporations[15] and some early commentators that endorsed the ideal[16] did not explain why and how corporations ought to be distinct persons in law. This certainly pushed other commentators like Thurman[17] to contend that the idea was similar to that of the divine right of kings in a much earlier day.[18]

---

to past standards to such an extent that "like cases are treated alike" in line with the contentions of Perelman (1963); Hart (1994); and Ashworth (2000).

[15] *Salomon v Salomon and Co Ltd* [1897] AC 22, hereinafter referred to as *Salomon*; *Lee v Lee Air's Farming* [1961] AC 12.

[16] See Freund, 1897: 52-55; and Maitland, 1900b: 335.

[17] 1937: 185.

[18] This is also supported by Brickey (1988: 593) who contends that "just as primitive art and artefacts depicted inanimate beasts and gods as creatures possessed of human traits, so did common-law courts breathe life into the corporate form." See also Maitland, 1900a: xxx; Dewey, 1926: 655; and Radin, 1932: 643.

As such, the failure to seek justification for rules such as the separate personality of corporations has led to much confusion with regard to the nature of the corporate person within criminal law discourse. It has nonetheless been posited that any theorists attempting to premise their study with an answer to the question of what is a corporation would be confronted with an ideological battle at the onset.[19] However, Fisse and Braithwaite make an interesting remark which may be deemed to advise the contrary. They state that "[i]f we understood how organisations decide to break the law or how they drift into breaking the law, we might be able to prescribe legal accountability principles which are consonant with organisational realities."[20] Wells[21] equally advances that questions about the nature of the corporation are indispensable to the establishment of corporate fault and deplores the fact that many commentators have readily assumed that these questions were settled by the recognition of the corporation's separate personality by courts and Parliament.[22] Nonetheless, in order to avoid a dogmatic assertion,[23] attempts at justifying the corporation's entity status have often focussed on distinguishing between individualist (or atomic or reductionist) and collectivist (or holistic) perspectives of the corporate entity[24] and "fiction" and "realist" explanations.[25] As such, it may be posited that the absence of a theoretical base (and the lack of integrity) is due to the inability of courts and legislators to make a clear choice between these competing theories or to harmonise and standardise them.

This is exemplified by the fact that a corporation was held to be identifiable only with senior officers in one case,[26] but in another case it was identified with a junior employee.[27] However, in *Belmont Finance*

---

[19]Hart, 1983: 25-32; and Orts, 1993: 1567-1574.

[20] 1993: 101. See also, Schlegel, 1990: 14; and Gobert and Punch, 2003: 17-18.

[21] 2001: 2 and 74-75.

[22] Wells (2001: 75) cites Holdsworth (1944: ix and 70) to this effect. Her view also echoes that of French (1984) who argues that corporations are morally competent. See Wells, 2001: 155-160.

[23] Marmor (2006: 691) notes that the "essence of dogmatism is the refusal to revise one's conclusion in light of contrary evidence."

[24] See Hessen, 1979: xiv-xviii; Donaldson, 1982: 14-16; French, 1995: 10-13 and 34-35; Wells, 2001: 75-78; and Gobert and Punch, 2003: 17-18.

[25] See Png, 2001: 6-8; and Laufer, 2004: 48-52.

[26] *Tesco Supermarkets Ltd v Nattrass* [1972] AC 153, hereinafter referred to as *Nattrass.*

[27] *R v British Steel* [1995] 1 WLR 1356, hereinafter referred to as *British Steel.*

Corporation Ltd v Williams Furniture Ltd and Others,[28] the court held that a corporation will neither be identified with a junior employee nor a senior officer where it was the agent's targeted victim. Thus, there is no thread linking different decisions but the fact that each judge puts her unique interpretation on the relevant statute or precedent. In the first of these three cases, Lord Reid advanced that the "purpose of this Act must have been to penalise those at fault, not those who were in no way to blame."[29] However, even though equally deciding a case on a corporation's criminal liability, Stein LJ in the second case found no difficulty in holding that "the decision in [*Nattrass*] does not provide the answer to the problem of construction before us. The answer must be found in the words of section 3(1) of the Act of 1974 read in its contextual setting."[30]

As such, whether criminal liability may be imposed on a corporation may be deemed to be strictly a question of interpretation. This means that the prospect of achieving coherence and integrity would be much higher not where judges have to consider whether it would be "irrational" to impute acts and intents to corporations[31] but where their interpretations of the relevant statute or precedent is guided not only by uniform rules governing imputation but also by uniform rules governing interpretation. In the absence of both sets of uniform rules what judges actually do is well illustrated in Lord Hoffmann's dictum in *Meridian Global Financial Management Asia Ltd v Securities Commission*. He posited thus:

> [it] is always a matter of interpretation: given that it was intended to apply to a company, how was it intended to apply? Whose act (or knowledge, or state of mind) was for the purpose intended to count as the act etc. of the company? One finds the answer to this question by applying the usual canons of interpretation, taking into account the language of the rule (if it is a statute) and its content and policy.[32]

This statement begs the question of whether interpretation is solely a matter of the judge's impulse. Equally, it may be important to determine whether the same canons that govern the interpretation of statutory provisions would govern the interpretation of the precedent. Generally, it seems each court has taken the liberty to formulate its own rules of interpretation in order to justify its decision. The result as mentioned

---

[28] [1979] Ch 250. This case is hereinafter referred to as *Belmont*.
[29] *Nattrass* at 174.
[30] *British Steel* at 1361.
[31] Buckley LJ in *Belmont* at 262.
[32] [1995] 2 AC 500 at 507. This case is hereinafter referred to as *Meridian*.

above is that it has been remarkably difficult to predict courts' decisions and ascertain objective standards for fair outcomes. In the words of MacCormick "if everyone has convictions of her or his own, who is to say which subjective conviction is better?"[33] There is no denying that non-legal issues would always influence the contextual interpretation by the judge.[34] However, a judge may not be said to be entitled to curtail or expand legislation in light of her moral leaning.[35] Allan argues that where a common thread may be identified in different interpretations the idea of formulating rules that ought to govern interpretation[36] becomes trivial.[37] In spite of the fact that this may be understood to be a tacit endorsement of judicial activism, if it is deemed to be true then it may be said that the argument ironically works against judge-made rules of interpretation in areas where there is no common thread linking different interpretations in a rational manner. As mentioned above, corporate criminal law is marked by such incoherence.[38] As such, my objective is to show how internal coherence and integrity may be achieved by limiting the interpretive authority of judges.

This limitation must however take into consideration what Allan deems should be the benchmark for assessing the cogency of judges'

[33] 2008a: 150.

[34] Naffine (2003: 361) posits that when judges are required to assign a meaning to the term "person" used by a statute they seek to ascertain how Parliament intended to define such a term and the process of ascertaining Parliament's intended meaning involves "quasi non-legal" and metaphysical questions.

[35] *Cf* Blackstone (1765-1769); and Allan, 2004: 710. Opponents to limitations of the judge's interpretive authority adhere to the doctrine of the equity of the statute that was inspired by Plowden's commentaries on *Eyston v Studd* (1574) 75 ER 688 (hereinafter referred to as *Eyston*) that were in turn inspired by Aristotle's doctrine of valid inference. Plowden's commentaries are discussed succinctly by Behrens (1999).

[36] What Hart (1994: 100-110) called "rules of recognition."

[37] The common thread thus justifies the objectivity of the judges' moral values. See Allan, 2004: 709-711. He seeks to justify Blackstone's (1765-1769) claim that judges have a moral duty to either eliminate a "mischief" created by the statute or provide a "remedy" where it may be just and reasonable to do so.

[38] It may be advanced that the claim that judges are entitled to modify statutes while interpreting them may be deemed to be a rule requiring judges to improvise where they deem it necessary. Thus, whichever way one looks at it judges may be said to be guided by rules governing interpretation although rules that require improvisation favour incoherence and inconsistency. However, Dworkin (1986: 225) maintains that questions about whether a judge is guided by pre-established rules or invents the law are unhelpful because interpretation is a function of the judge's moral capacity.

interpretations: "the reasons of policy and principle that inspired them."[39] These policies and principles constitute the premises of judges' arguments and narrow their lines of reasoning and restrict the scope of their conclusions. Thus, where Coke began with the assumption that "the corporation itself is only in abstracto" and corporations "have no souls" it is only fair that he concluded that a judge cannot interpret a statute as imposing liability on a corporation for treason or any offence that is punished by excommunication.[40] Equally, where Lord Hoffmann premised his dictum on the contention that "[a] company exists because there is a rule (usually in a statute) which says that a persona ficta shall be deemed to exist" it is fair that he concluded that if the judge successfully fits an improvised rule into the legislator's "intended meaning"[41] to the effect that employee X acted as the corporation, then the corporation would be liable for employee X's action.[42] Although sometimes the premise adopted by the judge may be true or even axiomatic,[43] there is the danger that the extent of the corporation's liability would depend not on what the law says a corporation can or cannot do but actually on what the judge thinks the

[39] 2004: 710. This reflects what Dworkin (1986: 225 and 243) described as "principles about justice and fairness and procedural due process."

[40] *Sutton's Hospital Case* [1558-1774] All ER 11 at 22. This case is hereinafter referred to as *Sutton's Hospital*. It must be noted that although this reflected a statement made by Pope Innocent IV in 1245 during the first council in Lyon (See Coffee, 1981: 386, n. 2; Lizee, 1995: 136; and Weismann and Newman, 2007: 419) Coke did not cite any previous authorities to support his contention. He cited two cases which approved of the statement that a "corporate aggregate" cannot do fealty or swear an oath of loyalty: *Duchy of Lancaster Case* (1561) 75 ER 325 (hereinafter referred to as *Duchy of Lancaster*) and *Willion v Berkley* (1561) 75 ER 345. However, a corporation and its members (proprietors) who were assignees to the Corporation of Bath had been jointly indicted for failure to repair a bridge. See 3 Chit. Cr. Law 600 cited by Lord Denman in *R v Birmingham and Gloucester Railway Company* 3 QB 224 (hereinafter referred to as *Birmingham and Gloucester Railway Co*) at 225. As such, Coke's decision was not guided by any legal principle but by his moral leaning.

[41] For discussion on how such an "intended meaning" may be ascertained, see Fuller, 1969: 82-91.

[42] Lord Hoffmann called such an improvised judge-made rule "special rule." See *Meridian* at 506-507.

[43] See for example, Lord Blackburn in *Pharmaceutical Society v London & Provincial Supply Association* (1880) 5 App Cas 857 (hereinafter referred to as *Pharmaceutical Society*) at 870. He posited that "[i]f you could get over the first difficulty of saying that the word 'person' here may be construed to include an artificial person, a corporation, I should not have the least difficulty upon those other grounds which have been suggested."

corporation can or cannot do. As such, a judge held that the word "person" in a statute cannot be understood to mean a corporation where it is impossible for the corporation to perform the duty imposed by statute such as voting at meetings.[44]

This furtive advancement towards judicial activism in corporate criminal law has not only motivated judges to ordain the enforcement of their feelings about the nature of corporations but also to modify the principles of the criminal law to suit such feelings. As such, at the time when the consensus was that corporations could not be held liable for *mens rea* offences,[45] Channel J in a bid to pursue the policy goal of the relevant statute noted thus:

> [b]y the general principles of the criminal law, if a matter is made a criminal offence, it is essential that there should be something in the nature of mens rea, and therefore, in ordinary cases a corporation cannot be guilty of a criminal offence, nor can a master be liable criminally for an offence committed by his servant. But there are exceptions to this rule in the case of quasi-criminal offences, as they may be termed – that is to say, where certain acts are forbidden by law under a penalty...and the reason for this is that the legislature has thought it so important to prevent the particular act from being committed that it absolutely forbids it to be done.[46]

This decision was later on used by Viscount Reading[47] to justify the disregard of the requirement of *mens rea* on the ground that the legislator forbade the act absolutely.[48] Thus, judges may create makeshift offences (quasi-crimes) in order to circumvent the *mens rea* requirement and avoid giving the impression that vicarious criminal liability was imposed. However, even when judges eventually decided that corporations could be guilty of *mens rea* offences they still proceeded to alter criminal law principles. They declared that they were imposing direct or personal

---

[44] See *Wills v Tozer* (1904) 53 WR 74, hereinafter referred to as *Tozer*. This position is criticised in Chapter 3.

[45] For the historical development of corporate criminal law, see Schlegel, 1990: 5-17; Wells, 2001: 86-99; and Gobert and Punch, 2003: 53-68.

[46] *Pearks, Gunston and Tee, Ltd v Ward* [1902] 2 KB 1 at 11. This case is hereinafter referred to as *Pearks, Gunston and Tee.*

[47] *Mousell Bros v London and North Western Rail Co* [1916-17] All ER Rep 1101 at 1105. See also Atkin J (as he then was) at 1106. This case is hereinafter referred to as *Mousell Bros.*

[48] However, absolute liability implies that the legislator has stated that neither *mens rea* nor *actus reus* is required to prove guilt. See Chapter 3 for a brief discussion on absolute liability.

liability but they imposed vicarious liability indirectly. Viscount Caldecote was the first in a long line of judges that proceeded thence.[49] He was inspired by Lord Blackburn's statement in *Pharmaceutical Society* that was to the effect that although a corporation could not obtain competent knowledge independently, it could ("for all substantial purposes of protecting the public") be said to possess competent knowledge of something if it had employed competent agents to obtain such information.[50] Given that the counsel for the respondent company did not object to this proposition,[51] Viscount Caldecote had the leeway for contending that: "[a] company is incapable of acting or speaking or even of thinking except in so far as its officers have acted, spoken or thought." He then proceeded to impute the liability of two officers to the corporation because they were the corporation for this purpose.[52] The precedent on the imposition of criminal liability on corporations for crimes of intent (excluding corporate manslaughter or corporate homicide) and the invocation of the defence of due diligence by a corporation[53] was built around this restricted form of vicarious liability.[54] However, many subsequent decisions have departed from this precedent because judges have defined the nature of a corporation in a different manner and interpreted the relevant statutes as intending that another pattern of imputation be employed.[55]

The undue focus by *Nattrass* on the acts and intents of a few individuals has also left prosecutors in a difficult position given that in most cases the *actus reus* is the result of the combination of the acts of several agents while the *mens rea* is often reflected in the policies and practices adopted within the company. As such, if like cases ought to be treated alike and the accused corporate person is treated as any other accused, the case against a corporation may become unmanageable. Where a corporation invokes the right to silence for example, the few senior

---

[49] *Director of Public Prosecution v Kent and Sussex Contractors Ltd* [1944] 1 KB 146. This case is hereinafter referred to as *Kent and Sussex Contractors*.
[50] *Pharmaceutical Society* at 870.
[51] *Kent and Sussex Contractors Ltd* at 149.
[52] *Kent and Sussex Contractors Ltd* at 155.
[53] *Nattrass*. This case is discussed in Chapters 3 and 5.
[54] The fact that courts do not impute acts and intents of agents to corporations but the liabilities of the agents (even though the agents whose liabilities are imputable are fairly restricted) is no doubt vicarious liability that is still imposed on the corporation.
[55] Thus, *Belmont, Meridian* and *British Steel* do not follow the pattern of imputation affirmed in *Nattrass*.

officers that could be identified with it may not make any statement incriminating it. This is confounded by the fact that in most corporate cases these officers are in possession of the bulk of documents that may be used to prosecute and convict the corporation. However, Parliament has stepped in incuriously. It has given criminal justice agencies such as the Health and Safety Executive (HSE), the Serious Fraud Office (SFO) and the Financial Services Authority (FSA) the power to compel agents to provide incriminating statements. The HSE on its part would not use such evidence against the agent although her act may be imputed to the corporation for the purpose of imposing criminal liability on it; and SFO inquiries are marked by an obligation of those investigated to provide answers. The legislator has equally provided that documentary evidence is admissible during trial provided that the person that supplied the information comprised in the document had or is reasonably expected to have had personal knowledge of the material discussed in the document. Thus, such information will not be hearsay even if it was supplied by an agent that would normally not be identified with the corporation.

Also, given the ambiguity of the corporation's nature it is difficult to determine who or what constitutes its 'peers' or 'fellow citizens' in order to enforce its right to be tried by a jury of its peers. It is uncertain whether other senior officers of other corporations or other employees of other corporations may constitute such a jury. Courts readily use natural persons selected randomly as jurors and so there is apparently no difference between a jury of an artificial person's peers and a jury of a natural person's peers. The ambiguity of the corporation's nature has equally complicated the process of deliberation by a court during trial. It is uncertain which sanction would effectively rehabilitate or incapacitate or deter the corporate offender and other corporations in similar circumstances. The effects of a heavy fine may spill over to employees and even the community; the effectiveness of remedial orders and punitive injunctions is hinged upon the threat of a fine if the corporate offender fails to comply; and suspension and revocation of licence and public censure may also have very severe consequences on the community.

In light of the above, it may be said that when judges seek to answer the question of how the relevant statute or precedent is intended to apply to a corporation they are required to first of all ascertain what a corporation 'is' and whose act or intent would count as that of the corporation. However, in the absence of specific rules guiding the determination of the nature of the corporation and providing for the imputation of acts and intents to corporations they have arbitrarily invoked principles and policies (fairness and justice) which they believe provide 'rational' answers. This arbitrary invocation has been the source of incoherence and inconsistency and has deprived the subject of corporate criminal law of a cogent theoretical base. Thus, it may be important to check the interpretive authority of judges by ascertaining rules that would guide the interpretation of relevant statutes and precedent[56] and also circumscribing the nature of a corporation and delineating a pattern of imputing acts and intents to corporations in defined circumstances.

As such, in Chapter 2 an attempt will be made to circumscribe the nature of the corporation within criminal law discourse. Nonetheless, the urge to begin this study with an inceptive description of the term 'corporation' is met with the fact that legal concepts are generally not amenable to precise definitions.[57] This is compounded by the fact that each word that is used in defining the 'corporation' bears complex meanings within different legal categories.[58] However, there are certain features that are recognised as pertaining to corporate entities by courts and commentators and these features may provide an indication of what a corporation 'is' in criminal law. Hence, a number of 'pedigreed' theories (legal and non-legal) explaining the nature or essence of corporate entities will be discussed. In other to keep focus on the criminal law, the theories will be discussed in light of whether they favour or are resistant to the use of the criminal law to regulate the activities of corporations. A general concept of the nature of a corporation as an entity in *esse* will then be formulated by abstracting properties from these different theories. Equally, the concept of legal personality will be examined and an attempt will be made to determine whether the corporation has the features that may be said to be representational of legal personality. Finally, an attempt will be made to show the relationship between some accounts of responsibility and punishment within the criminal law and the concept of the corporate person. These accounts will be analysed in respect of the two recurrent questions of why a corporation is responsible and why it is punished.

---

[56] This will restrict the inspiration provided by policies and principles (that are neither legal nor relevant) that judges are wont to use as premises.

[57] See Hart, 1983: 47; Nesteruk, 2002: 441; and Lord Hoffmann's foreword to Pinto and Evans, 2003. The second edition (Pinto and Evans, 2008) does not contain Lord Hoffmann's foreword.

[58] Examples include: contract, freedom, public interests, market, managers and employees.

With an ascertained meaning of the term 'corporation' as used in the criminal law (and how it ought to be used) the second problem discussed above, the incoherent and inconsistent use of the criminal law to regulate corporate behaviour, will be addressed. Chapter 3 will discuss the adaptability of the criminal law as reflected in the different forms of liability and offences that Parliament and courts may impose on corporations. The discussion will centre on how the corporation as a legal person and in a system where vicarious liability is not applicable may be held personally or secondarily liable. Different kinds of offences including strict and absolute liability offences and *mens rea* offences (including corporate manslaughter and corporate homicide) will be examined in relation to the sequence in which they have been imposed on corporations over the past 400 years. The principles that have been developed and used by Parliament and courts to justify the imposition of these forms of liability will also be examined. Recommendations will then be made about the need to modify the way these forms of liability are imposed in order to be consistent with how corporate entities function in the eyes of judges and legislators. However, as noted above, there is a disjunction of rules applied by courts to impose different types of liability. As such, it will be submitted that the effectiveness of the criminal law in regulating corporations is largely dependent upon the imposition of appropriate forms of liability through the coherent use of related rules within mechanisms of imputing acts and intents to corporations.

Chapter 4 will show how such mechanisms may be identified and will suggest ways in which they may be evaluated from a substantive perspective. An attempt will be made to expatiate on the notion of 'rules of attribution' given that commentators and judges have variously contended that courts are guided by these rules when imputing acts and intents to corporations. Impediments on the consistent imputation of acts and intents to corporations due to this terminology will be discussed and it will be submitted that in order to avoid a confused usage it may be preferable to refer to the use of "rules" by Hart. Thus, there is a primary rule that plays an expressive function (stating whose act or intent counts as that of the corporation) and imposes an obligation on courts to impute in a given way. This is the rule found in the relevant statute or precedent and it ought to be interpreted and implemented in accordance with the secondary rules (rules of recognition and rules of adjudication) and what Dworkin referred to as legal principles. In other words, the secondary rule may enable the court to find the "best" theory or unequivocal interpretation of the primary rule. A mechanism of imputation is a comprehensive term describing the consistent relation of both rules. Parameters for evaluating mechanisms of imputation from a substantive perspective or with regard to the discovery stage of the criminal justice process will be suggested.

In Chapters 5 and 6, the applicable mechanisms in the United Kingdom and some alternative mechanisms will be evaluated with reference to the parameters established in Chapter 4. The objective will be to determine whether any single mechanism captures both the reality of corporate structures and the adaptability of the criminal law in order to serve as a template for the imposition of liability and sanctions on corporate entities. Where no such mechanism is identified the most appropriate mechanism will be deemed to be that which can best be aligned with propositions of how the criminal liability of corporations may be established on a coherent and consistent basis. Such a modified mechanism will thus provide the prosecution with an arsenal consisting of diverse weapons to deal with the diverse forms of corporate entities and corporate offending under justifiable circumstances.

Chapter 7 will be concerned with the evaluation of the mechanisms of imputation with reference to the rules of adjudication or rules governing the proof and deliberation stages of the criminal justice process. As regards the proof stage, this Chapter will examine the logical connection between rules of adjudication and the mechanisms in light of how prosecutorial decision-making in criminal cases (involving corporations) is and ought to be influenced. With regard to the deliberation stage, emphasis will be placed on how the mechanisms of imputation guide courts and/or criminal justice agencies through the processes of deciding whether to convict or not and which sanction to impose.

In light of the above, it will be evident that the criminal law ought to be enforced in such a way that the rights that are incidental to the recognition of the corporation's personality are respected and there is a logical connection between the different ways in which corporations are held criminally liable and sanctioned. This will achieve coherence and integrity in the way in which courts impute acts and intents to corporations for the purposes of imposing criminal liability and penalties on them. Thus, an appropriate mechanism of imputation is the linchpin that prevents the concept of corporate criminal liability from sliding off the axles of the criminal law and the rule of law. Chapter 8 of this book will conclude with the presentation of such an appropriate mechanism and I will make recommendations for further research to consolidate and enhance this position.

CHAPTER TWO

CIRCUMSCRIBING THE NATURE OF THE CORPORATION WITHIN CRIMINAL LAW DISCOURSE

2.1 Introduction

As mentioned in Chapter 1, the first major cause of the incoherent use of the criminal law to regulate the behaviour of corporations is the failure to elaborate the concept of corporation or company. Thus, there is no clear authoritative reference. Section 1 of the Companies Act 2006 provides that a company is a company formed and registered under the Act or registered under the Companies Act 1985 or the Companies (Northern Ireland) Order 1986 or existed as a company for the purposes of that Act or that Order. Section 832(1) of the Income and Corporations Taxes Act 1988 is to the effect that a corporation is "any body corporate or unincorporated association but does not include a partnership, a local authority or a local authority association." Section 12 of the Fraud Act 2006 reduces the corporation to the acts of directors, managers, secretaries or other officers or persons acting in such capacities. Also, leading cases in corporate criminal law have indicated that a corporation has no metaphysical or material existence[1] and there is no thing as a corporation as such.[2] These references show that it may be close to impossible to ascribe a precise meaning to the concept of corporation.[3] However, the recognition of its right to exist as a legal person and capacity to affect legal relationships is an indication of the conception of 'corporation' by Parliament and courts. Hence, this Chapter seeks to give an ostensive definition of the term 'corporation' by pointing to the role the concept plays within criminal law discourse. It will do so by ascertaining why the 'corporation' or 'company'

---

[1] Lord Reid in *Nattrass* at 170.

[2] Lord Hoffmann in *Meridian* at 507.

[3] See *Stanley Tenant v Stanley* [1906] 1 Ch 131 at 134. See also Lord Hoffmann in the Foreword to Pinto and Evans (2003).

exists in the legal world as a legal person that may be criminally responsible and punishable. The objective is to establish that if it is assumed that the concepts of existence, legal personality, responsibility and punishment may be employed to describe a rational and autonomous person then the use of the word 'corporation' in relation to these concepts may enable one understand what it is and why it may be amenable to the criminal law on coherent and consistent basis.[4] As noted in Chapter 1, although the analysis will be restricted to the internal point of view, the examination of some normative propositions pertaining to some non-legal categories (external point of view) may be required in some instances. For the purposes of consistency and predictability, it was also noted that such important external points of view will be limited to principles of non-legal categories that may be deduced from the *obiter dicta* of criminal law judges.

2.2 Ascertaining the corporation as an entity in *esse*

About four centuries ago, Coke advanced that a corporation "rests only in intendment and consideration of the law." He also stated that a corporation is a "thing not in esse [but] in apparent expectancy is regarded in law as a [person]."[5] This statement although categorical was more of a factual supposition that he offered as justification for his choice among a set of different rival legal principles. As such, it was deployed as a legal fiction.[6] The idea that corporations are fictitious was also sanctioned by influential commentators such as Savigny[7] and Hallis.[8] However, it may be argued that the idea that a corporation exists falls short of meeting the requirement of legal fiction today. This is because unlike in the days of Coke, to say that a corporation exists will not be deemed today to be a

---

[4] This means that corporations may be labelled as members of a criminal class treated by the criminal justice system in a particular way. *Cf* Hessen, 1979: xvii – xviii.

[5] *Sutton's Hospital* at 22. As noted in Chapter 1, this view reflected that enunciated by Pope Innocent IV and was later echoed by Blackstone and then Lord Reid in *Nattrass* and Lord Hoffmann in *Meridian*.

[6] See Smith, 2007: 1441-1442 on some of the reasons why courts offer new legal fictions. Thus, the factual supposition offered by Coke enabled him to make a normative choice between holding the accused corporation criminally liable or not.

[7] 1884: 176-177, 184.

[8] 1930: 11. See also Austin, 1885; and Nesteruk, 2002: 439. See also Chief Justice John Marshall in the United States case of *Dartmouth College v Woodward*, 4 Wheat 518 (1819) at 636.

descriptively inaccurate assertion aimed at justifying normative choices.[9] Some studies have shown (with some degree of persuasion) that a corporation as a collective unit has a separate existence from its individual members[10] and its existence is therefore reality.[11] Nonetheless, even if one maintains that a corporation exists only in the intendment of the law one may still be held to imply that the law consists of a set of experiences that determines how behaviour is governed and since a corporation provides input to this set of experiences and is governable, its existence is confirmable.[12] Thus, it is factual in the legal domain and may perform actions and affect relationships and legal systems are left with little choice but to recognise the *fait accompli.*[13] As such, it may be contended that irrespective of the perspective endorsed a corporation's existence may not be questioned.[14] Hence, the gamut of theories explaining the nature of the corporation from either the fiction or realist perspective or a combination of both are simply geared towards describing different aspects of its existence as the proverbial blind men and the elephant.

I will therefore attempt to formulate a general concept of the corporation as an entity in *esse* by abstracting properties from some of these different theories. However, since there are more theories than can be discussed here and my objective is to circumscribe the concept of corporation within criminal law discourse, the standard for selecting the theories discussed below (assuming they are all pedigreed principles)[15] is whether they favour or eschew the regulation of the behaviour of corporations by the state.[16]

---

[9] The designation of "fiction" implies that the judge's choice is guided by something false or which the judge thinks to be false. See Smith, 2007: 1441-1442 and 1472-1478.

[10] See the discussion below.

[11] The realist theory of corporations was inspired by Gierke (see Maitland, 1900a) who was categorical about the corporation's existence. See also Geldart, 1911: 96.

[12] In other words, to say that it is a fiction that has been created by court or Parliament is to imply that it exists. See Machen, 1911: 255; and Winfield, 1950: 91.

[13] See Laski, 1916: 404-405.

[14] Wells (2001: 75) even advises that the bifurcation between the fiction and realist perspectives is unnecessary.

[15] They will be deemed to be pedigreed because they are deducible from the *obiter dicta* of the judgments cited above.

[16] However, this must not be taken to imply that if a theory does not favour regulation it would be deemed here as less accurate or adequate. Other analyses can and have been made from economic or political and legal (especially

2.2.1 Some prevalent theoretical approaches

The various interweaving and sometimes conflicting approaches adopted by different theorists give a somewhat vivid picture of the complexity of the corporate entity and no doubt fuel claims about the futility of beginning such a discourse with an attempt to ascertain its meaning.[17] This is compounded by the fact that each word that is used to describe the corporation bears complex meanings within different legal systems. Thus, the legal enquirer may avoid more ambiguities by limiting her search to the edicts of a given legal system.[18] Also, it is difficult to ascertain what Parliament or courts ordain without involving non-legal questions, especially if one seeks to assemble different statutes and *dicta* within a rational whole.[19] Hence, the objective of discussing these approaches is not to pick the most adequate approach and/or expose its theoretical depth, which should be convoluted, but simply to explore the practical value that the approaches bring as interlocking pieces of a jigsaw puzzle.[20] As mentioned above, the focus is on whether a theory favours the regulation of the activities of corporations by the state or not and this question may be said to be related to that of whether a theory purports that a corporation exists as an expression of individual freedoms (opposing regulation) or as an institution created by the state and therefore under its control (favouring regulation). Theories discussed below are grouped into these two blocks.

---

contractual) perspectives with different conclusions about the accuracy and adequacy of the theories. See for example, Nesteruk, 1990: 453; and 2002: 438-456.

[17] Paton (1972: 409) says that there have been so many theories that it is possible to arrive at any result with any theory. See also Radin, 1932: 643; Wolff, 1938: 494; and Pound, 1959: 22.

[18] See the Supreme Court of Canada in *Tremblay v Daigle* [1989] 2 SCR 530 at 552-553 on the task of the Court as regards philosophical and theological debates and legal questions.

[19] See Finnis, 2003: 134; and Naffine, 2003: 361.

[20] This means that there will be no claim to a solution to the problem of which theory or theories are better in absolute terms. Coyle (2006: 278) advises that "the function of lawyers lies in 'dealing with' the perennial problems of social life through the exploration of established understandings, technical definitions and doctrines, rather than offering solutions to those problems in the light of political principles for which wisdom, or especially desirability, is claimed."

2.2.1.1 The Corporation exists as an expression of individual freedoms

The acceptance of membership of a group by natural persons is a voluntary act of these persons and the assumption of the corporate form by that group is a consensual act by its members.[21] Thus, the corporation is a voluntary exercise of the freedom of association by a group of persons seeking to achieve a common objective, usually making of profits.[22] These persons enter into an agreement and it is from this agreement that the corporation is born.[23] This view is supported by a number of theories, including the aggregate theory and the bracket theory. The aggregate theory lays emphasis on the right of individuals to consociate in order to achieve common goals and the role of the law of contract to delineate this right and the correlative obligations.[24] The bracket theory equally places emphasis on the rights of individuals that have formed an association and holds the corporation to be a convenient way of addressing this group of persons.[25] These theories can all be described as different approaches to the "inherence theory" that describes a corporation as the consequence of the exercise of individual rights such as the freedom of association and the freedom to contract.[26] As such, the idea of the corporation as an expression of individual freedoms is centred on the right of people to enter into contracts and the consequences of exercising such a right. Thus, these theories support in different ways the proposition that a corporation exists simply as a nexus of contracts. This proposition has generally been explicated from two perspectives: legal and economic.[27]

The legal contractual theorists conceive of the corporation as a subject of private law emanating from the willingness of its members to take risks and employ their skills to further a common purpose.[28] The members spell

---

[21] See Davis, 1905: 15. This conception rests on principles such as choice, consent and contractual authorisation. See also Hessen, 1979: xiii.

[22] Nesteruk, 2002: 440- 441. The objective may also be extended to include the maximisation of happiness. See McConvill, 2005.

[23] See Hessen, 1979: xi; and Dine, 2000: 3.

[24] See Bottomley, 1990: 208.

[25] See Pound, 1959: 250. Austin (1885) also advanced that collective entities may be described as subjects only by "figment" and for purposes of "brevity of discussion."

[26] See Hessen, 1979: xiv.

[27] See the distinctions drawn by Dine (2000: 3-17). See also Parkinson, 1995: 75-76.

[28] Dine, 2000: 8.

out their intentions in the articles of association or company's constitution which constitutes a binding contract between them. Thus, in *Eley v Positive Government Life Security Assurance Co*, Lord Cairns defined the articles of association as "an agreement *inter socios*" and a "covenant between the parties."[29] Section 8(1) of the Companies Act 2006 also defines a memorandum of association as a proposal stating that the subscribers would like to form a company and have agreed to become members of the company.[30] As such, tasks beneficial to the society may or may not be part of the terms of members' agreement and imposing such tasks on them would be tantamount to imposing a burden or tax on them.[31] There is therefore little need for state intervention given that that the corporation is the natural expression of the members' freedoms and obtains its status independently of the state.[32] Jensen and Meckling give a clear picture of the theory. They advance that a corporation is a legal fiction that embodies the complex process by which different goals of individuals are assimilated into a structure of contractual relations.[33] In other words, it is just a means of connecting the different contracts that link members and agents.[34]

The much vaunted and deplored influence of the school of law and economics on the study of corporate law[35] has also given much impetus to the treatment of the corporation as a nexus of contracts.[36] The neo-classical liberal economics school that seeks to understand all legal precepts in economic terms therefore developed the economic contractual theory. Easterbrook and Fischel describe the corporation as a complex collection of contracts, express and implied, by which parties choose the best arrangements for different risks and opportunities.[37] These contracts

---

[29] 1876 1 ExD 88. See also *Hickman v Kent or Romney Marsh Sheep-Breeders' Association Ltd* [1915] 1 Ch 881; and *Salmon v Quin and Axtens Limited* [1909] AC 442.

[30] See also Griffiths (2005: 5) as regards the Companies Act 1985.

[31] Dine, 2000: 7.

[32] See Mark, 1987: 1470. See also Dine, 2000: 4. However, individual freedoms are expressed within a framework such as contract law and this framework is built by the state.

[33] 1976: 311.

[34] Orts, 1993: 1568.

[35] Especially in the United States, see Cheffins, 1999: 202-208; and McCrudden, 2006: 639-640.

[36] See Bratton, 1989: 407; and Easterbook and Fischel, 1989: 1416.

[37] Easterbrook and Fischel, 1989: 1416. See also Easterbrook and Fischel 1991: 12.

constitute the lifeblood of the corporation[38] and depict a sort of restricted market wherein buyers and sellers freely engage in exchange.[39] As such, benefits of free enterprise such as increased wealth may be obtained[40] if the law on corporations is deemed to be a substitute for private contract that efficiently saves the costs associated with negotiating, drafting and redrafting contracts with the different members and employees.

Efficiency is achieved through the separation of ownership and control whereby the directors and other senior managers of the corporation are agents[41] or fiduciaries[42] that are accountable to the shareholders who are the beneficiaries of the actions of the former.[43] The decision of shareholders to vest managerial powers in directors who have the requisite skill smacks of a rational exercise of freewill that may benefit all the parties and even society subsequently.[44] As such, the exercise of freedoms by individuals in pursuit of private goals eventually benefits society without any state intervention. This means that if the corporation causes harm to the community through pollution, efficiency would be achieved if the corporation can potentially compensate the affected community.[45] The role of the law and the state is restricted to facilitating the operation of the market[46] by delimiting the type of contracts into which individuals may enter without regard to possible civil liability or criminal prosecution.[47] Direct state intervention is deemed illegitimate and counterproductive due to the inalienability of individual freedoms such as the freedom of

---

[38] See Jensen and Meckling, 1976: 305, 310; and Eugene, 1980: 288.

[39] Cheffins, 1999: 209. See also Cheffins, 1997: 38- 41; and Easterbook and Fischel, 1991: 8- 22.

[40] Orts, 1993: 1580.

[41] See Black, 1992: 811; and Jensen and Meckling, 1976: 311.

[42] O'Connor, 1991: 1189; and Millon, 1991: 223.

[43] See the discussion on this separation by Berle and Means, 1968. See also Hill, 2000: 42- 44.

[44] See Butler, 1989: 106-108; Orgus, 1994: 24; Stapledon, 1996: 14; and Cheffins, 1997: 499- 500. This is in line with the Kaldar-Hicks criteria whereby the beneficiaries of economic transactions can potentially compensate those that bear some of the costs and do not benefit directly. See generally Ray, 1984; Johansson, 1993; Hausman and McPherson, 1996; and Dine, 2000.

[45] This may be contrasted with Pareto efficiency whereby one party is better off but no one is worse off.

[46] Hessen, 1979: 32- 33; and Dine, 2000: 10.

[47] Jensen and Meckling, 1976: 311, footnote n. 14.

association and the defects in the enactment and administration of legal rules.[48]

Orts however criticises the contractual approach as a crude description of contract law that is quite innocent of the substantive and procedural complexities of this branch of law.[49] In light of a number of commentators including Welch and Turezyn,[50] Klein and Coffee[51] and Manning and Hanks,[52] Orts discusses a number of notions that the contractual approach equally simplifies such as shareholders, stock, bonds, debentures, employees, directors and managers.[53] The treatment of these notions is superficial because they bear different meanings when invoked in legal and economic contexts. Equally, even when discussed only within a legal framework, they may be supplied not only by contract law but also by laws on employment, security, bankruptcy and taxation.[54] Moreover, the contractual theorists do not provide any clear-cut distinction between "originating" and "operational" contracts[55] and the preferences of individual members (which are treated separately from the broader community in which these members exist) are simplified.[56] These shortcomings may thus be blamed on the "metaphorical" use of the concept of contract.[57]

As such, it is difficult to substantiate the argument that a corporation exists simply as a nexus of contracts. Even if this approach was not liable to such debilitating criticisms it would still be important to note that persons who are not members of a corporation do not willingly agree to be affected by its activities.[58] This is especially true with regard to persons

---

[48] Cheffins, 1997: 163.
[49] 1993: 1576.
[50] Welch and Turezyn, 1993: 254 -272. See also the 5th edition of 2006 with Saunders.
[51] Klein and Coffee, 1990. See also the 10th edition of 2007.
[52] Manning and Hanks, 1990: 98- 105.
[53] 1993: 1576-1577.
[54] See also Eisenberg, 1989: 1487; and Blair, 1995: 16.
[55] The rights and duties that emanate from "operational" contracts are often regulated by different legal rules that emanate from different sources and which may in some cases be outside the scope of company law. See Bodoleoku, 2002: 412, 418. See also Dine, 2000: 2.
[56] See Nesteruk, 2002: 450.
[57] See Braucher, 1990: 698. See also Clark, 1985: 59-71; and Kornhauser, 1989: 1449.
[58] Davis, 1905: 15.

that cannot be compensated by the corporation.[59] Thus, the interests of stakeholders who are not members or creditors of the corporation must also be taken into consideration when determining the nature or essence of the concept of corporation.[60] A situation must be averted where members may simply limit their accountability and liability by structuring their contractual relationships strategically.[61] Also, the extension of the privilege of legal personality to corporations enables the criminal justice system to target the corporate person given that it represents the qualities of an entity that can breach the law and be sanctioned. Conceiving of the corporate person as an array of contracts negates such personification[62] and contradicts the treatment of corporations as separate persons.[63]

Nonetheless, it may be argued that members of a corporation limit their liability and that of the corporation when drafting the articles of association. However, this argument may only be true if it is thought that corporations cannot be liable for *ultra vires* acts.[64] Not only is the doctrine of *ultra vires* obsolete but also one cannot contract to avoid criminal liability.[65] Moreover, it is difficult to see why a third party may enter into a contract with a corporation but be required to institute legal proceedings against its members (who were acting as agents) in the event of breach.[66]

---

[59] Examples include where the corporation is insolvent and where the consciences of the senior managers cannot bring them to make reparations.

[60] Millon (1993: 1388) posits that there is need for a "multifiduciary" mechanism that redefines the duties of the corporation's management in order for them to serve the interests of all stakeholders affected by the corporation's activities.

[61] See Nesteruk, 2002: 451. Van Eeghen (2005: 57) contends that modern liberals have hardly examined the issue of legitimacy because if individuals are granted such freedom as to pursue their interests without accompanying responsibilities, irresponsible behaviour would be encouraged. Arthur (1940: 247) had also deplored the use of the 1862 incorporation laws in Great Britain by individuals "to purchase freedom from responsibility." See also Aubrey, 1982: 42; and Frazer, 1998: 129.

[62] Jensen and Meckling, 1976: 310-11. See also Stoljar, 1973: 40; and Bottomley, 1990: 211.

[63] See Blumberg, 1993: 3- 25; and Cheffins, 1999: 209.

[64] It has also been contended that all crimes are *ultra vires* because a crime cannot logically be part of a legally binding contract as no action may arise from such an agreement. See Clough and Mulhern, 2002: 14.

[65] Even in jurisdictions where plea bargaining is recognised, the defendant does not avoid criminal liability but pleads guilty to a lesser charge.

[66] Also, to say a corporation has contractual capacity implies that it has an autonomous mental capacity.

As such, just as corporations may themselves enter into and breach contracts, they may transact business fraudulently, make fake payments and disregard health and safety legislation. There is an independence of thought and action that courts and legislators recognise and this cannot be explained only by the logic of a nexus of contracts.[67] When judges and legislators talk of a 'corporation,' they are referring to something whose responsibility is even more important than the furtherance of its members' interests.[68] The change of emphasis from natural persons being responsible for corporate activities to the corporation itself gives the corporation some degree of autonomy to act in its own interests.[69] Hence, in the absence of any independent force that may compel corporations to act responsibly (in terms of furthering the interests of both members and society) state intervention may be important. This means that the state and the corporation may associate their activities to achieve socially responsible objectives.[70] In this light, it may be possible to define the corporation by referring to its distinct interest, the shared purposes of its members[71] and the benefits of all stakeholders.[72] Thus, it may be posited that theories that view the corporation as social institutions enhance the awareness of corporate person's responsibility for corporate activities that also affect non-member constituencies and facilitate regulation by the state.

---

[67] This is illustrated by *Duchy of Lancaster* where it was held that the King as a "body politic" could be piloted by a nine year old and thus the latter could sell land while acting within such a "body politic." This decision is not absurd when it is deemed to connote the body politic's intentionality and separateness. Thus, French (1995: 34-35) contends that if members automate the functioning of a corporation and leave, the automated corporation will continue to act rationally.

[68] See Wedderburn, 1985: 16. See however Deakin and Hughes (1997: 4) who posit that the diffusion of objectives of members and the corporate entity is both inefficient and irrelevant. See also Hessen, 1979: 22. See also Fischel's (1982: 1259 and 1273) contention that there is a fundamental error in assuming that inanimate objects such as corporations are capable of having social and moral obligations. Friedman (1962: 133) also argues that accepting that corporations have any responsibility other than to maximise profits for shareholders undermines the foundations of a free society. However, Friedman's argument begs the question of what is freedom?

[69] See Teubner, 1988: 139. See also the discussion below on corporate personality and the "collectivising" of reason.

[70] However, regulation of activities of private businesses may blur the distinction between public and private institutions. See Dine, 2000: 19-20. See also Stone, 1982: 1506.

[71] Pound, 1959: 254; and Baty, 1919: 361- 365.

[72] Stokes, 1986: 177.

2.2.1.2 The corporation exists as a social instrument

Davis sees the grant and protection of rights to individuals or groups as social expressions.[73] Dahl professes that corporations exist simply because society allows them to exist[74] and Dine begins her discussion on the theoretical underpinnings of the concept of corporation with a claim that understanding the concept involves ascertaining its construction as a social phenomenon.[75] Thus, where public sentiment is in favour of restricting or extending the powers of corporations the probability that legislation will be to that effect is high. The charter granted to the corporation would not be the product of a bargain between the members but an expression of the state's desire to make this group of persons more efficient by providing it with a form more appropriate for its activities.[76] It may therefore be contended that the existence of a group of persons as a collective body is founded on an obligation, whether implied or express, to perform a social function.[77] The corporate form and the nexus of relationships[78] (whether contractual or otherwise) existing between members of a corporation or between the corporation and the society constitute a concession by the state.[79]

However, it may be argued that the grant of corporate status is not a concession by the state *stricto sensu*.[80] This is because it is difficult to contend that the grant of a charter or the registration of a corporation is analogous to what Maitland describes as the state blowing "the breath of a fictitious life" into the "nostrils" of the corporation.[81] Thus, the conception of the corporation as essentially a creature not of its members but of the state reflects the absolutist feudal system where the Crown was deemed to

---

[73] 1905: 16.

[74] 1973: 11.

[75] 2000: 1.

[76] See Davis, 1905: 16, 18; and Bottomley, 1990: 203. See also the contention of Nader and Green MJ (1973: 80) that the corporate charter is an implied agreement between the state and the corporate entity seeking existence.

[77] Davis, 1905: 18. See also Dodd, 1932: 1145; Smith TA, 1999: 214; and Blair, Margaret and Stout, 2001: 416-418

[78] McConvill, 2005: 35-36.

[79] Concession here is held to mean some benefit or privilege accorded by the state in exchange for some services rendered or to be rendered to the state. See Hessen, 1979: 28.

[80] Dine, 2000: 17.

[81] 1900a: xxx.

have omnipotent powers.[82] The inalienability of individual freedoms such as the freedom to contract and to associate is undeniable and the fact that they are inalienable implies that they existed before the state. Hence, the state cannot create something that emanates from the exercise of freedoms when such an emanation naturally precedes it.[83]

The recognition of a group or its entitlement to certain advantages does not entail creating that group.[84] Thus, if it is said that the corporation is a fiction recognised (and not created) by the state in exchange for the performance of social functions then it may be advanced that there is a pre-existing corporate form (that can perform functions) to which the state simply gives official approval. As such, the registrar of companies recognises the existence of a group of persons wishing to undertake business activities by issuing a certificate of incorporation and can do no more.[85] Nonetheless, although the law does not create that group it cannot be claimed that the latter may act as a 'corporation' before its members have been granted authority by the duly designated state institution. This means that it is the quality of 'corporateness' that is attached to the group of persons that act as a collective body following the registration of that collective body or the grant of a charter that enables the group to metamorphose into a 'corporation.'[86] However, the quality of 'corporateness' may not be said to be tantamount to a 'corporation' with regard to its origin and function.

The recognition of foreign bodies as corporations also buttresses the argument that a corporation's existence does not depend on the state. In the United States case of *Liverpool and London Life and Fire Insurance Company v Commonwealth of Massachusetts*, Justice Miller noted that courts may consider the power and rights and privileges exercised by collective bodies and the capacity in which they are exercised in order to determine whether corporate status has been granted by implication or

[82] Carr, 1913: xiv-xv; Thurman, 1937: 185; and Hessen, 1979: 10-11.

[83] van Eeghen (2005: 55) however thinks that corporations were originally seen as agencies of the state because legal personality naturally belongs to the state.

[84] See Maitland's (1900a: xxxviii) comparison of the state's power to make corporations and its power to make marriages. See also Hessen, 1979: 33.

[85] See Stevens and Henn, 1965: 307-312; and Hessen, 1979: 25-26.

[86] According to section 1(1) of the Companies Act 2006 for example, unless a collective body is duly registered under this Act or under the previous statutes or registers it may not be held to be a company.

not.[87] This may sometimes be seen as a pragmatic approach impelled by the desire to do justice between the parties.[88] Such pragmatism is also reflected in the fact that courts are required to recognise foreign companies in given instances. Article 43 of the Treaty establishing the European Community (Consolidated Version of 2001) provides for the freedom of establishment of both natural and artificial persons. Hence, a corporation is capable of moving from the jurisdiction in which it was incorporated to another jurisdiction without losing its status as corporation. This is similar to the approach adopted by English courts to recognise foreign incorporated companies[89] and shows that the idea that a corporation is essentially a concession by the state is very much open to debate.[90] Thus, in cases of foreign incorporated companies, in the absence of international comity,[91] courts may decide the question of their recognition by looking at certain attributes that substantiate the entity status of corporations.[92] Such attributes may include separate personality, limited liability and perpetuity, which are often conferred by law to corporations as "privileges"[93] or "powers"[94] or as a "legal convenience."[95] Accordingly, the entity status of the corporation may also have been acquired by contractual agreement or any other means.[96] The important thing is that the state recognises the corporate form that has been created by the actions of its members.

---

[87] 77 US 10 Wallace 566 (1870). See also *Sutton's Hospital* at 30.

[88] See Townsend, 2006: 593.

[89] See Scrutton LJ in *Banque Internationale de Commerce de Petrograd v Goukassov* [1923] 2 KB 682 at 691. This case is hereinafter referred to as *Goukassov*. See also Rammeloo, 2001.

[90] See also *Cartesio Oktató és Szolgáltató bt* [2008] BCC 745 where the European Court of Justice held that the Hungarian rules (reflecting the 'real seat' theory) that allow companies to transfer their headquarters only within the country was in contradiction with articles 43 and 48 of the European Community Treaty. The judge advanced (at 759) that "it is impossible, in my view, to argue on the basis of the current state of Community law that Member States enjoy an absolute freedom to determine the 'life and death' of companies constituted under their domestic law, irrespective of the consequences for the freedom of establishment. Otherwise, Member States would have *carte blanche* to impose a 'death sentence' on a company constituted under its laws just because it had decided to exercise the freedom of establishment."

[91] See Scrutton LJ in *Goukassov* at 691.

[92] See Drucker, 1968: 42.

[93] Nader, Green MJ and Seligman, 1976: 63.

[94] Orts, 1993: 1578, footnote n. 49.

[95] Berle and Means, 1968: 120, footnote n. 2.

[96] See Paton, 1972: 409. See also Hessen, 1979: 15 – 22.

In light of the above, it may be posited that the communitarian and concession theories are to the effect that incorporation is what the state barters in exchange for social services[97] or the furtherance of public interests or those of all 'stakeholders.' However, this is not of much help because concepts such as stakeholders and public interest are equivocal.[98] They may mean a variety of things including the respect of individual freedoms to associate or contract. Even if they are said to imply that consideration must be given to the wellbeing of the community, contractual theorists may still argue that individuals may contract to pursue a broad range of interests including those of other stakeholders such as consumers, employees, creditors and debtors and eventually contribute to the amelioration of communal values.[99] However, Deakin and Hughes warn that if the social function of corporations should involve serving a wide variety of interests including those of all consumers, as well as the environment, there is a risk that the function itself would become diffused and less relevant.[100] Nonetheless, a concise definition of the social function would always exclude things such as environmental pollution and the marketing of defective and potentially harmful products. In such cases, corporations would be required to make separate cost-benefit tests based on actual and not potential compensation of those affected.[101] Given that it may be close to impossible to achieve Kaldor-Hicks or Pareto efficiency in all of such cases, the state may have to intervene to ensure that beneficiaries actually compensate those that bear the costs of the activities of the corporation. Nonetheless, the registration of such a corporation bespeaks the state's recognition of the fact that it has a right to exist as well as the capacity to perform the incidental social function.

---

[97] This means that the legislator conceives of a corporation as an instrument for promoting social wellbeing and ordains that the state must recognise any group that is structured to perform such functions as a corporation. Thus, a group is structured to perform such functions if it meets the requirements set out in the Companies Act 2006.

[98] Hessen, 1979: 27.

[99] See McConvill J, 2005: 35-36, 44. See the reference to the Kaldor-Hicks criteria and Pareto efficiency above.

[100] 1997: 4. See also, Braithwaite and Ayres, 1992: 23. It is also true that if the interests of shareholders are not prioritised the corporation may become a major target for a take-over bid. See Malkiel, 1972: 4; and Van Eeghen, 2005: 64.

[101] See Farrow, 1998: 27, 183-188.

2.2.2 Abstracting from the theoretical approaches

As mentioned above, these theories represent different perspectives of the reality of the corporate entity. Hence, drawing a conclusion solely from any single set of related theories would be tantamount to establishing the relative truth. Contractual theories describe the corporation as a voluntary enterprise founded on individual rights and freedoms. Thus, a corporation exists independently of the state as a fabrication of private individuals to further their interests or as a linguistic tool for identifying the group of natural persons that have entered into related contracts. This means that when the state recognises this group by the name (corporation) chosen by the contractual parties it buys into the fiction. However, a corporation is more than just a reflection of the exercise of basic rights or a nexus of contracts. The communitarian and concession theories talk of persons that do not enter into any contract with any of the members of the corporation but are affected by the activities of the corporation. As such, the state will not recognise any group as a corporation unless it is satisfied that members of the group have taken the interests of all stakeholders into consideration. Nonetheless, the recognition of the corporate form is not always the state's prerogative as this can be imposed upon it by rules of international law or courts may even grant such status in accordance with some accepted norms.[102] Moreover, given that what the state demands in exchange for official approval (the promotion of social welfare) is quite ambiguous and may even overlap with the interests of shareholders, it may be said that the state simply recognises the corporate form when the group fulfils certain variable requirements in the circumstances.

As such, a definition of the concept of corporation ought to reflect the contention that it rests in the contemplation of the law although it does not rest solely there given that it may also exist outside the law under consideration.[103] This implies that one may not provide an ostensive

---

[102] The idea that the corporate form is a concession by the state therefore leaves courts confronted with unincorporated associations and foreign corporations in the position of the King and Queen of hearts before the Cheshire cat.

[103] The European Court of Justice is cited above as stating that a state does not have the absolute freedom to decide on the life and death of corporations. However, it may be argued that international law is still considered the law and this case was more about the precedence of fundamental rights enshrined in the European Community Treaty than about the precedence of the normative institutions. In such an instance one may talk of an internal conflict between legal norms. See Westen, 2008: 564.

definition of the term ‘corporation’ by pointing solely to legal rules since in some cases the relevant legal rules may conflict with each other. However, what is certain is that legal rules tell us what corporations may or may not do. As such, even if everybody within a legal system would not readily understand what it means when a judge or legislator talks of a ‘corporation,’ they are likely to understand what the judge or legislator means when she says a ‘corporation’ may or may not perform an action in a given instance. This means that it may be possible to define the term ‘corporation’ in each given instance with regard to say the different legal rights and duties recognised in the European, Scottish and English jurisdictions, as well as the way in which these rights and duties have been enforced. Nonetheless, this book will not attempt to define the ‘corporation’ in the context of all the rights and duties of these legal systems because such an attempt will not be adequately informed on the complex theories and usages of these systems. That notwithstanding, a definition may be attempted within the context of corporate criminal liability, that is, the criminal context in which the corporation is essentially related.

A common feature of both sets of theories discussed above is that corporations may by themselves perform certain activities, whether it is to enter into contracts or perform social functions. To a certain extent these theories may be said to reflect the notion of the corporation’s distinct identity. Equally, the Criminal Law Act 1827, the Interpretation Act 1899 and section 48 of the European Community Treaty affirm this distinct identity to the effect that a corporation may be said to be a body vested with legal personality and upon whom the state may impose obligations. However, this notion is furtherer from the contractual theories because the boundaries of the agreements between the members are not recognised by the state and criminal liability may be imposed in circumstances where the court believes that the corporation (as an autonomous entity) may have perpetrated an offence or failed to perform a duty. On the other hand, to say that a corporation may not violate the law because it is a concession by the state is a weak argument. Nonetheless, the conclusion that may be drawn from the discussion above is that when a judge or legislator talks of the imposition of criminal liability on a corporation, she is referring to two things, *viz.* the imposition of criminal liability on an entity that exists *simplicter* (whether as the embodiment of several related contracts or the state’s concession); and the imposition of criminal liability on an entity that exists as a legal person with the capacity to perform actions and affect relationships. However, it is uncertain whether issues of expediency impelled Parliament and courts to grant and recognise the corporation's existence as legal person[104] or the decision was based on conviction.

2.3 Ascertaining the corporate entity in *esse* as a legal person

The discussion here is based not on the motivations of earlier and present courts and legislators to recognise the concept of corporate personality but on whether such recognition is justified. Given that the objective is to determine what the law 'is' (as regards the meaning of the term 'corporation'), I will seek to determine whether there is an adequate definition or definitions of the term 'legal personality' and whether the corporation can fit into such a definition or definitions, thereby justifying the postulate of courts that a corporation 'is' a legal person. However, the term 'legal personality' is sinuous and controversial and this may be attributed to the fact that some commentators tend to borrow the literary meaning of the term 'person' for legal use.[105] This reinforces Hohfeld's statement that some jurists often make metaphorical use of terms that were not intended for use in connection with legal relations.[106] Thus, cognisant of the term's philosophical depth, I will employ an ordered but simplified analysis proposed by Naffine that identifies three ways in which the term 'legal person' is used in connection with legal relations. The approaches include: firstly, defining a legal person as the subject of rights and other legal relations; secondly, the inclusion of non-legal moral essence in defining legal personality because a legal person is a reasonable creature

[104] For example, ecclesiastical courts used to excommunicate corporations until the practice was abrogated by Pope Innocent IV in 1245. See Lizee, 1995: 136; and Coffee, 1981: 386, footnote n. 2. Thus, prior to the abrogation, corporations were treated as distinct legal persons and Weismann and Newman (2007: 419, footnote n. 14) although providing no evidence surmise that there could have been an economic motivation to stop this practice given that the assets of the excommunicated corporation were moved out of the jurisdiction of the Church. Thus, Pope Innocent IV's espousal of the fiction theory may have been guided by economic expediency and not principle.

[105] Poole (1996: 38) for example says that the term 'person' designates what humans are or ought to be in reference to the most significant aspects of their existence. However, it is unclear whether the literary meaning of 'person' is synonymous to human being since etymologically the term was used to describe a mask worn by actors.

[106] 1923: 31.

in *rerum natura*; and thirdly, the conception of the legal person as a rational and competent moral agent.

2.3.1 The subject of rights and other legal relations

Proponents of this approach eschew metaphysical presuppositions because they believe that moral, political and social characters do not in any way constitute the requirements for legal personality[107] and there are no "natural substrates" that may be identified as a common feature of legal persons.[108] The law therefore recognises certain entities as legal persons simply because they have a capacity to bear rights and the recognition of this capacity conveys the practical benefit of fashioning legal relationships in the law's logical system.[109] Legal personality may therefore be deemed to be a basic unit of a mathematical equation that simplifies calculations.[110] Thus, where judges or legislators talk of a legal person they may be said to be referring to any entity that is a subject of rights or other legal relations.[111] This means that an entity is a legal person simply because the law extends that privilege to it.[112] As such, there is a great assortment of entities that can become legal persons ranging from animals, the environment, idols, partnerships, cultural organisations and cartels.[113] Thus, in legal parlance there is no natural person and no artificial person *per se* but only legal persons.[114]

---

[107] Naffine, 2003: 351. See also the Canadian case of *Tremblay v Daigle* [1989] 2 SCR 530 where it was held that where the Court is called upon to decide on the question of whether a foetus is a legal person "metaphysical arguments may be relevant but they are not the primary focus of inquiry."

[108] See Nekam, 1938.

[109] See Derham, 1958: 1 and 5.

[110] In this case we would talk of the simplification of legal calculations. See Lawson, 1957: 915.

[111] See Lawson, 1957: 915.

[112] Naffine, 2003: 351.

[113] As noted above, Tur (1987: 123) lends support to this approach by stating that one cannot talk of a general law of persons but of sets of rules governing relationships and establishing liabilities. See also Naffine, 2003: 351.

[114] Smith B (1928: 283 and 293) thus advanced that legal persons are abstractions of legal science in the same vein as title, possession and duty. *Cf* Maitland, 1900b: 335.

One may however question the rationale of this approach given that it may be held to imply that the term legal person may mean anything.[115] This is because if any entity can become a legal person due to the enjoyment of a single right provided by a law, where such an entity is out of the set of relations created by that law under consideration it loses its legal personality and "there is no more left than the smile of the Cheshire Cat after the cat had disappeared."[116] In other words, a person would be said to exist in law only to the extent that she has rights and duties, apart from which such a person has no legal existence whatsoever;[117] and in order to know whether an entity is a legal person or not courts simply have to look at the provisions of the law under consideration.[118] Nonetheless, it may be argued that this merely conveys the reality of how the term is used in the practice of many legal systems.[119] As such, there are cases where courts have recognised the legal personality of corporations[120] and cases where they have disregarded this attribute in corporate bodies.[121] The same may be said of fully developed human beings, foetuses, dead persons and cartels. However, this does not discount the fact that mountains would also be legal persons, as well as dolphins, trees and rivers due to the existence of large numbers of legal rights and relations.

As such, Naffine thinks that it would not be possible for proponents of this approach to enforce strict linguistic vigilance in order to ensure that commentators do not blend legal and non-legal attributes.[122] This is because the capacity to bear a right or be subject to legal relations does not only invoke the need to give empirical content to the entity but also presupposes a being that is real and concrete and can perform an action.[123] In this light, a number of commentators have simply concluded that legal persons are only human beings because they are the only real and concrete entities that can perform actions in a rational manner.

---

[115] This approach is described by Naffine (2003: 351) as "an empty bracket, capable of being filled and refilled in any way."
[116] Smith B, 1928: 294 cited in Naffine, 2003: 353.
[117] See Kelsen, 1945: 93.
[118] Tur, 1987: 121-122.
[119] In the words of Hart (1983: 25, footnote n. 17) it may be said that this approach "conveys the formal availability of the [empty] slot to anyone" in any given legal system. See also Naffine, 2003: 355.
[120] See *Salomon*.
[121] See *Gilford Motor Company Ltd v Horne* [1933] Ch 935; *Agrotexim Hellas SA and Others v Greece* (1996) 21 EHRR 250; and *Belgium v Spain* ICJ Rep (1970) 3.
[122] 2003: 355. *Cf* Hohfeld, 1923: 27.
[123] Naffine, 2003: 355.

2.3.2 A reasonable creature in rerum natura

It has been argued that each individual acquires a set of rights and duties at birth and loses them at death and these rights and duties constitute the privilege of legal personality. Moreover, such a privilege can only be enjoyed by human beings because they are reasonable creatures in *rerum natura*[124] or in being.[125] Reasonable creatures in *rerum natura* fulfil certain biological and metaphysical requirements[126] that convey the status of legal personality to them. They are reasonable because they have a naturally endowed ability to choose[127] and since rights and duties involve rational choices, they are the only ones that can acquire such status.[128] This approach therefore uses the terms 'human' and 'person' as synonyms,[129] something which Kelsen decries as misguided.[130]

It must however be noted that this approach is not fundamentally opposed to that discussed above. It agrees with the fact that a legal person is an entity that has the capacity to bear rights. However, it contends that if this capacity is analysed critically (both scientifically and metaphysically) the logical conclusion would be that only human beings have the capacity to bear rights and thus only human beings can be legal persons. This approach is therefore not derailed by the blending of legal and non-legal quantities. As noted by Finnis, juristic knowledge must be informed by both metaphysical and natural truths about persons that are supposed be served by the law.[131] This no doubt fuels the temptation of judges to look beyond the provisions of statutes and legal practice and seek answers from non-legal subjects. However, given that there is no limit to the scope and

---

[124] See Coke, *Co. Inst., Pt. III, ch.7*, at 50. There is no connection between this conception and the term as used by Lucretius in his poem defending the Epicurean philosophy, *De rerum natura.*

[125] See also Waller, 1987: 37.

[126] See Kester, 1994: 1607. Naffine (2003: 357) warns that giving regard to contributions from non-legal commentators such as Kester represents an "irritant to jurists" that wish to ensure the legal purity of legal concepts.

[127] Ducor (1996: 200) in the same vein sees the human being as the "paradigmatic subject of rights." See also Kinley, 1998: 4; and Kramer, 2001: 29 and 36.

[128] See Fitzgerald, 1966: 298. However, the measure of reasonableness is controversial because it may be extended to include decisions that would otherwise be unreasonable but are made because they are voluntary and do not cause harm or encroach upon the freedom of others. See also Feinberg, 1986: 67.

[129] See McHugh, 1992: 445; and Naffine, 2003: 358.

[130] 1945: 94.

[131] 2000: 13.

depth of non-legal knowledge that a judge may import, such a process may legitimise value judgments at the expense of the letter of the law. Also, there is no steadfast metaphysical and scientific truth about any entity[132] and there is even an ongoing debate about what it means to be 'human.'[133]

Moreover, if the capacity to bear rights involves the ability to choose, then it may be said that the subject of rights is an autonomous individual.[134] However, not all humans are separate and distinct[135] and many do not possess individualism.[136] Equally, there are non-human entities that demonstrate the qualities of separateness and individualism[137] and may even be held to be more deserving of legal personality if autonomy and reasonableness were the cardinal features. Nonetheless, this approach may be summarised as postulating that the only quality needed to qualify for legal personality is existence as a human being.[138] Thus, it would be to no avail that a non-human entity is autonomous or reasonable or intelligent. If such an entity is not a human being it does not qualify.[139] This shows that this approach is dogmatic and lacks a rational underpinning[140] and it is important that focus should shift to another approach.

---

[132] Such truth is often influenced by cultural ideas. See Naffine, 2003: 360-361.

[133] See *Attorney-General's Reference (No 3 of 1994)* [1997] 3 All ER 936 on the personality of foetuses. See also the New Zealand case of *Baby P (An Unborn Child)* [1995] NZFLR 577.

[134] Autonomy in this sense may be described as separate, distinct and possessing individualism. See Naffine, 2003: 360.

[135] See the case of conjoined twins in *Re A (Children) Conjoined Twins: Surgical Separation* [2004] 4 All ER 961.

[136] For example, foetuses and mentally unbalanced persons.

[137] See the discussion below on rational and autonomous corporate persons.

[138] See Naffine, 2003: 361.

[139] As shown above, the reasons for attributing legal personality to human beings only are quite contentious. Thus, it may be held that there is no cogent justification for this stance, whether from a legal or scientific perspective.

[140] See Naffine, 2003: 361. Courts have therefore extended the protection of traditional human rights under the ECHR to corporations and other private business undertakings. See the cases of *Pudas v Sweden* (1998) 10 EHRR 30; *Autronic AG v Switzerland* (1990) 12 EHRR; and *Demuth v Switzerland* (2001) 31 EHRR 772. See also Emberland, 2006: 17.

2.3.3 A rational and competent moral agent

A third approach conceives of legal personality as a privilege that is conferred to rational and competent entities only.[141] Hence, a legal person is an entity that has the ability to perform an action in a rational manner.[142] Empirical content may be ascribed to such a person because of both moral and legal reasons. Morally, the person is an individual that can make decisions and execute them independently.[143] Legally, the person has a right to make decisions and execute them.[144] Proponents of this approach therefore espouse an idea that proponents of the previous approaches fail to adopt. Entities that are not rational to the extent that that they can judge their behaviour from both moral and legal perspectives are excluded.[145] However, it is uncertain what amount of rationality would suffice and what measure is used. Harris says that legal persons should have the requisite cognition to sustain biographical life[146] and Naffine contends that the legal person ought to have the ability to mentally perceive the nature of her situation and assume the responsibilities for her actions.[147] This means that not only are non-living organisms excluded but equally entities that have invariably been defined as 'humans' such as foetuses, very young children and the mentally unbalanced may be excluded.[148] In this light, Naffine contends that individuation and physical integrity are prerequisites for claiming and enforcing rights and these qualities best describe the adult human.[149] However, it is uncertain why the adult human's occasional infirmity and dependence is ignored. Thus, this approach may be described as an alluring but illusory attempt at categorically excluding entities other than humans from the broad expanse of legal personality. The end result is another dogmatic declaration that humans are the paradigmatic subject of rights.

---

[141] Naffine, 2003: 362.

[142] Smith, 1928: 287. It is however questionable whether mere legal competence is sufficient for an entity to qualify as a legal person following this argument.

[143] See Wolgast, 1992: 65. In this book, this may be understood to mean the decision to breach the law.

[144] Moore (1984: 48) however thinks that both perspectives are basically the same.

[145] See Moore, 1984: 66; and Naffine, 2003: 363.

[146] 2001: 235-236.

[147] 2003: 364.

[148] See Moore, 1984: 65. This is in light with the "Will Theory" that is to the effect that each right holder must be a competent and rational agent that can enforce her rights. See Kramer, 1998: 62; and Steiner, 1998: 262.

[149] 2003: 364 and 365.

2.3.4 Abstracting from the legal personality theories

The corporation may rightly be held to be a legal person if regard is given to the approaches discussed above. Following the first approach (the subject of rights and other legal relations), it may be said that a corporation enjoys the status of legal personality because it is entitled to claim rights and has duties in respect of a broad range of rules under both substantive and adjectival law.[150] Thus, if legal personality is an abstraction that exists only in the intendment of the law we may simply refer to the law under consideration to determine whether a corporation is a subject of rights and thus a legal person. As such, we may refer to the laws of England and Scotland, as well as European law and deduce that the corporation in these systems has been treated as a subject of legal relations.[151] However, as noted above, this approach opens a floodgate to the ingress of entities that can claim the privilege of legal personality and may thus be seen an "empty bracket" in which any entity may be inserted.

Hence, if it is not appropriate to simply define a legal person as the subject of legal relations, it is worth mentioning that the corporation equally fits (to a certain extent) the second definition, that is, a reasonable creature in *rerum natura*. The corporation fits the requirement of "reasonable" in this definition, except where the approach is summarised by the categorical claim that only humans can be reasonable and natural and thus legal persons. However, it must also be noted that proponents of this conception of legal personality vehemently oppose the extension of any form of personality to corporate entities on the ground that it would be tantamount to imputing judgments, intentions, beliefs, emotions and attitudes to a social group; something which proponents of the bracket and aggregate theories (discussed above) believe is metaphorically a summative way of attributing these "predicates" to the individuals in the social group.[152] Nonetheless, although it is true that when people blame Shell or British Petroleum for environmental pollution or supporting human rights abuses they are indirectly blaming the managers of these companies,[153] it cannot be said that when people say that Shell or British

---

[150] This is supported by Lord Hoffmann in *Meridian* at 506.

[151] *Solomon*. See also *Uberseering BV v Nordic Construction Company Baumanagement GmbH* (*NCC*) C-208/00 ECJ 2002.

[152] See also Kerlin, 1997: 1436-1437.

[153] *Cf* Gobert and Punch, 2003: 49. Nonetheless, blaming the corporation (corporate liability) does not in any way negate the individual liability of directors and managers.

Petroleum supports human rights violations by the Nigerian or Burmese government they are indirectly saying that all the shareholders, senior managers and junior employees of Shell or British Petroleum support these human rights violations.[154] Thus, a corporation is not synonymous to the sum of its individual members and may have different objectives and judgements that are reasonable in their own right. [155]

As regards the third approach relating a legal person to a rational and competent entity, it may be said that the requirements of rationality and competence invoke so many things that it is difficult to ascertain what measure is used to establish these facts. Nonetheless, it may be argued that the legal person described in this approach is one that consistently acts intentionally and in a rationally permissible manner.[156] Pettit[157] set out to justify the claim that collective bodies are psychologically autonomous by employing what he termed the "discursive dilemma"[158] to show how group identity and rationality emerge in collectivising reason within an organisation. As such, although collective bodies come in different shapes and sizes they deserve to be recognised as intentional subjects.[159] The discursive dilemma describes in general terms a number of possibilities that are available to decision makers within a group in a situation where there are more than two members and more than one premise.[160] In a situation where collective bodies are required to make decisions, they do so by either placing emphasis on a "conjunction of premises" or a

---

[154] Although there is much animosity directed towards managers of hedge funds in the present economic crisis, the resentment does not extend to junior managers and operational employees although they are also part of the organisations.

[155] See Gold and Sugden, 2007. See also Bratman's (1999) discussion on "shared intention" and the criticism of "singularism" by Pettit (1992).

[156] However, a problem with such understanding is that the focus is often on the properties of the mind rather than on the mental processes by which intentions are formed. See Gold and Sugden, 2007.

[157] 1992: 167-193.

[158] This is a variation of the doctrinal paradox first identified by Kornhauser and Sager. See Kornhauser and Sager, 1986: 82-117; and Kornhauser and Sager, 1993: 1-59. This is discussed further in Chapter 8.

[159] Pettit, 1992: 173. See also Rock, 2005: 3 and 25.

[160] Pettit, 1992: 170. It must be noted that it is assumed that people in other social groups would often reach decisions on "an incompletely theorized basis." Pettit's (1992: 178-179) analysis thus suits only "purposive groups" such as corporations. Thus, legal personality is only necessary for corporate bodies because as posited by Rock (2005: 23-24) "the corporation (much more than the partnership) has the institutional capacity to constrain the discursive dilemma."

"disjunction of premises." A "conjunction of premises" arises where premises concur such as whether to adopt a procedure to make a decision involving two steps, while a disjunction of premises is a negation of a conjunction such as whether the procedure would not involve one of such steps.[161] In both instances, the group may make a decision in two distinct ways. It may adopt a "conclusion-centred procedure" where the votes of members in respect of the conclusion are aggregated and the majority view on the conclusion determines the decision or it may adopt a "premise-centred procedure" where the votes of members in respect of individual premises are aggregated and the majority view on each premise determines whether or not the premise is collectively endorsed.[162] Pettit also identifies three less obvious ways in which possibilities available to decision makers within a group can be generalised, *viz.* social generalisation, diachronic generalisation and *modus tollens* generalisation.[163] It must be noted that the decision-making procedures identified by Kornhauser and Sager and Pettit are in no way exhaustive. There are several other possibilities available to decision makers within a group in a situation where there are more than two members and more than one premise.[164]

What these commentators have sought to show is that there is a group identity or personality that emerges that is different from the identities of

---

[161] See Pettit, 1992: 168-170.

[162] See the examples of the court panel of three judges having to make decisions in a tort case and on a retrial in Kornhauser and Sager, 1993: 11 and 40. See also the example given by Rock (2005: 9) on a decision in the firm to expand into specialty chemicals.

[163] Social generalisation occurs where the collective body is required to decide on an issue that is essentially related to other issues such as where a company owned by employees has to decide whether to forfeit a pay-rise and use the money saved to improve upon safety at the workplace. The diachronic generalisation occurs where the collective body is confronted by a choice between deciding on a new issue based on previous decisions taken collectively and deciding on the new issue in a manner that is inconsistent with previous decisions. The *modus tellens* generalisation occurs where the collective body is faced with a choice between ignoring the majority view on the conclusion and let the majority view on the premises dictate the decision (*modus ponens)* and ignoring the majority view on one of the premises and let the majority view on other premises and the conclusion dictate the decision. See Pettit, 1992: 170-175.

[164] The procedure to be followed in order to adopt a decision in this particular situation may even be a lot more complex than demonstrated by these commentators. The complexity of the procedure for the adoption of one procedure for making decisions over another is for example not discussed.

individuals that constitute that group.[165] Thus, the majority of members may decide to adopt a certain course of action in an instance where there is no consensus among them.[166] The group manifests collective rationality (and disregards responsiveness to individual members) by imposing the discipline of reason at a collective level in order to maintain coherence and credibility.[167] Therefore, a member may very well be happy with a conclusion adopted but not with the procedure employed to arrive at that conclusion given that each member votes for a particular course of action for reasons related to her own interests or judgments.[168] This implies that members of a group run the risk of endorsing a decision that a majority or even all of them individually reject and this is what Pettit calls "collectivising reason."[169] As such, if regard is given to the process in which reason is formed or the decision-making pathology, one may find similarities between purposive social groups such as corporate bodies and purposive natural persons.[170] In the words of Gold and Sugden "[w]hen an agent deliberates about what she ought to do, the result of her reasoning is an intention. An intention is interposed between reasoning and action, so it is natural to treat intentions that result from team reasoning as collective intentions."[171]

This means that whether legal personality is a legal mask that is worn to play a designated role in the legal system (such as enforcing certain rights) or power conferred to certain rational and moral creatures to facilitate their enforcement of rights or the process of holding them accountable, the corporation fits every definition of legal personality to a

---

[165] The group can therefore be a subject of rights and other legal relations of which the members of that group are not privy in their individual capacities. See *Foss v Harbottle* (1843) 2 Hare 461. See also the case of *Agrotexim Hellas SA and Others v Greece*.

[166] Pettit, 1992: 172. See the distinction between collective intentions and mutually-consistent individual actions (often described as "nash equilibrium" behaviour) drawn by Gold and Sugden, 2007.

[167] Pettit, 1992: 174; and Rock, 2005: 6.

[168] Pettit, 1992: 173.

[169] It is the natural response of groups under pressure when confronted with the discursive dilemma. See Pettit, 1992: 175- 176; and Rock, 2005: 11.

[170] Rock (2005: 24) contends that "corporations are a paradigmatic example" of what Pettit refers to as "groups with a mind of their own."

[171] 2007: 111. See also the analysis of collective intentionality by Tuomela and Miller, 1988: 375. However, they have been criticised by Searle (1990: 404) for proposing a "primitive" notion with a "distinct phenomenology" that includes cases where there is no collective intentionality.

reasonable extent. It can individuate and enforce rights, as well as be autonomous and "sufficiently rational" to adjust its actions in accordance with legal and moral norms.[172] There is in fact nothing that comes between the corporation and legal personality. This reflects the common feature shared by the theoretical approaches on the nature of a corporation discussed above: a corporation may by itself perform an action, whether it is to enter into contracts or carry out some social activity. As such, the corporation may be deemed to be a medium through which different groups of people including shareholders, managers and employees exercise individual rights such as the freedom of association and the freedom to contract, contribute "essential" resources[173] and learn to become part of the community.[174] However, the medium is not given empirical content by the exercise of these rights or the contribution of resources but by the members' collectivisation of their efforts.[175] As such, a corporation has no definite shape or purpose and does not represent a specific set of attributes. It is an amorphous entity that exists somewhere between the abstract and the concrete, the imaginary and the perceived, the Cheshire cat and the proverbial elephant. Its form changes according to the circumstances and it may be described accurately as any changeable entity (existing in the legal world) that is recognised either by the legislator or the court as a person because of its independence (collectivisation) of thought and action.

Nonetheless, this definition does not tell us what the term corporation actually means within criminal law discourse. This is because despite its separate existence and independence of thought and action, a corporation

---

[172] In fact some commentators have even gone further by stating that humans to a certain degree acquire their personality from the corporation and not the reverse. See Scruton, 1989.

[173] See Blair and Stout, 1999: 275.

[174] See generally Fort, 2001.

[175] This explains why recognising corporations by looking solely at essential features such as corporate personality or limited liability may be controversial. Maitland for example advanced that the operation of a trust whereby property is managed by trustees for the benefit of other individuals can be used to describe the corporate form. However, other commentators have disagreed on the ground that any definition that follows the consideration of the nature of trusts cannot apply to "profit-oriented" business corporations. Also, the process or processes of identifying the essential attributes may be as dauntingly complex as they are important given that each attribute has to be discussed in great detail in order to understand the reasons that found its choice. See Maitland, 1911: 279 and 321. See also Goebel, 1946: 389; Hessen, 1979: 9; and Davis, 1905: 10.

is not necessarily a responsible agent in the criminal law that may be deserving of punishment. Children under the age of eight and even some animals exist separately and may to a certain extent be said to exercise rational thought and perform actions[176] although the criminal law cannot be used to regulate their behaviour. In the words of Robinson,[177] these children have "exculpatory defences," and in line with Duff,[178] they cannot be "answerable" or accountable.[179] This means that a corporation may be a person with regard to other legal categories but not as regards the criminal law.[180] As such, it is important to consider what is required by criminal law courts to recognise a thing or an entity as a 'person' in order to establish whether a corporation equally fulfils this requirement. Given that the criminal law is concerned only with 'persons' capable of conducting themselves in such a manner as to breach criminal law standards, criminal law courts will recognise as 'persons' only entities that are responsible and punishable.

2.4 Ascertaining the corporate entity in *esse* as a responsible legal person

In the first three sections, I have sought to define the term 'corporation' by abstracting properties of rival theories on the essence of a corporation and legal personality. As mentioned above, an assemblage of these different properties depicts something close to the reality of the corporate person in law although not particularly in criminal law. Given that this book examines corporate criminal law it is important to determine what the term 'corporation' actually means in criminal law. I will do this by showing the relationship between some accounts of responsibility and punishment within the criminal law and the concept of the corporate person. I will employ the same approach of limiting the discussion to

---

[176] As noted above there is no steadfast degree of rationality that is required to make an entity a person.
[177] 1997: 71-81.
[178] 2007: 206.
[179] See also Westen, 2008: 565-566.
[180] In the French jurisdiction, prior to the *Code Pénal* of 1992, the corporation was recognised as a legal person (or *personne morale*) although it was generally not amenable to the criminal law. The German position is also similar where only administrative sanctions can be imposed on corporations. This shows internal incoherence within the system.

descriptive and analytical theorising centred on both legal edicts and some 'pedigreed' non-legal prescriptions.[181]

2.4.1 Who should be responsible?

Responsibility in criminal law may be said to be founded on two postulates. The first concerns the maxim *actus non facit reum nisi men sit rea.*[182] This maxim lays stress on the criminal law components of *mens rea, actus reus,* knowledge, causing injury and fault, in order to determine whether the accused may be said to be responsible for the commission of the offence[183] and thus liable.[184] Hence, the court may impose criminal liability on a subject if her responsibility is established by showing that she performed the physical act with a guilty mind and lacks an exonerating excuse.[185] This approach can readily be observed in criminal law monographs and statutes in the United Kingdom.[186] The second postulate on which criminal responsibility is based is to the effect that an act does not make a person criminal unless the law so provides. This places emphasis on the actions of the accused and the wordings of the relevant precedent or statute (including the equity or spirit of the *dictum* or statute).

These two postulates also represent two ways in which criminal liability may be ascribed to persons, *viz.* attributing liability to the morally blameworthy person and attributing liability to a person in accordance

---

[181] It must be noted that the choice of an account of responsibility, as well as a perspective on who deserves to be punished, has also heavily influenced the development of corporate criminal liability. See Gobert and Punch, 2003: 44 and 46.

[182] This may be translated roughly as an act does not make a person criminal unless the mind is guilty. Lacey (2001: 352) however questions the grammatical correctness of this maxim.

[183] Lacey, 2001: 350-351.

[184] Responsibility is understood here to mean the defendant's obligation and the province or the extent of her actions. As such, liability may be said to refer to the defendant's lack of justification or excuse for her actions. See Duff, 2007: 39. This implies that liability is responsibility coupled with the lack of an appropriate defence. See Westen, 2008: 565-566. However, where the offence charged is absolute then liability and responsibility may be treated as synonyms.

[185] See Dresser, 1993: 41, 85; and Todarello, 2002-2003: 853.

[186] See for example, draft Codes by the English Law Commissions No 413, 1985 (Codification of the Criminal Law); and Law Commission No 177, 1989 (A Criminal Code for England and Wales). See also the draft Code for Scotland in Clive, Ferguson, Gane and Smith (2003).

with the objective of a statute. These patterns of ascription may be said to represent the deontological and teleological rationales in criminal law theory. The deontological rationale describes legal and moral precepts of responsibility as deserts or warrants and constraints on the criminal justice system and the teleological rationale conceives of responsibility as representing a mechanism devised to meet a target defined by the law.[187] It may therefore be posited that courts (and even commentators) elect for a particular way in which the criminal law distributes (or ought to distribute) liability based on their understanding of responsibility[188] and such understanding is based on a set of ideas held to constitute morality or the objective of a statute or common law practice.[189] Given that the criminal law may be theorised in several ways including the philosophical, sociological, psychological and historical, the notion of responsibility (moral and legal) may be addressed from multiple perspectives. However, the objective of these different analyses would almost always be to determine whether liability may be imposed on a morally acceptable ground.[190] In other words, they seek to establish whether liability may be imposed only where the accused is shown to be responsible or both responsible and culpable.

Nonetheless, in corporate liability literature not much emphasis has been placed on the personal (non-derivative) responsibility and culpability of the accused corporation. This may be blamed on three things. Firstly, crimes that occur in relation to corporate activities have historically been treated as lesser crimes or illegal activities that do not warrant a strict observance of traditional standards of proof of intent.[191] Secondly, given

---

[187] Both perspectives also represent what have been termed constraint-driven enforcement and objective or target-driven enforcement. See generally Braithwaite and Pettit, 1990; Schlegel, 1990; Fisse and Braithwaite, 1993; and Wells, 2001.

[188] See Nobles and Schiff, 2006: 207.

[189] Examining responsibility and deriving its meaning from both legal and moral precepts does not necessarily take exception to the argument put forward by some commentators such as Hart (1983: 25) and Orts (1993: 1574) that legal concepts can only be defined and understood within the confinement of an established legal practice. See however Lacey, 2001: 358.

[190] Standards that are legally acceptable overlap with standards that are morally acceptable because it is morally unacceptable to disregard the law.

[191] It has for example been noted that Sutherland introduced the concept of "white-collar crime" to distinguish between traditional crimes such as theft and murder from activities within the corporate world that happen to breach criminal law standards. See Schlegel, 1990: 3. A number of cases were discussed above where

that corporations were deemed to be legal fictions or entities existing only in the intendment of the law, courts for many centuries imposed criminal liability on corporations only where proof of guilt was not deemed as important as policy objectives.[192] Thirdly, the difficulty of finding an appropriate mechanism for the attribution of responsibility (acts and intents or causal relationships) to the corporate entity pushed some judges and commentators to conclude that the most effective way of holding corporations criminally liable was to simply disregard the notion of responsibility and any rules or mechanisms incidental thereto and treat corporations as *de facto* blameworthy agents.[193] However, with the increase of systematic studies of the behaviour of the corporation and the attribution of empirical content to its entity status, courts have felt the need to impose liability directly on corporations as responsible[194] or culpability-bearing agents.[195] Nonetheless, despite the failure of earlier courts to address direct or non-derivative responsibility, it may not be claimed that the subject of corporate criminal liability did not constitute a legitimate branch of the criminal law. This is because responsibility simply binds the accused to the relevant course of action and the prosecution may do so by either showing that the accused entertained and performed the requisite *mens rea* and *actus reus* or simply performed an act prohibited by the law or failed to perform one required by the law. As such, a corporation may

---

the courts declined to require the prosecution to show proof of intent and held the corporate defendants liable for what they termed "quasi-crimes."

[192] This is also the reason why corporations are held vicariously liable in some jurisdictions. See for example *New York Central and Hudson River Railroad v United States* 212 US 481 (1909), hereinafter referred to as *New York Central.*

[193] Sullivan, 1995: 283. Such an approach would no doubt fuel arguments about the lack of theoretical foundation of corporate criminal law and its legitimacy as a branch of the criminal law.

[194] Although some commentators cited in Chapter 4 suggested that the identification doctrine employed to impose direct liability on corporations for crimes of intent was inspired by the organ theory and German Law, there is little evidence to substantiate this claim. The judges that first imposed this form of liability on corporations in 1944 did not allude to any empirical studies. Only Stable J in *R v ICR Haulage* [1944] 1 KB 551 (hereinafter referred to as *ICR Haulage*) at 556 suggested that the courts' attitude had "undergone a process of development" making it likely that in 1944 Finlay J's decision in *R v Cory Bros* [1927] 1 KB 810 (hereinafter referred to as *Cory Bros*) acquitting a corporation of manslaughter, could have been otherwise.

[195] The conflict between consequentialist (including utilitarian) values and retributive values becomes apparent when the notion of responsibility is examined. See Schlegel, 1990: 75-90.

be deemed to be a responsible agent in criminal law if it can be shown to have breached the law in one or both of these ways, representing the deontological and teleological patterns of ascription.

2.4.1.1 The deontological pattern: responsibility based on moral agency

The function of the criminal law has been described as restricted to punishing only persons who have committed a morally reprehensible action and are deserving of blame.[196] This means that only persons that appreciated or ought to have appreciated the moral content of their actions may be criminally liable.[197] This position is generally related to methodological individualism and individual justice[198] and viewed from a 'person-centred' standpoint whereby the criminal justice system is constrained to treat a person faced with a choice in a particular manner.[199] It is also related to what Norrie describes as the "Kantian model of justice" whereby a person free from the exigencies of her surrounding environment chooses to commit a morally reprehensible act. It is not important to explain the person's choice of action in light of ambient social factors;[200] and when questions of criminal liability are addressed in court the number of excuses available to the person is limited only to those that concern her state of mind.

This perspective of responsibility has always been confronted with questions about the source and definition of moral agency. It has been posited that moral agency may be discovered through careful reasoning on the relation between the agent and her conduct (irrespective of social values or the interests of the wider community).[201] This is because moral agents are endowed with the capacity to recognise the rightness and

---

[196] See Schlegel, 1990: 75; Moore, 1997: 33 and 35; Norrie, 1999: 111; and Duff, 2005: 356.

[197] See Nobles and Schiff, 2006: 208.

[198] This is to the effect that the rights of the individual should not be unduly sacrificed in favour of the interest of the community. See Braithwaite and Pettit, 1990: 54; Schlegel, 1990: 75; Fisse and Braithwaite, 1993: 17-19; and Gobert and Punch, 2003: 44.

[199] See generally Braithwaite and Pettit, 1990: 26-31.

[200] See Norrie, 2000: 47-49. See also the review article by Sullivan (2002).

[201] See Watkins' (2006: 601-604) discussion of the "Ledger View" where the agent's responsibility is deemed to be a function of her moral conduct and not necessarily the expectations of other members of her community.

wrongness of conduct.[202] Thus, courts have to look at the judgement made by an agent in order to impose liability for the conduct chosen.[203] It may therefore be said that the rules of responsibility and liability are enacted in light of the agent's right to choose and the operation of defences such as undue influence, automatism and insanity constitute a constraint on the criminal justice system to refrain from ascribing responsibility under circumstances where the agent was not autonomous and could not have exercised her freewill to choose otherwise. These defences thus provide the affected agent with a warrant to non-culpability.[204]

With regard to the question of moral blameworthiness, two major ideas are recurrent in the literature of responsibility and morality which are of particular interest to the corporate entity. Firstly, a morally responsible agent is essentially a human being;[205] and secondly, the mental element relevant to convict is subjective, that is, it must be established that the moral agent in the dock intentionally carried out the blameworthy act in such a manner that it could be said that she was certain or ought to have been certain of the outcome.[206] Before testing these ideas on the corporate person it is important to look at the second pattern of ascription employed in criminal law which can be described as teleological.

---

[202] See Lacey, 2001: 353; Cane, 2002: 4 and 23; and Gobert and Punch, 2003: 46-50. However, this would be a good example of a materialistic fallacy if the concepts of rightness and wrongness are not understood here to relate to legality and illegality.

[203] This means that courts are constrained to impose liability on agents that exercise poor judgement. Such constraints may be called deserts. See Schlegel, 1990: 66-67; and Braithwaite and Pettit, 1990: 29-30.

[204] These are the "exculpatory defences" discussed by Robinson (1997) and Duff (2007).

[205] Hayek, 1949: 6. See also Fisse and Braithwaite, 1993: 19-24; Lacey, 2001: 357; and Cane, 2002: 4, 23.

[206] Norrie (2000: 1) describes this approach as "orthodox subjectivism." Horder, (1997: 95) on his part contends that this approach was the orthodox custom in the 20th century. See also Norrie, 1999: 532; Simester, 1999: 17; Lacey, 2001: 350; and Sullivan, 2002: 749. See also the cases of *R v Scartlett* [1993] Crim LR 288; and *B v DPP* [2000] 1 All ER 833. However, the orthodox custom has not always been observed by courts and Parliament.

2.4.1.2 The teleological pattern: responsibility based on social interest

Social conflict may emanate from discordant moral views and such a conflict may sometimes be resolved by turning to the law for a compromise solution. Given that the law (when compared to morality) imposes more effective sanctions and attends to diverse social and cultural complexities in real life,[207] relying solely on notions such as 'freewill' and 'moral blameworthiness' would be tantamount to using them as articles of faith.[208] This may result in the disregard of certain rights that conflict with those of the accused such as the right of the victim and the right of society to security. Hence, the teleological perspective pays attention to other types of offences that do not necessarily require proof of moral blameworthiness or subjective intent. These include absolute and strict liability offences.[209] As such, all offences existing within each jurisdiction cannot be brought together and measured with regard to an independent set of moral ideas and may sometimes be better understood when discussed within a teleological or consequentialist frame whereby regard is given to the functions they play and the objectives they are required to meet.[210] Thus, there are values[211] that the criminal justice system seeks to promote and in so doing targets an agent to whom responsibility is ascribed. The agent is therefore liable because this promises the best of consequences.[212]

It is however important to note that the teleological facet of the criminal law hardly enjoys consensus among commentators. Leonard for example contends that this approach is simply unjust as the defendant is used as a "means to an end."[213] Hippard on his part contends that any form of criminal liability without fault is oxymoronic and unconstitutional.[214] Nonetheless, this approach of responsibility is concerned with the dynamics of the interaction between the agent, the victim and the society

---

[207] See Watkins, 2006: 596.
[208] Sullivan, 2002: 753.
[209] See Cane, 2002: 105-110.
[210] See Cane, 2002: 56-60; and Gobert and Punch, 2003: 47.
[211] In this case social (utilitarian) values such as the happiness of most members of the society.
[212] See Braithwaite and Pettit, 1990: 31-32; and Gobert and Punch, 2003: 47.
[213] 2003: 692 and 697. He however notes that *mens rea* is not always an essential component of an offence. For criticisms of similar approaches, see Horder, 1997.
[214] 1973: 1040.

at large because this interaction defines the function of the criminal justice system. Thus, there are instances where the interests of the society may determine an agent's "prospective responsibilities."[215] To hold a person responsible in such instances would imply that she has breached her "prospective" duty by causing harm to the community or to a neighbour that is the beneficiary of the prospective duty.[216] There are two recurrent ideas under this approach which are of particular interest to the corporate entity. Firstly, a person is held responsible due to society's perception of the importance of holding her responsible for her action.[217] Secondly, the ascription of responsibility should be based on an objective test. This means that responsibility relates not to the intention or mental disposition of the accused but to the risk inherent in the activity that she carried out.[218]

2.4.1.3 Ascertaining the responsible corporate person

Two perspectives of responsibility have been discussed. They are based on different sets of rationale that are sometimes contradictory given that one approach advocates for holding only the morally blameworthy agent responsible while the other advocates for holding agents responsible when a designated objective will be achieved irrespective of whether she is morally blameworthy or not. Both perspectives are important and it is submitted here that neither of them should be presented as the criminal justice system's only concern.[219] Just as in the case with defining the corporation as an entity in *esse* and as a legal person, the advocacy for a "grand theory" or a unitary and cosmopolitan view of responsibility is ill-conceived due to the fact the operation of such criminal law concepts cannot be captured by a single set of principles.[220]

Hence, as regards the deontological approach, a corporation may be shown to have entertained the blameworthy motive via an established

---

[215] Cane, 2002: 36. See also the discussion of the "Practice View" by Strawson, 1974, where the agent's responsibility is held to be a function of expectations within her community. See also Watkins, 2006: 601-604.

[216] The fact that the duty-holder did not intend the consequences of her action is immaterial. See Cane, 2002: 55-56.

[217] See for example Wells' (1993: 551) claim that corporate criminal liability represents "cultural attitudes" toward technological ventures. See also Miers, 1983.

[218] See Wells, 1988: 797; and 1993: 553.

[219] This book therefore endorses the dual view of Braithwaite and Pettit (1990) that includes both the retributive and the consequentialist or utilitarian perspectives.

[220] See Duff, 2005: 356.

mechanism of attributing the knowledge and intents of agents (or causal relationship) to the corporation.[221] In other words, such a mechanism will be based on the fact that a corporation (through its agents) is capable of cognition and may be morally blameworthy. This means that the corporation's liability will not be established by evidence showing that one of its agents was responsible but by showing that the corporation itself was responsible.[222] As such, the individuals that make up a corporation may be innocent and yet the corporation is guilty. As noted above, some researchers such as Kornhauser, Sager, Pettit and Rock have shown how collective groups such as corporations act with a specific intent. Thus, if corporations are moral persons or intelligent machines that distinctly manifest reason, bear intentions and carry out positive actions, the criminal justice system ought to be constrained to hold them liable where the intent manifested corresponds to the *mens rea* of the offence charged.[223]

The corporation may equally be said to be a responsible subject in criminal law theory from a teleological perspective. In fact, corporate liability has historically developed along the lines of target or objective-driven enforcement.[224] Judges have readily turned to the existing criminal legislation, as well as values and doctrines established through precedent in order to determine whether these relate to the values of the wider society to which the criminal justice system appeals for legitimacy.[225] Thus, a corporation has been held liable for obstructing a road and causing harm through pollution even though no subjective test showed that its board of directors or senior management actually intended or foresaw that their activities may have resulted in harm to members of the community.[226] This is because the values of the wider society as well as the statutes creating the offences dictated that society must be protected

---

221 See Schlegel, 1990: 75-90; and Sullivan, 1995: 283.

222 See Wells, 2001: Chapter 8, especially the specific references made to the metaphysics of corporations developed by French, 1984; and Dan-Cohen, 1986. See also Schlegel, 1990: 78-79; and Sullivan, 1995: 283.

223 Sullivan, 1995: 283.

224 See the historical development of corporate criminal liability in Schlegel, 1990; Wells, 2001; and Gobert and Punch, 2003.

225 See Gobert and Punch, 2003: 54. This demonstrates the influence of social and cultural forces on the development of the criminal law. See Wells, 1993: 551-556.

226 *R v The Great North of England Railway Company* (1846) 115 ER 1294. This case is hereinafter referred to as *The Great North of England Railway Co.*

from harm resulting from public works and such values would have been defeated if liability was not imposed on the corporation.[227]

However, it must be noted that terms such as 'goal of the statute' and 'social interest' are as equivocal as 'moral blameworthiness' and 'freewill' and it is uncertain what measure is used to determine how statutory provisions relate to the values of the wider society. Public perception of responsibility may influence the imposition of liability on agents on the ground that the public thinks the agent's act is morally blameworthy.[228] This has been the case with corporate defendants. Before the capsize of the Herald of Free Enterprise and the Southall train crash for example, there was more tolerance for "accidents" and "chance" disasters directly related to corporate activities although they registered scores of deaths.[229] The deaths were seen as tragic and unfortunate.[230] Wells[231] also talks of the then British Prime Minister describing a deranged gunman shooting and killing 16 people as a tragic crime and the capsize of the Herald of Free Enterprise and the fire at the King's Cross Station as accidents. As such, it is only after scathing media reports placing blame for financial scandals at the door of the practices and policies of Enron, WorldCom and Arthur Andersen and showing that better management would have avoided the disasters that communities' perception of the responsibility of corporations began to change. Under pressure, the British Parliament has seemingly reacted to the clamant calls for stricter regulatory measures by enacting the Corporate Manslaughter and Corporate Homicide Act 2007 (CMCHA)

---

[227] However, this does not imply that judges are required to disregard important words in a statutory provision in order to enforce what they deem to be the equity of the statute. See the recommendation by the Criminal Law Revision Committee (1980) on the need to circumscribe the mental element for manslaughter.

[228] This shows that morality, a deontological instrument, may sometimes play an important role in the teleological construction of legal concepts.

[229] Carson (1982: 30) suggests that economic rationality might have played a role in the tolerance towards corporate crime. See also Taylor, 1983: 10.

[230] Box (1983: 26) intimates that the number of deaths from occupational hazards is seven times higher than those of homicide. See also the gory figures presented by Hair (1971: 5-24); and Beattie (1986: 86) cited in Wells, 1988: 788. Thus, corporate activities that had a high propensity of resulting in injury or death seemed to preoccupy the public far less than routine violent crime by humans. See also the survey conducted by Prescott-Clarke (1982: 13) that showed that 51 percent of people surveyed were concerned by road and traffic accidents compared to 8 percent by crime and violence.

[231] 1988: 791, citing The Guardian, August 21, 1987.

and creating an offence targeting corporations which requires only an objective test.

Nonetheless, in light of the above, it may be advanced that a corporation may be shown to be criminally responsible on both deontological and teleological bases. This is because although amorphous and incorporeal it can distinctly manifest reason, bear intentions and carry out positive actions. Although such reason, intentions and actions may overlap with those of an individual agent they are often the products of collectivisation and are therefore motivated by the corporation's independent interests. The discussion above is therefore consonant with the contention that a corporation is a changeable entity (existing in the legal world) that is recognised by the legislator or court as a corporation because of its independence of thought and action. What this definition tells us is that a corporation is capable of using its agents or encouraging and assisting them in the commission of offences and may be responsible either directly (non-derivatively) or as an accessory. However, this description is not complete because an entity may be all of these and yet criminal liability is not imposed upon it owing to the fact that it cannot be punished. In other words, there is no criminal sanction that may deter or rehabilitate or incapacitate the entity.[232] As such, ascertaining the essence of a corporation within criminal law discourse also involves determining whether the corporate person is amenable to criminal sanction.

2.4.2 Who can be punished?

The discussion below adopts the same methodology employed to analyse the use of responsibility in criminal law theory. Hence, the question of punishment will be addressed from the deontological and teleological perspectives. Deontological theories conform to the notion of constraint-driven enforcement discussed in the previous subsection and submit to the assertion that moral blameworthiness is the purpose of punishment. This reflects the criminal law goal of retribution and just deserts. As such, deontological or retributive theories are geared towards the redistribution or a just distribution of the varied burdens and benefits in society according to moral criteria.[233] They constitute a system of blame

[232] For example, although Coke (*Sutton's Hospital*) conceived of a corporation as existing in the intendment of the law and capable of performing a few acts, he held that it could not be prosecuted and convicted for offences such as treason because it could neither be excommunicated nor executed.

[233] Braithwaite and Fisse, 1993: 45.

that empowers society to respond to crime by imposing something unpleasant on the wrongdoer[234] that provides her with moral reasons not to indulge in a similar act.[235] Thus, the wrongdoer should have the capacity to appreciate the social disapproval communicated through the sanction. However, it is uncertain whether the imposition of a criminal sanction on the offender solely because her act deserves to be punished would in theory preclude other persons from committing the same offence.[236] Thus, although the reasons for imposing a criminal sanction on a person include the person's moral blameworthiness and the need for society to make a moral statement, it would be otiose to impose a sanction that does not deter the wrongdoer and others from indulging in the same offence.[237] As such, where criminal sanctions are imposed to punish blameworthiness there is a concomitant objective to reduce the incidence of the offender or other persons committing the same offence.[238] This means that the theory of retribution may to a certain extent serve the utilitarian goals of deterrence and rehabilitation[239] and shows that both accounts are not always mutually exclusive and sometimes overlap.[240] However, from a purely deontological perspective a judge is constrained to impose a sanction where the accused is morally blameworthy or does not have an exculpatory defence and utilitarian goals are nonessential.

---

[234] Irrespective of whether the person displays feelings of regret or not. See Byam, 1982: 583; and Fisse and Braithwaite, 1993: 45.

[235] See Kant, 1965: 101-107; Packer, 1968: 9; Ezorsky, 1972: 102-34; LaFave and Scot, 1972: 5; Byam, 1982: 583; Murphy J, 1985: 158; Lacey, 1988: 22-24; Fisse and Braithwaite, 1993: 45, 128; Wells, 2001: 19; and Todarello, 2002-2003: 854.

[236] Fisse and Braithwaite, 1993: 44.

[237] This is because the moral statement would be deemed unheeded.

[238] And also minimise human suffering, a goal influenced by the 'harm principle.' See Wells, 2001: 14, 15.

[239] This type of deterrence is often referred to as "weak" or "negative retributivism." It is to the effect that the fact that a person is deserving of punishment is not sufficient justification to punish her lest there is a utilitarian goal to be achieved. See Hart, 1968: 77; Fisse and Braithwaite, 1993: 46; and Wells, 2001: 19.

[240] These accounts may also be said to reflect Duff's (2007) contention that a person is punishable because she is responsible and does not have an exculpatory excuse. As such, the defender that has an exculpatory defence is not blameworthy and does not need to be deterred or rehabilitated.

On the other hand, teleological or consequentialist theories[241] concord with the notions of target-driven and objective-driven enforcement and support the statement that the criminal law should punish the wrongdoer in order to meet the social objectives of security and crime reduction. Proponents of teleological theories see punishment as more than a vengeful act perpetrated by society[242] and believe that it must be defined in consequentialist terms. Some of the consequentialist objectives in this regard include deterrence, rehabilitation and incapacitation.[243] Deterrence seen through a teleological lens is distinguishable from deterrence discussed under retribution in that it does not seek to attribute blame or make a moral statement but simply dissuade the criminal offender (specific deterrence) and other potential offenders in similar situations (general deterrence).[244] There is some uncertainty as regards the extent to which a form of punishment effectively deters offenders and thus, the idea of imposing sanctions on persons merely for the purpose of deterring them may be said to actually favour despotism. However, it may be argued that this line of reasoning is ineluctable where society is constrained to deter a particular criminal offender due to a high propensity of the latter to perform injurious actions.[245] As regards rehabilitation, it may be said to be geared toward educating and training the target criminal offender so that she may reintegrate into society after serving the penalty as a law-abiding citizen. The objective is equally to reduce the number of criminals.[246] This may also be said to be the objective of incapacitation although it is thought that incapacitation is achieved by simply removing the offender from

[241] They may also be referred to as instrumental or symbolic and relate more effectively to the "harm principle." See Wells, 2001: 14.
[242] Gibbs, 1975: 82-83. See also Lacey, 1988: 96; Wells, 2001: 18; and Todarello, 2002-2003: 854.
[243] See Packer, 1968: 11; Note, Harvard, 1979: 1231-1243; and Byam, 1982: 583.
[244] Todarello, 2002-2003: 854. As such, if no moral statement is made but the objective is achieved, the sanction is justifiable.
[245] This is another example of the intersection of retributive and consequentialist rationales. The criminal statute that places such a constraint on society may be said to have a retributive as well as a consequentialist objective and such statutes include those that provide for the proof of intent of the accused.
[246] See Gibbs, 1975: 72; and Todarello, 2002-2003: 854. It has nonetheless been invariably described as an unrealistic goal (see Blecker, 1990: 1149) and a totalitarian regime that seeks to rearrange the mind and thoughts of prisoners through coercion. See Fisse and Braithwaite, 2002: 124. These commentators however recommend rehabilitative services for offenders who are found to need them and who freely ask for them.

society[247] and protecting the public from the danger posed by the offender.[248] This means that the incapacitation should be proportionate to the crime committed.[249]

From the above, it may be advanced that there is no cosmopolitan theory of punishment. Both deontological and teleological perspectives discussed above present credible opportunities for the criminal justice system to reduce crime. They are not mutually exclusive[250] and have serious loopholes that in certain circumstances undermine the objective of the criminal law. They may however be said to represent a holistic view of the purpose of punishment in criminal law theory. A person may be punished if she is morally blameworthy and/or if socially desirable objectives may be achieved. Thus, on the one hand it is fair to impose punishment for past acts and on the other hand it is socially useful to impose punishment for the future.[251] The question that this section seeks to address is whether it is logical to impose criminal sanctions on the responsible corporate person and why. It is expected that the answer to this question will provide another indication to the essence of the corporate person.

---

[247] See Zimring and Hawkins, 1973.

[248] This is often described as selective incapacitation.

[249] However, there are few accurate predictions of recidivism and the absence of precise data seriously undermines the importance of selective incapacitation. An offender would thus be incapacitated for a period based on a decision founded on questionable variables. Moreover, if an offender is deemed to remain dangerous and the period of her incapacitation has to be extended this would be tantamount to an infringement upon her right to non-interference beyond the maximum sentence prescribed by legislation. Another shortcoming is the lack of sufficient fiscal resources to imprison the number of criminals that would be enough to have a substantial impact on crime rate. See Braithwaite and Pettit, 1990: 3 and 125.

[250] Punishment is a complex concept and attempts at formulating cosmopolitan theories to explain the nature of punishment should not be encouraged. See Wells, 2001: 20.

[251] If it is established that a corporation is punishable the question that follows is what is the most appropriate punishment for corporate entities given their artificial nature? This question is not addressed below but in Chapter 7 dealing with the applicable sanctions in the United Kingdom.

2.4.2.1 Ascertaining the essence of the corporate person as a punishable entity

Some commentators have contended that punishing the corporation represents a total disregard of the theoretical bases on which the criminal law is grounded, *viz.*, criminal intent and positive action.[252] However, it is shown above that the argument that corporations have intentions of their own and carry out positive rational actions holds water in certain instances. Thus, where a corporation intentionally breaches criminal law standards it is just and fair to impose criminal sanctions on it.[253] The argument here is that a corporation is punishable because it has the capacity to relate to the consequences of its actions and decisions, as well as the capacity to appreciate the social disapproval of its act communicated through the sanction.

In the same vein the imposition of criminal sanctions can effectively deter corporations,[254] as well as rehabilitate and incapacitate them[255] in order to achieve the goals of crime reduction and furtherance of social interests. Deterrence no doubt enjoys consensus as the main purpose of punishing corporations given that even opponents of corporate criminal liability accept that corporations may be deterred by criminal sanctions,[256] although they also claim that there is unfortunately no standard to determine whether a sanction effectively deters corporate defenders.[257] Nonetheless, it is manifest that corporations are most likely to be deterred

---

[252] See Spurgeon and Fagan, 1981: 400, 424; and Byam, 1982: 585.

[253] See French, 1995: 160, 166; Note, Harvard, 1979: 1243; and Fisse and Braithwaite, 1993: 45.

[254] See Wells, 2001: 13-14.

[255] *Cf* Byam, 1982: 586. The thought that fines are the only sanctions that may be imposed on corporate defenders may have influenced Byam's conclusion that corporations may only be deterred.

[256] See Packer, 1968: 356; and Byam, 1982: 585 and 586.

[257] See Coffee, 1981: 408; and Byam, 1982: 585. This argument has more to do with the practicality of sanctions than their legitimacy because the same claim may be made of human defenders. See Fisse and Braithwaite, 2002: 148; and Wells, 2001: 19. However, Byam (1982: 584-585) employs economic efficiency as a standard to specify a deterrent penalty for corporations (which he thinks should be civil damages) but his analysis is premised on contestable assumptions: a system of enforcement that reduces the incidence of corporate crime will cost less to society and will be more efficient and more effective; and corporations naturally respond to threats of economic sanctions (irrespective of the likelihood of prosecution and conviction).

by sanctions that may cause considerable economic loss[258] or by an indictment and prosecution and/or a sanction that carries public stigma.[259]

Rehabilitation has in some instances (when coerced) been deemed to be more appropriate to corporate entities than natural persons.[260] A remedial order may incite a corporation to put in place a compliance programme to correct a defective operation in accordance with the order and re-establish its reputation. In such an instance the corporation may be said to have been rehabilitated or reformed. This is also the case where the court thinks that it is appropriate in the circumstance to order a re-organisation of the managerial structure.[261] This may be achieved in part through orders disqualifying negligent company directors[262] and compelling other directors to act responsibly and exercise sufficient skill and care with regard to the interests of all the company's stakeholders.[263]

Comments for and against the theory of incapacitation have been based on the assumption that imprisonment and execution are the only penalties that can be used to incapacitate an offender. Although these penalties are not applicable to the corporate criminal,[264] there are a host of other penalties that may effectively incapacitate a corporation. When its license privileges are withdrawn or the license is temporally suspended or the corporation is temporally or permanently disqualified from carrying on

---

[258] This is logical for profit-making corporations given that they are driven by the desire to maximise profit and might be tempted to commit the crime and include it in their costs if the crime will enable them maximise profits or the sanction is not hefty. See Note, Harvard (1979): 1365; and Byam, 1982: 587.

[259] See Stone, 1975: 43.

[260] See Braithwaite and Pettit, 1990: 124.

[261] See Chapter 7.

[262] See for example the Company Directors Disqualification Act 1986, the Insolvency Act 2000, and the Enterprise Act 2002.

[263] This may be stated as the reason why criminal sanctions should target the responsible individuals rather than corporations. However, there are instances where no single director may be shown to be at fault. Thus, although targeting the corporation only may not always achieve the goals of the criminal law, in many cases involving corporate activities, it remains the most efficient strategy. See Khanna, 1996: 1496.

[264] Nonetheless, it has been suggested that the dissolution of the corporation may be imposed as a corresponding sentence for execution. See Bouzat and Pinatel, 1970: 312. Such a decision would however take into consideration the repercussions on the community: loss of jobs and revenue and may be the provision of essential services.

specific activities, it may be said to have been incapacitated. Also, if a corporation is placed under judicial supervision whereby it reports its activities and cannot act without prior authorisation, such a corporation may be said to have been incapacitated.[265]

It may therefore be contended that a corporation is not only a responsible agent but it is equally punishable under certain circumstances.[266] It is punishable because on the one hand, it has the capacity to relate to the consequences of its actions and decisions, as well as the capacity to appreciate the moral blemish of the criminal sanction (therefore it does not have an exculpatory defence) and on the other hand, it can be deterred, rehabilitated and incapacitated. However, given that it invariably acts through natural persons, the courts and legislators must devise a means of punishing it only in situations where it would react accordingly through such agents.

2.5 Conclusion

I set out to circumscribe the nature of the corporation within criminal law discourse and in the course of doing this I established that although courts have often asserted the fictitious nature of the corporation they have treated it as a real entity that bears legal rights and has the capacity to affect relationships. This dual view of the corporation is also consonant with a number of theories (both legal and non-legal) that describe different facets of the corporate reality. Thus, these theories may help in elucidating the features by which courts may recognise a corporation. Courts may refrain from intervening in the operation of the activities of a corporation because it is an expression of fundamental individual freedoms, although an intervention may be necessary in some instances because the state and the agents of the corporation had an agreement that the former will recognise the existence of the corporation in exchange for the performance of some social functions by the latter. The proposition that follows from both theoretical positions is that corporations may by themselves perform

[265] Where a corporation without expert staff and the requisite resources obtains a license to carry out public operations such as waste disposal or building of a bridge, its license may be revoked to prevent it from breaching the criminal law (through misfeasance or nonfeasance) and to protect public interests. See Gobert and Punch, 2003.

[266] The question of what forms of punishment achieve the deterrence, rehabilitation and incapacitation goals requires an extended empirical study that should examine the effects of each sanction on a large number of corporations.

certain activities, whether it is to enter into agreements or perform some social functions. Nonetheless, when a judge or legislator talks of the imposition of criminal liability on a corporation she is not simply referring to the imposition of criminal liability on an entity that exists *simplicter* (in the sense of entertaining ideas and performing positive actions) but that exists as a legal person. This is because in the legal world only legal persons may be deemed to have the capacity to perform actions and affect relationships. Thus, theories describing the concept of legal personality are also important in elucidating the features by which criminal law courts may recognise a corporation. After abstracting different properties from some of these theories, I submitted that criminal law courts conceive of a corporation as an amorphous entity that exists somewhere between the abstract and the concrete, the imaginary and the perceived, and the Cheshire cat and the proverbial elephant.

This implies that there is no substantive element that may be used to define a corporation and to distinguish it from other non-human entities. Van Eeghen posits that legal personality is the distinguishing element.[267] However, in some jurisdictions such as Scotland, partnerships are legal persons and cannot be said to be corporations. Equally, features such as limited liability and perpetuity cannot be said to be the distinguishing factors given that a person's liability cannot be limited under the criminal law and the concept of perpetuity has no bearing on either criminal responsibility or punishability.[268] Thus, given its amorphous nature the only defining feature of the corporation may be said to be the fact of its recognition as a corporation by the court or legislator. This implies that the reason why a court or legislator recognises an entity as a corporation is the most cogent indicator to the nature of the corporation, although such reason would change in light of the circumstances. However, in light of the above, the common reason that gives courts and legislators incentive to recognise a collective entity as a corporation is its ability to think and act independently and relate to the consequences of such thought and action.[269] It may then be submitted that the entity recognised by courts and

---

[267] Van Eeghen, 2005: 52-53.

[268] Moreover, there are other means by which limited liability and perpetuity may be acquired other than forming a corporation. See Hessen, 1979: 15-22.

[269] Nonetheless, it must be noted that although Rock (2005) is cited above as saying that the corporation is the paradigmatic example of what Pettit (1993) calls "purposive groups," it is not the fact of acting autonomously and with a purpose that makes an entity a corporation (as other associations of persons may also be deemed to be "purposive groups") but the fact of acting autonomously and with a

legislators as a corporation is logically amenable to the criminal law. However, there is no guarantee of optimum results for the criminal justice system. This is because the fact that a corporation is capable of committing a crime does not imply that the criminal law is necessarily structured to deal with such a changeable entity. Thus, it may also be important to determine whether the criminal law has the requisite tools to effectively regulate such an entity.

---

purpose and being recognised by the court or legislator as a corporation. Although the insistence on the fact of the recognition of an entity as a corporation (in the circumstances) by a court may be deemed dogmatic, there is hardly any other sustainable argument justifying the extension of legal personality to an artificial entity while rational animals and plants that may also relate to the consequences of their independent actions are not granted such a privilege. Some commentators like French (1995: 56-80) have premised their analyses (in favour of granting the privilege to corporations) on the idea that animals and plants cannot be moral agents although the idea is not explicated.

CHAPTER THREE

THE ADAPTABILITY OF THE CRIMINAL LAW IN DEALING WITH THE CORPORATE PERSON

3.1 Introduction

In Chapter 2, it was submitted that a corporation is anything recognised by Parliament or courts as a corporation due to its ability to think and act independently and relate to the consequences of such thought and action. However, it was noted that courts may not be able to convict and sanction corporations on a consistent basis if the criminal law lacks the requisite tools to deal with such peculiar entities. This means that the criminal law ought to be adaptable to such an extent that it may be used it to prosecute, convict and sanction corporations of different shapes and sizes perpetrating different offences in different circumstances. This Chapter looks at the way the different forms of liability (and criminal offences) may be modified to suit the nature of the corporate entity in circumstances where the crime is shown to have been committed *qua* corporation.[1] The discussion below is premised on two assumptions. Firstly, the criminal law is a legitimate means of regulating the activities of corporations.[2] Secondly, given that a corporation is an independent person and vicarious liability is shunned by the criminal law regimes of the United Kingdom, a corporation may only be held directly (non-derivatively) or secondarily liable. These assumptions will reinforce other propositions from which I will be able to draw the conclusion that the coherence and integrity of the criminal law (as regards regulating corporations) are directly related to the appropriateness of the mechanism of imputation used by the court or prescribed by Parliament.

---

[1] Chapter 7 discusses the different forms of punishment that may be imposed on different types of corporations for crimes committed *qua* corporation.

[2] With regard to the justification of the use of the criminal law, see Clarkson, 1996; and Wells, 2001: Chapter 2.

The discussion proceeds with an examination of the direct and secondary liability of corporations and four different kinds of offences related thereto in the sequence in which they have been imposed on corporations over the past 400 years,[3] as well as the principles that have been developed and used by Parliament and courts to justify their imposition. I will then seek to determine whether these forms of liability and the offences are appropriate to deal with the 'corporation' as defined in Chapter 2. Finally, I will consider ways in which the use of these forms of liability may be adapted to reflect other legal principles and enable courts to impute acts and intents (or causal relationships) to corporations on a logical and consistent basis.

3.2 Direct (non-derivative) liability

Over the past 400 years, the practice in the United Kingdom has been to hold corporations liable for offences perpetrated by guilty agents. Although it is the guilt and not the act or knowledge of the agent that is imputed to the corporation in order to hold it liable, the latter's liability is held to be direct and not vicarious. The argument is that the guilt of an agent that is identifiable with the corporation is the guilt of the corporation. However, the station of the agent that is identified with the corporation depends on the interpretation of the relevant law by the court and the offence charged.[4] I will examine some of the offences that are enforced against corporations directly in order to determine whether the criminal law has the appropriate tools to deal with the corporate offender.

---

[3] This sequence is determined not by the endorsement of the fact that corporate criminal liability did not exist before then (which is contrary to what this book propounds) but by the difficulty of finding data on corporate criminal liability in the United Kingdom prior to the 17th century.

[4] This idea was propounded by Stable J in *ICR Haulage* but dismissed by Lord Reid in *Nattrass*. However, Lord Reid's rejection of the idea is unfounded given that where the offence charged is an absolute or strict liability offence the corporation may be liable for the act of any employee (performed within the scope of employment) that breaches the strict or absolute duty. Equally, where the offence charged is corporate manslaughter or corporate homicide the corporation may be liable for the act of any employee that breaches the relevant duty of care provided it was motivated by the way the collective of senior managers organised or managed the corporation's activities.

3.2.1 Strict and absolute liability offences

These are offences that generally do not require proof of intent or knowledge and awareness of risk or any form of *mens rea*.[5] Strict liability offences often require what may be termed "minimum culpability,"[6] where the defendant knows or has reasonable cause to know that there is a risk in the activity carried out and was in a position to prevent the risk but did not prevent it.[7] Absolute liability offences on the other hand involve the breach of an absolute duty or carrying out of a prohibited activity[8] and require no standard of culpability.[9] The rationale for enforcing strict and absolute liability offences has been the subject of much debate.[10] They may however be said to delineate a crime prevention scheme instituted by Parliament because it has enough information to believe that modes of carrying out particular activities or the activities themselves have serious consequences on public welfare[11] and thus seeks to prohibit these modes or activities by compelling persons in control to be vigilant and/or to refrain from using the modes or performing the activities.[12] The absence of *mens rea* would not make such persons 'innocent,'[13] because they held the

---

[5] See Wells, 2001: 67; Gobert and Punch, 2003: 94; and Simester, 2005: 22.

[6] Gross, 1979: 372; Braithwaite and Pettit, 1990: 99; and Schlegel, 1990: 87.

[7] Thus, the defendant is not entirely blameless. This has however been described as "formal strict liability" as opposed to "substantive strict liability" where the defendant is blameless. See Green SP, 2005: 1-20; and Husak, 2005: 81-103. See also Simester, 2005: 21-50. However, the idea of "substantive strict liability" reflects absolute liability and will be treated as such in this book.

[8] See *Mousell Bros* at 1101.

[9] Braithwaite and Pettit, 1990: 99.

[10] See generally, Hart, 1968; Singer and Husak, 1999; Ashworth, 1989; and Simester, 2005. Wells (2001: 68) notes that it was a response to the growing abuses by entrepreneurs during the development of industry in early 19th century Britain. However, she cites Singer (1989: 339-353) who differs from this view by pointing out that strict liability offences were enforced against many minors and drunks at the time. See also Gobert, 1994: 396-397.

[11] Braithwaite and Pettit, 1990: 100; Gobert and Punch, 2003: 94-95; and Leonard, 2003: 696. This is consonant with the "harm principle." See Simester, 2005: 25.

[12] See *Gammon (Hong Kong) Ltd v Attorney-General of Hong Kong* [1985] AC 1, hereinafter referred to as *Gammon*. See also *Harrow London Borough Council v Shah* [1999] 3 All ER 302.

[13] The term 'innocent' is used here to refer to the state of mind and act that do not amount to *mens rea* and *actus reus* and not necessarily the state of mind and act that are completely blameless. This is because a number of employees may be negligent in the way in which they carry out their activities although none of their

duties that were breached.[14] Hence, although there is uncertainty as regards their state of mind, they failed to be vigilant and tolerated or encouraged the breach of their duties.[15] As such, attaching the stigma of criminal conviction to such a failure is not unjust or objectionable from a social perspective.[16] As mentioned in Chapter 2, the concepts of justice and morality are to a certain extent social constructs. Thus, criticisms directed at strict and absolute liability on the ground of society's encroachment on the freedom or personal autonomy of duty-holders[17] may only be justified if such power is used to compel persons to perform activities that have no direct connection to public welfare. However, the decision to impose strict and absolute liability is made after careful consideration by Parliament on the need to prohibit certain acts or omissions and the consequences of the accused evading liability (due to the difficulty of proving *mens rea*) on public welfare.[18] Thus, there is good reason to impose strict and absolute liability without the establishment of blameworthiness. The criminal law is not based solely on deontological theorems of constraints and just deserts. Utilitarian or consequentialist theorems of punishment also justify the use of the criminal law. As such, the defendant is liable if she is shown to have performed the prohibited act and unless relevant to the defence of the case, the reasons for performing the prohibited act are not important.[19]

---

negligent acts amounts to the gross negligence required by the law to hold a person liable. These employees are thus innocent although not completely blameless.

[14] *Cf.* Singer and Husak, 1999.

[15] Parliament may also be said to have intended to wipe out the unjust benefit gained by such persons. See Braithwaite and Pettit, 1990: 100; Schlegel, 1990: 87; and Wells, 2001: 70.

[16] See Hart, 1968: 120; Ashworth, 1989: 52; and Simester, 2005: 33-37.

[17] See Simester, 2005: 37-39.

[18] As such, suggesting that it should be a matter for the courts to decide whether societal interests should prevail (see Horder 2002: 461) may be deemed to be tantamount to arguing that courts should make value judgements and disregard Parliament's objective if and when they deem necessary.

[19] Gobert and Punch, 2003: 94. This should however be distinguished from decisions of courts, some of which are cited below, that displace the presumption of *mens rea* where the applicable statute is silent on the issue or simply ignore the express statutory requirement of proof of intent and impose liability on the duty-holder in order to avoid defeating the purpose of the statute. It is argued below that this is unjustified and relates to judicial activism since the intention of the legislator in such situations is to ensure that liability is imposed only on the person that entertained the relevant *mens rea*.

What is important to note here is that if the ideas of strict and absolute liability are taken out of the historical context in which they were formed, there is no reason why they cannot be applied to both natural and artificial persons given that the criminal law is concerned with enforcing a strict or an absolute duty irrespective of the nature of the person on whom it is imposed.[20] Therefore, it may be logical to disapprove of the contention that different standards for strict and absolute liability ought to be applied for natural and artificial persons.[21] This is because the same argument may be used in reverse to justify the impossibility of enforcing offences requiring proof of intent against artificial persons. Moreover, not all corporations are similarly structured; they come in different sizes and shapes and some wield more power and influence than others.[22] The argument for different standards relates to the idea that strict and absolute liability imposed on corporations are not strict and absolute liability *simpliciter* but a form of cost-efficient regulation whereby the burden of proof is reversed and placed on the corporation that has the requisite knowledge and expertise.[23] Nonetheless, as mentioned above, corporations do not constitute a homogenous group and enacting laws affecting all corporations because of the nature of a category of corporations would be highly exceptionable. Thus, it may be submitted that strict and absolute liability offences involve the imposition of liability directly on the person that owed the duty, whether such a person is natural or artificial. There is no ground for applying different standards. This position is well illustrated by Smith JC:[24]

> [w]here a statutory duty to do something is imposed upon a particular person (here, 'an employer') and he does not do it, he commits the *actus reus* of an offence. It may be that he has failed to fulfil his duty because

---

[20] Nonetheless, a duty cannot be imposed on a person that cannot perform it by virtue of her nature.

[21] See Ashworth 1989: 52; and Wells 2001: 68.

[22] Horder (2002: 472-474) for example, posits that imposing strict liability on small businesses that have intrinsic value to individuals or small groups of individuals impacts upon their quest for personal autonomy.

[23] See Simester, 2005: 27-28. The shift of the onus of proof to the accused in such cases is in the opinion of Lord Reid (*Nattrass* at 170) important because it helps avoid instances where it is very difficult for the prosecution to prove *mens rea* and Parliament does not intend that a blameless person should be convicted. However, as deplored in Chapter 7, shifting the burden of proof to the accused because of the prosecution's lack of resources is tantamount to sacrificing fundamental rights on the altar of expediency.

[24] 1995: 655.

> his employee or agent has failed to carry out his duties properly but this is not a case for vicarious liability. If the employer is held liable, it is because he, personally, has failed to do what the law requires him to do and he is personally, not vicariously, liable. There is no need to find someone - in the case of a company, the 'brains' and not merely the 'hands' – for whose act the person with the duty can be held liable. The duty on the company in this case was to 'ensure' - i.e. to make certain - that persons are not exposed to risk. They did not make it certain. It does not matter how; they were in breach of their statutory duty and, in the absence of any requirement of *mens rea*, that is the end of the matter.[25]

As such, even though it was generally accepted in the 19th century that corporations could not commit acts of treason and felony,[26] they were still liable where they failed to perform their duties.[27] Thus, where a duty was imposed upon sellers not to sell any article of food or any drug which was different in terms of nature, substance and quality from that requested by the customer, a corporation was prosecuted for acting contrary to such a provision.[28] The practice has continued over the centuries and today there are hundreds of strict and absolute duties created by statutes that can be enforced against corporations. Thus, where a section engineer did not plan and supervise the operation properly and this resulted in the death of a worker (although provided by a sub-contractor), a corporate employer was held liable for violating the provisions of section 3 of the Health and Safety at Work etc Act 1974 (HSWA).[29]

However, even if it is accepted that strict and absolute liability offences may be enforced directly against the corporate duty-holder,[30] it

---

[25]Smith JC's logic could even be taken further by positing that whether the offence is a strict liability offence or one requiring proof of *mens rea*, the corporation's liability remains direct or non-derivative and not vicarious. *Cf* Gobert, 1994: 396.

[26] In light with Coke's *dictum* in *Sutton's Hospital.*

[27] See *Birmingham and Gloucester Railway Co*. See also *Russell v Men of Devon* 100 ER 359 (1788); *R v Corporation of Stanford upon Avon* (1811) 14 East 348; *R v Steven and Wye Railway Co* (1819) 2 B & Ald 645; *R v Inhabitants of Dorset* (1825) 77 ER 1442; and *The Great North of England Railway Co.*

[28] *Pearks, Dunston and Tee*. See also *Chuter v Freeth and Pocock Ltd* [1911] 2 KB 832, hereinafter referred to as *Chuter v Freeth.*

[29] *British Steel*. See also *R v Associated Octel Co Ltd* [1996] 4 All ER 826, hereinafter referred to as *Associated Octel*. Also important is *R v Great Western Trains Co Ltd* [2000] QB 796 (hereinafter referred to as *Great Western Trains*) where manslaughter charges against the company were dismissed at the preliminary ruling although it pleaded guilty to the HSWA charges.

[30] See Lord Denman in *The Great North of England Railway Co* at 1298.

has been argued that where the legislator uses words such as "use," "permit," "wilfully" and "knowingly," evidence of the guilty state of mind of the person on whom the duty is imposed is required.[31] Hence, where there is no ascertained way of proving the corporation's state of mind, enforcing such duties would be problematic. As such, courts in the 19th and early 20th century generally showed reluctance to consider theories of corporate knowledge and *mens rea* and the significance of words such as "wilfully" and "knowingly" was conveniently ignored. Avory J in *Moses* v *Midland Railway Co* for example held that irrespective of the words "every person who causes or knowingly permits," the offence under section 5 of the Salmon Fishery Act 1861 was an absolute offence that did not require proof of *mens rea*.[32] This shows that the extension of corporate liability to include statutory offences inevitably requires evidence of the accused corporation's knowledge or intent.[33] Lord Campbell considered this in 1858 and concluded that "there may be great difficulty in saying that under certain circumstances express malice may not be imputed to and proved against a corporation."[34]

The paragraph above notwithstanding, it may be said that strict and absolute liability offences constitute a valid way of imposing criminal liability directly on corporations. Although these offences have been the subject of scathing criticisms, they may be justified on consequentialist

---

[31] There is nothing wrong in permitting wilfully or knowingly the disposal of waste (in case of pollution) but it is the attendant recklessness or disregard of the consequences of permitting wilfully or knowingly such a disposal that gives the innocent state of mind a criminal character. See Simester, 2005: 25.

[32] (1915) 113 LT 451 at 453. This case is hereinafter referred to as *Midland Railway Co*. See also Lord Esher MR and Bowen LJ in *Kirkheaton District Local Board* v *Ainley, Sons & Co* (1892) 2 QB 274 with regard to the construction of the Rivers Pollution Prevention Act 1876. Other interesting decisions include that of Lord Shaw in *Leyland Shipping Co* v *Norwich Union Fire Insurance Society* [1918] AC 350; Viscount Simon in *Yorkshire Dale Steamship Co Ltd* v *Minister of War Transport, The Coxwold* [1942] AC 691; and Lord Diplock in *Sweet* v *Parsley* [1970] AC 132. Despite the development of theories of corporate *mens rea*, some courts still circumvent statutory requirements in like manner. See *Meridian* discussed in Chapters 1, 4 and 8.

[33] Another question that courts need to address is whether such words should be construed as implying that all elements of the *actus reus* should correspond to the *mens rea* that is proved. See Manchester, 2006: 214-222. However, Simester (2005: 22) suggests that it is sufficient that at least one "material element" of the *actus reus* corresponds to the *mens rea*.

[34] *Whitfield v South Eastern Railway Co* (1858) 120 ER 451 at 453.

grounds given that they are imposed only where Parliament seeks to prohibit activities that have serious consequences on public welfare. Thus, they may be said to adopt what is described in Chapter 2 as the teleological pattern of ascribing liability to corporations. The fact that they do not require proof of intent or knowledge and awareness of risk or any form of *mens rea* implies that courts do not need to concern themselves with the metaphysics of the accused corporations.[35] Pre-20th century courts therefore readily held that no other kinds of offences could be enforced against corporations.[36] However, given the difficulty of adequately defining many offences without reference to the mind of the accused it was inevitable that courts had to consider the corporation's state of mind and devise mechanisms for dealing with deontological patterns of ascription.

3.2.2 Offences with an element of intent or defence of due diligence

The scope of enforcement of statutory offences expanded considerably in the 19th century following the enactment of the Criminal Law Act 1827 (section 14) and the Interpretation Act 1889 (section 2) indicating that the term "person" in statutes should be construed as including a corporation unless the contrary was stated.[37] These statutes were however understood to imply that unless the contrary was provided in the applicable provision, a corporation could be convicted if it was capable of committing the act prohibited by the provision.[38]As such, courts were confronted with an

---

[35] However, many strict liability offences provide for a defence of due diligence and a corporation as a defendant may invoke this defence to show that it was compliant with the law and the offence was caused by another person. In such cases, courts are required to consider questions of the corporation's mind and body. This is actually the situation that pushed the House of Lords to delineate the applicable mechanism of imputation in the United Kingdom in *Nattrass*.

[36] See Lindley, 1863: 34-35; and Khanna, 1996: 1484.

[37] See also section 5 of the Interpretation Act 1987.

[38] See the interpretation of sections 98 and 99 of the Railway Clauses Consolidation Act 1845 by Viscount Reading CJ in *Mousell Bros* at 1104-1105. The question of whether the term "person" in statutes should include corporations has thus been the subject of much controversy both in criminal law and in the law of tort with regard to acts that courts believe cannot be performed by corporations or where courts believe that Parliament had no intention of extending the application of the statute to corporations. Some criminal cases are cited below. With regard to the tort cases, see *R v London (North) Industrial Tribunal, ex Parte*

influx of cases whereby statutes imposed duties on persons as owners or occupiers and created offences that required evidence of the state of mind of the owners or occupiers and such owners or occupiers were corporations. In the proceedings, the prosecutors had to prove and the courts had to accept that the accused corporations had a mind and had disposed of it in a certain way. It was especially difficult to overlook this element where the objective of the statute was to sanction the responsible 'person' and the proceedings under the applicable section required a measure of proof that had an element of *mens rea*. However, Channell J had this to say:

> By the general principles of the criminal law, if a matter is made a criminal offence, it is essential that there should be something in the nature of mens rea, and, therefore, in ordinary cases a corporation cannot be guilty of a criminal offence, nor can a master be liable criminally for an offence committed by his servant. But there are exceptions to this rule in the case of quasi-criminal offences, as they may be termed – that is to say, where certain acts are forbidden, by law under a penalty, possibly even under a personal penalty, such as imprisonment – at any rate, in default of payment of a fine; and the reason for this is that the legislature has thought it so important to prevent the particular act from being committed that it absolutely forbids it to be done; and if done the offender is liable to a penalty whether he had any mens rea or not, and whether or not he intended to commit a breach of the law.[39]

It must be noted that the prevailing conception of corporate criminality at the time when Channell J made this statement was still in line with Coke's contention that a corporation could be charged and convicted of criminal offences that did not require proof of blameworthiness and were not punished by execution or banishment or imprisonment. In light of this conception, Channell J postulated that even where the statutory provision creating the offence required proof of intent to commit, liability could still be imposed on the corporation on the ground of the objective of the legislature.[40] As such, a few years later, Lord Alverstone (Pickford J and Lush J concurring) cited *Pearks, Gunston and Tee* and held that a company was a "person" within section 20(6) of the Sale of Food and

---

Associated Newspapers [1998] ICR 1212; *M v Vincent* [1998] ICR 17; and *Leicester University v A* [1999] ICR 701.

[39] *Pearks, Gunston and Tee* at 11.

[40] See also Avory J in *Midland Railway Co.* However, some courts in the last quarter of the 20th century still maintained this view. See Lord Scarman in *Gammon* at 14. Equally, it is not too dissimilar from the idea of "special rules" propounded by Lord Hoffmann in *Meridian*.

Drugs Act 1899 and was liable for the offence of giving false warranty in writing to a purchaser in spite of the impossibility of proving the intent required to commit the offence.[41] Viscount Reading in *Mousell Bros* cited both cases and upheld a magistrate's decision to convict a corporation of the offence charged under section 98 and 99 of the Railway Clauses Consolidation Act 1845.

However, although it was stated in Chapter 2 that decisions prioritising the objectives of statutes are sufficiently justified, the teleological enforcement of the law may not be said to entail such disregard of certain parts of the statutory provisions. Such a piecemeal application is no doubt opportunistic, odd and whimsical.[42] There is no need to seek to distinguish between ordinary crimes and what Channell J called "quasi-crimes" on the ground that the statute requires proof of a mental element but imputes proof of *actus reus* only.[43] It is true that if such a distinction could hold there would be no need to satisfy all the requirements of a traditional or ordinary crime when prosecuting a corporation for a quasi-crime. However, such a distinction breeds inconsistency and smacks of state tyranny.[44] Hence, it is submitted that statutory provisions ought to determine the outcome of cases by virtue of the words they use.[45] As such, if there is a requirement for proof of a mental element the court must give effect to such a requirement.[46]

---

[41] *Chutter v Freeth* at 138.

[42] The argument that the judge has a moral duty to disregard unfair provisions of the statute is countered by the assumption stated in Chapter 1 that morality concerns the need to comply with the law. Thus, if the statute states that proof of intent is required, the judge's moral duty is to request such proof.

[43] Simester (2005: 23) on his part defines what he calls "quasi-criminal regulations" as offences that are non-stigmatic or that do not carry the usual moral blemish of serious crimes. See also Stanton-Ife's (2007: 152-154) discussion on "stigmatic offences" and "non-stigmatic offences.

[44] Wells (2001: 8-9) suggests that the spurious distinction may be due to the fact that the work carried out by the police in investigating regulatory or quasi-crimes is readily ignored.

[45] *Cf* Blackstone (1765-1769); and Allan, 2004: 709-711.

[46] In such an instance Parliament intends to impose liability only on persons shown to have guilty minds. A piecemeal application of the statute would not render the statute effective for its declared purpose. See Lord Russell in *Coppen v Moore (No 2)* (1898) 2 QB 306 at 314; and the House of Lords in *Alphacell Ltd v Woodward* [1972] AC 824, hereinafter referred to as *Alphacell*.

Unfortunately, courts to this day still sometimes use the same artificial distinction between acts that are "truly criminal" and acts that are not "sufficiently criminal" or what they call "regulatory crime" in order to justify their decisions to disregard the proof of *mens rea* that is required.[47] The uncertainty seems to stem from the fact that it is sometimes difficult to determine when *mens rea* would be presumed in a statutory provision and when the provision would be interpreted as creating a strict liability offence. Lord Reid in *Sweet v Parsley* ordained that where the statute is silent, *mens rea* would be presumed unless the relevant circumstances show that the legislator intended otherwise. Lord Reid may not be said to imply that where the statute provides for *mens rea* the court's interpretation is left to be dictated by policy considerations. Nonetheless, the argument that quasi or regulatory crimes are those that attract little or no moral stigma is weak. Although there are offences that may be judged (objectively) to involve higher degrees of moral turpitude, the determination of such offences and the level of social stigma that attaches would depend on the cultural norms and attitudes prevailing within each community. Thus, terms such as "stigma" and "moral blemish" are used to develop arguments only as a matter of convenience.[48] Courts employing Channell J's erstwhile distinction are simply trying too hard to circumvent the obstacle of proving the element of *mens rea* against corporations. His *dictum* was redolent of objective-driven enforcement although the classification of offences into traditional criminal offences and quasi-criminal offences was without doubt a glib response to a very complex question.[49] If the legislator only intended to prevent an absolutely

---

[47] See Lord Scarman in *Gammon* at 14; Lord Diplock in *Sweet v Parsley* at 163; and Dyson LJ in *R v Muhamad* (2003) QB 1031.

[48] See Horder, 2002: 459, footnote n. 4. See also Leonard, 2003: 831.

[49] However, given that the provision that Channell J considered (section 6 of the Sale of Food and Drugs Act 1875) clearly provided for the proof of intention, his disregard of this requirement even for the purpose of avoiding to frustrate the statute may be said to amount to nothing more than a piecemeal application of the statutory provision. Channell J could have adopted a similar position to that of the court in *Tozer* some two years later, which was to the effect that the word "person" in a statute cannot be understood to mean a corporation in instances where it is impossible for the corporation to perform the duty imposed by statute, such as voting at meetings. See also Lord Hoffmann in *Meridian* at 507. However, *Tozer* may be subject to debate given that a company holding shares in another company may be represented by a senior manager at the board meeting of latter company and this senior manager may vote in the former company's name. As such, the solution lies in the way courts impute acts and intents (or causal relationships) to

prohibited action or inaction then she could have simply said so. Equally, if the prohibited act may not be described by statute without the use of words that point to a mental element,[50] the legislator would clearly indicate that proof of *mens rea* is not required for the establishment of guilt if this is her objective lest the she is creating a vicarious criminal liability offence.[51]

As such, it may be advanced that if the corporate master or owner cannot be vicariously liable for the criminal acts of its agents and if criminal statutes are not concerned with the action or omission of the agents but with that of the corporate master on whom the duty is imposed,[52] then direct or non-derivative liability is what was contemplated by the statutes that were enforced in the cases cited above. The corporation's direct liability invariably involves proof of its intent unless the statute provides otherwise. Thus, in the 19th and early 20th centuries, the direct liability of corporations could hardly blossom into a fully developed model for holding corporations criminally liable because of the conceptual obstacle of *mens rea*.[53] However, two convenient options were available. Parliament and courts could have rigorously restricted the concept of corporate criminal liability to strict and absolute liability offences (teleological pattern of ascription) or they could have made a pragmatic appraisal of the idea of direct or non-derivative liability of corporations in order to determine how it ought to be materialised when a statute or the common law required proof of a mental element (deontological pattern of ascription). As we will see in the next subsection, a judge chose the second option and although he was not entertaining a

---

corporations given that an effective mechanism of imputation should enable courts establish different ways in which a corporation may perform the duty imposed.

50 The use of words such as "false warranty" by themselves indicates promises or undertakings that are deliberately deceptive. See Simester (2005: 25, footnote n. 16) on the difficulty of defining "theft" without reference to the defendant's state of mind.

51 See Khanna, 1996: 1482, footnote n. 26. However, some of the judges cited above vehemently denied that vicarious criminal liability was intended. See for example Channell J in *Pearks, Gunston and Tee* at 11. See also the opinions of Viscount Reading and Atkin J in *Mousell* at 1104-1107. See also Lord Reid in *Nattrass* at 170.

52 Stern (1987: 126) intimates that it was due to this difficulty that the concept of accessory was created. See also Kadish and Paulsen, 1975: 369-371.

53 Many offences could not be enforced against corporations because the applicable statutory provisions required proof of *mens rea* and courts were not always willing to circumvent this requirement.

criminal case, his appraisal was marked by the parturition of what was to become the bedrock of corporate criminal liability in the United Kingdom: the identification doctrine.

3.2.2.1 The use of the identification doctrine

A ship called *Edward Dawson* and its cargo were destroyed at sea by fire caused by defective boilers. The ship was owned by the appellant, Lennard's Carrying Company Ltd, and its cargo was owned by the respondents. The applicable statutory provision was section 502 of the Merchant Shipping Act 1894 (now repealed) which provided that the owner of a ship would be exculpated if she could show that the loss or damage occurred without her actual fault or privity. Given that the owner of *Edward Dawson* was a company, the question that arose was whether it was possible for such an artificial entity to show that the loss happened without its fault or privity and if yes, which mechanism to employ to show this. Viscount Haldane sitting in the House of Lords assessed the personal liability of the company on the basis of his understanding of the structure and functioning of corporations.[54] Thus, in his words (Lord Dunedin, Lord Atkinson, Lord Parker and Lord Parmoor concurring) this is what reflected the reality of a corporation:

> [m]y Lords, a corporation is an abstraction. It has no mind of its own any more than it has a body of its own; its active and directing will must consequently be sought in the person of somebody who for some purposes may be called an agent, but who is the directing mind and will of the corporation, the very ego and centre of the personality of the corporation….the fault or privity is the fault or privity of somebody who is not merely a servant or agent for whom the company is liable upon the footing of *respondeat superior*, but somebody for whom the company is

[54] As mentioned in Chapter 1, this is the first rung towards addressing the question of how to hold corporations criminally liable. Fairly recently, there have been scathing criticisms of the applicable mechanisms in the United Kingdom and recommendations have geared towards blending principles of legal liability with the realities of contemporary corporate structures. However, the attempts made by commentators have hardly provided mechanisms with cogent solutions on how the law, both substantive and procedural, is supposed to accommodate the corporate theories (especially non-legal theories). Thus, commentators have been able to point out the weaknesses of Viscount Haldane's mechanism but have fallen short of providing a more cogent template indicating how Viscount Haldane ought to have made a diagnosis of Lennard's Carrying Company Ltd's actions.

> liable because his action is the very action of the company itself.[55] [No emphasis added]

It may be understood from this statement that a corporation is a formal structure consisting of employees performing specific tasks that have been allocated to them by one or many persons who may be termed the corporation's "directing mind and will." This is related to a mechanistic organisation with clearly defined hierarchical levels and little or no discretion to front-line employees.[56] Holding a corporation with a mechanistic structure liable for the wrongful act of the empowered senior manager is justifiable since such a senior manager is indeed its "directing mind and will"[57] or as coined by Denning LJ some 40 years later, its "brain and nerve centre which controls what it does."[58] Viscount Haldane logically rejected vicarious liability as the basis for identifying the mind of the corporation given that the onus to prove that the loss was not due to the corporation's fault was on the corporation itself and not its agents.[59] His use of the words "ego" and "centre of personality" shows that he purported to have discovered the part of the corporation from which conscious urges and desires arose and which shaped its behaviour and personality. However, the contention that agents that qualified as the "directing mind

---

[55] *Lennard's Carrying Co Ltd v Asiatic Petroleum Co Ltd* (1915) AC 705 (hereinafter referred to as *Lennard's Carrying Co*) at 713-714.

[56] See Chapter 4.

[57] See Fisse and Braithwaite, 1993: 105.

[58] *HL Bolton (Engineering) Ltd v TJ Graham & Sons Ltd* [1957] 1 QB 159 (hereinafter referred to as *Bolton Engineering*) at 172.

[59] This obligation reflected the rule of common employment (repealed by section 1(1) of the Law Reform (Personal Injuries) Act 1948) whereby a master was not liable for the injury to a worker caused by the negligence of another worker where both workers were in common employment. The liability of the master depended on the proof of his own personal negligence. See Welsh, 1946: 353. See also *Fanton v Denville* [1932] 2 KB 309. See also *Rudd v Elder Dempster and Co* [1933] 1 KB 566, where it was held that the negligence of the "general manager" and "persons having authority from the board of directors" could be attributed to companies to hold them liable. In this light, Wells (2001: 96) contends that there is "an irony in the origin of the criminal liability of corporations [for crimes with an element of intent or defence of due diligence] being found in the oppressive and management serving doctrine of common employment." It may thus be advanced that the influence of doctrines such as common employment on the development of corporate liability for crimes of intent tells us two things: firstly, this branch of the criminal law is based on the concept of direct or personal liability; and secondly, "oppressive and management-serving" schemes defined corporate structures at the time when the identification doctrine was developed.

and will" are those that may be said to be the corporation's "centre of personality" or "ego" betrays a circularity that underscores the main weakness of Viscount Haldane's model. Thus, his understanding of corporate action although grounded in logic was demonstrably flawed in the measure of who within the corporate structure was to be identified with the corporation and why. He had actually postulated that a corporation must be liable only for the fault or privity of those that may be considered its "directing mind and will" and they may be considered thus because they are its "ego" and "centre of personality." Unfortunately, this circularity was to be exacerbated by subsequent interpretations and undue restrictions (for purposes of clarity) placed by criminal law courts which espoused this model on a later date. In *Kent and Sussex Contractors*, Viscount Caldecote stated that there was no authority to the effect that a company could not be criminally liable for the offences with which it was charged[60] and then intimated that there was an axiomatic connection between the acts of the transport manager and the company that employed him. Moreover, given that there was ample evidence showing that he was one of "the only people who could act or speak or think for [the company]" he could be identified with the company to make it criminally liable.

With no information pointing to the contrary, it can safely be assumed that the prevailing conception at the time of Viscount Caldecote was still in line with the abovementioned contentions by Coke in *Sutton's Hospital*, Patteson J in *Birmingham and Gloucester Railway Col* and Channell J in *Pearks, Gunston and Tee*. Hence, a corporation could be criminally liable unless the offence charged was treason or perjury or an offence against the person or other offence that was only punishable by death or imprisonment. One therefore struggles to see anything revolutionary in the decision in *Kent and Sussex Contractors* given that the offence charged was neither treason nor an offence against the person and was punishable by fine.[61] Viscount Caldecote was certainly not in Finlay J's position in *Cory Bros*[62] and did not consider questions about collectivisation of actions. As stated in Chapter 1, Viscount Caldecote was inspired by

[60] Making use of a false document with intent to deceive and making a statement which was known to be false in a material particular contrary to the Defence (General) Regulations 1939 and the Motor Fuel Rationing (No 3) Order 1941.
[61] *Cf.* Png, 2001: 14 and 63.
[62] Where the company was charged with an offence under the Offences Against the Person Act 1861 and Finlay J could only identify one previous case where the Court of Common Pleas had held that a corporation may be sued in trespass.

Pharmaceutical Society[63] and dealt with the theoretical impediment of proving the corporation's intent by substituting it for its criminal agent. Although this may be commendable on the ground that he applied the law fully and not selectively, compelling the corporation to substitute for its criminal agent does not correspond with the description of the deontological pattern of ascription provided in Chapter 2. This is because it was the agent that was morally blameworthy and not the corporation, unless the corporation was shown to have assisted or motivated the criminal agent, in which case its liability would have been secondary and not direct. Nevertheless, Viscount Caldecote stressed that the question of the company's *mens rea* was irrelevant to the case although he went ahead to hold that the company was liable because the only people who could act and speak for it had knowingly made a false statement with the intent to deceive.[64] As such, just like Viscount Haldane, he was equally flawed in the explanation of why the corporation was responsible and punishable in that given instance.

In *Moore v I Bresler Ltd*,[65] a company was identified with the company secretary (who doubled as general manager of the Nottingham branch) and the sales manager and convicted for making use of a document which was false in a material particular with the intent to deceive contrary to section 35(2) of the Finance (No 2) Act 1940. The court also endorsed imputation as a valid form of locating the corporation's mind and held that these officers were of sufficient station to be identified with the company, not because they were the only persons that acted or spoke or thought for the company but because they were senior officers acting within the scope of their employment. Even though the officers had acted without the knowledge of the board of directors and the senior management and had defrauded the company in making sales of handbags, the Divisional Court contended that the goods were the property of the company intended for sale and the officers were acting as agents of the company.[66] Due to the

---

[63] It has also been intimated that Viscount Haldane's seminal remarks in *Lennard's Carrying Co* supplied the inspiration. See Gower, 1992: 193; and Wells, 2001: 97.

[64] He seemed to have implied that the company was vicariously liable for the criminal acts of the officers because they were the only ones that could speak and act for it, which is rather confusing.

[65] [1944] 2 KBD 515, hereinafter referred to as *Bresler*.

[66] See the criticisms of this case by Welsh, 1946: 360; and Williams, 1961: 858-859. However, Wells (2001: 95-96) contends that their criticisms are not cogent because they are based on a restrictive construction of the term "within the scope of employment" and whether the officers were of sufficient station to be identified

fact that the officers were agents of the company acting within the scope of their authority, their criminal minds and acts were imputed to the company to render it liable.

The court did not consider whether section 35(2) of the Finance (No 2) Act 1940 could be construed as imposing a duty on the company and whether it had breached such a duty. Equally, the court did not consider the principle in *re Hampshire Land Co*[67] (approved by the House of Lords in *J C Houghton and Co v Nothard, Lowe & Wills Ltd*)[68] which was to the effect that an agent's dishonesty will not be imputed to the corporation where the latter was the target of the dishonest scheme and would be disadvantaged as regards enforcing its rights. In fact, these cases later on provided justification for the House of Lords to take exception from *Nattrass* in *Belmont.*[69] Thus, *Bresler* dealt with the *mens rea* obstacle by simply ignoring it and holding the corporation vicariously liable. It may serve only as a historical reference point for commentaries on corporate criminal liability since where the corporation was the targeted victim *Belmont* will apply. However, it is uncertain whether if the agent that defrauded the company was the sole agent who acted and spoke for the corporation, the court may hold that the company was not a victim because one cannot commit an offence against oneself. This raises questions about the cogency of the criminal law courts' conception of the corporation and the pattern of ascription adopted. However, what is certain is that courts in the United Kingdom impose liability directly on corporations by compelling them to substitute for their guilty senior officers. There is little or no distinction between this way of holding corporations liable (which

---

with the company. Based on the inordinately broad interpretation of the term "within the scope of employment" by civil courts (discussed in Chapter 4), it may be advanced that Wells is right in dismissing these criticisms. Equally, based on *Nattrass*, as regards the officers that can be identified with a corporation, it may be said that the company secretary and general sales manager were sufficiently high. However, we may find fault in the fact that the court in *Bresler* identified these officers as "agents" of the company and not necessarily as its "directing mind and will," and on this ground, holding the company liable for their acts amounts to vicarious criminal liability. Nonetheless, *Belmont* subsequently provided that where the corporation was the targeted victim of its officers, the rule in *Nattrass* would not apply.

[67] [1896] 2 Ch 743.

[68] [1928] AC 1.

[69] See also *Attorney General's Reference (No 2 of 1982)* [1984] QB 624; and *Stone & Rolls Ltd (in liquidation) v Moore Stephens (a firm) and another* [2008] 3 WLR 1146, hereinafter referred to as *Stone & Rolls*.

ought to be non-derivative) and vicarious liability except for the restriction of the agents that may be identified with the corporations. Nonetheless, there is also much uncertainty as regards the requisite station of the guilty senior officer. In *The Lady Gwendolen*,[70] the court cited *Kent and Sussex Contractors* and also held that the transport manager was the directing mind of the company, and in *National Coal Board v Gamble*,[71] the company was identified with a weighbridge man.[72]

The House of Lords sought to provide a frame of reference in *Nattrass*. It was advanced that a branch manager may not be identified with a company that owned a chain of several hundred supermarkets across the country. Their Lordships construed the applicable provision, section 24(1) of the Trade Descriptions Act 1968, as placing the onus of proof on the corporation itself to show that it had exercised all due diligence and the offence was due to the fault of another person or an accident or some other cause beyond its control. They then sought to determine what the corporation needed to show in order to be exculpated from the fault of its guilty branch manager. In line with Viscount Haldane's decision in *Lennard's Carrying Co*, Viscount Caldecote's position in *Kent and Sussex Contractors* and Lord Denning's *dictum* in *Bolton Engineering*, they held that the company only needed to show that the guilty agent occupied a relatively low position. Although an agent, senior or junior, is certainly not the duty-holder in such an instance, it is difficult to understand why only the state of mind of a senior officer is imputable to the accused corporation. Their Lordships may be faulted for failing to seek to understand how and why corporations break the law beyond the prescriptions of Viscount Haldane, Viscount Caldecote and Lord Denning. In other words, they did not employ any means of ascertaining the nature of the corporate entity beyond legal precepts. So they ended up endorsing a very restricted form of vicarious liability which as will be shown in Chapter 5 is rigidly adapted to mechanistic corporate structures.[73]

Nonetheless, if we take into consideration the facts that where the corporation is a victim it is instead *Belmont* that applies and also that the

---

[70] [1965] 2 All ER 283.

[71] (1959) 1 QB 11.

[72] See also *R v Blamires Transport Services Ltd* (1963) 3 WLR 496. However, in *John Henshall (Quarries) Ltd v Harvey* [1965] 2 QB 233, the court declined to identify a corporation with a weighbridge man.

[73] A small window was however left open with the recognition of the delegation of managerial functions.

rule in *Nattrass* does not direct courts on how to draw a line across the corporate structure dividing agents that may be identified with the corporation and those that may not, it may be advanced that in the United Kingdom, the deontological pattern of ascription is employed for the same purpose as the teleological, *viz.* to impose liability on the corporation under circumstances where the court thinks it is fair and just to do so. Whether the corporation was morally blameworthy is not as decisive as the judge's value judgement. This position is buttressed by Lord Hoffmann's *dictum* in *Meridian*. He sought to ascertain the legislator's intention with regard to imposing liability directly on the corporate defendant. However, in an attempt to break with the rule in *Nattrass* he also stopped short of seeking to understand how and why corporate entities break the law. Seated in the Privy Council, he entertained an appeal from the Court of Appeal of New Zealand regarding whether an investment management company had violated the New Zealand Securities Amendment Act 1988 as a result of the failure of its chief investment manger and senior portfolio manager to comply with the statutory obligation to give notice of the acquisition to the Securities Commission. These two officers had acquired the shares without the authority and knowledge of the board of directors and managing director. Lord Hoffmann proposed three ways of determining whether the company could be said to have committed the offence via the agency of these officers. The first involved considering whether the applicable statutory provision was intended to apply to corporations. The second involved adopting Lord Diplock's approach (*Nattrass*) of consulting the company's constitution and memorandum and articles of association.[74] He however warned that there are situations where neither of these two options will yield satisfactory results.[75] Thus, he propounded a third step that involved looking at the words of the applicable statutory provision and fashioning "special rules" of attribution that conformed to the inferred objective of the statute.[76]

---

[74] Lord Hoffmann called the rules in these documents the "primary rules of attribution" and extended their scope to include principles of company law and to a certain extent agency law. The concept of primary rules is discussed further in Chapter 4.

[75] As stated above, in light with *Tozer*, a convenient but unprincipled way of avoiding the intricacy of establishing the corporation's guilt is to hold that it is impossible for a corporation to perform the duty imposed by the applicable statute.

[76] This proposition is discussed further in Chapter 4.

Lord Hoffmann may be understood to have contended that the effectiveness of a statute (as regards regulating corporations) depends entirely on the judge's interpretation. Thus, where a statute provides for corporate liability, it is incumbent upon the judge to decide whether it applies to corporations (whether they can commit the offence created) and how it would apply (fashioning a special rule). This takes us back to the beginning of the 20th century where Avory J (*Midland Railway Co*) held that certain essential words of a statute may be ignored and Channell J (*Pearks, Gunston and Tee*) advanced that the court may create new offences (quasi-crimes) for the purpose of furthering the legislator's objective. Thus, judges can ignore clear statutory prescriptions and apply what they think is right. This is no doubt the recipe for incoherence and inconsistency given that disparate decisions are taken by different judges although addressing similar facts. The uncertainties discussed above as regards how the identification doctrine applies may therefore be explained by this penchant towards judicial activism.

As such, in *Meridian*, the statute required that both the *mens rea* and the *actus reus* be proved against the accused. Since the accused was a corporation, Lord Hoffmann disregarded the statute by not referring to the established rule of proving a corporation's guilt for an offence that is not absolute (*Kent and Sussex Contractors* and *Nattrass*). Hence, Lord Hoffmann may be said to have changed an offence with an element of intent into an absolute liability offence since a corporation will almost always be liable if what is applied is a special rule that is fashioned to make it liable.[77] The above notwithstanding, it was later on noted that Lord Hoffmann did not dismiss the identification doctrine after all. Rose LJ seated in the Court of Appeal in *Attorney-General's Reference (No 2 of 1999)*[78] pointed out that Lord Hoffmann's speech proceeded on the basis that the identification doctrine remains the applicable mechanism although there are exceptional cases in which other mechanisms could be invoked. Thus, *Attorney General's Reference (No 2)* was arguably not a major

[77] Nonetheless, it may be argued that the fashioning of special rules for the circumstances implies that the nature of a corporation depends on the circumstances and this is a better reflection of the reality of the concept of corporation (as shown in Chapter 2) than the identification doctrine. However, since the identification doctrine is the applicable rule for determining whether a corporation has acted or not, ignoring this doctrine amounts to acting *per incuriam*.
[78] [2000] 3 All ER 182 CA at 257. This case is hereinafter referred to as *Attorney-General's Reference (No 2)*.

obstruction to the development of the common law by the courts[79] because the interpretation that Rose LJ put on *Meridian* has served as a pretext for many courts to deviate from the rule in *Nattrass* and impose liability (in accordance with *Meridian*) on corporations in circumstances that can only be explained by the recourse to the statute's intended meaning.[80] The influence of *Meridian* is strong in recent cases where the tradition of citing *Nattrass* and applying *Meridian* has been abandoned in favour of simply citing and applying *Meridian*.[81] Nonetheless, it remains that the identification doctrine as established in *Nattrass* is the mechanism that applies where a corporation is on trial for the commission of an offence, the exceptions being where the offence charged is absolute[82] or is deemed to be corporate manslaughter or corporate homicide created by the CMCHA. The offence of corporate homicide (Scotland) or corporate manslaughter (England and Wales) was created against a backdrop of calls for a better mechanism of imputation. However, there is a worrisome similarity between the mechanism of imputation that the CMCHA has introduced to enforce corporate manslaughter or corporate homicide and the identification doctrine.

3.2.3 Culpable (corporate) homicide and (corporate) manslaughter

The offences of culpable homicide and manslaughter had proved to be a quagmire for the identification doctrine. A corporation was charged with manslaughter in the 1920s[83] and in the early 1930s it was held that corporations could be imputed with the personal negligence of the general manager or other person having authority from the board.[84] In 1965,

---

[79] *Cf.* Gobert and Punch, 2003: 69.

[80] This was described as a "pragmatic approach" by Nourse LJ in *El Ajou v Dollar Land Holdings Plc* [1994] 2 All ER 685, hereinafter referred to as *El Ajou*. See also Millet J at the first instance: *El Ajou v Dollar Land Holdings Plc* [1993] 3 All ER 717 at 740.

[81] See Arden LJ in *Real Estate Opportunities Ltd v Aberdeen Asset Managers Jersey Ltd and others* [2007] Bus LR 971 (hereinafter referred to as *Real Estate Opportunities*) at 986-989.

[82] Given that a corporation's liability is established by default where an absolute duty has been breached by its agent, there is no need to consider questions of imputation.

[83] *Cory Bros.*

[84] See *Fanton v Denville* and *Rudd v Elder Dempster and Co.* See also Wells, 2001: 96.

although Streatfield J acquitted a company on the merits of the case he held that it could be indicted for manslaughter.[85] In 1986, Maurace J also observed that a company could be held guilty of manslaughter.[86] These remarks concur with Bingham LJ's judgment in *R v HM Coroner for East Kent, Ex parte Spooner and Others*.[87] Following Sheen J's Report on the capsize of the Herald of Free Enterprise near the Zeebrugge Harbour that caused the loss of 192 lives, Bingham LJ ruled that the company could be charged with manslaughter but stated that the *mens rea* and *actus reus* of the offence should not be established against all the agents who acted on behalf of the company but against only those who were to be identified as the embodiment of the company.[88] Persuaded by the coroner's inquest and Sheen J's report the prosecution however brought a case against the company without establishing the guilt of any senior officer that could be said to embody the company.[89] Turner J reiterated the observation made by Bingham LJ that a company could be indicted for manslaughter but may only be convicted by the imputation of the guilt of a senior officer to the corporation. Both judges had thus re-emphasised the primacy of the identification doctrine as established in *Nattrass* as the true basis for analysing a corporation's behaviour and establishing its liability for manslaughter.[90]

As mentioned above, *Nattrass* requires courts to impose liability on corporations only where the prosecution proves the guilt of the directing mind of the corporation. Thus, in *R v OLL Ltd and Kite*, where no distress flares were provided and coastguards were not informed of a fatal canoeing trip and the prosecution could establish the gross negligence of Peter Kite, the managing director of OLL Ltd, his guilt was imputed to the company for the purpose of convicting it of manslaughter.[91] In *R v Jackson Transport (Osett) Ltd*, Jackson Transport (Osett) Ltd and its sole

---

[85] *R v Northern Strip Mining Construction Co Ltd* (1 February1965, Unreported).
[86] This was however a civil suit: *S and Y Investments (No 2) Pty Ltd v Commercial Union Assurance Co of Australia Ltd* (1986) 82 FLR 130.
[87] (1989) 88 Cr App R 10, hereinafter referred to as *HM Coroner for East Kent*.
[88] *HM Coroner for East Kent* at 16.
[89] *R v P & O European Ferries (Dover) Ltd* (1991) 93 Cr App R 72, hereinafter referred to as *P & O European Ferries*.
[90] *P & O European Ferries* at 81-84. This case together with *Attorney-General's Reference (No 2)* was the landmark case with regard to the mechanism of holding corporations liable for negligent manslaughter.
[91] [1996] 2 Cr App R 295. This is however not a report of the case but of Kite's appeal. For proceedings instituted by OLL Ltd against the coastguard, see *OLL Ltd v Secretary of State for Transport* [1997] 3 All ER 897.

director Alan Jackson were convicted for the manslaughter of an employee that had neither been provided with protective equipment nor trained and had used steam pressure to clean a valve in a tanker blocked with toxic substances.[92] Equally, in spite of the unsuccessful challenge (by judicial review) of the Crown Prosecution Service's decision not to prosecute Fewston Transport Ltd, a heavy goods vehicle operator whose vehicle was involved in an incident that resulted in the death of five persons, the court intimated that it was nevertheless in the interest of the public that companies are prosecuted for manslaughter in such instances.[93] As such, the prospects for the identification doctrine as a means of imputing liability to mechanistic and small and medium-sized corporations in manslaughter cases looked bright. Also, following a coroner's inquest verdict of unlawful killing of an unattended disabled woman by a care home, Popplewell J observed that if the jury had been properly directed there was a possibility that they could have convicted the care home of manslaughter.[94] It is important to note that the requirements for the common law offence of gross negligence manslaughter have evolved over the years. In 1925, the position was that the test should be whether the accused showed flagrant disregard for the life and safety of others as to amount to conduct that deserves to be punished.[95] However, in 1994 the test had evolved and the court was required to determine whether the extent to which the accused departed from accepted standards was unreasonable.[96]

---

[92] 1996 (Unreported) 18 *Health and Safety at Work*, November 1999 at 14.

[93] *R v Crown Prosecution Service, Ex parte Waterworth* [1996] COD 277.

[94] *R v HM Coroner for Reading ex parte West Berkshire Housing Consortium Ltd* 11 July 1995 (Unreported) CO/2994/94. This is true because in *Stone v Dobinson* [1977] QB 354, the defendants, natural persons, took Stone's anorexic sister into their home but isolated her and failed to appreciate the seriousness of her situation. They were convicted of manslaughter because she died as a result of their gross negligence. As regards the successful use of the identification doctrine to convict small and mechanistic structures, see also *R v English Brothers Ltd & Melvyn Hubbard* (Northampton Crown Court, 30 July 2001, Unreported); *R v Dennis Clothier and Sons Ltd* (Bristol Crown Court, 23 October 2002, Unreported); *R v Teglgaard Hardwood (UK) Ltd* (Hull Crown Court, 24 February 2004, Unreported); and *R v Alan Mark, Nationwide Heating Services Ltd* [2004] EWCA Crim 2490.

[95] See *R v Bateman* (1925) 19 Cr App R 8, hereinafter referred to as *Bateman.*

[96] *R v Adomako* [1995] 1 AC 171, hereinafter referred to as *Adomako*. Also pertinent is the decision in *R v Prentice* [1993] 4 All ER 935 (hereinafter referred to as *Prentice*) that a breach of duty amounts to 'gross negligence' where there is "indifference to an obvious risk of injury to health; actual foresight of the risk

It was nevertheless uncertain whether the progressive stance of *Adomako* applied to the corporate defendant.[97] What was certain was that a corporation could be prosecuted successfully for manslaughter or culpable homicide if the evidence showed that officers of the corporation knew (subjective) or ought to have known (objective) about a risk of injury to health but failed to address it.[98]Against this background, the Great Western Trains Company was indicted on seven counts of manslaughter when seven people died as a result of injury sustained in the collision between a High Speed Train and a freight train. The company was also indicted on one count (of breach of duty) under section 3 of the HSWA. There was a preliminary ruling on how the prosecution may put up its case against the Great Western Trains Company because the judge, Scott-Baker J, disagreed with the prosecution on the fact that the company was guilty of gross negligent manslaughter based on the failure of its management to set up and maintain an acceptable safety system that could deal with mistakes such as the driver's fatal mistake. The prosecution was apprehensive because the case against P&O European Ferries (Dover) Ltd had been unsuccessful due to the failure to prove that the directors had been reckless.[99] Nonetheless, given that the House of Lords in *Adomako* had ordained that a person could be convicted of involuntary 'gross negligence' manslaughter (which did not require proof of subjective intent) on the basis of an objective test, there was no need to look for a guilty state of mind among the senior officers for the purposes of identification.[100] Hence, the prosecution's argument was that the

coupled with the determination nevertheless to run it; appreciation of the risk coupled with an intention to avoid it but also coupled with such a high degree of negligence in the attempted avoidance as the jury consider justifies conviction, and inattention or failure to advert a serious risk which goes 'beyond inadvertence' in respect of an obvious and important matter which the defendant's duty demanded he should address."

[97] This question is an unfortunate consequence of the artificial distinction often made between the guilty individual and the guilty company as regards the criminal law's objectives.

[98] See the optimism expressed by Wells (1999: 11).

[99] However, Turner J (*P&O European Ferries* at 73) did not consider the subjective and objective tests owing to the fact that he was called upon to determine whether a corporation could be guilty of manslaughter under English law, how such guilt had to be proved and whether the corporate defendant was guilty.

[100] The Director of Public Prosecution (DPP)'s decision to prosecute only the company (Great Western Trains) and a front-line employee (the driver) was based on the fact that the director had no knowledge of the train in question travelling on

company's guilt could be established by showing that it had departed from reasonable standards to such an extent as to be judged criminal.

Scott-Baker J disagreed. He rightfully pointed out that the test as established in *Adomako* was not entirely objective. However, he regretfully maintained that *Adomako* did not in any way address the circumstances in which a corporation may be held liable for manslaughter. Thus, the prosecution was required to apply a subjective test to establish that the corporate defendant's guilt. In other words, the prosecution had to prove that the company was aware of the particular risk and went ahead to take the risk; and this could only be established by showing that an individual sufficiently senior to be identified with the company knew of the particular risk. Although the learned judge was right in requiring that a subjective test was equally necessary, his judgement hinged solely upon the satisfaction of the subjective test. He did not in any way consider the possibility of proving the company's guilt via an objective test. Likewise the commentators that contend that the criminal law was historically an instrument to address the behaviour of natural persons, hc failed to understand that the House of Lords in *Adomako* established the way in which gross negligence manslaughter may be proved against a defendant *simpliciter*. The question of the nature of the defendant is a different matter altogether.

It is however surprising that the counsel for the prosecution referred the question whether a defendant can be convicted of gross negligence manslaughter in the absence of evidence as to the defendant's state of mind to the Court of Appeal for its opinion[101] rather than whether *Adomako* had any place in the law of corporate manslaughter. The Court of Appeal advanced that a defendant can be convicted of gross negligence manslaughter in the absence of evidence as to the defendant's state of mind, which could nonetheless be understood to imply that *Adomako* governed the law of corporate manslaughter. However, the prosecution also referred the question whether a non-human defendant could be convicted of gross negligence manslaughter in the absence of evidence

---

that particular date due to the malfunctioning Advance Warning System. Thus, given that *Adomako* had changed the test of establishing negligence from a purely subjective standard (*R v Caldwell* [1982] AC 341; and *R v Seymour* [1983] 2 AC 493) to the objective standard (*Bateman*), the company's negligence may have been established by showing that the fatal crash was caused by the failure of its management to set up and maintain a viable safety system.

[101] *Attorney-General's Reference (No 2).*

establishing the guilt of an individual that is its directing mind.[102] As stated earlier, Rose LJ answered in the negative and upheld the identification doctrine as the sole basis for holding corporations criminally liable. The decision begs the question of why a human defendant can be convicted of gross negligence manslaughter in the absence of evidence as to her state of mind and yet a corporation or non-human defendant cannot be convicted of the same offence in the absence of evidence its guilty mind (the guilt of the individual that is its directing mind)? In other words, if a human defendant can be convicted of gross negligence manslaughter based on an objective test, why is the corporate defendant's guilt restricted to a subjective test? A possible answer would be that the Court of Appeal, in line with *Nattrass*, deemed that that the identification doctrine was the required avenue for analysing the criminal behaviour of corporations. Thus, a corporation may only act or think through its senior officer and in order to determine whether it had performed the *actus reus* of an offence, the evidence must show that a senior officer had acted recklessly.[103] Equally, although *Adomako* does not apply in Scotland, the identification doctrine as established in *Nattrass* was upheld by the Scottish High Court of Justiciary in *Transco* about a decade later. However, the High Court of Justiciary sought to distinguish between gross negligence manslaughter that applies under English law and involuntary culpable homicide as applicable in Scotland in the process.[104]

It is nonetheless of no relevance today to consider whether gross negligence manslaughter should be established in accordance with the test laid out in *Adomako* or whether the opinions of the Court of Appeal in *Attorney-General's Reference (No 2)* and the High Court of Justiciary in *Transco* should direct the course of establishing the corporation's guilt in

[102] The DPP blamed the failure of the manslaughter charges against Great Western Trains company on the rigidity of the identification doctrine and this may have influenced his decision not to prosecute the Thames for manslaughter when one of its trains went through a red light and collided head on with a train belonging to the Great Western Trains in the Paddington station at Ladbroke Grove. See Christian, 2001: 343.

[103] However, this line of reasoning is not consonant with Lord Denning's dictum in *Bolton Engineering* (approved by their Lordships in *Nattrass*). He had intimated that a corporation may also act through low-level employees that represent its "hands" although it may not be liable for such actions. As such, in the absence of evidence of the subjective guilt of the "directing mind," a corporation ought to be liable for the negligent acts of the "hands" that were tolerated by senior managers where an objective test is applied.

[104] See Chapter 5.

the law of manslaughter or culpable homicide. This is because of the enactment of the CMCHA. As mentioned above, the prevailing opinion prior to the enactment was that the identification doctrine was obsolete. The CMCHA therefore moves away (albeit slightly) from the identification doctrine by adopting a mechanism of holding corporations liable that may be called the senior management failure test. A corporation is guilty of corporate homicide or corporate manslaughter if the way its activities were managed or organised by its senior management caused a person's death and is judged to amount to a "gross breach" of a relevant duty of care owed by the corporation to the victim.[105] The CMCHA also departs from *Great Western Trains* and *Attorney-General's Reference (No 2)* by adopting an objective test for establishing the "gross breach." Hence, the prosecution is not required to show that someone within the corporation had knowledge of the breach and acted in spite of such knowledge. The argument of the prosecution that did not sway the opinion of the judges in *Great Western Trains* and *Attorney-General's Reference (No 2)* is vindicated by section 1(4)(b) which is to the effect that the corporation's "gross breach" will be established by showing that it had departed from accepted standards to such an extent as to be judged criminal and there is no need to prove subjective *mens rea.*[106]

That notwithstanding, the "gross breach" must have been that of the "senior management." This organ is defined as a collective of persons who manage or organise the "whole" or a "substantial" part of the activities in

---

[105] See section 1(1) and (3).

[106] However, it will be interesting to see the interpretations put on the CMCHA as regards the legislator's true intentions. This is because adopting the objective test of *Adomako* also involves adopting a circular standard that requires juries to decide a legal question (degree of negligence) based on their assessment of the facts of the case. See Gardner, 1995: 23. See also Law Commission No 237 (1996): paras. 3.8-3.10. This is similar to the circular standard for establishing involuntary culpable homicide under Scottish criminal law propounded by Lord Justice-Clerk Atchison in *Paton v HM Advocate* 1936 JC 19 at 22. He said what was required was evidence of "gross, or wicked, or criminal negligence, something amounting, or at least analogous, to a criminal indifference to consequences." Although Lord Osborne in *Transco* moved away from this definition, the definitions that he adopted are similar, *viz.* "total disregard of what the consequences of the act in question may be so far as the public are concerned" (*Quinn v Cunningham* 1956 JC 22); and "total indifference to and disregard for the safety of the public" (*W v HM Advocate* 1982 SLT 420). These standards are certainly clearer than what is required by *Adomako* but they are also equivocal given that it is still up to the jury to decide what "total" or "utter" indifference is.

question or who play significant roles in directing policy or making decisions about the management or organisation of such activities.[107] Unfortunately, this subsection may be said to be reminiscent of Lord Reid's description of the "directing mind" of a company in *Nattrass*: the board of directors, the managing director and other superior officers that carry out the functions of management or officers to whom the board of directors has delegated some part of their functions of management and given full discretion to act independently of instructions from the board of directors.[108] Lord Reid contended that this was an exhaustive list of individuals that manage or organise the activities and act and speak for the company. The wordings of the CMCHA also suggest that such is the case.[109] It may therefore be advanced that the senior management failure test is a re-statement of the identification doctrine as established in *Nattrass* except for the aggregation of the acts of all senior managers and the test of establishing the gross breach by the "senior management." It is an objective test based on how the actions of this organ compare with accepted standards in the industry and not the subjective recklessness of any individual member of the group.[110]

Nonetheless, it must be noted that the identification doctrine and the senior management failure test are the only mechanisms for imputing acts and intents to corporations for the purposes of imposing criminal liability and sanctions directly on them, the exception being where the offence charged is an absolute or strict liability offence. However, these mechanisms were not necessarily adopted because they were the most appropriate devices for determining a corporation's criminal intentions and actions (non-derivatively) given that their mechanistic basis is not always consonant with the description of the concept of corporation in criminal law such as that put forward in Chapter 2, *viz.* an amorphous entity

---

[107] Section 1(4)(c).

[108] *Nattrass* at 171.

[109] If the statute had omitted the words "whole" and "substantial" then it could be interpreted in light of the decisions of Stable J in *ICR Haulage* and Nourse LJ in *El Ajou* that the senior management includes the employee or director that had control over the activities that caused the death of the victim. This is unfortunately not the case.

[110] It is however unclear whether in construing the term "senior management" only the collective actions of the persons that manage or organise the activities of a corporation should be taken into consideration or the action of one of such persons may be sufficient to establish the corporation's guilt given that the CMCHA uses and defines only the term "senior management" and not "senior manager." This is discussed further in Chapters 5 and 8.

recognised as a corporation because of its independence of thought and action. The question of the suitability of the identification doctrine for imposing liability on corporations that do not have mechanistic systems has been addressed in several forums over the past decades and many commentators have concluded that this mechanism is a rudimentary legal tool for enforcing crimes against complex corporate entities.[111] Nonetheless, given that the crux of the problem is the complexity of the nature and personality of the accused, criminal justice systems may avoid direct (non-derivative) liability and still target the corporation without recourse to vicarious liability.[112] This may be the case where liability is imposed on a corporation for encouraging or assisting its agents to perpetrate the offence charged.

3.3 Secondary (derivative) liability

In *R v Robert Millar (Contractors) Ltd and Robert Millar*,[113] a lorry driver employed by Robert Millar (Contractors) Ltd carried heavy loads from Scotland to England with a tyre which he knew to be defective and which the managing director, Robert Millar, equally knew to be defective. While in England the tyre blew out, the driver lost control of the lorry, crashed into a motor car coming from the opposite direction and killed an entire family of six in the motor car. The Crown Court convicted both Robert Millar (Contractors) Ltd and Robert Millar for counselling and procuring the driver to cause death by driving in a manner dangerous to the public. Also, citing previous convictions of natural persons as accessories,[114] the Appeal Court held that there is an offence of counselling and procuring (involuntary) manslaughter and such an offence could be enforced against corporations.[115] Similarly, in *R v JF Alford Transport Ltd*,[116] it was held that a company that knew that its drivers were falsifying their tacograph records but omitted to stop or sanction them had deliberately done nothing to prevent the illegal activity from

---

[111] The doctrine and the senior management failure test are evaluated in Chapter 5.
[112] An attempt is however made in Chapter 6 to show how vicarious liability may be used to target corporations directly.
[113] (1970) 1 All ER 577, hereinafter referred to as *Robert Millar*.
[114] *R v Buck and Buck* (1960) 44 Cr App R 213; and *R v Creamer* [1965] 3 All ER 257.
[115] See Fenton Atkinson LJ *Robert Millar* at 578-581. See also Gobert and Punch, 2003: 71.
[116] [1997] CLR 745.

being repeated and had intended to encourage the repetition.[117] The form of liability on the corporations in these cases was secondary liability because as contended by Fenton Atkinson LJ "[they] are guilty of participating in that crime and not of some self-subsisting crime on their own account."[118] As such, this form of liability may be used to enforce crimes against corporations in instances where the senior officers were not guilty but tolerated or encouraged the non-compliant acts of junior employees.

What is important is that the prosecution shows that the guilty agent was encouraged by the corporation (senior management) to perpetrate or to attempt to perpetrate an offence.[119] The corporation may then be said to be an accessory to the offence. Its liability is derivative because it aided and abetted its agent (the principal offender) to perpetrate the offence charged.[120] Such liability may include (although it is not synonymous to) inchoate liability involving an attempt,[121] where the corporation may be guilty for encouraging its agent to attempt to commit the offence; conspiracy,[122] where the corporation may be said to have conspired with the agent to perpetrate an offence; and incitement,[123] where the corporation may be said to have incited the agent to engage in criminal acts. As such, rather than seeking to show evidence of the corporation's intent to perpetrate the offence charged, it may be easier for the prosecution to

---

[117] The conviction was however quashed on the facts due to the trial judge's misdirection to the jury.

[118] *Robert Millar* at 580.

[119] See Law Commission No 300 (2006): 4-7; and Law Commission No 305 (2007): para. 1.32.

[120] See Law Commission No 300 (2006): 1-3; and Law Commission No 305 (2007): paras. 1.1-1.4.

[121] See section 1(1) of the Criminal Attempts Act 1981. See also the common law position in Scotland in *HM Advocate v Camerons* 1911 2 SLT 108; and *Docherty v Brown* 1996 SLT 355. See also section 18 of the Draft Criminal Code for Scotland discussed in Clive, Ferguson, Gane and Smith, 2003.

[122] Section 1 of the Criminal Law Act 1977. For the common law position in Scotland, see *Maxwell and Others v HM Advocate* 1980 JC 40. See also Clive, Ferguson, Gane and Smith, 2003: 56-58.

[123] For examples of statutory offences of incitement, see Law Commission No 300 (2006): 4. However, incitement is still a common law offence in England and Wales. For the common law position in Scotland, see *HM Advocate v Tannahill and Neilson* 1943 JC 150; and *Baxter v H.M. Advocate* 1998 SLT 414. See also section 19 of the Draft Criminal Code for Scotland discussed in Clive, Ferguson, Gane and Smith, 2003.

show that the corporation simply provided inchoate assistance to the agent that perpetrated the offence. In other words, the corporation encouraged or incited or conspired with the agent to perpetrate the offence.

However, accessorial liability may be another slippery avenue for the enforcement of corporate crime. Where the liability imposed is inchoate, the corporation's liability stems from the fact that it is shown to have encouraged the perpetration of the offence even if the offence was not committed subsequently.[124] Equally, where the corporation was unable to control the guilty agent, it may nevertheless be said to be guilty because it had committed to a joint enterprise with the former.[125] It is however uncertain whether evidence of the existence of a defective compliance programme or poor internal disciplinary system would suffice.[126] If it is said that a corporation provided inchoate assistance to the agent's attempt to commit the offence this would imply that a corporation may be liable if it has a defective compliance programme irrespective of the fact that no agent has actually committed an offence as a result of the defective programme.[127]

---

[124] Law Commission No 305, 2007: para. 1.33. The Law Commission distinguishes between inchoate liability and secondary liability by pointing to the question of whether the accessory either merely encouraged or assisted the perpetrator. However, it is uncertain whether a fine line can be drawn between the notions of "assisting" and "encouraging" especially as different words such as "counselling," "abetting," "aiding," and "art and part" are used in other instances. Given that these words generally overlap in their literal meanings, it may be contended that there is truly no distinction between inchoate and secondary liability except for the fact that in the first instance the principal offence is not intended. However, the complexity of the corporation's nature confounds the situation because offences are often committed as a result of the pursuit of a collective goal with no intent to commit the principal offence. Thus, to say that the pursuit of a collective goal provided inchoate assistance would be to imply that a corporation ought to be guilty of any offence committed by any of its employees while seeking to further the corporation's interests.

[125] See Simester, 2006: 591-600; and Wilson, 2008: 11.

[126] The question here is whether having a defective compliance system may be sufficiently blameworthy to found a criminal charge. This is discussed further in Chapters 5 and 6 as regards the use of the senior management failure test and corporate culture doctrine as mechanisms of imputation.

[127] If the corporation argues that there were instructions that forbade the agent from performing the wrongful act, the court may say that proof of the principal's approval of the agent's specific illegal objective is not necessary. See *DPP of Northern Ireland v Lynch* [1975] AC 653.

It may therefore be advanced that accessorial liability represents a departure from the common law rule that a 'person' cannot be convicted (where she does not owe a duty) as a result of an omission to act[128] or for simply standing and doing nothing.[129] Thus, liability is imposed on the corporation for its failure to exercise its entitlement (and not perform its duty) to control others.[130] There is no doubt that it would be easier for the prosecution to show that a corporation's policies aided, abetted or encouraged a crime or its management failed to control or stop the wrongdoing by its agents.[131] However, there is certainly a danger of overcriminalisation.[132] Accessorial liability would be established even where the accessory did not have specific knowledge of the principal's intention to commit the offence and only had knowledge of the possibility of the latter committing an offence.[133] Thus, a corporation may be liable if it was aware of the possibility of a maverick agent violating the law even though the latter would have done so while acting outwith the scope of her agreement with the corporation (delegated duties).[134] Gobert and Punch[135] have therefore sought to dampen the optimistic view as regards the use of accessorial liability. They advance that accessorial liability is not the much-sought-after panacea because of the requirement of identifying a senior manager (that was aware of the wrongdoing) with the corporation.[136]

---

[128] Law Commission No 305 (2007): para. 2.25.

[129] Law Commission No 305, 2007: para. 3.25. This is one of the consequences of the lack of distinction between an accessory that encouraged the principal offender and one that assisted the principal offender.

[130] See Glazebrook, 2002: 408. However, see the court's remark in *Rubie v Faulkner* [1946] 1 KB 571 that a driving instructor could be secondarily liable for a learner's dangerous driving.

[131] See Gobert and Punch, 2003: 71-72.

[132] This is a problem with secondary liability in general and not only when corporations are concerned. See Wilson, 2008: 13.

[133] See *DPP of Northern Ireland v Maxwell* [1978] 1 WLR 1350.

[134] See Wilson (2008: 4) on the difficulty of justifying the imposition of liability on the accessory in instances where the principal offender's action was greater than the former may be said to have encouraged or tolerated.

[135] 2003: 75-77.

[136] In *Robert Millar*, the managing director was in charge of the day-to-day running of the business and was fully aware of the dangerous state of the front offside tyre of the lorry and was sentenced to nine months imprisonment. That notwithstanding, any serious senior management should have reasonable cause to be aware of the mode of carrying out activities used by the junior employees, especially where such a mode could have serious consequences on the wellbeing of other employees and other members of society. Thus, the senior management may be said to have had constructive knowledge in such cases. See Chapter 4 for

Moreover, the act of the junior employee must amount to an offence.[137] This is because accessorial liability involves procuring the breach of the criminal law and not simply the breach of corporate ethics or policies.[138] Also, as mentioned above, a corporation may be held liable for providing inchoate assistance[139] although the degree of blameworthiness in such an instance is questionable.[140] Nonetheless, given that the CMCHA provides for the imposition of liability based on a low level of blameworthiness (poor management and organisation of activities), the question of blameworthiness will certainly be tested in the implementation of the CMCHA. It must be noted that the level of blameworthiness for crimes such as negligence may be low because as posited by Lord Lane, "manslaughter ranges in its gravity from the borders of murder right down to those of accidental death." [141] However, as regards other crimes of intent such as fraud, murder and theft, it is important that conviction should follow a reasonably high level of blameworthiness.

The challenge with regard to the use of accessorial liability may be summarised under two heads: firstly, ascertaining whether a corporation must only be shown to assist or encourage the commission of an offence or it may also suffice to show that it encouraged a number of negligent acts that cumulatively resulted in an offence; and secondly, ascertaining the degree of blameworthiness that is required to establish the corporation's guilt. However, given the prevailing uncertainty with regard to the way acts and intents (or causal relationships) may be imputed to a corporation in order to hold it liable personally, enforcing crimes of intent through accessorial liability may be worth the effort. Nonetheless, it would still be necessary to establish whose acts and states of mind ought to be imputed

---

discussion on constructive knowledge as a legal principle governing the use of rules of attribution.

[137] This is however based on a strict application of the principle governing secondary liability. See Law Commission No 305, 2007: paras. 2.8-2.13.

[138] As noted above, the prosecution of large and organic companies for manslaughter was (in part) unsuccessful because the prosecution could only adduce evidence of several acts of employees that were reproachable but did not amount to the offence charged when considered singly. This pushed the prosecution to call for the adoption of the aggregation doctrine (discussed in Chapters 6 and 8) adopted by some courts in the United States.

[139] Such as where its policies encouraged or tolerated non-compliance by its agents.

[140] Where the level of blameworthiness is very low the offence becomes a strict liability offence.

[141] *R v Walker* (1992) 13 Cr App R (S) 474 at 476.

to corporations for the purposes of showing that they assisted or encouraged their delinquent agents and why. In *Robert Millar*, the act and knowledge of the managing director was imputed to the corporation. However, in line with the CMCHA, only the collective acts of those that constitute the senior management may be imputed to the corporation. As such, irrespective of the form of liability imposed the determination of a suitable mechanism of imputation remains paramount.

3.4 Conclusion

This Chapter considered the adaptability of the criminal law in dealing with a peculiar class of criminals: corporate persons. Discussion was premised on the assumption that the criminal law is an effective means of regulating the activities of corporations. The forms of liability imposed on corporations over the past 400 years were analysed briefly and it was noted that given that vicarious liability is eschewed by the criminal law regimes of the United Kingdom and a corporation is a distinct person, its liability may only be direct (non-derivative) or secondary (derivative). As such, although a corporation invariably acts through natural persons it ought not to be liable for an offence committed *qua* agent but for one committed *qua* corporation. This means that criminal liability may only be imposed on corporations in two instances. Firstly, where the evidence shows that the corporation used its agents as instruments to perpetrate the offence charged; and secondly, where the evidence shows that it encouraged or assisted its guilty agent in the performance of the offence charged.

In the first instance, although the corporation acts through its agents, its liability is direct or non-derivative because the corporation is the only offender; it perpetrates the offence through agents that are innocent. This reflects the doctrine of innocent agency[142] but may be said to be an extension of this doctrine because in many cases the acts of the agents may not amount to an offence.[143] The corporation will be the only offender because the elements of the offence may only be established against it given that it controlled the set of facts that gave rise to the offence

[142]See Smith K, 1991: 94. This also reflects the defence of "employee necessity" where the employee was simply obeying instructions (see Wells, 2001: 165) and "member-responsibility" of individual agents. See Pettit, 2007.

[143] See however the discussion on the doctrine's simplicity by the Law Commission No 300 (2006: 25-26).

charged.[144] Gobert and Punch[145] cite the study published by Geis[146] on a number of anti-trust cases in 1961 in which company executives collectively fixed prices not for any personal gains but to further the interests of the companies.[147] Equally, other studies and reports such as Carson's[148] study of the practices and policies in the oil and gas industry and the Sheen Report on the sinking of the Herald of Free enterprise show that agents may actually collectively breach the law in order to meet company objectives or further collective interests. The agents in these cases were no doubt innocent agents that the companies used to perpetrate the offences charged.

However, it has been argued that to say that a person that did not perform the *actus reus* of an offence such as rape or bigamy was the principal offender would be a "violent wrench of the English language."[149] Nonetheless, it may be countered that to say that a corporation may perform any action or entertain any opinion would equally constitute a wrench of the language. The objective of this book is to achieve coherence and integrity within a given legal frame (corporate criminal law) and not within a literary one. Thus, as shown in Chapter 2, from a legal perspective, a corporation may perform actions and entertain intentions and may perpetrate any offence. Moreover, the corporation's use of innocent agents is axiomatic. Where for example the offence charged is an absolute liability offence, no agent may be held liable for the breach of the absolute duty.[150] Hence, the underpinning rationale of innocent agency is congenial to corporate criminal law.

---

[144] See Wilson (2008: 5). See also Wilson (2002: 218-222) on a solution to the problem of imposing liability on the accessory for an offence that she did not commit.

[145] 2003: 4-5.

[146] 1967.

[147] Despite the fact that these agents may be said to have had an ulterior motive of obtaining bonuses, the study revealed that their behaviour was acceptable within the industry.

[148] 1979.

[149] These are the words of Williams (1983: 371) criticising the use of the doctrine of innocent agency to hold a person liable for rape as principal offender in an instance where he encouraged the perpetrator but did not have sexual intercourse with the victim.

[150] This may also be true of strict liability offences given that the prosecution may only establish some "minimum culpability."

However, courts do not have such a leeway with regard to imposing liability on corporations for crimes of intent (excluding manslaughter and culpable homicide). They are required to convict only where the evidence shows that the accused entertained the relevant *mens rea*. Given the nebulousness of the concept of 'corporation,' some courts have simply held that the offence charged cannot be committed by a corporation while others have avoided the quandary by interpreting statutory crimes of intent as strict or absolute liability offences.[151] As shown above, dictates of coherence and integrity require that courts or Parliament should prescribe an appropriate mechanism of imputation. This is because the identification doctrine that ought to have given courts a way out of the predicament is itself a very rigid mechanism reflecting only the realities of mechanistic corporate structures. It has been heavily criticised in different avenues and although some judges employ its modified version (*Meridian*) readily, the rigid rule in *Nattrass* still applies. Moreover, there is always the danger that if the doctrine was modified to enable courts to hold corporations liable for the offences of all employees, the unreasonably broad nature of the mechanism would be undistinguished from vicarious criminal liability. The dire consequences of observing this rigid rule were noted especially in manslaughter and culpable homicide cases and Parliament introduced the senior management failure test, which as shown above (and in Chapter 5), is quite similar to the identification doctrine and may likely produce the same results.

It is therefore submitted that it may be pragmatic to consider imposing liability on a corporation as accessory in instances where the prosecution may identify the guilty agent but may not be able to impute her guilt to the corporation (using the applicable mechanisms) because the agent is not of sufficient station. Thus, the corporation is still personally liable but its liability is derivative as it is based on the fact that it encouraged or assisted the principal offender (guilty junior employee) in the commission of the offence. Equally, this form of liability may be appropriate where the prosecution is unable to distinguish between the accessory and the principal in a situation where both the corporation and the agent undertook the criminal activity together. This is because one of the main reasons for

[151] This is not only due to the fact that the language employed in statutes can often be open to many interpretations but also due to the deliberate disregard of certain essential words. Thus, the history of ascertaining the meaning of statutory provisions by courts has not been marked by consistency. Different reasons have been invoked ranging from policy considerations to semantics in a bid to achieve what the courts believe to be fair in light of the applicable statute.

the use of accessorial liability is to enable the prosecution to obtain a conviction where it is difficult to identify the principal offender in an apparently joint criminal venture.[152] As such, in cases where the offence was the result of a number of devious acts performed by agents seeking to further both personal and collective interests, the prosecution may consider proving the corporation's guilt by showing that it encouraged or assisted these agents. However, the fact that there have been few convictions since *Robert Millar* shows that the option of accessorial liability may be arduous.[153] Nevertheless, the problem of ascertaining whose acts and intents are imputable to the corporation remains. This is because the prosecution would be required to show that the corporation was an accessory while acting via certain agents. Given the rigidity of the applicable mechanisms of imputation it may be important to devise other mechanisms that will provide the avenue to impute the acts and intents of certain or all agents in defined circumstances for the purpose of showing that one set of agents were innocent instruments used by the corporation (another set of agents) or that one set of agents (the corporation) aided or encouraged another set of agents in the commission of the offence charged. Such a mechanism would therefore give the criminal law the flexibility to deal with corporations of different shapes and sizes committing different offences in different circumstances.[154]

---

[152] See Wilson, 2008: 3-4. See also the case of *R v Forman and Ford* [1988] Crim LR 677.

[153] Accessorial liability may be subject to much controversy as shown in the Reports by the Law Commission No 300 (2006); and Law Commission No 305 (2007).

[154] As mentioned above, Lord Hoffmann's contention that judges should be able to fashion special rules to address the circumstances before them is not appropriate because it predicates the arbitrary interpretation of statutes by judges rather than the use of a single flexible mechanism on a consistent basis. *Meridian* is analysed further in Chapter 4.

CHAPTER FOUR

GENERATING PARAMETERS FOR DETERMINING AN APPROPRIATE MECHANISM OF IMPUTATION

4.1 Introduction

In Chapter 2 it was advanced that although a corporation may be accountable for its actions or omissions, its existence is manifested in the substance of other persons (natural). In Chapter 3 it was established that imposing criminal liability on the corporation presupposes that it has either used or assisted one or many of such natural persons to perpetrate an offence.[1] As such, the challenge for the criminal justice system is to consistently distinguish between on the one hand, acts that are particular to a corporation (for corporate liability) and those that are particular to its agents (for innocent agency) and on the other hand, acts that are common to the secondary corporate offender (for corporate accessorial liability) and those that are particular to the agent who is either the principal offender or a maverick (for individual liability). A convenient way of achieving this is by establishing a convention of imputing acts and intents of agents[2] to corporations under specified circumstances. This convention is referred to as a mechanism of imputation and it will be shown that the absence or

---

[1] This does not imply that both the corporation and its employee cannot be liable for the same offence. Where this happens it should simply be understood as either coincidence or conspiracy or incitement.

[2] Although I talk often of the imputation of acts and intents of agents to the corporation, what is actually imputed is the causal relationship between the agent's act or intent and the offence. This is because the court is interested in determining whether the corporation caused the offence and not whether it performed the act or entertained the intention. That is why it is argued in Chapter 3 that a corporation may be the principal offender without necessarily performing the *actus reus* of the offence. Nonetheless, in order to reduce the complexity of the discussion, the imputation of acts and intents of agents is interchanged with the imputation of causal relationships.

inconsistent use of such a mechanism renders the criminal law unpredictable and incoherent as regards the imposition of liability on corporations.

This Chapter therefore dwells on the importance of developing mechanisms of imputation and suggests ways in which the process may be assessed and standardised. Discussion here follows the factual supposition offered in Chapter 1 that all criminal jurisdictions have an applicable mechanism of imputation that courts and criminal justice agencies employ or ought to employ. This Chapter consists of two phases. The first phase will expatiate on the notion of "rules of attribution" given that mechanisms have habitually been referred to as rules or models or principles of attribution. Emphasis will be placed on Lord Hoffmann's concise description of rules of attribution in *Meridian* and obstacles to their consistent use. It will be submitted that in order to avoid a disconnected usage of rules of attribution it may be preferable to return to Hart's conception of primary and secondary rules. In the second phase, parameters for evaluating such mechanisms from a substantive perspective will be suggested. I will then conclude that the diverse ways in which courts may impute acts and intents to corporations for the purpose of imposing liability directly or secondarily on them ought to be linked to a combination of primary and secondary rules; and an effective link is an appropriate mechanism of imputation.

4.2 From rule of attribution to mechanism of imputation

> Any proposition about a company necessarily involves a reference to a set of rules. A company exists because there is a rule (usually in a statute) which says that a persona ficta shall be deemed to exist and to have certain powers, rights and duties of a natural person. But there would be little sense in deeming such a persona ficta to exist unless there were also rules to tell one what acts were to count as acts of the company. It is therefore a necessary part of corporate personality that there should be rules by which acts are attributed to the company. These may be called 'the rules of attribution.'[3]

This statement by Lord Hoffmann highlights the significance of attribution and rules that define its processes in corporate personality and liability discourse.[4] It has rightly been influential over the years for it may be lauded for simplifying (and making flexible) the conduct of criminal

[3] Lord Hoffmann in *Meridian* at 506.
[4] See Png, 2001: 27.

proceedings against corporations, a task that was notoriously made arduous by the House of Lords in *Nattrass*. Hence, it is thanks to Lord Hoffmann that it is generally accepted today that whenever a court of law talks of a corporation's act or thought it is alluding to a particular way of imputing acts and thoughts (or causal relationships) to the corporation.[5] However, the gist of his assertion is that since a corporation is a fiction created by the law (*persona ficta*), it is also important that the law outlines the aggregate of its interactions with its environment. Thus, rules of attribution are devised to serve this purpose. Nonetheless, if it is shown that a corporation is an objective reality and not the legislator's creation,[6] the contention that the truth of its behaviour (whether legal or otherwise) may be found only in legal edicts may be questioned. Also, Lord Hoffmann distinguished between three types of rules of attribution, namely: primary, general and special; and noted that the primary rules emanate from the corporation's constitution or may sometimes be implied by the operation of company law, while the general rules may be inferred from principles of agency and vicarious liability.[7] However, if this is understood to imply that there are rules governing a corporation's existence and behaviour outside legal rules (such as the corporation's constitution), then relying solely on legal prescriptions for knowledge about the behaviour of corporations may be unjustified. Thus, emphases on the fiction theory and the sovereignty of the statute only tugs corporate criminal law further into the maze of dogma, circularity and material fallacy ('is-ought' problem). This may be blamed (in part) on the theoretical approach employed (strictly doctrinal analysis or internal approach) given that the process of attributing acts and intents to corporations is far too complex (involving other processes that do not necessarily have to satisfy legal rules) and mutable to be enshrined in fixed legal rules.

A fixed legal rule may be said to describe the way in which a court is required to invest a corporation with a body for the purposes of convicting

---

[5] See Bartlett, 1998: 463; and Hawke, 2000: 54. It may therefore be claimed that the conception of rules of attribution is as old as those of corporate personality and liability.

[6] Or at least that the *persona ficta* stance is highly debatable. The idea that a corporation is simply a fiction created by the state reflects the concession theory. This was shown in Chapter 2 to be only partially true as regards the corporation's origin and nature.

[7] *Meridian* at 506-507.

and sanctioning it. This may be a statute or precedent.[8] However, given that corporations may act (via their agents) in more ways than can possibly be envisaged by legislators and judges, the application of these legal rules ought to be directed by other legal principles as well as factual considerations or explanations of the corporate phenomena. As such, in order to avoid the circularity and material fallacy of rationalising legal propositions by appealing solely to legal rules, courts are required to look beyond the prescriptions of the relevant statutes and precedent (fixed legal rules) and also apply other rules and principles[9] in order to ascertain the "best interpretation."[10] This implies that they ought to appeal to both legal and non-legal considerations of what would reasonably justify the imputation of acts and intents to a corporation in any given instance; the legal consideration being the rule of attribution enshrined in the statute or precedent and the non-legal consideration being propositions that judges may deduce from the observations of previous judges. Thus, the question of how to allocate criminal responsibility to corporations is a function of how a court on the one hand, interprets the relevant law (with its rule of attribution) and other related legal principles, and on the other hand, appraises the facts of the case; the objective being to determine whether the accused corporation acted through its agent or whether the latter acted in her individual capacity.[11]

As such, a judge may not devise "special" rules of attribution merely to achieve the objective of a statute.[12] Where the wordings of the statutory provision provide for a specific pattern of attribution, the judge is required to impute acts and intents to corporations in accordance with such a pattern. Where no pattern may be deduced from the wordings of the statute, the judge must give regard to the pattern prescribed by the precedent. Although there may be some differences in the ways in which

---

[8] The identification doctrine may then be referred to as the rule of attribution in *Nattrass* and the senior management failure test may be referred to as the rule of attribution in the CMCHA. Equally, in the United States, vicarious liability may be referred to as the rule of attribution in *New York Central*.

[9] See Hart, 1994: 81 and 260.

[10] See Dworkin, 1986: 337.

[11] This means that irrespective of the dictate of the rule of attribution, a corporation may only be held responsible if the facts of the case show that the corporation caused (or induced) the act of the agent who ought to be identified with it according to the rule of attribution.

[12] As posited by Lord Hoffmann in *Meridian* at 507. Dworkin (1986: 338-339) notes that the judge must seek the best substantive outcome and not that she should seek the best justification of her own convictions about policy and justice.

courts interpret both statute and precedent,[13] it may be submitted that in both instances the judge would have to refer to other legal principles and factual suppositions in order to determine whether the prescribed pattern is the right way of distinguishing the acts of the corporation from those of its agents.[14] Thus, where neither the applicable statute nor precedent provides for a pattern of imputing acts and intents to corporations, it may be submitted that the judge should simply consider other legal rules and principles and factual suppositions. As such, Lord Hoffmann's recommendation that judges fashion "special rules" to deal with the cases before them concerns only cases where neither the applicable statutory provision nor precedent provides for a pattern of attribution. However, it is highly unlikely to find such cases.[15] Thus, judges that fashion special rules to address the peculiar circumstances before them do so through lack of concern for the prescription by precedent.[16]

---

[13] See Dworkin, 1986: 276-313.

[14] This does not imply that if the judge considers that the prescribed pattern is not the right way of attributing acts to the corporation she may part with it and fashion special rules. What the judge may consider wrong in such an instance is not the actual prescription but the interpretation put upon it by previous courts. Thus, the judge rejects such an interpretation and not the prescribed pattern. This means that a judge may not for example assert that a statute that provides for the imputation of the acts of agents performed outside their scope of employment is not morally correct. She may however submit that the previous definitions of 'scope of employment' are not accurate as this statute does not broaden the meaning of this concept. It may therefore be contended that the approach adopted here is similar to that of Raz (1975 and 1979), Perry (1987) and Hart (1994) whereby precedent may be deemed to be exclusionary but not absolute. Thus, we may agree with Schauer (1991:196-206) that it is important for a judge to be able to sometimes find recourse in "non-pedigreed" rules in order to arrive at the right answer. However, we will disagree with the contention that "pedigreed" rules of precedent may be disregarded in certain instances. This is similar to what Lord Hoffmann suggested in *Meridian* and it is suggested here that this will lead to judge-made laws and inconsistency given that "non-pedigreed" rules are not legitimate and are largely ambiguous.

[15] This is because criminal law courts within each jurisdiction have a customary way of imputing acts and intents to corporations. Such is the pattern prescribed by precedent. Thus, in the United Kingdom, the imputation of acts and intents of only senior managers to corporations sanctioned by the House of Lords in *Nattrass* may be said to be the pattern prescribed by precedent.

[16] The prescription by precedent is also understood here to imply other legal rules or principles that may determine the outcome of the case. Hence, the judge has to decide which rule or principle outweighs the other in the circumstances. See Raz, 1972: 832-834; and Dworkin, 1986: 240-244.

It may then be advanced that the process of attributing acts and intents to corporations involves interpreting and applying rules embedded in statutes or precedent in accordance with related legal rules, principles and factual suppositions. This indicates a union between rules that impose obligations on courts and rules that specify how the courts ought to fulfil such obligations. Following Hart's[17] conception of rules, the first type of rules may be called the "primary rules" and the second type of rules may be called the "secondary rules." There is a clear distinction between the use of "primary rule" here and the use of the term by Lord Hoffmann in *Meridian*. It is unfortunate that his Lordship did not explain why rules that may be deduced from a company's constitution or the operation of company law may be referred to as "primary rules." If "primary rules" as described by Lord Hoffmann ought to be supplemented by the "general rules,"[18] then the "primary rules" may be deemed to take precedence over the "general rules." However, it cannot be said that the rules in the company's constitution or articles of association take precedence over the principles of agency (general rules). In fact, courts enforce strict liability offences against corporations on the basis of the actions of agents of the corporations irrespective of what is written in their constitutions or may be implied by company law. It is therefore submitted here that for heuristic purposes it may be preferable to refer to Hart's terminology and designate the rule that imposes an obligation on courts to impute acts and intents to corporations in a particular way as the "primary rule" while the rules that enhance the understanding of the primary rule and inform the legislator on its shortcomings as "secondary rules."[19] This implies that the primary rule of attribution is embedded in a statute or precedent while the secondary rules are standards established by other legal rules and propositions. These propositions represent what Dworkin calls "legal principles" and are important because they provide a test for determining the validity of the primary rule by content-based and pedigree-based tests.[20] However,

---

[17] 1994: 79-99.

[18] See also Png, 2001: 27.

[19] The secondary rules referred to here are therefore those that constitute what Hart called the "rules of recognition" and "rules of adjudication." This is because the "rules of change" are not required to ascertain the validity of the primary rule. However, both conceptions of "secondary rules" of Hart and Lord Hoffmann favour the discretion of judges to put their interpretations on laws.

[20] See the contention by Hart (1994: 259-263) that nothing in his description of the secondary rules suggests that content-based tests (such as those implied by Dworkin's legal principles) may not be included. See also Leiter, 2003. Hart then

owing to the fact that the secondary rules may not always provide the meaning of an essential word used in expressing the primary rule, the judge may be required to consider what is acceptable or not in light of the legislator's intention and other policy considerations. It is submitted here that she should apply the "commonsense" meaning of such a term[21] and this may involve having recourse to an "external" perspective[22] that may include for example knowledge about group or corporate behaviour from some non-legal categories.[23] Nonetheless, given the ambiguity of non-legal perspectives, the process of having recourse to the meanings they provide ought to be within a framework built by precedent.[24]

In *Nattrass*, Lord Reid ordained that "it must be a question of law whether, once the facts have been ascertained, a person in doing particular things is to be regarded as the company or merely as the company's servant or agent."[25] This implies that the question of law as regards whose act or intent counts as that of the corporation is answered by the primary rule of attribution, while the question of fact as regards whether the agent's act that is considered by the court should be attributed to the corporation in accordance with the primary rule is answered by the secondary rules. Hence, Dworkin's Hercules[26] would arrive at the right answer (of how to impute acts and intents to corporations) by interpreting the primary rule in accordance with the secondary rules. This shows that attribution is a complex process that involves examining the conclusive legal rule (rule of attribution) and the factual context of the case in light of

---

showed how difficult it is to distinguish between secondary rules as he saw them and legal principles as described by Dworkin. Thus, for the purpose of clarity, I will consider legal principles to be part of secondary rules.

[21] See for example the recommendation of the Home Affairs and Work and Pensions Committee in their joint report on the Draft Bill of 2005 (paras. 145 and 153) with regard to defining the term "substantial" as used in the CMCHA. See also the "commonsense" meaning attributed to the term "causation" by Lord Wilberforce and Lord Salmon in *Alphacell* at 834 and 847 respectively.

[22] It is described as "external" because it often involves a non-legal view of the legal phenomena.

[23] See Fisse and Braithwaite, 1993: 15.

[24] This means that the judge may not seek commonsense meanings of the terms "causation" and "foreseeability" out of the scope of common sense meanings of these terms delineated by the House of Lords in *Alphacell*. As noted in Chapter 1, specifying instances where judges may invoke non-pedigreed and non-legal knowledge augurs well for coherence and consistency.

[25] *Nattrass* at 170.

[26] The infinitely wise arbiter in the "Law's Empire."

what may be understood as the accepted wisdom (non-conclusive principle).[27] It may therefore be contended that when one talks of the "rule of attribution" one is strictly referring to the primary rule embedded in the statute or precedent and not the process of attribution that also involves secondary rules. Thus, it may be better to talk of "mechanism" and not "rule" given that courts do not simply apply the primary rule of attribution as set out by the relevant statute or precedent but they also consider other rules (secondary rules) that modify the application of the primary rule.[28] As such, although the primary rule may take precedence over the secondary rules, it is non-conclusive and may be outweighed in certain circumstances. This may explain why the rule of attribution affirmed in *Nattrass* was disregarded in *Belmont* as the court in the latter case deemed it unfair that the act of a fraudulent senior manager should be imputed to his corporate victim. However, it must be noted that, within the set of rules, the primary rule is fixed in terms of content and pedigree while the secondary rules are only fixed in terms of pedigree, since their content may vary according to the facts of the case.[29] Thus, within each jurisdiction there is a mutable mechanism that describes the ascertained processes of imputation involving primary rules embedded in statutes or precedent and secondary rules. As will be shown below, a defective mechanism is likely to compromise the consistent imposition of liability on corporations while an entirely adequate one enhances the process. This book is focused on the ascertainment of an adequate mechanism.

4.2.1 Understanding how the mechanism operates

Where an offence has been committed or a wrong suffered most people would say that it is unacceptable not to impose liability on the individual (or entity) that committed the offence or ought to have prevented the offence from being committed.[30] Principles such as these often guide the customary use of legal edicts by officials[31] and may provide the

[27] This is similar to a court's deliberation that involves looking at the legal rule and normative considerations. See Marmor, 2006: 699.

[28] I will also talk of mechanism of 'imputation' and not mechanism of 'attribution' in order to distinguish both concepts further and avoid any confusion that may arise from using the term 'attribution' when referring to both concepts.

[29] See Hart, 1994: 264-265. As noted above, the secondary rules must equally be "pedigreed" in order not to patronise a system of arbitrary judge-made laws.

[30] This is further accentuated by the belief that if responsibility is not attributed the harm will not be eradicated. See Miller, 2001: 453.

[31] See Marmor, 2006: 686.

framework for normative law.[32] Hence, they may be deemed to justify an enactment or the creation of a precedent.[33] However, the justification of the use of legal rules in a certain manner by normative principles would depend on the judge who is required to exercise discretion in invoking the latter, understanding the former and establishing a link between both.[34] Nonetheless, despite the fact that one judge's evaluation of a law from a given perspective may probably be different from that of other judges, there is likely to be consensus on the fact that judges are empowered to interpret and modify laws with reference to diverse considerations[35] and it may be possible to determine whether these laws are appropriate or not by referring to a framework of such considerations.[36] In other words, we may ascertain the effectiveness of a law by referring to the elucidation of judges' moral constructs used in understanding what problems such a law is required to solve.[37] As such, what is described above as primary rules may be deemed to be the "formal reason"[38] or "first-order reasons"[39] of the judgment and what is described as the secondary rules may be deemed to be the "substantive reason."[40] By analysing the "substantive reason" of a statute or precedent it may also be said that we are seeking to understand

---

[32] See Green, 2005: 567.
[33] See Coleman, 2001.
[34] See Honoré, 2002: 489-495.
[35] See Marmor, 2006: 689-688; and Berger, 2002: 30. The contentions of Schauer (1991) and Perry (1987) to the effect that precedent is dispensable and those of Raz (1979) and Hart (1994) that precedent is exclusionary thus overlap with regard to the judge's discretion in considering non-legal prescriptions. However, they differ on the amount of discretion that judges may enjoy.
[36] This does not mean that non-legal considerations are *sine qua non* for the determination of the law. However, there is no intention here to take sides or justify any stance in the long-drawn-out battle between positivists and those against positivism as regards the correlation between moral constructs and legal validity. What is important here is that given the ambiguity of legislative intention and the limits of legal language (which many positivists do underscore), it is likely that the law will often be a "prophecy of what the courts will do." See Marmor, 2001: 81-88.
[37] It may also be said that the Government often explains laws and the explanations are affected by certain norms that are not strictly legal. However, since legislators have largely abandoned their casuistic style of yore and only state the general principles or the rule without further illustrations on the implementation and intended consequences (see Hunt, 2002: 25), it is less likely that such notions may be had from legislators' enactments and explanatory notes.
[38] See Atiyah and Summers, 1987: 2.
[39] Perry, 1989: 944.
[40] Atiyah and Summers, 1987: 5-6.

the law by looking at the interaction of the formal reason with other rules and principles, as well the law's description from an "internal point of view" or by those that play the most active role in the practice. Thus, when legislators or judges make decisions about the acceptability or not of a way of imputing acts and intents to corporations, we are able to better understand their choices by referring to the internal point of view.[41] Similarly, where the internal point of view neither explains nor justifies the use of a primary rule, commonsense may dictate that the presiding judge considers the viewpoints expressed by some non-legal commentators. These may equally constitute "secondary rules" although they ought to be relevant to the case, that is, they ought to have been invoked by or discussed as *obiter dicta* of the precedent.[42]

It may therefore be posited that an appropriate mechanism of imputation is one that also enables the judge to examine the "substantive reason" that underpins the "secondary rules" (consisting of other legal principles and other judges' "internal point of view" and related theorists' "external point of view") in order to arrive at the right answer. In other words, the mechanism of imputation ought to enable the judge to look at the way previous judges understood and applied the primary rule and how corporate structures function in practice (secondary rules). In essence, the "internal point of view" reflects what Lord Hoffmann described in *Meridian* as the "special rule of attribution for the particular substantive rule" to the extent that each judge is empowered to give an explanation of the way the primary rule ought to apply in the case before her. As such, Lord Hoffmann understood the applicable section 20 of the New Zealand Securities Amendment Act 1988 (primary rule) as prescribing that the agent that acquired the interest on behalf of the corporation and with its authority may be deemed to have acted as the corporation.[43] However, the interpretation of the primary rule in Lord Hoffmann's context was guided completely by his moral considerations and not by a "pedigreed" set of customary rules (secondary rules) as advanced above. The discretion exercised was almost as large as that which only the legislator should

---

[41] Marmor, 2006: 701-702. This is in line with the theoretical approach adopted in this book: the interpretive legal theory or internal approach.

[42] Although *obiter dictum* is not binding, it is nevertheless persuasive authority and may therefore guide other courts on how to enforce certain laws in certain peculiar instances. In fact, some *obiter dicta* may be so persuasive that it is sometimes difficult to say whether they were not one of the major premises from which the judge drew her conclusion. See Cross R and Harris, 1991: 75-81.

[43] See *Meridian* at 511.

exercise. Hence, Lord Hoffmann's "special rule" truly reflects only his "internal point of view." For the purposes of consistency and coherence, it is important that this point of view conforms to other relevant legal principles and the outlook of other judges and some related non-legal theories. It is therefore submitted that there is need for a framework of such principles and views (secondary rules) that would limit a judge's discretion and guide her interpretation of the primary rule. This framework of secondary rules by which the primary rule may be ascertained consists of rules of recognition and rules of adjudication.[44] The content of these rules may be said to vary positively with the effectiveness of the mechanism of imputation. This is because the larger or more pertinent the content the more relevant information there will be at the judge's disposal to interpret and explain the primary rule in light of the facts that she addresses.

Building a framework of secondary rules may however be problematic owing to the fact that in seeking to ascertain the "substantive reason" or "internal point of view" one must be able to distinguish the *rationes decidendi* and the *obiter dicta* of the applicable precedent.[45] This may be too broad and complex for analysis[46] and may impede the consistent and coherent application of the secondary rules that ought to guide the interpretation and implementation of each primary rule. In other words, it may be quite challenging to group the "internal points of view" of different judges entertaining similar cases in order to determine a proposition that justifies the interpretation and implementation of primary rules in a particular way.[47] However, given the uniqueness of each judgment, the actual challenge consists of showing that the explanation of the primary rule upon which a particular judgment is based reflects the propositions embedded in secondary rules and the trial judge did not interpret and apply the primary rule *per incuriam*.[48] Equally, the internal

---

[44] With regard to how the validity of these rules may be determined, see Hart, 1994: 96-110.

[45] As explained above, although both types of rules ought to be "pedigreed," the primary rule ought to be deduced from the *ratio decidendi* and the secondary rules from the *obiter dictum*.

[46] See Siems, 2008: 149. This is especially the case where the *obiter dictum* is very persuasive. See Cross R and Harris, 1991: 76-77.

[47] See the discussion on consistency and coherence by MacCormick (2005: 189, 190, 206). See also Berger, 2002: 30.

[48] The task may be much easier where there is a clear and weighty legal principle that a judge may not disregard. An example is the unfairness of imputing the

point of view of judges is much broader than can be envisaged and the external point of view (especially of non-legal commentators) is even broader and more complex. Moreover, not all public officials (courts and enforcement agencies) may accept an external point of view.[49] Nonetheless, it may be submitted that secondary rules can hardly be delineated with mathematical precision and the idea here is to develop a framework by which the primary rules embedded in statutes and precedent may be interpreted and applied on rational and consistent bases. The link between this framework and the diverse ways in which courts may impute acts and intents to corporations is what I refer to as the mechanism of imputation. An effective mechanism of imputation would enable courts to consistently impute acts and intents to corporations in accordance with both primary and secondary rules.

4.3 Parameters for determining the appropriate mechanism

In light of the discussion above, there are two major factors that may delineate a mechanism of imputation and determine its efficacy. Firstly, the compatibility of the mechanism's primary rule with legal principles that set standards which are essential to the determination of the case. Secondly, the compatibility of the mechanism's primary rule with patterns of imputation embedded in the secondary rules that guide the implementation of the primary rule. As mentioned above, the patterns of imputation may be deduced from the outlook of judges expressed in the *obiter dicta* of their judgements and also from the factual propositions of non-legal theorists (equally alluded to by judges in the *obiter dicta* of their judgements) where the outlook of judges does not provide an adequate explanation. I will now expound on these factors and show how an appropriate mechanism of imputation may be determined with reference to them.

---

fraudulent act of a senior manager to the corporation where the latter was the former's targeted victim. See also the United States case of *Riggs v Palmer*, 115 NY 506 (1889) discussed by Dworkin (1986: 15-20) where a boy murdered his grandfather and the Court held that although the victim's will that devolved most of his estate to the murderer did not violate any of the provisions of the applicable statute, this law could not take precedence over another legal principle that was to the effect that no one may benefit from his own wrong.

[49] The non-acceptance of a non-legal viewpoint by legal officials may hinder the development of such a viewpoint into a secondary rule.

4.3.1 The congruity between the mechanism's primary rule and related legal principles

As mentioned above, the legal principles referred to here involve standards deduced from the operation of related branches of law. As regards corporate criminal liability in the United Kingdom, such standards include (although not exclusively) those derived from company law, agency law (excluding vicarious liability) and criminal law. Standards derived from these branches are used as reference points because the branches essentially scaffold the extension of the criminal law to corporate entities.

Company law was devised to delineate the interaction of the different persons that have agreed to be bound by the internal rules of the corporation, as well as between these persons and other stakeholders. Hence, the corporation is the focus of company law rules and it is only logical that any judge required to impute the acts and intents of agents to a corporation should weigh the rule prescribing such a pattern of imputation against the standards of company law. Also, due to the fact that a corporation may only form an intention or perform an action through the agency of natural persons, the judge should equally be satisfied that the rule reflects principles of the law of agency. Finally, given that what is intended is the imposition of criminal liability and punishment on the corporation, it is crucial that the rule conforms to criminal law standards. As such, where a mechanism's primary rule does not concur with principles that derive from the operation of these branches of law, the mechanism may be deemed unsuitable for enforcing crimes against corporations. However, standards set by such principles may not conclusively resolve a case but guide the judge through the process of interpreting and applying the primary rule. Thus, where a statute provides for the imposition of criminal liability on the duty-holder and the corporation happens to be the duty-holder, such a statute may be understood to imply that the accused corporation is liable if there was an agency relationship between the person whose action breached the duty and the corporation. Owing to the fact that several related legal principles may be deduced from these branches of law (as well as other branches), the parameters for evaluating mechanisms of imputation (in order to determine the most appropriate mechanism) will be limited to some prominent principles, *viz.* corporate personality (company law), scope of employment/maverick agent and constructive knowledge (agency law) and proof of *mens rea* and/or *actus reus* and the imposition of personal liability (criminal law).

4.3.1.1 Compatibility with the principle of corporate personality

In Chapter 2, it was established that courts do not necessarily recognise a corporation as a result of its incorporation but because it may act and think independently (at least in the legal world) and can bear rights and affect legal relationships. Thus, corporate criminal liability is concerned with the corporation's personal liability although such liability is predicated on the confluence of several actions and decisions of one or several of its agents. Thus, an appropriate mechanism of imputation ought to operate in such a way as to distinguish acts and intentions that are particular to the corporate person from those that are particular to its agents.

4.3.1.2 Compatibility with the criminal law rules of culpability and responsibility

In Chapter 2, it was shown that the prosecution may use the principles of culpability and responsibility to bind the accused corporation to the relevant course of action by showing that it entertained and performed the requisite *mens rea* and *actus reus* or it performed an act prohibited by the law or failed to perform one required by the law. Thus, in Chapter 3, it was established that liability may be imposed on a corporation directly for strict and absolute liability offences that require only breach of a duty and also for offences that require proof of both *actus reus* and *mens rea*. In both instances, it is important to show that the guilty act was that of the corporation or that it was responsible. However, in the second instance, it is important to show that the negligence or intent to commit the offence (*mens rea*) was actually that of the corporation and not of its agent. In other words, it is important to show that the corporation was both culpable and responsible. It was also suggested that this may be achieved by showing how a corporation used a number of innocent agents to perpetrate the offence or encouraged or assisted the agents that are primarily responsible for the offence.

4.3.1.3 Compatibility with principles implied by agency law

An important principle that may guide courts in the interpretation and application of the primary rule is that exemplified by the maxim *qui facit per alium facit per se*. This common law maxim may be roughly translated as he who acts through another acts himself. The maxim is fundamental to the law of agency as it operates to hold a principal liable for the acts of the agent performed within the scope of the agency. Etymologically, it depicted the convergence of the legal personae of both the principal and the agent creating the impression that the principal actually performed an act through the agent.[50] Hence, although the corporation and its agent are distinct persons there are instances where their legal personae may merge to such an extent that a corporation acting through the agent may be said to act itself.[51] This means that the judge ought to interpret the primary rule of attribution in a statute or precedent as merging the legal personae of the corporation and the agent.[52] As such, an appropriate mechanism of imputation ought to provide the requisite flexibility to the court to weigh the primary rule against the pattern of imputing liability to the principal in agency law.[53] The court may refer to such a pattern by considering a number of questions including whether the agent was a maverick that acted outwith her scope of employment and whether the corporation could be said to have had constructive knowledge of the agent's action. We will now see how the judge may address these questions.

4.3.1.3.1 The exception of the maverick agent

In civil law, the agent's act or knowledge may only be imputed to the principal if such an act or knowledge is relevant both to the agent's duties

---

[50] See Fuller, 1967: 19. He however described the maxim as a fiction and noted that it was a "superfluous and wasteful intellectual operation" to contrive readers to pretend that the act was actually performed by the principal. See also Demott, 2003: 293.

[51] It should nonetheless be noted that even though the agency relationship is invoked in this instance the corporation's liability remains direct and not vicarious. It is however challenging drawing a fine line between agency and vicarious liability as they sometimes overlap in both their legal and normative applications. It is thus common to find some commentators treating both concepts as synonyms. See for example, Lederman, 2000: 652; and Watts, 2001: 309.

[52] However, the delineation of circumstances where the principal will be liable for the agent's act is still subject to debate. See Watts, 2001: 300.

[53] A good example of how judges weighed the primary rule against principles deduced from the operation of agency law is *El Ajou*. See especially Nourse LJ at 698 and Hoffmann LJ (as he then was) at 702-705.

to the principal and the principal's relations with other parties.[54] Thus, a principal acts through its agent to the extent that the latter's act alters the former's legal status within the boundaries of the delegation. If the agent's act falls outside these boundaries, the act cannot be imputed to the principal. In criminal law, this has hardly been addressed owing to the fact that the concept of scope of employment is mostly invoked when determining a principal's vicarious liability and the criminal law eschews this form of liability. However, this concept is important to the enforcement of the criminal law against corporations because the latter can only act via natural persons acting within the scope of their employment or agency. Nonetheless, although the concept of 'scope of employment' encompasses conventionalised principles that facilitate imputation to principals, it hides a perplexing complexity that may extend the principal's liability to such great lengths that the criminal lawyer could be rendered dizzy.[55] It is for example uncertain whether the agent must be shown to have furthered the principal's interest or simply performed an act that was in line with the principal's business irrespective of whether the act was beyond the bounds of the agent's specific authority.[56] Lord Steyn[57] intimated that the English position was put into perspective by Salmond.[58] The latter had advanced that the act was within the scope of the agent's employment if it was authorised by the principal or if it was not, it was a "mode" of performing a task assigned by the principal. Thus, the principal may be liable for acts that she did not authorise but were "so connected" with acts that she authorised.[59]

---

[54] Demott, 2003: 293. This may equally be the case in criminal law although in lieu of the principal's relations with other parties we will talk of the principal's legal obligations. See for example, the CMCHA.

[55] The term 'course/scope of employment' has been widely expanded in civil law over the last century to include the employee's "ostensible authority" (*Harvey v Whitehead* (1911) 30 NZLR 795) or the "improper" or "unauthorised or prohibited" modes she used to perform her duties. See *Canadian Pacific Railway v* Lockhart (1942) AC 591, hereinafter referred to as *Canadian Pacific Railway*; *Irving and Irving v Post Office* [1987] IRLR 289, hereinafter referred to as *Irving*; and *Marjowski v Guy's and St Thomas' NHS* Trust [2007] 1 AC 224, hereinafter referred as *Marjowski*.

[56] See Nana, 2008: 253-258.

[57] *Lister and Others v Hesley Hall Ltd* [2002] 1 AC 215 (hereinafter referred to as *Lister*) at 223-224.

[58] Salmond, 1907: 83. See also Heuston and Buckley, 1996: 443.

[59] This position was affirmed by the House of Lords in *Dubai Aluminium Co Ltd v Salaam and Others* [2003] 2 AC 366, hereinafter referred to as *Dubai Aluminium*.

It is difficult to justify the imputation of an unauthorised act to a principal especially where the agent neither sought to further the former's interests nor acted in line with her business.[60] Nonetheless, it may be argued that the agent's act was relevant to the principal's relation with third parties or in the case of the criminal law, the principal's legal obligation. However, the fact that the principal did not intend to achieve anything incidental to this act makes it difficult to argue that the principal used the agent to perform the act that is then imputed to the former. As noted above, these cases were based on the employers' vicarious liability and this concept is not deemed to be derived from legal propositions but conceived as an abstraction from the nebulous notion of public policy.[61] However, owing to the fact that vicarious liability and agency are not entirely synonymous, the public policy argument underpinning the sort of vicarious liability with no outer limit may be ignored. As such, where an employee's action is out of the boundaries of her agency to such an extent that the corporate employer cannot be said to have acted through her, the court may hardly justify the imputation of her act to the corporation given that such an act breaks the link between the agency relationship and the offence.[62] This is exemplified by the fraud exception to the imputed knowledge rule. The fraud exception operates to exculpate the employer from the fraud where the agent was defrauding her.[63] Nonetheless, it must be noted that this exception lacks definite form and may not always be constituted as an exception to imputation because in many cases the agent's fraudulent act is only part of a whole transaction and the principal is willing to reject the fraud but maintain the general transaction.[64] Equally, criminal law courts find it difficult severing the fraudulent act from a whole transaction when imputing such a transaction to the

---

See Lord Nicholls at 375-379 and Lord Millet at 400. See also Lord Nicholls in *Majrowski* at 229.

[60] However, see Lord Pearce in *Williams v A&W Hemphill Ltd* 1986 SC (HL) 31 at 46; and Diplock LJ (as he then was) in *Morris v CW Martin & Sons Ltd* [1966] 1 QB 716 at 736-737.

[61] The employer has often been vicariously liable because it is "fair" to hold her liable in the circumstances. See the Canadian cases of *Bazley v Curry* (1999) 174 DLR (4th) 45; *Jacobi v Griffiths* (1999)174 DLR (4th) 71 cited by Lord Steyn in *Lister* at 223-224. See also Chapter 6.

[62] See Lord Chelmsford in *Espin v Pemberton* (1859) 3 De G & J 547 at 554-555.

[63] This exception was established by Lord Brougham in *Kennedy v Green* (1834) 3 My & K 699. See also *Re European Bank* (1870) LR 5 Ch App 358; and *Stoneleigh Finance Ltd v Phillips* [1965] 2 QB 537.

[64] See Watts, 2001.

corporation.[65] However, *Belmont* gives good reason to believe that fraudulent acts targeting the corporation would not be imputed to it. This implies that only acts that are incidental to the achievement of the objectives of corporations as defined in their constitutions are imputable to corporations (in accordance with the *ultra vires* doctrine).[66] As such, if a crime perpetrated by an agent benefits a corporation whose major objective is to make profit, it ought to be held criminally liable for that crime[67] on the basis that the crime was perpetrated by the agent within the "scope" of her authority.

It follows from the above that the delineation of the principles of maverick agent and scope of employment that may be implied by agency law depends on the test of whether the agent conferred some advantage or benefit upon the corporation.[68] In *Bresler*, although the two officers defrauded the company they enabled it to make more money by evading taxes.[69] However, in such cases it is likely that the corporation benefits in the short-term but ultimately suffers a much bigger loss in the long-run following the stigma of prosecution and conviction and the burden of sanctions, making it less likely that the corporation would benefit from the crime.[70] It is uncertain whether courts are then required to weigh the corporation's potential or actual loss against its potential or actual gains in order to determine whether it benefited from the crime. This would be unfair to the corporate defender that seldom has the full benefit of hindsight since concealing the offence is *sine qua non* to the fraudulent agent's enterprise.

A more justifiable stance may be to hold the company liable for formulating and implementing policies that encouraged or tolerated the

---

[65] See Humphreys J in *Bresler* at 517.

[66] *Ultra vires acts* may be defined as acts that are outside the scope of the corporation's powers as stated in its constitution. See Leigh, 1969: 3; and Todarello, 2002-2003: 856.

[67] See Wells, 2001: 135.

[68] See Braithwaite and Pettit, 2003: 13.

[69] Nonetheless, given that there was no representation from the board of directors or senior management endorsing the tax evasion, reliance was placed on the representation of the fraudulent officers. This means that courts would have to rely on "bootstraps" agency and corporate culture in order to establish such a link.

[70] See Braithwaite and Pettit, 2003: 13. Nevertheless, where crime detection is low and punishment is not certain the corporation is more likely to benefit from the short-term benefit and less likely to suffer from the long-term harms of prosecution, conviction and sanctioning.

commission of crimes.[71] In this light, it may be said that the agent did not deviate from her scope of authority by using an unauthorised mode to perform her activities since such an unauthorised mode was motivated by the policies and practices of the corporate employer. The agent may then be said to have had apparent authority to use such a mode. As noted in Chapter 3, in such an instance it may be preferable to say that the corporation was an accessory to the offence committed by the agent and not that it was the offender. However, if courts restricted themselves to corporate policies then corporations would simply instruct their employees never to commit any form of crime.[72] Nonetheless, where it is shown that the agent acted outwith the scope of her agency and against clear instructions and no benefit was conferred upon the corporation, the latter may still be liable if it ought to have been aware of the reasonably high risk of its agents breaching the criminal law due to the nature of their tasks. In other words, the corporation would be liable because it had constructive knowledge of the agents' wrongful acts or propensity to perpetrate wrongful acts and ought to have taken steps to prevent the performance of such acts. Its failure to do so may be interpreted as tolerating or encouraging the wrongful acts.

4.3.1.3.2 The corporation's constructive knowledge

The primary rule of attribution embedded in the statute or precedent may be interpreted as imputing acts and intents to a corporation on the ground that the latter ought to have known of its agent's intention to perpetrate an offence or the possibility of the perpetration of such an offence. In the civil law case of *Compania Maritima San Basilio SA v Oceanus Mutual Underwriting Association (Bermuda) Ltd*,[73] Lord Denning gave a brief narrative description of the common law position on the requisite degree of involvement that would absolve the principal from her agent's fault. The old position was that a wrongful act perpetrated by an agent within the scope of her authority and with the intention of benefiting the employer was imputable to the latter irrespective of whether

[71] See Braithwaite and Pettit, 2003: 38.

[72] See Wells, 2001: 135; and Note, Harvard, 1979: 1227. That is why corporations cannot always rely on the defence of having a compliance programme or that they practised due diligence. See *Re Supply of Ready Mixed Concrete* [1995] 1 AC 456.

[73] [1977] QB 49 at 67-68. This case is hereinafter referred to as *Compania Maritima*.

she commanded or had actual knowledge of the act.[74] Lord Denning intimated that subsequently a number of Merchant Shipping Acts were passed mitigating the harshness of this position and these culminated in the enactment of section 503(1) of the Merchant Shipping Act 1894 which provided that the principal's liability could be limited by evidence showing that her agent had not performed the wrongful act by her "command" or with her "privity."[75] He then contended that the word "privity" in these statutes may be said to imply that the owner's liability was dependent on whether she had personal knowledge or ought to have had personal knowledge (in which case she turned a "blind eye"). In other words, the owner was liable because a hypothetical reasonable person in her place would not have recklessly omitted to make such an inquiry.[76] Thus, she had constructive knowledge of the facts and ought to have taken steps to prevent the perpetration of the wrongful act.[77] However, the diligence required of the defender should not be extraordinary. Hence, the sheriff held that a gulf club was not liable where one golfer with a high handicap hastily mis-hit a golf ball and injured another golfer.[78]

That notwithstanding, if this principle is transplanted to the criminal law (in terms of the agency relationship between the corporation and the agent) and even if evidence of the corporate employer's knowledge of the likelihood of the incident happening will be sufficient to convict, the prosecutor may still face an uphill task owing to the fact that she must convince the court that the corporation acquired knowledge or failed to

---

[74] See *Morse v Slue* (1674) 1 Vent 190; *Tuberville v Stampe* (1697) 1 Ld Ray 264; and *Huzzey v Field* (1835) 2 CM & R 432.

[75] See also Article 2 of the Convention on the Limitation of Liability for Maritime Claims 1976 limiting the owner's liability for loss or damage to property that occurs on board the vessel or that is connected with its operation. This Convention may be read together with section 185 of the Merchant Shipping Act 1995. Also important is section 186(2) of the Merchant Shipping Act 1995 that absolves masters and/or members of the crew from liability for loss or damage that arises from acts they performed in the course of their employment.

[76] This is related to the duty of the principal to investigate. See Lord Hoffmann in *El Ajou* at 702-703. See also *Baldwin v Casella* (1872) LR 7 Exc 325.

[77] See *Baden v Société Générale Pour Favoriser le Développement du Commerce et de l'Industrie en France* [1993] 1 WLR 509 at 575-576. Denning J (as he then was) had equally applied a similar test to the effect that the defendant had notice because a reasonable man would have perceived the want of authority and the defendant was negligent in failing to do so. See *Nelson v Larholt* [1948] 1 KB 339 at 343.

[78] *Lewis v Buckpool Golf Club* [1993] SLT 43.

inquire about a fact via certain agents that must be identified with it. Lord Denning advanced that it should be a question of whether the company's *alter ego* had knowledge or ought to have inquired about the facts.[79] The reference to the company's *alter ego* is in line with the *alter ego* rule adopted (in part) within the framework of the identification doctrine, the applicable mechanism of imputation in the United Kingdom, which Lord Denning had sanctioned in an earlier case.[80] However, as will be shown in Chapters 5 and 8, the identification doctrine is an unduly restrictive mechanism and unless the concept of a company's *alter ego* is extended to include middle-level managers, corporations would escape liability by simply delegating the management of criminogenic activities to such managers. Nonetheless, it may be contended that irrespective of the meaning that one gives to the term *alter ego* (only senior managers or both senior managers and empowered middle-level managers), Lord Denning's contention that a company's knowledge or negligence is that of its *alter ego* is true. Thus, an effective mechanism of imputation should provide for such flexibility as to enable a court to identify a corporate defender with its truc *alter ego* in order to determine whether it had constructive knowledge of another agent's intention or propensity to perpetrate the offence.

In light of the discussion above, it may be advanced that the primary rule embedded in statutes or precedent often provides for a pattern of imputation in ambiguous terms. However, there are other legal principles that may guide a judge in finding the "best" theory or unequivocal interpretation of the primary rule. Some of these include principles deduced from the operation of criminal law, company law and agency law. Thus, where a corporation is charged courts ought to ensure that it is treated as a distinct legal person that may be personally liable and the *actus reus* (and *mens rea* where required) of the offence is proved against the corporation and not its agent. Equally, the crime (or acts constituting the crime) ought to have been perpetrated by the corporation's agents while acting within the scope of their employment and/or the corporation ought to have had constructive knowledge of the possibility of that happening. However, it is not in every instance that the act of an agent (even though within the scope of her employment) will be imputed to the corporation. Thus, there are other rules of recognition that ought to guide

---

[79] *Compania Maritima* at 68.

[80] *Bolton Engineering*. This case is discussed below.

the court in interpreting the primary rule as regards whose act and intent is imputable to the corporation and why.

4.3.2 The congruity between the mechanism's primary rule and other rules of recognition

It is important to note that relying solely on other legal principles may be recursive in many instances given that legal principles may not always explain or justify the application of a primary rule. This may lead to circularity (is-ought problem) whereby the court seeks to explain a legal concept by referring to legal rules although the legal concept represents an actuality that transcends information contained in legal edicts. There are for example many more forms of corporate structures than judges and legislators can ever envisage. Thus, their failure to consider extraneous knowledge when entertaining cases involving corporations would surely defeat the purpose of legal rules fashioned to deal with corporations. As mentioned above, the test of validity (and efficacy) of the primary rule (referring to related legal principles) is a pedigree-based test. However, a content-based test is also important. The latter test as defined here differs from Dworkin's test given that it seeks justify the application of the primary rule of attribution from a much narrower perspective than Dworkin enunciated.[81] This is because the large width of morality and non-pedigreed principles increases the likelihood of inconsistency (judges invoking all sorts of principles). As such, although a content-based test is also important it ought to be based on pedigree. This means that although judges are not required to appeal to principles that do not form part of the *rationes decidendi* of the precedent, they may appeal to principles that form part of the persuasive observations made by previous courts (*obiter dicta*). In this light, the content-based test may be restricted to the outlook (normative conceptions) of judges and non-legal theorists that previous courts discussed or alluded to. These may be said to be secondary rules deduced from both the internal points of view and the external points of view. The internal points of view here are deemed to be the normative perspectives of other judges while the external points of view include the viewpoint of some non-legal categories (referred to by previous judges). As such, a mechanism of imputation may also be evaluated by weighing its primary rule against such secondary rules.

[81] See Hart, 1994: 263-268.

4.3.2.1 Rules of recognition deduced from the normative perspectives of judges

Given that secondary rules ought to be arranged systematically it is likely that the same problem of "open texture" encountered in the interpretation of statutes (primary rules) by judges may be encountered in the interpretation of secondary rules. There is also a possibility that what the legislator (that created the offence that is being enforced) intended may be completely different from the proposition implicit in the secondary rules. However, a judge is required to show that the hermeneutics at the various stages of interpreting both the primary rule and the secondary rules was meticulous to such an extent that her decision may be said to reflect the rules in a fair and accurate manner. A tool often used in this regard is the metaphor. It helps to reduce the complexity of arguments in order to affect ordinary good consciousness[82] and has been said to have modelled jurisprudence in a furtive manner.[83] As such, judges use metaphors to provide suitable means of ascertaining the normative secondary rules that ought to guide the interpretation and explanation of primary rules. This implies that metaphors may provide a suitable avenue for identifying a specific category of rules (secondary rules) since they reflect judges' outlook on laws providing for or implying the imputation of acts and intents to corporations. A number of metaphors have played this role in corporate criminal law and have enhanced the consistency of the interpretation and implementation of its rules. They are described here as enforcement-generated metaphors.[84]

4.3.2.1.1 Enforcement-generated metaphors

A judgment is often made of conjectural statements illustrating a point of law (*obiter dictum*) and the reasoning on which the conclusion is based (*ratio decidendi*). The *obiter dictum* may therefore involve the specification of a number of premises while the *ratio decidendi* may involve the movement from the premises to a conclusion. However, this does not mean that a judge is required to infer a conclusion only from the established premises. That notwithstanding, she must provide legal and logical (moral) explanations for the specification and use of these

---

[82] See Lawley and Tompkins, 2005: 4-5.

[83] Berger, 2002: 30.

[84] These are metaphors that are used specifically for the purposes of explaining how corporations function and how liability ought to be imposed upon them with regard to such modes of functioning.

premises[85] in order to protect the law's integrity and satisfy the onlooker that justice has taken its course.[86] In this regard, judges have often had a predilection for what has been described as the "argumentative method and justificatory rhetoric."[87] The rhetoric has often been embedded with metaphors especially when judges are stepping on new ground. This is because metaphors confer the apposite message[88] and enable judges to convey different meanings and distinguish different experiences.[89]

Metaphors are literary devices that suggest similarities between different experiences.[90] They are more than just a play of words or devices used to embellish language because they are indicative of cognition[91] and involve the features of human consciousness.[92] They are often expressed as imaginative expressions and comprise several units such as words and objects (which may be called "symbols") that connect the experiences by a pattern that may be termed "isomorphism."[93] Given the difficulty of determining the essential quality of abstract and intangible concepts, there is a natural tendency to define such concepts using metaphors and then act upon them,[94] since people are more likely to understand the nature of abstract concepts through the isomorphic connection between the concepts and the metaphor.[95] As such, a convenient way of understanding corporations and their actions has been to compare corporations with familiar objects in order to underscore their peculiarity and appeal to a given logic.

---

[85] See Perelman, 1980: 150.
[86] Berger, 2002: 31. This augurs well for certainty and coherence and enables subsequent courts of equal or lower standing to apply the decision when confronted with a similar set of facts.
[87] Goodrich, 1987: 123.
[88] Berger, 2002: 32.
[89] Perelman, 1980: 156. Thus, where a judge intends to take exception to a particular rule (used by a previous judge) providing for the imputation of acts and intents to corporations in a particular manner metaphors may be suitable tools for justifying the taking of exception.
[90] Lakoff and Johnson, 1980: 5.
[91] Richards, 1936: 90, 96 and Berger, 2002: 34.
[92] Capara, 1996: 170.
[93] See Lawley and Tompkins, 2005: 6-7.
[94] Lakoff and Johnson, 1980: 158. This however means that perceptions and actions are restricted to those that may be specified within the realm of the metaphor's logic. See Lawley and Tompkins, 2005: 9.
[95] Patry, 2008: 2. See also Berger, 2002: 34.

Hence, given that a corporation is deemed by many judges to be an abstraction the language they employ to describe its actions or explain their decisions is often laced with metaphors.[96] A cursory look at judgments imposing criminal liability on corporations over the past 400 years therefore reveals a substantial number of metaphors employed to explain and justify the imputation of acts and intents to corporations in a certain manner or the taking of exception from the legally prescribed way of imputing acts and intents to corporations. As such, if it is assumed that the majority of these judges sought to describe the primary rule of the applicable law and justify their interpretation by making reference to metaphors, a close examination of the metaphors may enable us to construct a model that is consonant with courts' outlook of the way in which acts and intents ought to be imputed to corporations. Such a model may then be said to describe the secondary rules that guide the interpretation and implementation of primary rules that provide for imputation. It may thus be possible for other judges to invoke these secondary rules when seeking to determine how to impute acts and intents to corporations in the cases before them.[97]

As noted in the previous Chapters, the first challenge that both civil law and criminal law courts grapple with is that of explaining the abstract concept of 'corporation.' Some 400 years ago, Fineux advanced that "[a] corporation is an aggregation of head and body: not a head by itself, nor a body by itself; and it must be consonant to reason, for otherwise it is worth nought."[98] As Maitland rightly pointed out, Fineux intended to link the attribute of "corporateness" or the abstraction that is characteristic of corporations to that of a number of different concrete concepts. He therefore used an isomorphic pattern consisting of symbols such as "aggregation," "head" and "body" to connect the abstract concept of corporation to the tangible structure of an organism in order to appeal to

---

[96] They contend that it may be easier to understand the abstract legal concept of 'corporation' through these metaphors. For discussion on the importance of using metaphors in such instances, see Lakoff and Johnson, 1980: 115.

[97] As will be shown below, the result is not simply a model but the "bringing forth" of a "world" of corporations through the operation of the judicial system. Lawley and Tompkins (2005: 17-18, 29-39) describe such a mental viewpoint as a "Metaphor Landscape." This "world" or "Metaphor Landscape" is the same legal world described in Chapter 2 in which corporations are entities in *esse*.

[98] 14 Hen. VIII f. 3 (Mich. pl. 2) cited in Maitland, 1900a. Fineux sought to dismiss the idea that the corporation sole that consisted of just one person qualified as a corporation.

the logic of a system of interdependent units that constitute a whole. In the same epoch, Coke endorsed the use of these metaphors on the basis that a corporation is "invisible, immortal and rests only in intendment and consideration of the law." He also asserted that a corporation has no "soul" and cannot appear in "person" and then he compared it to a "bishop who is elect before he is consecrated" and an "infant in his mother's womb before his birth."[99] The last thing these judges may have been accused of was trying to embellish their opinions with metaphors. It is obvious that they struggled to underscore the peculiarity of corporations and thus appealed to commonsense logic by suggesting similarities between the corporation and an organism or a bishop before consecration and a foetus.[100] Nonetheless, the message conveyed was that a corporation corresponds to something intangible (an abstract whole) but functions like a living organism.

The most problematic metaphor that has been used to describe a corporation is that of "person."[101] In line with section 14 of the Criminal Law Act 1827, section 2(1) of the Interpretation Act 1899 ordained thus:

> [i]n the construction of every enactment relating to an offence punishable on indictment or on summary conviction, whether contained in an Act passed before or after the commencement of the Act, the expression "person" shall, unless the contrary intention appears, include a body corporate.

In a landmark civil suit a few years earlier, Lord Halsbury seated in the House of Lords had stated emphatically that "once the company is legally incorporated it must be treated like any other independent person with its rights and liabilities appropriate to itself"[102] Lord MacNaghten acquiesced and introduced metaphors of his own. He contended that "[t]he company attains maturity on its birth. There is no period of minority - no interval of incapacity. I cannot understand how a body corporate thus made "capable" by statute can lose its individuality."[103] Although there is no evidence that Lord MacNaghten took Coke's metaphorical expression into consideration, the use of words such as birth, maturity and individuality

---

[99] *Sutton's Hospital* at 22.

[100] However, the logic of these metaphors may be questioned since a bishop before consecration and a foetus are both in existence although in another form.

[101] See Chapter 2 for discussion on the corporation's entitlement to legal personality.

[102] *Salomon* at 30.

[103] *Salomon* at 51. See also Lord Davey at 56.

connotes the actuality of the corporation and the need to treat it as a "person" with incidental rights and duties.[104] These words were thus used as symbols to connect the abstract notion of corporation to the less abstract notion of "person"[105] in order to communicate the essential qualities of a corporation in plain language. Drafters of the abovementioned sections of the Criminal Law Act 1827 and the Interpretation Act 1899 may also have intended to use the word "person" for similar reasons.

The prevailing current of thought still flows towards the recognition of corporate personality and the view of this personality as representing a body existing in the legal world (contemplation) and analogous to a human body. Although this viewpoint is far from comprehensible, it certainly justifies the enjoyment of rights by corporations as well as the enforcement of duties against them. However, it does not help in ascertaining a course of action for the enforcement of crimes against corporations. As noted in Chapter 3, criminal law courts initially found niche in the regimes of strict and absolute liability, as well as expediently interpreting regulatory laws as providing for such liability. But when they were called upon to convict and sanction corporations for (clearly defined) crimes of intent or negligence they simply averred that corporations could not be criminally liable for such offences. Thus, the stumbling block was the adduction of relevant evidence showing a corporation's criminal intention or negligence. The analogy with the human body soon proved valuable. Judges readily introduced new metaphors or expounded those introduced by previous judges to strengthen the comparison. In another landmark civil law suit that also subsequently influenced criminal law courts, Viscount Haldane decided the case before him on the logic of this comparison but noted that a corporation does not really have a body of its own but has a "directing mind and will" that is also its "ego" and the "centre of its personality."[106] These symbols were used not only to connect the abstract corporation to the human "person" but also to facilitate the identification of the corporation's locus of control. Hence, as the mind is purportedly responsible for a human being's thoughts and as the will and ego represent a human being's conscious choices and decisions, there are individual agents that embody all these features that typify the corporation.

[104] They may have been influenced by the contention that legal personality is predicated on humanness. This contention is however shown to be flawed in Chapter 2.

[105] Less abstract because it was considered as being synonymous to 'individual' although 'person' is equally a tortuous concept.

[106] *Lennard's Carrying Co* at 713.

About three decades later, Viscount Caldecote contended that "[a] company is incapable of acting or speaking or even of thinking except in so far as its officers have acted, spoken or thought." As such, in order to hold a corporation liable for intent to deceive under the Defence (General) Regulations 1939 he concluded that these "officers are the company for this purpose."[107] In the following decade, Denning LJ's (as he then was) comparison was aboveboard. He said that:

> [a] company may in many ways be likened to a human body. It has a brain and nerve centre which controls what it does. It also has hands which hold the tools and act in accordance with directions from the centre. Some of the people in the company are mere servants and agents who are nothing more than hands to do the work and cannot be said to represent the mind or will. Others are directors and mangers who represent the directing mind and will of the company, and control what it does. The state of mind of these managers is the state of mind of the company.[108]

This was no doubt a concise explanation of the analogy between the corporation and the human body as a means of describing how a corporation functions in the eyes of the law and how its liability ought to be established. In the words of Denning LJ this meant that "the fault of the manager will be the personal fault of the company." However, as stated above, the isomorphic pattern that connected the abstract corporation to the human body did not provide a vivid picture (as secondary rules) to such an extent that judges could consistently identify the natural persons that represented the corporation's "mind or will" in cases where the relevant law imposed criminal liability on corporations. As such, different agents at different levels were recognised in the abovementioned cases. In the landmark case of *Nattrass*, the House of Lords upheld this comparison and sought to clarify the uncertainty as regards the agents that ought to be identified with the corporation. Lord Reid stated that:

> There have been attempts to apply Lord Denning's words to all servants of a company whose work is brain work, or who exercise some managerial discretion under the direction of superior officers of the company. I do not think that Lord Denning intended to refer to them. He only referred to those who "represent the directing mind and will of the company and control what it does."[109]

---

[107] *Kent and Sussex Contractors* at 155.
[108] *Bolton Engineering* at 172.
[109] *Nattrass* at 171.

Despite the circularity of this contention, Lord Reid later on narrowed the meaning of the metaphors employed by the previous judges and noted that agents that constitute the "brain" of the corporation are those that have managerial functions with full discretion to act.[110] He equally discounted Viscount Haldane's use of the word "ego" or the less abstract concept of *alter ego*. In his opinion, this concept did not give a clear image of what was required given that courts ought to seek officers that could be identified with the accused corporation and not those that were in some way the corporation's alternate persona.[111] Lord Morris on his part complemented Lord Reid's interpretation with another metaphor. He said the company in the case before them could not be liable for the acts of the store manager because the latter was "a cog in the machine which was devised: it was not left to him to devise it."[112] As such, there was a furtive shift from Viscount Haldane's "directing mind and will" or "ego" that represented a corporation's conscious choices and decisions or that typified the set of attributes that characterised a corporation in a given instance to the conception of the "directing mind and will" (excluding the "ego") representing not only the choices and decisions but also the decision-making process itself. In other words, courts are now required to look beyond the set of attributes that characterise the corporation to the instrumentality that combines these attributes.[113] There is no doubt that *Nattrass* was based on surmise and not any evidence of how corporations function or ought to function.[114] But that notwithstanding, their position was and to a certain extent still is what obtains (primary rule) in the enforcement of offences in the United Kingdom except where the statutory provision provides for another pattern of attribution.

---

[110] See Chapter 5 for further discussion on Lord Reid's position.

[111] Some phrases used by Lord Reid however require further explanation. An example is: "the directing mind speaks through the *persona* of the company" (no emphasis added) at *Nattrass* at 170.

[112] *Nattrass* at 181.

[113] This means that the "brain" would always remain the "brain" and the hands would always be construed as the "hands." This is no doubt a classic case of anthropomorphism whereas the previous courts seemed to have intended to make an analogy and not simply ascribe uniquely human features to corporations. This is because the human being's organs do not switch roles to suit the circumstances. In other words, if Viscount Haldane and Denning LJ had intended to define the corporate person based on the human anatomy they would have directed courts to stick to labels and titles because the brain remains the brain and the hand remains the hand whatever the circumstances.

[114] See discussion on the criticisms of this approach in Chapter 5.

The parochiality of this position has no doubt resulted in the lack of certainty and coherence in the way in which laws (primary rules) providing for the imputation of acts and intents to corporations ought to be interpreted and implemented (secondary rules).[115] This may be blamed in part on the disregard of the metaphorical nature of the communication of earlier judgements (especially Viscount Haldane's) and the contamination of the experiences they described by the introduction of new metaphors.[116] However, given that metaphors are embedded in most sentences made by people[117] it is difficult to conceive of an express interpretation by one judge that would not include many new metaphors.[118] The problem seems to stem from two things: firstly, the failure to closely examine only those metaphors that may be described as 'enforcement-generated metaphors' in order to decipher what the judges actually described; and secondly, the introduction of new enforcement-generated metaphors. However, given that *Nattrass* may be said to represent the ascriptive primary rule, only a close examination of the enforcement-generated metaphors used by their Lordships in *Nattrass* and not those used by earlier judges such as Viscount Haldane and Viscount Caldecote may be important in determining the normative secondary rules.[119] This is because *Nattrass* is the precedent and other courts are bound by its rules. As such, it may be said that the applicable mechanism of imputation in the United Kingdom requires courts to impute only the offence committed (in part or in whole) by a senior manager with full discretion to a corporation.

However, when the identification doctrine is evaluated by referring to the outlook of *Nattrass* judges it is shown to be a rigid form of anthropomorphism that is not appropriate to the enforcement of crimes against all types of corporations. Nonetheless, it may be argued that Lord Reid's dictum was based on the premise that a corporation is a legal fiction and acts and intents are imputed to it by a fiction. Thus, he stated that "[a] living person has a mind which can have knowledge or intention or be negligent and he has hands to carry out his intentions. A corporation has none of these: it must act through living persons, though not always

---

[115] See for example Nourse LJ in *El Ajou* at 695.

[116] The introduction of new metaphors is a major impediment to understanding the experience described. See Lawley and Tompkins, 2005: 27.

[117] Lawley and Tompkins, 2005: 11-12.

[118] Even my explanations above do include metaphors that were unintentionally introduced.

[119] Even though *Nattrass* does not seem to have complied with the secondary rules that derived from previous judgements. See Chapter 5.

one or the same person."[120] This means that he did not espouse the idea of attributing human traits to a corporation to such an extent that the agent that is considered a corporation's "brain" would be its "brain" under all circumstances. Instead, he may be understood to imply that a corporation can act through different persons and whether an agent is identified with the corporation must depend on the circumstances of each case although such an agent must be sufficiently senior.[121]

The confusion as regards the flexibility of *Nattrass* is depicted by Turner J's strict interpretation of *Nattrass* in *P&O European Ferries* and the broad interpretations by Nourse LJ and Lord Hoffmann in *El Ajou* and *Meridian*. Lord Hoffmann's interpretation is particularly important as he advanced that the "misunderstanding of the true principle" on which *Lennard's Carrying Co* was decided had favoured a strict interpretation of Viscount Haldane's words in all circumstances.[122] That notwithstanding, Lord Hoffmann equally added to the confusion of how the primary rule ought to be interpreted by introducing his own metaphors. He said "[t]here is in fact no such thing as the company as such, no ding an sich, only the applicable rules."[123] He therefore premised his dictum on the fiction theory and this may have pushed him to the conclusion that Viscount Haldane's internal point of view was simply about how the rule embedded in the relevant statute ought to apply to the accused corporation and not about how such a corporation's functioning and nature ought to be ascertained by the court.[124] However, if courts are required to consider only the wordings of the relevant statute, then it is uncertain what they will do where such wordings do not provide any pattern for the imputation of acts and intents to corporations. As such, there is need for a primary rule that applies in all circumstances together with a set of secondary rules (informing judges on how corporations are structured and how they

---

[120] *Nattrass* at 170.

[121] It is then uncertain why Lord Reid took exception to the statement by Stable J in *ICR Haulage* to this effect. Stern (1987: 134-5) describes Stable J's position as "pragmatic" but however warns that too much discretion should not be given to courts.

[122] *Meridian* at 506 and 509-510. The assumption is that both *Lennard's Carrying Co* and *Nattrass* established the same rule and the latter (although more important to criminal law courts) simply elaborated on the rule established by the former.

[123] *Meridian* at 507.

[124] Thus, Lord Hoffmann described Denning LJ's metaphors (cited above) as a form of anthropomorphism that diverted attention from the objective that Viscount Haldane sought to achieve. See *Meridian* at 509.

function) guiding their interpretation and explanation of the primary rule.[125] As mentioned above, the machinery through which both sets of rules function is the mechanism of imputation and it is submitted here that an efficacious mechanism of imputation must have a primary rule that reflects the secondary rules. The normative perspective of judges presented through metaphors is thus shown here to be a good example of secondary rules.

It must however be noted that the picture depicted by the framework of metaphors is neither an accurate reflection of how corporations are truly structured nor of the outlook of all criminal law judges. It is simply an explanation of the primary rule from a normative (moral) perspective describing the rule as it is and not necessarily an explanation from an objective (beyond legal bias) perspective describing the rule as it ought to be.[126] The framework of metaphors is supposed to help avert the fallacy of defining a good or appropriate mechanism on the basis of legal provisions only although it does so to a very limited extent. It merely represents some established standards of some participants in the criminal justice practice (judges) and the fact that the properties of these standards are largely undefined leaves much room for uncertainty in the processes by which courts may impute acts and intents to corporations. It is thus still uncertain what should count as the corporation's act and mind. One finds little justification (from an objective viewpoint) for imputing acts and intents in a particular way in any given instance by referring solely to this outlook of judges. The judges may be accused of having over the years simply deduced an "is" from an "ought" by bringing forth a spurious system of proving a corporation's guilt since they consider the corporation to be a legal abstraction. However, if it is accepted that knowledge of corporate behaviour stretches well beyond the confines of legal categories,[127] then it

---

[125] If courts were required to examine the relevant law and fashion "special rules" where necessary as contended by Lord Hoffmann, then Viscount Haldane and subsequent judges would not have bothered employing the abovementioned enforcement-generated metaphors to explain the nature of the corporation and how the relevant law ought to be implemented as regards such nature.

[126] The overlap of the discussions on the law as it operates and as it ought to operate stems from the fact that there is no clear-cut distinction between the law as it "is" and as it "ought to be." See Marmor's (2006: 690-693) discussion on ethical positivism and legal positivism.

[127] That is why judges readily use metaphors to compare legal experiences to other experiences outside the realm of law such as biology and mechanics. Equally, that is why Lord Hoffmann referred to a corporation's constitution as its "primary rules of attribution."

is only logical that recourse be had to a number of non-legal disciplines explaining the relationship between a corporation and the natural persons that it uses to perform actions.[128] Such knowledge may broaden the view of judges and legislators and guide their interpretation and explanation of primary rules. However, as noted above, describing principles deduced from non-legal categories as secondary rules solely because of their content may lead to inconsistency especially where judges may be empowered to disregard the primary rule. Thus, it is important that principles are deduced only from non-legal categories that previous courts referred or alluded to.[129]

4.3.2.1.2 Rules of recognition deduced from non-legal categories

In *Nattrass*, Viscount Dilhorne stated that:

> [*Lennard's Carrying Co* and *Bolton Engineering*], I think clearly indicate that one has in relation to a company to determine who is or who are, for it may be more than one, in actual control of the operations of the company, and the answer to be given to that question may vary from company to company depending on its organisation.[130]

Lord Pearson also noted that:

> It was suggested in the argument of this appeal that in exercising supervision over the operations in the shop Mr Clement was performing functions of management...But supervision of the details of operations is not normally a function of higher management.[131]

These judges were no doubt alluding to the fact that the court has to examine a corporate structure and determine whether the agent who performed the act under consideration exercised the requisite amount of control in order to be deemed the directing mind of the corporation.[132] As such, courts are advised to consider the system of management and control adopted by the accused corporations and may therefore look beyond legal edicts (statutes and *rationes decidendi* of the precedent) to obtain

---

[128] This knowledge will no doubt help avert the fallacy described above.

[129] This may enable courts to avoid diluting the legal tenets to such an extent that the integrity of the applicable law is brought into disrepute. See a similar problem discussed by Legrand and Munday, 2003: 126.

[130] *Nattrass* at 187.

[131] *Nattrass* at 193.

[132] See also Nourse LJ in *El Ajou* at 696 and Eveleigh J in *R v Andrews-Weatherfoil Ltd* [1972] 1 All ER 65 at 70.

knowledge of the different types of systems that corporations may generally adopt. There are for example, four functions of management commonly cited in management studies: planning, organising, controlling and leading.[133] Planning involves devising strategies for the future to foresee problems and decide on actions to evade these problems; organising involves designating individuals for different tasks or responsibilities in order form them to work together to accomplish the goals of the corporation;[134] controlling involves ensuring that plans are being implemented properly; and leading involves guiding, directing and overseeing of employees to achieve the goals of the corporation. As such, a simple overview of the functions of management in management studies may lead to the suggestion that corporations are instruments designed to control and coordinate human activities in order to achieve defined goals.[135] Thus, the manager that plans strategies, organises other agents and leads them towards specific goals may be said to represent the corporate entity.

Organisation theory also presents a gamut of conceptions of management systems. The existence of so many conceptions is indicative of a number of things: firstly, there are diverse forms of corporations; secondly, there are different ways in which organisations use their agents to perform defined actions (and thus breach the law);[136] and thirdly, it is difficult, if not impossible, for a single conception to capture the complexity of the structure and functioning of corporate entities to such an extent that it may be said to be a blueprint for ascertaining corporate action.[137] A number of legal researchers have examined a number of these conceptions with the objective of deducing conventions from them that may guide the processes of imputation by judges. Fisse and Braithwaite for example present four typologies tied to different ways in which different types of organisations act and think via their agents. They advise that a model for regulating corporations must harmonise these varieties of conceptions in order for the criminal justice system to diagnose corporate crime in its complex and paradoxical setting and impose liability in a justified manner. Unfortunately, they embarked instead on a search for the magic bullet that would serve as

---

[133] See Higgins, 1994: 7.
[134] See Bateman and Snell, 2007: 16 -18.
[135] Abell, 2006: 9-10.
[136] See Fisse and Braithwaite, 1993: 101-132.
[137] Kriesberg, 1976: 1100; and Fisse and Braithwaite, 1993: 122. See also Morgan, 1986: 348.

ultimate guide for imposing criminal liability on all corporations.[138] Equally, the Accountability Model that they introduce, as well as its regulatory framework (pyramidal enforcement), seems to negate the use of the primary rule of attribution in spite of the fact that the essence of the use of knowledge from non-legal categories is to determine how acts and intents ought to be imputed to corporations in accordance with the primary rule.[139] Kriesberg also discusses three models of organisational behaviour but omits discussing how the knowledge of these different types of models ought to be used by courts in given instances and why.

Following the expositions of these commentators, it may be safe to submit that seeking to put a finger on the model that stands out as the blueprint for corporate decision-making and actions is to thrash straw. In other words, no single theory deduced from organisation theory may be held to represent the secondary rules (to guide the interpretation of primary rule by courts). A more reasonable approach may be to ascertain a means of determining how knowledge obtained from organisation theory may help courts in understanding the nature and functioning of corporations. Thus, if such knowledge is shown to be helpful to the court's obligation to punish the corporation for an offence particular to the corporation (and not its agent), then it may provide good guidance as a secondary rule. However, given the complex nature of the agency relationship, as well the diverse number of management structures that corporations may adopt, it may be difficult to build a clear framework of conceptions that justify the imputation of acts and intents to corporations in different instances. Moreover, such a framework ought to enable courts to consistently implement the primary rule of attribution irrespective of the size and structure of the corporation and the offence committed. Nonetheless, penetrating the intricate structure of corporations and identifying the agent or agents at fault is already an arduous task assigned to judges by the applicable primary rule (*Nattrass*). This is exacerbated by the fact that the same corporation's structure and functioning may reflect different conceptions of organisation theory at the same or different times.[140] As such, where in the first year, senior manager A was responsible

---

[138] See Fisse and Braithwaite, 1993: 104, 122.

[139] Fisse and Braithwaite seem to have placed too much reliance on the notion that corporations are entities controlled entirely by their agents and less on the fact that corporations are autonomous and rational entities. See Chapter 7 for discussion on some of the shortcomings of this model and its regulatory framework.

[140] Different departments may adopt different decision-making models. See Fisse and Braithwaite, 1993: 104.

for general transactions in departments X and Y, and in the second year, changes in the market or other circumstances pushed the senior management to delegate (unofficially) the management of department Y to junior manager B, it may be difficult to identify the agent at fault if the criminogenic transaction was carried out in department X in the first year and completed in department Y in the second year.

It is submitted here that organisation theories on the restructuring of corporations to suit contingencies or external circumstances may be helpful in this regard. Some theorists have established that the behaviour of organisations is a function of the relationship between the organisation and the system in which it operates. Thus, where the market becomes unpredictable a corporation may be impelled to move from a rigid hierarchical management system to a system of project management by specialists. This is referred to as the contingency approach to organisational behaviour and management.[141] The crust of this approach is that managers should not believe in panaceas given that there is no single best way to structure and manage an organisation.[142] The same advice may be given to judges. As such, it is submitted here that rather than engage in a futile search for a panacea it may be preferable to borrow (albeit a small part of) the explanation of contingency theorists to justify a court's decision to impute the action and intent of senior manager A to the accused corporation in a given instance and the act and intent of junior manager B in another instance. Given that there are different explanations for the different processes and interactions that may result in the performance of an action by a corporation, these different processes and interactions may be deemed to reflect the different ways in which corporations may modify their structures in order to cope with contingencies.[143] As such, the contingency approach may guide the court's interpretation of the primary rule of attribution. It may enable the court to consider how the senior management of the accused corporation assessed the different contingencies and which system (processes and interactions)

---

[141] See generally Legge, 1978 and Tosi, 1990.

[142] See Wood, 1979: 334. See also Burns and Stalker, 1990: 253; and Burns and Stalker, 1966: vii.

[143] It must nonetheless be pointed out that this is in no way an attempt to broaden the scope of the already expansive organisation theory. Focus here is simply on how the relationship between a corporation and its agent may be institutionalised to such an extent that the corporation's actions may be distinguished from those of its agent on a consistent basis. See the boundaries of organisation theory drawn by L Donaldson (1985: 119).

the senior management deemed most appropriate to adopt in order to cope with these contingencies. Thus, actions of agents that may be explained on the basis of this system would logically be imputed to the corporation.[144] It may then be submitted that an appropriate way of imputing acts and intents of agents to corporations should be via a mechanism whose primary rule provides sufficient flexibility to courts in order for them to establish a link between the corporations and their agents irrespective of the system adopted or the way activities were organised.

The above notwithstanding, it may also be important for the court to have knowledge of the different systems that different corporations may adopt when dealing with contingencies. Kriesberg, Fisse and Braithwaite, cited above, discuss different ways in which organisations may be structured and how these may (to a certain extent) be harmonised with rules of corporate criminal accountability. Given that an exhaustive analysis of theories explaining the structure and functioning of organisations is both unrealistic and unnecessary, I will group a few theories discussed by these commentators under two heads representing two major management systems regularly adopted in contingency thinking. These are the mechanistic and the organic systems. Thus, a corporation seeking to adapt to its environment may either adopt a mechanistic or an organic system. These systems are important because they describe the agent's commitment to the corporation with regard to her role and responsibility and the mode she adopts to perform her role or further the corporation's interests.[145]

Mechanistic systems are characterised by clearly defined hierarchical levels (often vertical) with well-established policies and procedures and little or no discretion to operational agents that often have low levels of skill.[146] Each agent knows what is expected of her and how she is required to perform tasks assigned to her although she may not always be aware of her job's end goal. Nonetheless, her loyalty and compliance with the instructions from the hierarchy are bigger motivations and quite crucial for the smooth functioning of the system.[147] This implies that low-level employees are largely dependent on their superiors (senior managers) who

---

[144] This reflects the idea of "organization culture" where agents rely on an existing culture to justify their actions. See Tosi, 1990: 19. See also the discussion of corporate culture as a mechanism of imputation in Chapter 6.
[145] See Burns and Stalker, 1990: 248.
[146] See Tosi, 1990: 18-19.
[147] Burns and Stalker, 1990: 248-250 and Tosi, 1990: 18-19.

are required to have a panoptic view of the activities of the former. It is the same senior managers who from the viewpoint of the psychologist, as shown by Abell,[148] use incentives and other motivating factors (which shape values and experiences) to induce junior employees to contribute to defined objectives.

Organisation theories that are concerned with centralised decision-making and simple structures may therefore be described as mechanistic.[149] Equally, the models discussed by Kriesberg[150] may be said to describe (to a certain extent) mechanistic organisations: the Rational Actor Model describes the corporation as an entity whose decisions (taken by senior officers) are based on the rationale of maximising benefits; and the Organisational Process Model and Machine Bureaucracy Model favour the placing of emphasis on values and experiences that emerge from established standard operating procedures (SOPs) within the corporation and the bargaining process involving different persons of the hierarchy. Although the question of corporate liability is unfortunately given less regard in the illustration of the Organisational Process Model and Machine Bureaucracy Model, it may be argued that they require the court to impute the acts and knowledge of the officers that formulate, implement and monitor the SOPs.[151] However, where the formulation of defective SOPs was done by a collective unit (as it is often the case), it is uncertain whose acts and possibly knowledge would be imputed to the corporation. Also it is uncertain which act would be attached to the corporation where the offence was the result of a combination of the formulation, enactment and implementation of the SOPs by different agents at different stations and departments. Unsurprisingly, after a thorough analysis of these theories and several others (mentioned above), Fisse and Braithwaite[152] remarked that they shed little light on how legal principles of accountability ought to be patterned to suit corporate behaviour. However, they may also be said to show that if a corporation had adopted a mechanistic system, it is less likely to be identified with a low-level employee unless her attitude was

---

[148] 2006: 14, 23.

[149] Examples include Mintzberg's Simple Structure Model, Max Weber's conception of bureaucracy (Professional Bureaucracy), the *Noblese Oblige* Model, the Fault-based Individual Responsibility Model, and the Autopoiesis Model all discussed by Fisse and Braithwaite (1993: 105-117).

[150] 1976: 1091-1029.

[151] This may be said to concord with French's (1995) "corporate internal decision structure" (CID).

[152] 1993: 118.

one of allegiance and her act that breached the law was influenced by practices and procedures established by the senior managers.[153]

Organic systems on the other hand are characterised by a more flexible structure where the power to create practices and implement procedures is proportional to the agent's competence and skill or what she contributes.[154] The established practices and procedures are less influential in this system given that agents enjoy much wider discretions in planning and performing their tasks.[155] The commitment of an agent stems from the community of interests she has with other agents and the corporation.[156] The agent is therefore more likely to take responsibility for omissions or failures given that she has control of the planning and implementation. As such, the organic system has no defined locus of command and control as changes in the surrounding circumstances dictate which department or person with the requisite knowledge and competence should guide the concern.[157] This system is akin to a number of theories discussed by Fisse and Braithwaite. The Nominated Accountability Model operates to attach the acts and intents not of the titular head but of the person that was charged with the function of managing or performing a task within the corporation.[158] Equally, the Divisionalised Form may be said to describe an organic structure because it operates to attach the activities of different semi-autonomous departments that are simply required to meet defined targets by the senior management or board of directors.[159] This is also similar to Adhocracy where loosely related experts are brought on ad hoc projects and established practices and procedures have little or no influence on the experts.[160] Also, it reflects the Dramaturgical Model that operates to hold a corporation liable for the acts of agents performed in a makeshift manner following general guidelines.[161] Given that the focus here is on imputation, it may be said that once it is ascertained that the accused corporation had adopted an organic structure, the court ought to

[153] This implies that a hypothetical reasonable worker would have acted likewise in similar circumstances given that workers in a mechanistic setting are interchangeable.
[154] Tosi, 1990: 19.
[155] Tosi, 1990: 19.
[156] Burns and Stalker, 1990: 250.
[157] Burns and Stalker, 1990: 250.
[158] Fisse and Braithwaite: 1993: 116.
[159] Fisse and Braithwaite, 1993: 106. See also Mintzberg, 1979: 380-387.
[160] Fisse and Braithwaite, 1993: 106-108.
[161] Fisse and Braithwaite, 1993: 109-111. See also Mangham, 1978: 27.

allow the imputation of the knowledge or act of the nominated person or department that had control over the transaction under consideration and not the executive head or senior management.[162]

It must however be noted that there is hardly any organisation that is simply mechanistic or organic. The adoption of either system is often not an objective reality since corporate managers may adopt one system or the other in short intervals or even a hybrid of both systems to deal with different contingencies.[163] As such, organic organisations are not always adhocracies and are more often than not stratified while mechanistic systems may also sometimes allow greater discretion to operational employees.[164] It is therefore important that emphasis is placed on the transaction that allegedly breached the law and the motivations and objectives of the various persons that were involved. Thus, the court ought to refer to this approach to determine how the accused corporation reacted to contingencies and how the reaction affected its structure and functioning as regards the relevant transaction. In other words, the court would determine whether in allocating responsibilities with regard to that transaction the accused corporation acted as a mechanistic or organic organisation and whether the agent or agents that acted were motivated or influenced by established practices and procedures or they were empowered to use their discretion to meet the objectives of the corporation. The actions of these agents should logically be imputed to the corporation because they are particular to it and not the agents who were instruments that were used to achieve set goals.

It may then be contended that a mechanism of imputation is not supposed to enable the court to identify the guilty agent with the corporation but simply to link the wrongdoing of one or many agents (as well as the acts and the variables that motivated the acts) to the corporate principal to such an extent that it may be said that the latter perpetrated the

[162] The likelihood of other persons or departments that did not have control to claim responsibility for the transaction (Fisse and Braithwaite, 1993: 117) will be considerably low since it is the whole corporation that will nevertheless bear the brunt and there is often a community of interests shared by most agents and departments.

[163] Burns and Stalker (1990: 251) advance that both systems represent two opposite tendencies and not mutually incompatible attributes.

[164] The leadership often seeks to respond to the contingency in the most effective manner.

wrongdoing through the agent.[165] Thus, the court should not dwell on the question of whether the surgeon that performed the operation was at fault (which should be the concern of individual liability and not corporate liability) but on the question of whether the surgeon performed the operation in a setting created by the hospital that tended to encourage negligence on her part. In other words, it is not the surgeon's fault that is imputed to the corporate principal[166] but the relationship between the surgeon's negligent act and a number of different variables that tolerated or encouraged the negligent act and the breach of the law.[167]

What the discussion above shows is that the theoretical and practical understanding of the nature and functioning of corporations imported from non-legal disciplines may help in establishing reasonable parameters for showing how and why the acts of certain agents may be imputed to a corporation in a given instance. These may therefore constitute secondary rules that guide the interpretation and implementation of a primary rule of attribution by courts. However, they must not only be considered because of their content but also because of their pedigree. Hence, given that it is submitted that they must be derived from the *obiter dicta* of previous judgements, the knowledge they provide may be said to be persuasive. As such, they may be used to evaluate a mechanism of imputation in order to determine whether the pattern of imputation embedded in the mechanism is justifiable from an objective perspective.

4.4 Conclusion

It is argued above that when one talks of "rule of attribution" one is strictly referring to the primary rule embedded in the statute or precedent and not the whole process of attribution. However, the law compromises

---

[165] As noted above, even though I talk of the imputation of acts and intents to corporations, it is actually the causal relationship between the agent's acts and intents and the offence that is imputed to the corporation and not the whole acts and intents. This is because a corporation does not actually perform the act or entertain the intention but incites the agent to perform the act or entertain the intention.

[166] This would be tantamount to vicarious criminal liability.

[167] This does not imply that the imputable act of a single agent may not suffice to render a corporation guilty. Nonetheless, there will seldom be sufficient justification to impute only the one act of a single agent to the accused corporation since a corporation is a complex of several acts of several agents. See Chapters 6 and 8 for discussion on aggregation.

legal rules and normative notions established by courts in the process of interpreting and implementing the former.[168] Thus, Dworkin's Hercules would not arrive at the right answer (of how to impute acts and intents to corporations) by having recourse solely to the primary rule since this rule plays only an expressive function.

Within each jurisdiction there is a mutable mechanism that describes an ascertained process of attribution involving both the primary rule embedded in the applicable statutory provision or precedent and other rules that explain or modify the primary rule. These other rules are referred above as secondary rules (following Hart's use of these terminologies) because they confer the power upon judges to interpret and explain the primary rule in a particular way. The mutable mechanism is referred to as a mechanism of imputation. It has been shown that a defective mechanism is likely to compromise the consistent imposition of liability on corporations while an entirely adequate one enhances the process. Thus, in order to determine whether a mechanism is appropriate or not, some substantive parameters for evaluating mechanisms are suggested.

The parameters are shown to determine the efficaciousness of mechanisms on two bases. Firstly, the primary rule of a mechanism ought to correspond with other legal principles (following Dworkin's terminology) that are implied by the operation of related branches of law such as criminal law, company law and agency law. This test is a pedigree-based test, assessing legal rules by referring to legal edicts. Secondly, a mechanism may be also evaluated by looking at how its primary rule corresponds with rules of recognition (secondary rules).[169] The rules of recognition here are divided into two, *viz.* rules that may be inferred from the normative outlook of judges and rules that may be deduced from non-legal categories. Although this is a content-based test, the use of "non-pedigreed" principles is limited to their referral by previous courts. This reduces ambiguity (moral considerations), enhances consistency and averts a situation where judges may depart from the precedent by "plucking ideas literally from the air."

---

[168] See Cohen FS, 1933: 11. See also Gray, 1921: 84 cited in Golding, 1981: 1034-35.

[169] In Chapter 7 the mechanisms are evaluated with reference to other secondary rules called the rules of adjudication.

As regards rules inferred from the normative outlook of judges, the focus was on devices that judges often use to confer the apposite message in cases where they are dealing with abstract concepts such as corporations and where they are stepping on a largely undeveloped ground such as corporate criminal liability. These devices are metaphors (narrowed down to enforcement-generated metaphors) and tend to reveal a figurative legal world wherein a corporation exists in the form of an entity with a head, a brain and body but no soul or conscience. However, the metaphors direct courts (when interpreting and applying a primary rule) to ensure that a corporation is liable because an agent that may be described as its directing mind (because she controlled the corporation as the mind controls the body) was at fault. With regard to the rules that may be deduced from non-legal categories, emphasis was placed on organisation theory and its contingency approach to management because of the allusion to such theories in the *obiter dicta* of their Lordships in *Nattrass*.[170] This approach directs the court to consider how a corporation structured itself (whether in a mechanistic or an organic way) in order to deal with contingencies at the time when the offence was committed. Thus, if the agent or agents at fault were motivated by the way the corporation's business was conducted, it is logical that their fault be imputed to the corporation.

As stated above, these secondary rules are not legally valid as courts are not obliged to invoke them and the framework is not watertight as many more rules may be included. As such, there is truly no universal litmus test for an effective mechanism of imputation given that corporations come in different sizes and carry out diverse activities and may commit a range of crimes in diverse ways.[171] Nonetheless, where the primary rule of a mechanism reflects the substantive parameters established above it is more likely that courts would impute acts to corporations because the acts are particular to the corporations and not to their agents. Thus, in the next two Chapters five mechanisms describing different ways in which agents may be identified with corporations will be evaluated on the bases of these substantive parameters in order to

---

[170] The assumptions are that there are no orthogonal values influencing the judge's comprehension and explanation of the primary rule; and moral considerations involve turning towards the secondary rules.

[171] What this book seeks to establish is that the applicable mechanism of imputation ought to be mutable to such an extent it may be employed efficaciously in different circumstances and not that the applicable mechanism ought to be concordant with all possible secondary rules.

determine which mechanism is the most appropriate. However, given that courts apply the same procedural rules where the accused is a natural person and where the accused is a corporation, the evaluation of these five mechanisms on the bases of rules of recognition called rules of adjudication will be carried out by referring to the procedural rules governing the trial of natural persons. This will be done in Chapter 7.

CHAPTER FIVE

SUBSTANTIVE EVALUATION OF THE APPLICABLE MECHANISMS OF IMPUTATION

5.1 Introduction

As stated in Chapter 1, this book seeks to develop a template that consistently guides prosecutors and courts in the process of imputing acts and intents to corporations for the purposes of imposing criminal liability and sanctions on them. In Chapter 4, this template was termed mechanism of imputation and it was noted that each jurisdiction has such a mechanism given that courts are required to apply laws in a consistent manner. Substantive parameters for determining the suitability of such mechanisms were generated from an understanding of how courts impute or ought to impute acts and intents to corporations. Thus, they were generated as a guide towards evaluating mechanisms of imputation. This Chapter is focused on the evaluation of the mechanisms of imputation used by courts in the United Kingdom. These mechanisms are the identification doctrine and the senior management failure test. They are mechanisms of imputation because they are a logical consequence of the endeavours by courts and Parliament in the United Kingdom to ascertain (in accordance with prescription and practice) a measure of determining when the act or knowledge of an agent will be imputed to the corporation under defined circumstances. As such, they comprise primary rules that indicate the requisite pattern of attributing acts and intents to corporations and a number of secondary rules that explain and guide the implementation of the former rules. Both mechanisms (especially the identification doctrine) have been subjected to scathing criticisms by many commentators and judges. Thus, the evaluation below will also involve an appraisal of some of these criticisms. In the first part of this Chapter, I will examine the primary rule of the identification doctrine and evaluate this rule on the bases of the rules of recognition (guiding the interpretation and implementation of primary rules) generated in Chapter 4. In the second part, I will focus on the primary rule of the senior management failure test and evaluate this rule on the bases of the rules of recognition generated in Chapter 4.

5.2 The identification doctrine

The identification doctrine has invariably been referred to as the "directing mind and will" doctrine and the "alter ego" theory.[1] In Chapter 3, it was shown how the doctrine was imported from the civil law (*Lennard's Carrying Co*) by some criminal law courts in 1944 and later on developed by Denning LJ (*Bolton Engineering*), affirmed by the House of Lords (*Nattrass*) and furtively modified by Nourse LJ in *El Ajou* and Lord Hoffmann in *Meridian.* There is hardly any book or article on corporate criminal liability that has not reserved a number of pages or paragraphs for discussing and then lambasting this doctrine as a model for imputing acts and intents and/or liability to corporations. Some commentators have thus marvelled at its adoption by the House of Lords, while others have sought to remove what they consider irrational restrictions and expand its scope of application.[2] Equally, some judges have sought to distinguish the cases before them with *Nattrass* in order to avoid employing the restrictive form of the doctrine.[3] That notwithstanding, as mentioned in Chapter 3, the identification doctrine may be said to represent the legal position as regards the imputation of acts and intents of agents to corporations for the purpose of holding the latter criminally liable. Its primary rule may therefore be described as the primary rule embedded in the precedent for imputing acts and intents to corporations in the United Kingdom. However, this rule requires courts to impute not the acts or intents but the criminal liability of any senior officer that controls the corporation as the mind controls the body. As such, courts are required to dissect the body

---

[1] However, Stern (1987: 129), in line with Gower refers to the doctrine as the "organic theory." See also Hoffmann LJ (as he then was) in *El Ajou* at 705; and Gower, 1992: 194, footnote n. 36.

[2] See Stern, 1987: 142-147. See also Wells, 1995: 43-44; and 2001: 155-156.

[3] In addition to *El Ajou* and *Meridian*, see *Alphacell; Re Supply of Ready Mixed Concrete (No 2)*; *National Rivers Authority v Alfred McAlpine East Homes Ltd* [1994] 4 All ER 286, hereinafter referred to as *Alfred McAlpine*; and *R v Gateway Foodmarkets* [1997] 3 All ER 78, hereinafter referred to as *Gateway Foodmarkets.* This tendency has become the rule in many cases involving the enforcement of statutory offences as judges conveniently claim that policy considerations impel them to look past *Nattrass*. See also *Tesco Stores Ltd v Brent London Borough Council* [1993] 2 All ER 718.

corporate, identify the agent that was its "directing mind" and hold the corporation liable if such a "directing mind" is shown to be liable.[4] This primary rule may thus be said to provide straightforward instructions to the court and performs its linguistic or expressive function efficaciously. However, given that the rule ought to be invoked to impose liability on different types of corporations in a variety of circumstances, the efficaciousness of the rule would depend not on its linguistic clarity but on the possibility of courts to consistently interpret and apply it in diverse circumstances. In Chapter 4, it was advanced that the prospect of this happening is enhanced where the primary rule of the mechanism is consonant with the rules of recognition comprising some related legal principles and the viewpoints of both participants of the criminal justice practice and non-legal experts. As such, the first part of this Chapter will consider how the identification doctrine's primary rule concurs with these substantive rules of recognition.

5.2.1 The congruity between the doctrine's primary rule and related legal principles

As mentioned above, the primary rule of the identification doctrine may be said to be the principle directing a court to impute the guilt of an agent to a corporation where such an agent may be described as its "directing mind and will." This is what Lord Hoffmann described in *Meridian* as the basic principle in *Lennard's Carrying Co.* Criminal law courts have employed this rule as the "formal" or "first-order" reason for imposing liability on corporations for crimes of intent since 1944. As such, where courts have identified corporations with guilty persons not deemed to be the "directing minds" the convictions have been quashed on appeal.[5] From a formalistic perspective, this rule may be said to be consonant with other legal principles that are relevant to corporate criminal liability. Firstly, it is conformable with the recognition of a corporation's separate personality since liability is imposed directly or personally on the corporation. Secondly, it is congruent with the criminal law components of liability, *mens rea* and *actus reus,* given that a corporation is held liable only where it is shown to have entertained the relevant *mens rea* and

[4] The fact that courts are directed to impute the liability and not the acts and intents of agents to corporations may be said to imply that the identification doctrine cannot be employed to enforce strict and absolute liability offences against corporations. This is because corporate liability for these offences follows the breach of a duty owed by the corporation and none of its agents can be liable.

[5] See *Alfred McAlpine.*

performed the *actus reus* of the offence charged. Thirdly, it is congruent with the principle of agency since the corporation's liability is limited to offences committed by agents (directing minds) while acting within the scope of their authority.

With regard to the mechanism's compatibility with the principle of legal personality, it may be said that the identification doctrine provides an appropriate method of imputing acts of agents to corporate principals in order to hold them personally and not vicariously liable.[6] Although the agent may be called thus, she is actually "something more;"[7] she is the corporation's "directing mind and will" or the "very ego and centre" of its personality.[8] This means that a corporation qualifies for legal personality because, amongst other things, it may consistently act intentionally and rationally through its "directing mind"[9] and may therefore choose to either comply with the law or commit a crime. It is however uncertain why the corporation's personality is reduced to the attributes exhibited by a single agent in a given instance although a corporation often represents a complex network of several actions and decisions of more than one agent.[10] Some commentators also contemplate that the use of equivocal terms by courts (to describe such an agent) such as "brain," "nerve centre," "alter ego" and "directing mind and will" confuse the debate by merging and overlapping their context with the concept of vicarious liability.[11] The argument is that the identification doctrine does nothing more than compel a corporation to substitute for its delinquent senior manager, hence, the corporation's liability is essentially vicarious.[12] As such, the identification

---

[6] As mentioned in Chapter 3, this is equally the case where the corporate principal is held liable as an accessory. However, there is nothing in the historical development (see Wells, 2001: 86-105) to suggest that the identification doctrine was created as a convenient means of going around the difficulty of holding corporate principals vicariously liable for the crimes of their agents. *Cf* Lederman, 2000: 655; and Stern, 1987: 128.

[7] *Kent and Sussex Contractors* at 146.

[8] Viscount Haldane in *Lennard's Carrying Co* at 713; and Lord Reid in *Nattrass* at 171-172.

[9] Lord Reid in *Nattrass* at 170; and Denning LJ in *Bolton Engineering* at 175.

[10] See the criticism of the idea that corporate liability should be based on methodological individualism by Braithwaite and Fisse (1993: 19-31).

[11] See for example Stern, 1987: 132. See also Evans J in *Gateway Foodmarkets* at 84.

[12] Stern, 1987: 130; and Wells, 2001: 153-154.

doctrine may be said to bc inappropriate for holding corporations directly or personally liable.[13]

Gobert[14] also points out that if a corporation is an autonomous actor with distinct goals that do not necessarily agree with the goals of any particular manager and sometimes all managers and employees, it is awry for the corporation to take responsibility for the acts of any agent (derivatively or vicariously). It ought to take responsibility only for acts that can be identified as its own and it is of little importance that the agent that perpetrated the act was a top level executive or a junior employee.[15] The identification doctrine is therefore criticised for the unnecessary bifurcation that does not represent the reality of corporate structures given that a corporation's psychology is much broader than the thoughts of an individual senior manager in one instance.[16] In the same vein, Donaldson[17] argues that this stance is as good as focusing attention only on one part of the corporation or one aspect of its character. His argument is reinforced by the fact that in cases of strict and absolute liability, a corporation (as the duty-holder) is personally liable if the prohibited act was performed by a junior employee or was the result of the confluence of acts of several agents. As such, corporate activity in breach of a criminal law standard may be the result of the failure in more than one component of the whole corporate structure.[18] In other words, it may be the result of poorly conceived policies or poor monitoring of front-line employees by middle-level managers or poor implementation of policies or a combination of all of these in varying degrees.[19] Hence, seeking to identify the corporation with the blameworthy intent of one senior manager only is tantamount to deliberately ignoring other motivations and causes of corporate crime.

---

[13] Hill, 2003: 12; and Gobert and Punch, 2003: 64.

[14] 1994: 396.

[15] This implies that the court should be able to distinguish between acts that are particular to a given corporation or intentions that arise from its personality and acts and intentions that are particular to its agent.

[16] See also Field and Jorg, 1991: 158-60.

[17] 1982: 15.

[18] Gobert, 1994: 395.

[19] See *United States v Bank of New England*, 821 F 2nd 844, Court of Appeals (First Circuit) 1987 (hereinafter referred to as *Bank of New England*) where it was held that collectivism in the form of aggregation of fault is the basis of corporate criminal liability because the knowledge of corporations is separated into compartments. This position will be discussed further in Chapters 6, 7 and 8.

Corporations with management systems that are designed to diffuse and not centralise responsibility will escape liability.[20]

As such, it may be understood that collective responsibility ought to be the basis of corporate liability[21] and prosecutors ought to be able to prove their cases against the collective unit, the corporation, rather than strain to dissect the unit that may be very complex and show that the corporation is guilty because an officer that may be said to be its "brain" is guilty.[22] As mentioned in Chapter 3, the identification doctrine is based on mechanistic models of corporate structure and functioning and crumbles when faced with organic corporations that have complex decision-making structures. It may therefore be contended that the use of this doctrine may impel corporations to vest responsibilities for activities susceptible to prosecution in middle-level or operational managers in order to escape liability.[23] Even where there is no desire to circumvent the law, the fact that senior officers of large corporations are often remote from routine management means that restricting the liability of such corporations to the acts of senior officers makes it more likely for them to escape liability for crimes perpetrated by front-line employees under the supervision of junior or middle-level managers. Gobert[24] thus deplores the fact that something that invariably appears in business can be employed as a legal defence.[25]

---

[20] Fisse and Braithwaite, 1993: 112-113.

[21] See Wells, 1995: 44; Hill, 2003: 12; Archibald, Jull and Roach, 2004: 371; and Clark and Langsford, 2005: 30. See also Law Commission No 237, 1996: para. 7.11.

[22] Field and Jorg, 1991: 162.

[23] See Khanna, 1996: 1496. See also Law Commission No 237, 1996: para. 7.10. The temptation to pin the blame on junior employees or middle-level managers may be strong because the fault of the latter would not imputed to the corporation and the prosecution may be reluctant to prosecute the junior employee for an offence that was clearly the result of inadequate supervision and general sloppiness. Thus, in *P&O European Ferries*, although the company did not pin the blame on the driver, the CPS was quite reluctant to prosecute him after Turner J had directed the acquittal of the company.

[24] 1994: 401.

[25] In this light, the British Government in June 2000 undertook to develop a code for directors' responsibilities for health and safety that obliged organisations to appoint an individual director for health and safety (See the "Strategy Statement" by the Department of Environment, Transport and the Regions, 2000: 26, para. 68.) However, four years later, the Government declined to legislate in this manner and sought to encourage or persuade organisations via non-binding guidance to provide leadership on health and safety. The Voluntary Guidance for Leadership

Equally, where a corporation decides not to officially designate any senior officer as the person responsible for criminogenic activities it is unclear whether the prosecution would be able to identify the corporation with a senior officer that oversaw a range of activities comprising the criminogenic ones. This is because Lord Diplock in *Nattrass* and Lord Hoffmann in *Meridian* advanced that the corporation's constitution or other such document may be consulted to determine whether one of the negligent agents having control over the relevant transaction was a senior officer. *Admiralty v Owners of the Steamship Divina (The Truculent)*[26] and *The Lady Gwendolen* suggest that the corporation may be held liable because of the apparent failure of such a senior officer to supervise the middle-level managers and front-line employees, although it is uncertain whether her failure may be said to be negligent to such an extent as to be deemed criminal. Nevertheless, where a junior officer was officially designated to manage the relevant transactions, the identification doctrine cannot be used to convict the corporation.[27]

It may however be argued that although the identification doctrine is concerned with corporate liability and not individual liability, the former does not exclude the latter. Thus, if a junior officer is sufficiently blameworthy and deserving of punishment, she may be punished. This has nothing to do with either corporate liability or the identification doctrine. This is because the doctrine distinguishes between acts that are particular to a corporation and those that are particular to its agents on the basis that the acts and intentions of senior managers or other persons that may be called the corporation's "directing mind and will" are particular to the corporation and acts and intents of other agents are not. Thus, the question that should be asked is whether this is the most rational way of ascertaining acts and intentions that are particular to corporations. The answer to this question is that it would be ruinous to business and enterprise to burden corporations with all the wrongs of all employees

---

Action to Directors and Board Members published by the Institute of Directors and the Health and Safety Commission (2007) for example, entreats organisations to adopt an unambiguous health and safety policy and encourages them to ensure board level involvement in health and safety matters and appoint a senior manager that effectively oversees the implementation of such policies.

[26] [1951] 2 All ER 968, hereinafter referred to as *The Truculent*.

[27] See Law Commission No 237, 1996: para. 6.9. However, if the junior manager was given full discretion to act independently of instructions from the hierarchy, she may be deemed to be the directing mind.

(especially junior ones).[28] However, even if it is assumed that this is true, it may still be advanced that there are other ways (not synonymous to unlimited vicarious liability) of achieving the goals of holding corporations liable for the wrongs committed by their employees. Equally, the reductionist trend of the identification doctrine has been blamed not on the entreaty of business expediency but on the unfortunate proclivity of judges and legislators to imitate human criminal liability.[29] Such anthropomorphism is preposterous given that the nature and functioning of corporations are trenchantly distinct from those of human beings.[30] Nonetheless, irrespective of the judges' reasons for making comparisons between corporations and human beings, the fact that the primary rule of the identification doctrine relies solely on derivative liability makes it paradoxical for the mechanism to be used to impose liability directly on corporations.[31]

In spite of the difficulty of explaining the use of the identification doctrine as a mechanism for imposing liability directly on the corporate person, it must be noted that the corporate person is treated as morally blameworthy and deserving of punishment. Establishing its guilt by adducing evidence showing that its "brain" or "directing mind" entertained the *mens rea* and/or performed the *actus reus* thus means that the criminal law requirements of *mens rea* and *actus reus* are fulfilled. However, as a tool of the criminal law, the legitimacy of corporate criminal liability may

---

[28] See Estey J in the Canadian case of *R v Canadian Dredge & Dock Ltd* (1985) 19 CCC (3d) 1 at 29. Although Estey J described this explanation as "pragmatic," placing too much emphasis on business commonsense and very little on legal theory compromises the integrity of the criminal law.

[29] Thus, a corporation with senior and junior officers is similar to a human being with a brain and hands. See the discussion on metaphors used by judges in Chapter 4. However, it was argued that pre-*Nattrass* judges were not suggesting human features for corporations but rather drawing an analogy between the human and corporate systems.

[30] See Gobert, 1994: 393; Wells, 1988: 799, 801; Lederman, 2000: 655; Mays, 2000: 57; and Wells, 2001: 154.

[31] This is confounded by the fact that it is the agent's guilt or liability that is imputed to the corporation. Thus, it is deceptive to talk of the corporation's personal or direct liability since the liability was established against another person. If the doctrine allowed for the imputation of acts and intents that did not necessarily amount to an offence at the time they were performed or entertained then it would have been more logical to talk of the corporation's guilt or liability resulting from the confluence of these acts and intents. As noted in Chapter 2, two concepts come to mind in this respect: innocent agency and aggregation.

be said to rest on its ability to predict and punish corporate behaviour that is reprehensible (from a criminal law perspective). As shown above, the restrictive form of the identification doctrine as set out in *Nattrass* sanctions only simple predictions or those concerning mechanistic structures. This is because senior officers of corporations that have clear hierarchical structures would most probably be the ones that formulate and implement policies and monitor their implementation.[32] Gobert[33] therefore states that the doctrine "works best in cases where it is needed least and works least in cases where it is needed most."[34] In the same vein, Box[35] notes that an analogy may be drawn between the criminal justice system letting the largest (and organic) corporations that commit widespread calamities off the hook and a system ignoring the crimes committed by the majority of natural persons.

As regards the congruity between the doctrine's primary rule and the principles of agency (maverick agent/scope of employment and constructive knowledge), it may be contended that although a corporation can only form an intention or perform an act through its "directing mind," it may only be identified with the latter where she was acting within the scope of her employment and not as a maverick agent. However, the compatibility of the doctrine with agency law may be questioned because the "directing mind" is not identified with the corporation on the ground that she is the corporation's agent but because she is the corporation. This implies that crimes committed by the senior officer or "directing mind" outwith her scope of employment ought to be imputable to the corporation. Nonetheless, it may be argued that the doctrine is not incompatible with agency but represents a limited form of agency where the corporation is liable for the acts of certain agents that directs or controls its activities. However, if this were the case then Lord Reid would not have clearly stated that an officer should not be deemed to be the "directing mind" simply because her "work is brain work."[36] As such, it is uncertain whether a corporation may be identified with a rogue senior officer. As shown in Chapter 4, corporations have sometimes been identified with agents that defrauded them or acted contrary to directives from the board of directors. This may be justified by the contention that the corporations

---

[32] See for example the successful manslaughter cases cited in Chapter 3.

[33] 1994: 401

[34] See also Law Commission Consultation Paper No 135, 1994: 129-30, paras 5.77 and 5.80; Gobert and Punch, 2003: 63; and Hill, 2003: 12.

[35] 1983: 79.

[36] *Nattrass* at 171.

were deemed to have had constructive knowledge of the agents' dishonest acts. However, this would imply that the agents that had constructive knowledge were sufficiently senior for the courts to impute their knowledge to the corporation. Nonetheless, there was no contention to this effect and the accused corporations were identified with the dishonest senior officers because the latter were deemed to be the directing minds of the former. This shows another shortcoming of the identification doctrine given that the honest acts of other senior officers were ignored. It has been noted that the corporation has only one mind, which is the directing mind.[37] However, it is uncertain whether such a directing mind ought to be the dishonest senior officer or the honest one. Given that the identification doctrine is centred on the question of seniority, the most senior of both officers would logically be the directing mind. However, where they are at the same level and none of them had control over the relevant transaction the court may find itself in a quagmire.

An evaluation of the primary rule of the identification doctrine thus reveals a number of shortcomings. The liability that is imposed is essentially derivative and not personal and thus the doctrine is not conformable with the concept of corporate personality implied by company law. Equally, the doctrine is based on a parochial form of individualism that is counterproductive because the corporation is treated as the individual that committed the offence and not as a principal that used such an individual or encouraged or assisted her in committing the offence. The doctrine also lacks the sophistication required to deal with difficult and conflicting concepts such as maverick agents, scope of employment and constructive knowledge as regards the actions of agents that may not be deemed to be the directing mind. These weaknesses no doubt raise questions about the efficaciousness of the identification doctrine as a mechanism of imputation. Many commentators (some are cited above) have called for the dispensing with the doctrine or the expansion of its scope of application.[38] However, it would be assumptive to dismiss the primary rule of this mechanism on the basis of these inconsistencies without reference to other rules of recognition that may explain and justify its use. As such, although the doctrine's primary rule

---

[37] See *R v McDonnell* [1966] 1 QB 233.

[38] Such calls have been heeded in jurisdictions such as Canada and Australia where there has been a shift towards other mechanisms such as an expanded version of the identification doctrine and corporate culture. There has equally been a shift in the United Kingdom in culpable homicide and manslaughter cases involving corporations.

does not necessarily accord with the legal principles discussed above it may be shown to be valid from a normative perspective. This is because although many of these legal principles seem to outweigh the primary rule where a pedigree-based test is carried out, the primary rule may still apply on the ground that it has sufficient pedigree and outweighs these legal principles where a content-based test is applied.

5.2.2 The congruity between the doctrine's primary rule and other rules of recognition

As mentioned in Chapter 4, these rules constitute principles that enable courts to interpret and explain the primary rule. They may be deduced from the *obiter dicta* of criminal law judges and comprise a wide variety of internal and external viewpoints describing the normative perspectives of these judges and the prescriptions of organisation theorists within a model described as the contingency approach. As such, the evaluation of the primary rule of the identification doctrine will be based on how it corresponds with these rules of recognition.

As regards the internal point of view, the discussion in Chapter 4 was limited to the picture depicted by the framework of metaphors (enforcement-generated metaphors) used by judges to explain the appropriate pattern of attribution. Hence, a corporation is viewed as representing an entity existing in the legal world and analogous to the human body or a machine. Courts are then required to impose liability on it where the evidence shows that the offence was committed by an agent that does not represent the corporation's "hand" but its "directing mind and will." In other words, the agent must not simply be a "cog" in the machine. The identification doctrine certainly directs courts to impose liability in like manner given that many of these judges were interpreting and explaining the primary rule of the identification doctrine, which is the applicable mechanism in the United Kingdom. However, the reasoning of these judges (from a normative perspective) does not necessarily show that the identification doctrine is the suitable mechanism for the United Kingdom. A strict interpretation of *Nattrass* shows that it is tantamount to anthropomorphism although the outlook of pre- *Nattrass* judges suggests that a corporation is comparable to a human body and not itself a fictional body.[39] Thus, the "directing mind" or the "brain" may not always be the same person or organ as is the case with human beings or other biological

[39] *Cf* Hans: 2000: 60; and Minkes and Minkes, 2001: 245-6.

entities. This means that the primary rule of the identification doctrine is untenable unless it is interpreted to the effect that it would depend on circumstances of each case whether an agent is the "directing mind" or the "hand" of the corporation. However, as noted above, it was established in *Nattrass* that the corporation's "brain" is not simply any agent that does brain work but a senior officer with managerial functions and full discretion to act.[40]

As regards the external point of view, the perspective of some organisation theorists were subsumed within a model on the relationship between contingence, structure and performance called the contingency approach. The idea is that whichever structure the corporation adopts (contingency structure) and consequently whatever size it operates with, the prosecution should be able to use the mechanism of imputation to establish the corporation's guilt. Using this approach to determine whether the primary rule of the identification doctrine captures the reality of how corporations are diversely structured entails determining whether the doctrine is in concord with theories that delineate control and accountability within the corporate structure. Some of these theories were grouped under two heads representing two major conceptions of management systems regularly used in contingency thinking: the mechanistic and the organic systems.

The mechanistic systems are said to characterise clearly defined hierarchical levels (often vertical) with well-established policies and procedures and little or no discretion to operational agents. Thus, a corporation that has adopted a mechanistic system is less likely to be identified with a low-level employee. The identification doctrine as noted above corresponds with this system given that a corporation is said to be guilty only where a senior manager at the top of the hierarchy (directing mind) is shown to have perpetrated the offence charged. Lord Reid said a

---

[40]Nonetheless, in *Nattrass*, Viscount Dilhorne (at 187) also posited that the test for determining the directing mind may vary from one corporation to another depending on their organisation. Equally, Lord Reid (at 170) acknowledged that although the identification doctrine is a question of law, determining whether an officer is sufficiently senior to be identified with the corporation is a question of fact to be determined by the jury. As such, Lord Reid's grudge against Stable J (*ICR Haulage*) may be blamed on the fact that he thought the latter was inspired by *RC Hammet Ltd v London County Council* (1933) 97 JP 105, where it was established that the employer's liability was a question of fact and she was liable if she could not show that the due diligence was exercised by all her servants.

corporation's directing mind equally extends to other officers that have been delegated management functions with full discretion to act independently of instructions.[41] In the same light, Viscount Dilhorne[42] noted that the directing mind must be "a person who is in actual control of the operations of a company or of part of them and who is not responsible to another person in the company for the manner in which he discharges his duties in the sense of being under his orders." As well as Lord Pearson, he pointed to the list provided by the applicable statutory provision, the Trade Descriptions Act 1968 (section 20).[43] Lord Diplock on his part advanced that regard should be given to the memorandum and articles of association and actions normally taken by the directors, or by the company in a general meeting.[44] Such a directing mind is therefore the only one that is strictly accountable because she controls the corporate internal decision structure (CID) or formulates and implements or monitors established standard operating procedures (SOPs) or uses incentives and other motivating factors (which shape values and experiences) to induce junior officers or employees to contribute to defined objectives.

On the other hand, organic systems are characterised more flexible structures where the power to create practices and implement procedures is proportional to the competence and skill of agents or what they contribute. Hence, a corporation ought to be identified not with a senior officer but with any agent that was charged with the function of managing or performing a task even though she had little or no influence on other agents. Organic structures are therefore amorphous and are likelier to change in accordance with the dictates of contingencies. As such, the question of whether the identification doctrine shows flexibility in accommodating the structural changes that corporations may effect is an indication of whether the doctrine reflects the external viewpoint on the nature and functioning of organic organisations. However, the list of officers that constitute the directing mind provided by their Lordships in *Nattrass* may be said to support the idea that the identification doctrine was developed based on mechanistic models of corporate structure and functioning only. Criminal law courts in the United Kingdom are required to give importance to labels; and middle-level managers carrying out

---

[41] *Nattrass* at 171.
[42] *Nattrass* at 187.
[43] This list includes "any director, manager, secretary or other similar officer...purporting to act in any such capacity."
[44] *Nattrass* at 199-200.

functions of management without what their Lordships described as "full discretion" will not be identified with corporations.

As such, it may be posited that the identification doctrine may be used to enforce crimes of intent against organic structures only to the extent to which their Lordships may be said to have considered that the directing mind may also be the middle-level manager that had actual control over the relevant operations of the company or part of them. Such flexibility may be assumed on the ground that their Lordships did not establish what constitutes the "functions of management with full discretion." However, Lord Pearson stated that the supervision of the details of operation is not a function of management,[45] although he said nothing about the formulation and implementation of the policy, as well as general supervision.[46] Thus, it may be important to determine whether formulation and general supervision form part of the functions of management by implication or whether these functions require a lot more.

The Model Penal Code of the United States for example, specifies as a requirement for the imposition of criminal liability on corporations that

> the commission of the offence was authorized, requested, commanded, or performed by the board of directors, or by an agent having responsibility for formulation of corporate policy, or by a high managerial agent having supervisory responsibility over the subject matter of the offense and acting within the scope of his employment on behalf of the corporation.[47]

This section of the Model Penal Code adopts a two-pronged approach that involves determining whether the people that normally carry out management functions, the board of directors, authorised or tolerated the commission of the offence or whether other people designated to carry out management functions authorised or tolerated the commission of the offence. There is nothing to suggest that their Lordships in *Nattrass* established a more restrictive definition of the functions of management, excluding supervision and implementation.

---

[45] *Nattrass* at 193.

[46] In the Canadian case of *"Rhone" (The) v "Peter BB Widener" (The)*, [1993] 1 SCR 497, Iacobucci J sought to distinguish between "executive authority to design and supervise the implementation of corporate policy" and authority to "carry out such a policy." Lord Pearson in *Nattrass* may be held to have implied the latter when stating what does not constitute the functions of management.

[47] Section 2.07(1) of 1956 Proposed Official Draft.

Looking beyond the legal discipline, a simple overview of the functions of management in management studies is said in Chapter 4 to suggest that the agent that plans strategies and leads other agents towards specific goals ought to represent the corporate entity. Thus, in ascertaining whether the agent that acted is the corporation's directing mind, the judge may instruct the jury to consider whether the agent controlled and coordinated the activities of the corporation in such a manner irrespective of her official title. It must nonetheless be noted that their Lordships in *Nattrass* required that the officer in question must also have had full discretion to act, that is, she did not account to a superior officer for her actions. Given that corporations use a variety of models to organise their activities and achieve their goals, the functions of the manager may vary from corporation to corporation and may also depend on the transaction in question. The general manager with little or no expertise on health issues would naturally have little or nothing to do with the control and coordination of activities geared towards health and safety, especially in an Adhocracy. Thus, the requirement of full discretion when interpreted in this light may be deemed to be flexible and the identification doctrine may be used to regulate both mechanistic and organic systems. However, if identification is hinged upon the question of formulation and implementation of policy then courts may also be required to provide answers to other questions such as what constitutes corporate policy, what are its essential ingredients and when is it established.[48] It is nonetheless uncertain whether the identification doctrine is concerned only with officers charged with the implementation of corporate policy or whether the test of the directing mind requires less than or more than these or whether it may not even have anything to do with corporate policy.[49] That notwithstanding, it may be submitted that based on the analysis above the directing mind may be located at the second tier (upper management) and sometimes below (middle-level).[50]

The interesting question is whether the directing mind may be located at the operational or low-level since agents at different levels may be involved in the formulation of policy as well as its implementation and

---

[48] See Stern, 1987: 135-136 discussing related questions concerning the Model Penal Code of the United States.

[49] See *Bresler*; *The Truculent; The Lady Gwendolen*; and *Meridian*. However, refraining from discussing what constitutes policy and how it ought to be formulated may help in keeping the focus on the criminal justice process and also help in avoiding to delve further into the mire of organisation theory.

[50] *Cf* Sealy, 1992: 76.

supervision in varying degrees.[51] What their Lordships in *Nattrass* require is that a delegate (if she happens to be a middle-level manager) must have been assigned a task that would normally be performed by directors or senior managers and was expected to perform such a task with full discretion.[52] The danger in Lord Reid's eyes was that the term "delegation" may be given a very broad meaning to such an extent that the identification doctrine becomes synonymous to vicarious liability.[53] Lord Morris[54] also warned that the board of directors or senior management must not retain control over the person to whom the function of management is delegated. In *Bolton Engineering*, the board of directors only held one meeting per year and its mode of conducting business was to delegate the functions of management to three directors who did not act collectively but each played a designated part. Denning LJ cited *Austin Reed Ltd v Royal Assurance Co Ltd (No 2)*[55] to the effect that the decision of the board of directors must not necessarily be express and may be inferred from the way the corporation deals with important business matters. He went on to state that the three directors to whom the board had delegated functions of management were the "brain and nerve centre" of the corporation.

---

[51] In the Canadian case of *R v Safety Kleen Canada Inc* (1997), 145 DLR (4th) 276, it was held that a truck driver with "extensive responsibilities and discretion" was not the corporation's directing mind because he did not have the "power to design and supervise the implementation of corporate policy." Archibald, Jull and Roach (2004: 374) however contend that under the amendments of the Canadian Criminal Code 1985 by Bill C-45, courts would consider such a truck driver as the directing mind because he managed "an important aspect of the organization's activities." It is however difficult to see any major difference between the previous requirements and the amendments apart from the semantic analysis of the words "design," "implement" and "policy" on the one hand, and "manage" and "important aspect" on the other. Thus, Archibald, Jull and Roach (2004: 374-378) concede that they remain matters of fact.

[52] See Lord Reid at 174-5. See also *The Truculent*, where the Crown was identified with the Third Sea Lord who supervised the systems of navigation of its submarines because the task was one which an individual ship owner would normally be expected to perform.

[53] If we construe the term linguistically then we may agree with Laufer (1994: 654) that a corporation has delegated powers to all its employees and should be liable for their acts.

[54] *Nattrass* at 180-181.

[55] [1956] 3 All ER 490.

Thus, drawing a line between middle-level managers that perform the functions of the corporation's "brain but that have to routinely account for their actions and decisions" and middle-level managers that have been delegated functions of management with full discretion to act independently of directives is important because if no such distinction was made and each corporation's "directing mind" was a person that simply had control over a particular transaction, their Lordships would have had to squelch through a mire of intermingling concepts of vicarious liability and direct liability via the identification doctrine; a puddle they laboriously sought to avoid. Holding a corporation liable for the acts and states of mind of all employees that exercise management and control in relation to any particular transaction may invariably be synonymous to holding the corporation liable for the acts and states of mind of all or most of its employees. It is therefore submitted here that a corporation ought to be identified with the acts of a middle-level manager only where she managed and controlled the relevant transactions in a manner that they are traditionally managed and controlled by senior managers, that is, with full discretion and independently of instructions from above.[56] As such, where a director was accustomed to making arrangements for the receipt or disbursement of funds and signing agreements without prior authority from the board of directors, he was deemed to be the company's "directing mind" and his acts were the acts of the company.[57] As noted above, the management system adopted by the corporation or the relevant department may be a good indication of the amount of discretion enjoyed by such an

[56] It is difficult to envisage a situation where an operational or front-line employee would manage and control transactions that are normally managed and controlled by senior mangers and with full discretion to act independently of instructions. Not only would they seldom have such competence but it would equally be ruinous to the business to allow final decisions to be made at the operational level. However, there are exceptional cases such as the Canadian case of *R v Safety Kleen* where a person referred to as a "truck driver" was actually the only agent responsible for collecting waste oil, billing and attending to customers and regulators over a large geographical area. Given that waste oil collection was one of the main activities of the corporation, the "truck driver" had been given wide discretion and no business was conducted in the large area in his absence. As such, the Court of Appeal could certainly have contended that for the purpose of waste oil collection in the large geographical area, the said "truck driver" was not simply an operator of the corporation's vehicle but its directing mind. Unless it was shown that what the "truck driver" controlled and managed in terms of turnover and size of the market was reasonably small.

[57] See Nourse LJ in *El Ajou* at 696-697.

agent given that a middle-level manager seldom has full discretion in a mechanistic system.[58]

In light of the above, it is misleading to make categorical statements about the impossibility to prosecute corporations of different sizes and structures employing the identification doctrine.[59] The primary rule of the doctrine is shown to fit the bill of the contingency approach to a certain extent since it gives the jury the opportunity to examine the managerial structure of the accused corporation and determine whether in the circumstances a person's acts should be imputed to the corporation. In the words of Lord Reid, "the judge must direct the jury that if they find certain facts proved then as a matter of law they must find that the criminal act of the officer, *servant or agent* including his state of mind, intention, knowledge or belief is the act of the company."[60] Nonetheless, it remains uncertain whether a corporation will be identified with a middle-level manager where the board takes no interest in supervising her activities. Equally, there is no steadfast measure for determining whether the discretion exercised by a middle-level manager was full in order for her to qualify as the directing mind.[61] The internal point of view of the Court of Appeal (*El Ajou* and *Real Estate Opportunities*) and the Privy Council (*Meridian*) may be said to augur well for the doctrine in such cases although the views of these judges cannot be prioritised over those of higher courts (*Nattrass* and *Transco*) when ascertaining the rules of recognition. However, if the explanations of these different judges are synthesised, then it may be contended that the identification doctrine ought to operate to hold a corporation liable for the offence perpetrated by a person having control over the transactions generally where the corporation has adopted a mechanistic system or a person having control over the specific transaction that resulted in the offence where the corporation has adopted an organic system. In both instances, such a person controls the corporate body as the brain or mind controls the human body.

---

[58] The court should however consider the actual and not the official system since a corporation may have a mechanistic system on paper and yet its middle-level managers are sufficiently empowered in practice.

[59] *Cf* Ferguson, 2007: 251.

[60] *Nattrass* at 173. Emphasis added.

[61] If the negligent middle-level manager did not enjoy the requisite discretion, the court would have to determine whether the failure of the board of directors to supervise her and consequently prevent her negligent act is "sufficiently blameworthy."

5.3 Evaluating the senior management failure test

Although largely untried, the senior management failure test has been the subject of much discussion since the Law Commission recommended the creation of a new offence called "corporate killing."[62] The Government reacted with a Consultation Paper in 2000 and three draft Bills that focused on the liability of corporations for deaths caused by failure in the way in which their activities were managed or organised by their senior management.[63] As mentioned in Chapter 3, the high profile unsuccessful prosecutions of corporations for manslaughter and culpable homicide were invariably blamed on the rigidity of the identification doctrine[64] and gave an incentive for the consultation process that began in 1996, as well as the Draft Bills of 2005 and 2006 and the CMCHA. Thus, during the period between the introduction of the draft Bills and the enactment of the CMCHA, the senior management failure test underwent some scrutiny. This mechanism was introduced by the CMCHA on the ground that it is the appropriate instrument for holding corporations, large and small, mechanistic and organic, accountable for deaths that occur as a result of the reprehensible ways in which they conduct business. Equally, the Government stated in the Draft Bill of 2005 that the purpose of this mechanism is to replace the identification doctrine that is far removed from the complexities of decision-making and control in modern and large organisations.[65]

However, the Government's statement was premised to a greater extent on criticisms directed at the identification doctrine and the vehement calls for its disposal and to a lesser extent on an objectively established set of

---

[62] See Law Commission Report No 237, 1996: 8.1-8.44. See also Wells, 2001: 120-125.

[63] The Law Commission had proposed that the offence be based on wider management failures within the corporation. The Corporate Homicide Expert Group Report (Scotland) (2005: para. 6.1-6.2) even went further and proposed that the acts of individuals should be aggregated and attributed to the corporation on the basis of vicarious liability and the corporation should be liable unless it had put in place comprehensive management and health and safety systems.

[64] Although it is shown above that the identification doctrine is not certainly as rigid as contended by many judges and commentators.

[65] Draft Bill, 2005: para. 25. However, the official position is that the identification doctrine is appropriate for enforcing crimes of intent, except manslaughter and culpable homicide. Thus, the CMCHA is restricted to the latter cases and does not cover corporate criminality in its entirety. See the criticism by Gobert (2008: 414) of the limitation of the mechanism to an area that he deems "statistically minor."

parameters by which mechanisms of imputation may be evaluated. As such, in light of the evaluation of the identification doctrine above, the senior management failure test will be evaluated in order to determine whether it truly reflects the complexities of decision-making in contemporary corporations. If its primary rule is consonant with the rules of recognition identified in Chapter 4, the mechanism will be deemed to be a more appropriate mechanism (from a substantive perspective) for imputing acts and intentions to corporations for the purpose of imposing liability (for corporate manslaughter or corporate homicide) on them. Accordingly, it will be recommended that the mechanism be employed to enforce other criminal offences.[66]

5.3.1 The congruity between the mechanism's primary rule and related legal principles

Section 1 of the CMCHA provides that an organisation is guilty of the offence of corporate manslaughter or corporate homicide if the way in which its activities are managed and organised by its senior management causes a person's death and amounts to a gross breach of a relevant duty of care owed by the organisation to the deceased.[67] This section gives a

---

[66] It must be noted that the CMCHA is an example of a statute that has its own primary rule of attribution. Thus, unlike the recommendation by Lord Hoffmann that courts have to fashion a "special" rule for the statute, its rule is not "special" in the sense of being specific to any particular set of facts. It is systemic to the enforcement of corporate manslaughter or corporate homicide in all circumstances. As such, where the evidence adduced shows that the death of an agent was caused by the negligent management or organisation of the activities of a corporation, courts are obligated to refer to the rule embedded in the CMCHA (primary rule), as well as the rules that guide its interpretation and implementation (secondary rules) in order to determine whether the corporation is liable or not. That is why it is submitted here that the CMCHA actually introduces a new mechanism of imputation.

[67] The Government's decision to use the word "organisation" rather than "corporation" was an expedient way of allaying fears such as those expressed by the Home Affairs and Work and Pension Committee (2005: para. 62) that large unincorporated associations would not be prosecuted. However, it is shown in Chapter 2 that unincorporated associations may be deemed legal persons in certain instances given that incorporation is not the only source of legal personality for artificial entities. Nevertheless, the word "organisation" cannot be criticised for being unreasonably broad (*Cf* Gobert, 2008: 415) given that the activities of the vast array of organisations covered do sometimes result in unlawful deaths and the structure and functioning of corporations are often analysed based on general

concise presentation of the mechanism's primary rule because it describes what the courts require in order to establish the offence against a corporation. As such, the "formal" or "first-order" reason for holding a corporation liable for corporate manslaughter or corporate homicide is that its senior management's gross negligence caused the death of a person to whom the corporation owed a duty of care. A causal link is established between the corporation (duty-holder), the senior management failure and the death of the victim. The primary rule will be evaluated in terms of how it accords with some related principles implied by other branches of law, namely, company law, agency law and criminal law.

With regard to the rule's compatibility with company law, focus is on how the concept of corporate personality is accommodated. Section 1(4)(c) of the CMCHA ordains that the senior management of a corporation represents persons who play major roles in the making of decisions about how the whole or a substantial part of its activities are to be managed or organised, or who actually manage or organise the whole or a substantial part of its activities.[68] The practices adopted by the senior management also include attitudes, policies and systems within the corporation given that section 8(3) of the CMCHA provides that the jury may consider evidence of these in order to determine whether the senior management was in gross breach of the corporation's relevant duty of care.[69] The CMCHA can thus be given credit for not placing undue importance on labels but specifically defining the functions of the persons who may be identified with the accused corporation.[70] It may therefore be

---

organisation theories. However, since this book is limited to the criminal liability of corporations, the discussion below is focused on how the CMCHA affects corporations.

[68] In the Draft Bill of 2005 (para. 26), the Government stated that the liability of corporations will not be dependent on the negligence of operational managers and maverick employees that causes death but solely on the working practices adopted by the senior management.

[69] The idea of considering evidence of attitudes, policies and systems within the corporation reflects the corporate culture mechanism adopted in Australia. However, Part 2.5 of the Australian Criminal Code 1995 designates specific persons (members of the board of directors) that would normally "authorise" or "tolerate" and "encourage" such practices but also talks ambiguously of "high managerial agents" that should be considered. The corporate culture mechanism is discussed in Chapter 6.

[70] Nonetheless, the word "substantial" used in defining the functions of senior management is not defined by the CMCHA as recommended by the Home Affairs

contended that the legislator sought to impose liability directly on the corporation owing to the fact that it is a separate person. This may be distinguished from the identification doctrine that simply compels the accused corporation to substitute for its delinquent senior manager (thus overlapping with vicarious liability). However, as stated in Chapter 2, there is hardly any consensus on the nature of the acts that may be said to be particular to a corporation, whether they must be performed by a person that may be called its directing mind or by all agents within the scope of their authority. The important thing seems to be that the rule targets the corporate person and not its agents.[71]

Nonetheless, the senior management failure test is surprisingly not far from employing the same means to achieve the goal of direct corporate liability as the identification doctrine. Under the CMCHA, the failure of a restricted collective of the corporation's agents (the senior management) is the failure of the corporation.[72] However, it may be argued that the corporation is not liable for the gross negligence of an individual senior manager but for the gross negligence of the collective of senior managers. Equally, as noted above, the CMCHA directs juries to consider how existing attitudes, policies and systems within the corporation encouraged or tolerated the breach of health and safety standards.[73] Thus, it may be said that the CMCHA looks beyond the confines of the individual act of an agent (directing mind) in order to establish a corporation's guilty action. The senior management failure test is therefore an improvement upon the identification doctrine as regards actually holding corporations directly liable although the restriction of the aggregation of negligent acts to those

---

and Work and Pensions Committee in their join report on the Draft Bill of 2005 (paras. 145 and 153).

[71] There is no question that Parliament intended direct or primary liability of organisations. Section 18 of the CMCHA excludes individual liability.

[72] This may be deemed, with good reason, to be an appropriate definition of the "directing mind" required by the identification doctrine. Although, a codified definition of "senior management" may be said to be predicated on the need to avoid ambiguity, as mentioned above, the term "substantial" is left undefined and categorised as a question of fact meaning that the CMCHA does not bring anything new to the common law judge's table apart from the need to aggregate the acts of senior managers. Hence, just as the House of Lord ordained in *Nattrass*, the CMCHA may be said to provide that once the facts have been proved that the gross negligence of senior officers motivated or tolerated the manslaughter, it becomes a matter of law that their gross negligence be imputed to the corporation.

[73] It is unclear whether the identification doctrine may be used to hold corporations liable for criminogenic working practices.

of senior managers raises the question of whether the CMCHA accurately distinguishes acts that are particular to corporations from those that are particular to its senior managers.[74]

As regards the question of whether this mechanism's primary rule is in consonance with the rules implied by agency law, the discussion here is restricted to the principles of scope of employment/maverick agent and constructive knowledge. It must however be noted that the CMCHA talks of senior management and not of a single senior manager and the agency employed by the corporation to perpetrate the offence is that of the collective of senior managers. Hence, there is no agency relationship between the middle-level managers or frontline employees and the corporation. Like the identification doctrine, the senior management failure test does not provide any clear directive as regards whether the corporation's liability is limited to the gross negligence of the senior management that may be said to be within this organ's scope of authority or the corporation is liable simply because the senior management is shown to be grossly negligent *simpliciter*. It is for example axiomatic that actions of negligent directors ratified by the corporation in accordance with section 239 of the Companies Act 2006 will be imputed to the corporation under the CMCHA. However, this section of the Companies Act concerns commercial misjudgements or reasonably negligent decision-making to the extent that if the acts are grossly negligent they will be held against the directors and not the company.[75] The words of the CMCHA are not unequivocal about the corporation's liability for the grossly negligent acts or practices of the senior management that are not incidental to commercial misjudgements or within the scope of their authority. Thus, it is uncertain whether a corporation may be liable if an employee's family member is killed due to the failure of the senior management to issue proper warnings about the steepness of slopes of a mountain on which they had organised an excursion for both workers and their families. This is because it may not be said that the corporation owed to a duty to warn the employee's family member about the steepness of the slopes. This means that the corporation may be acquitted if the courts consider the question of whether the corporation owed a duty of care as paramount.

---

[74] Also, it may not be said that it is the liability of the senior management that is attributed to the corporation. This is because the prosecutor is not required to establish the liability of any individual manager. Thus, the senior managers are 'innocent' agents through whom the corporation perpetrates the offence.

[75] See Reed, 2006: 170-171.

Section 2(1) of the CMCHA provides a list of duties owed by a corporation that will be relevant for the purposes of the offence. This includes duties commonly owed by corporations such as the duty owed to employees or other persons working for the corporation or providing services on its behalf.[76] However, section 2(1) and (4) make reference to the duty owed under the law of negligence as the crux of what is required by the CMCHA. In the Draft Bill of March 2006,[77] the Government advanced that its decision to adopt the civil law approach of gross negligence was based on the need to clearly define the corporation's obligation and avoid a situation where the CMCHA will apply in wider circumstances than that delineated in gross negligence manslaughter cases after *Adomako*.[78] However, the CMCHA does not apply to all cases where a corporation may be said to have a duty of care but only to cases where the duty of care is defined as "relevant."[79] Nonetheless, this means that any senior management failure that falls outside the directors' scope of employment (exercising business judgments) cannot be imputed to corporations since they would not be imputed to the employer under the common law of negligence. As noted above, the CMCHA does not consider this fact.

Equally, placing considerable reliance on the law of negligence necessitates the invocation of nebulous standards that underpin negligence.

---

[76] This may be understood to include the employer's duties at common law such as the duty to provide a safe work environment, competent staff, appropriate tools and a safe system of work. See Saleem, 2007: 276-277.

[77] Paras. 13.

[78] It should be noted that the Government has sought to avoid the CMCHA overlapping with duties owed under the HSWA and under the common law which are normally duties under the law of negligence. However, the "relevant duties" of the CMCHA are broader than those covered by both regimes since some common law duties have been superseded by statute. An example is the duty owed in relation to a corporation's status as an occupier of premises which has been superseded by the Occupiers' Liability Acts of 1957 and 1984, the Defective Premises Act 1972 in England and Wales and the Occupier's Liability (Scotland) Act 1960 and the Carriage of Air Act 1961. See CMCHA – Explanatory Notes: para. 21; and Bill 220 – Explanatory Notes: para. 25. As such, section 2(4) and (7) of the CMCHA provide that the law of negligence will be interpreted as including these statutes (as well as the equivalent statutes in Northern Ireland).

[79] The word "relevant" implies duties commonly owed by corporations such as those described above or duties that may be determined by the judge with regard to the facts and duties that normally arise under the law of negligence.

The concept of duty of care was developed by English courts in the civil law of negligence as a means of determining whether the defendant's actions amount to gross negligence. However, there are many questions that remain unanswered by English courts.[80] Thus, section 2(6)(a) and (b) provide that common law rules (civil law) that may prevent claims being made such as those by afflicted parties that are part of the enterprise (*ex turpi causa non oritur actio*) or who knowingly placed themselves in positions where some degree of harm might result (*volenti non fit injuria*) are not applicable.[81] That notwithstanding, the underpinning logic seems to be that liability can hardly be established without the defendant owing a duty in law[82] although it has been held that an employer may be vicariously liable for the breach of a statutory duty owed by her worker and not the employer.[83]

As such, there is a real danger of pulling the criminal law into this quagmire of the civil law's duty of care concept. The Home Affairs and Work and Pensions Committee recommended the expunction of the duty of care requirement altogether and endorsed the proposal of the Law Commission that was to the effect that liability should be based solely on management failure.[84] Also, in *Transco*, Lord Osborne had difficulty ascertaining any contribution the civil law duty of care (imported via *Adomako*) makes in the assessment of guilt apart from delineating the defendant's responsibility, which does not provide much help in determining whether the defendant is liable in spite of being responsible. His argument is that since the criminal law is geared towards linking criminal intentions to actions, it is also important to address the state of mind of the accused.[85]

---

[80] The Report of the Corporate Homicide Expert Group (Scotland) (para 8.1- 8.2) clearly expressed concern with importing the civil law concept of "duty of care" into Scottish criminal law and deplored the fact the CMCHA leans towards this English formulation without stating (nor do the Explanatory Notes of the Draft Bill 220 of July 2006) the advantages that will accrue to Scottish criminal law for adopting the civil law concept. However, Ferguson (2007: 255) argues that the differences between the standards of care applicable in Scotland (culpable homicide) and England (civil law of negligence) are largely cosmetic.

[81] See also CMCHA – Explanatory Notes: para. 21. See also Clarkson, 2005: 683.

[82] Ferguson, 2007: 255. See also Lord Fraser in *R v Seymour* at 499; and *Donoghue v Stevenson* [1932] AC 562.

[83] *Majrowski* at [38] and [40].

[84] 2005: paras. 104-105.

[85] Unsurprisingly, the Court of Appeal in *R v Wacker* [2003] 1 Cr App R 329 rejected the application of the civil law maxim of *ex turpi causa non oritur actio*

This takes us to the question of whether the primary rule of the senior management failure test is in consonance with principles implied by the criminal law. In this case, the spotlight is on the proof of *actus reus* and *mens rea*. Proponents of the CMCHA may argue that although a criminal offence is predicated on the proof of criminal intent, the fact that the relevant statutory provision prioritises proof of the breach of a duty does not make corporate homicide or corporate manslaughter less of a criminal offence. In other words, the existence of a relevant duty of care although rooted in civil law conceptualisation is not a matter for the civil law of negligence because it is only an ingredient amongst many of the offence of corporate manslaughter or corporate homicide.[86] As such, in light of the abovementioned recommendations of the Law Commission and the Home Affairs and Work and Pensions Committee, emphasis should be placed on the way the corporation was managed and not how the scope of its duty may be delineated. This argument rests on the fact that it is better to avoid judging corporations on what they intended or could have foreseen because one of the major reasons for legislating on corporate offenders was the difficulty of imputing a state of mind to corporations.[87]

---

on the ground that civil law and criminal law have different objectives. However, as stated above, the CMCHA has specifically removed the obstacles posed by the civil law maxims of *ex turpi causa non oritur actio* and *volenti non fit injuria*.

[86] The prosecution must also show that the accused corporation's breach of such a duty was as a result of grossly negligent actions.

[87] See Law Commission Report No 237, 1996: para. 8.1. One may think that this position would put to rest questions of whether the corporation's mind should include the minds of its senior officers or its policies and practices and which senior officers and which policies and practices should count. However, to discount the consideration of the intentions of individual senior officers, as well as specific policies and practices will be synonymous to ignoring the complex of the attributes of the corporate person that is on trial. This position was most probably influenced by Lord Hoffmann's statement in *Meridian* that there is no such thing as a corporation given that it is a legal fiction. However, it is noted in Chapter 2 that the fiction theory propounds the idea of the corporation's existence (though in a fictitious legal world) and overlaps with the realist theory. Also, *dicta* such as those delivered by Lord Hoffmann were motivated to a greater extent by the fierce urgency of departing from the restrictive form of the identification doctrine and to a lesser extent by the entreaty of formulating a mechanism of imputation that reflects contemporary organisation theory. As such, the Law Commission may be said to have examined corporate criminal liability amiss given that there is compelling evidence that corporations can be brought within the ambit of the criminal law requirement of *mens rea*.

The legislator seems to acquiesce with the recommendation since the CMCHA does not require a subjective test of intent. However, the legislator also endorses the position that the common law duty of care as it applies in gross negligence manslaughter is an important stepping stone towards establishing senior management failure. The logic is simple: the test of duty of care will clarify circumstances where a corporation comes under an obligation to act and where it failed to act and if serious enough and if it resulted in death, the corporation will be liable. However, this reflects the teleological rationale of strict and absolute liability offences where the criminal law requirement of proving the state of mind of the accused is ignored in favour of punishing the accused because she has breached a duty based on promoting social welfare. As such, the prosecution of corporations would have been much more straightforward if the CMCHA had simply created a strict or absolute liability offence as advised by some commentators[88] rather than create an offence whose primary rule seems to conflict with a basic principle of the criminal law. It is therefore difficult to see the fairness of prosecuting and convicting corporations in instances where the evidence simply links a duty of care owed by the corporation and the omission or failure of its senior management. The CMCHA will certainly take us back to the question whether "any blame is enough."[89] If it suffices to pin the blame on the corporation's policies and practices or lack of, then a corporation may be liable where the death results from a practice adopted by operational employees. However, the fact that operational employees adopted a practice that was contrary to duties owed by a corporation does not necessarily imply that the senior management of the corporation directed or encouraged such a practice or acted in a grossly negligent manner.[90] Nonetheless, it may be argued that corporate homicide or corporate manslaughter is not a strict liability offence and the CMCHA is focused on the conduct of the corporation's senior management because this organ represents its "brain." Thus, unless it is shown that the senior management knew of the criminogenic practice or had decoupled its policies and practices, the corporation cannot be liable.

That notwithstanding, there may be difficulty agreeing on a test to apply with regard to whether the kind of discipline meted out to employees by the senior management although tenuous, is below reasonably

---

[88] See Home Affairs and Work and Pensions Committee, 2005: paras. 102-3.

[89] The rule that "any blame is enough" has certainly not been considered for a while.

[90] See *Gateway Foodmarkets*.

acceptable standards or is sufficiently blameworthy to found a conviction for a crime such as manslaughter or culpable homicide (if it is shown to have caused the death of one of them). If an employee dies due to a system of work that is below what would reasonably be expected in the industry but the employee happens to have contributed in some way to his own death by being reckless it is unclear how the jury will go about striking a balance. As stated Chapter 3, there is a growing divergence of opinion on how to establish negligence in culpable homicide and manslaughter cases. However, given that the offence created by the CMCHA is similar to gross negligence manslaughter (and to a certain extent involuntary culpable homicide) it may be safe to say that the victim's contributory negligence is of little or no importance and the court will be focused on the negligence of the senior management. Thus, in order to determine the seriousness of the failure of the corporation's senior management, the jury will be expected to use the measure of blameworthiness used in establishing gross negligence manslaughter. Equally, in order to determine the level of "risk of death" that the senior management failure posed, the jury will be expected to use the standard of risk assessment and perception used in establishing gross negligence manslaughter. As such, if the senior management failure is sufficiently serious or blameworthy and the senior management did not perceive an obvious and grave risk of death that the way they managed or organised the corporation's activities posed to the deceased, the jury may conclude that the conduct of the senior management was far below what may reasonably be expected of an organisation in the circumstances. In other words, their breach is a "gross breach" and the corporation is liable consequently.[91]

What the discussion above shows is that the CMCHA is largely based on the proof *actus reus* and not *mens rea*. As such, the jury may end up convicting a corporation based on objective standards although the senior management exercised all due diligence and the breach was caused by impediments beyond their control, such as a maverick employee furthering her selfish interests. Equally, a corporation may escape liability because it passes the objective test although its senior managers were indifferent to

[91]It is worth noting that the jury is left to determine whether the breach is a "gross breach" based on what they think is a reasonably acceptable standard in the industry under consideration. This connotes a circular process whereby it is a matter of fact that once certain facts have been proved, the jury will decide whether in the circumstances the accused should be guilty based on the facts proved. This reflects the much criticised circularity of *Adomako* and *Paton v HM Advocate* discussed in Chapter 3.

the consequences of their omission to supervise junior staff and provide adequate working tools.[92] The question of the subjective judgment of the senior management is therefore also important and its absence from the statute is a deplorable loophole.[93] However, the fact that section 8(4) calls upon the jury to consider whether any other matters may in their opinion be relevant leaves the door ajar for evidence that shows that in spite of the compliance system in place, the risk of death was unreasonably high because the senior management (or persons that form part of this organ) of that particular corporation were indifferent to the singular consequence of some of their policies and practices. As such, the door is ajar to the hope that the primary rule of this mechanism of imputation may reflect the principles of the criminal law as much as it does some of the principles of company law and agency law discussed above.

5.3.2 The congruity between the mechanism's primary rule and other rules of recognition

As noted in Chapter 4, the rules of recognition may involve the normative perspective of judges and the external viewpoint of some non-legal theorists. The normative perspective of judges was narrowed down to the picture depicted by metaphors (enforcement-generated metaphors) that judges used and the external viewpoint was narrowed down to organisation theories within a framework derived from the contingency approach to management studies. As regards the enforcement-generated metaphors, it may be said that the senior management failure test is at a disadvantage when compared to the identification doctrine because a good number of these metaphors were used to elucidate the identification doctrine. However, the metaphors are understood to imply that a corporation is a substantive person with no soul or conscience and laws can only be efficacious if they target the individuals (with souls and consciences) that control the body corporate as the brain controls the human body. It may be argued that the CMCHA's conception of the corporation's brain does not conform to the outlook of judges because it is a lot more complex than they envisaged. The CMCHA defines only the term "senior management" and provides for the imposition of liability on a

---

[92] See Wells' (1993: 554-9) discussion on what would have been the outcome of *P & O European Ferries* if the court had also applied an appropriate subjective test.
[93] This implies that evidence of the defender's total indifference towards the safety of the public required for proving involuntary culpable homicide as established in *Quinn v Cunningham* and *W v HM Advocate* and affirmed in *Transco* may have equally been important in proving the senior management's criminal negligence.

corporation only when failure by the "senior management" causes death. No mention is made of "senior managers." Thus, where a majority of the board of directors exercise all due diligence and one of them encourages or tolerates the breach that causes the death the corporation will not be liable. However, it may be said that the CMCHA equally treats the senior management as that part of the corporation that controls it as the brain and nerve centre controls the body and junior employees as the corporation's hands. Also, the fact that only an objective test of the corporation's guilt is required may be said to reflect the embedded conception of a corporation as an entity without a soul or conscience, making it unnecessary to prove subjective malice or intent. Thus, given that a corporation is like a "machine," what is required is that the prosecution shows that those that may be deemed to be its central processing unit failed in performing their duties.[94]

With regard to the contingency approach, the senior management failure test may be commended for attempting to strike a balance between the extreme conceptions of individualism (reductionism) and holism in such a way that it may be used to enforce crimes of intent against both mechanistic and organic corporate structures. On the one hand, the knowledge of a corporation is reducible only to the intentions and knowledge of a few individuals, *viz.* the senior managers (although aggregated).[95] On the other hand, the knowledge of the corporation is reducible to authoritative directives, policies and practices that encourage crime, whether contrived by any particular individual or not. Thus, theories such as the Organisational Process Model and the Machine Bureaucracy Model that favour the placing of emphasis on values and experiences that emerge from the CID or established SOPs also show that the senior management failure test can be employed to effectively enforce crimes against corporations.

However, the senior management failure test may be criticised for placing little emphasis on organic structures where decision-making is devolved. The failure that causes death may be the result of operations in

---

[94] There is no substantive person with a soul or conscience that is convicted nevertheless. The senior management is a collective unit just as a corporation and certainly represents Thurlow's conception of the corporation as having no "soul to be damned and no body to be kicked." Thurlow is cited in Coffee, 1981: 386, footnote n.1.

[95] This is in consonance with the Rational Actor Model and the Dramaturgical Model that focus largely on the individuals.

more than one component of the whole corporate structure and as noted above, the senior management may not even be aware of the failure. This will usually be the case where the board has vested responsibilities for activities in middle-level or operational managers that have the requisite expertise such as in Ad hoc or Divisionalised structures. The identification doctrine as shown above equally faces the same problem, lest the directing mind is interpreted in light of who was responsible for the transactions under consideration. Although the CMCHA may also be given credit for not placing undue focus on the job titles of agents that qualify as the senior management (such as director, managing director or secretary), the enshrined definition of the "senior management" is unduly restrictive. Only a handful of individuals may manage the whole or a "substantial" part of a corporation's activities and courts will find it very difficult to flex the word "substantial."[96] Thus, an individual that manages only a fifth of the corporation's activities will not render the corporation liable where the failure in the way she manages causes the death of an employee. As mentioned above, a way out of this tangle may be to seek to hold corporations liable for the omission of the senior manager that had responsibility to supervise the middle-level manager that was grossly negligent. However, it will be difficult to establish the moral blameworthiness of the senior manager for failure to supervise the negligent middle-level manager, especially because the jury is required to apply an objective test.[97] The corporation is more likely to be morally blameworthy if either the negligence of the middle-level manager is imputed to it or the supervising senior officer is shown to have been subjectively negligent. Nonetheless, as noted above, the management system adopted by the corporation should guide the process of imputation. As such, where it was a mechanistic system the failure of the senior officer should be considered, but where it was an organic system it is important to also consider the failure of the middle-level or operational managers that had control over the relevant transactions. The rigidity of the senior management failure test poses a formidable obstacle to this second pattern of imputation. The identification doctrine when interpreted as extending to

---

[96] It is possible to envisage situations where the directing mind would be a middle-level manager but to call a group of middle-level managers the 'senior management' sounds like a misnomer.

[97] Once again, if the test was a subjective one, as is the case with involuntary culpable homicide, courts would have had the option of holding the corporation liable where the senior management was utterly indifferent to the consequences of not supervising incompetent middle-level managers or unskilful front-line employees.

middle-level managers may provide a more pragmatic and flexible approach.[98]

5.4 Conclusion

The applicable mechanisms of imputation used by courts in the United Kingdom have been evaluated on the bases of the substantive parameters set out in Chapter 4. In the processes of these evaluations, a number of criticisms directed at the mechanisms were addressed and some were shown to be justified and others not. Thus, although both mechanisms are congruent (to a certain extent) with some important related legal principles such as corporate personality, agency and proof of *actus reus*, and they also reflect the normative outlook of judges, they are largely rigid and may not be suitable to enforce crimes of intent against organic and complex corporate structures. However, the identification doctrine has been modified by some courts and although the rule in *Nattrass* still obtains the modification has been held to reflect a correct interpretation of this rule. The modification (*Meridian*) no doubt leaves a door open for the efficacious use of the mechanism in cases where the accused corporation had adopted an organic management system and the agents that acted were middle-level managers. Nonetheless, it is submitted here that such middle-level managers ought to be identified with the accused corporation only where they had been delegated managerial functions over the relevant transactions, else the corporation's liability would be unlimited. As such, determining the directing mind may involve analyses of hierarchy and function and management systems.

The senior management failure test which is supposed to be an improvement upon the identification doctrine seems to be more rigid or similar at best. Corporate criminal liability is quite complex and no doubt raises many metaphysical subtleties that are not unwarranted in the development of the law,[99] else the subject would have developed solely on teleological or consequentialist bases of absolute and strict liability or Parliament would have simply endorsed the extreme reductionist or methodological individualistic approach of blaming individuals only. Thus, a better mechanism of imputation ought to have provided plausible answers to the difficult questions about the nature of the accused

---

[98] *Cf* Gobert, 2008: 428.

[99] *Cf* Lord Lindley in *Citizen's Life Assurance Co Ltd v Brown* [1904] AC 423 at 426.

corporation's mind and standards for establishing its culpability. The discussion above shows that both mechanisms do not provide any clear delineation of the intentions that are particular to the corporation in order to justify the imposition of punishment on a corporation for a crime committed *qua* corporation. It is then difficult to see how the prosecution can succeed where no individual senior manager or collective group of senior managers was sufficiently blameworthy or where the death of a person to whom the corporation owed a duty of care was caused by the acts and omissions of middle-level managers or operational employees. The prosecution seems to rely on two things: firstly, whether the judge or jury may be satisfied with the causal link established between the acts of the senior management and the offence; and secondly, whether the judge or jury may be satisfied with the evidence adduced to the effect that the acts of the senior management were sufficiently blameworthy. The CMCHA's requirements of "sufficiently blameworthy" conduct of the senior management and "what can reasonably be expected of the organisation in the circumstances" are quite nebulous. Hence, the legislator would have found clarity by requiring that the offence of corporate manslaughter or corporate homicide be established using the subjective test of *Quinn v Cunningham* (involuntary culpable homicide) rather than the circular and objective test of *Adomako* (gross negligence manslaughter).

Another major shortcoming of both mechanisms is the fact that what is imputed to the corporation is the agent's liability and not the agent's act or knowledge. Although the CMCHA does not apply to individuals, it nevertheless requires that the prosecution establish the gross negligence of the senior management and show how this caused the death of the victim. Thus, the corporation's liability under the CMCHA (and likewise under the identification doctrine) is vicarious and not direct. As such, where no agent is shown to be liable or no collective of agents is shown to be grossly negligent, these mechanisms cannot be employed because the prosecution would be unable to show that the collective of agents whose acts resulted in the breach were mere instruments that the corporation as the principal used to perpetrate the offence. This means that it is preferable that both mechanisms are used only to show that the accused corporation encouraged or assisted its agents to perpetrate the offence charged and is liable as an accessory. However, this would require the adduction of evidence substantiating the assertion that the corporation encouraged or assisted its agent, taking us back to the question of why the acts and intents of some agents and not others are imputable to the corporation. The question of whether alternative mechanisms applicable in other jurisdictions or devised by some commentators are in consonance with the substantive rules of recognition and may enable the criminal justice system overcome the shortcomings discussed above will be considered in the next Chapter.

CHAPTER SIX

SUBSTANTIVE EVALUATION OF ALTERNATIVE MECHANISMS OF IMPUTATION

6.1 Introduction

In Chapter 5, the applicable mechanisms of imputation in the United Kingdom were evaluated with regard to the substantive parameters established in Chapter 4. Although they were shown to require substantial development in certain areas, the recommendation that they should be dispensed with cannot be made unless an alternative mechanism is shown to be more amenable to these parameters. This Chapter is focused on the evaluation of some alternative mechanisms of imputation. Given that it would be neither possible nor reasonable to evaluate all the available alternatives or even most of them, three mechanisms will be evaluated. They were chosen because they have been referred to by criminal law judges in the United Kingdom, they are applicable in some jurisdictions that may trace their legal heritage to the United Kingdom and they have been endorsed by some prominent commentators.

Each alternative mechanism is thus deemed to be the logical consequence of the endeavour by foreign courts or Parliament to ascertain a measure of determining under specified circumstances when the act of an employee or agent may be said to have been that of the corporation that employed or directed her. The alternative mechanisms will be evaluated in light of the same parameters consisting of related legal principles and the internal and external viewpoints of judges and other non-legal theorists.

6.2 The vicarious liability doctrine

"Is corporate liability essentially more than a disguised form of vicarious liability?"[1]

---

[1] Leigh, 1966: 570.

Vicarious liability is founded on the maxim of *respondeat superior*[2] and to a certain extent *qui facit per alium facit per se.*[3] Although some commentators posit that it was developed in the medieval era,[4] it has been shown that the notion was recognised in ancient Rome,[5] as well as in African customary law.[6] In fact, it is a concept whose underlying principle may be said to be as ancient as civilization.[7] It is the applicable mechanism in some influential jurisdictions such as the United States[8] and South Africa[9] which do not only trace their legal heritage (or part of) to the United Kingdom but also have some important generic similarities such as adversarial court procedures and trial by jury (for the American legal system), amongst others.[10] Equally, commentators, courts and Law Commissions in the United Kingdom often review legal developments in the United States when considering the best line of approach for the United Kingdom.[11] However, vicarious liability evolved in its own right

---

[2] Let the master answer.

[3] As noted in Chapter 4, this may be translated roughly as he who acts through another acts himself. However, vicarious liability has shifted considerably from this maxim given that today it is more about the master answering for the offence of her servant as a result of their special relationship. Nonetheless, it was also noted in Chapter 4 that the imputation of acts and intents to the corporate master should rest on this maxim given that the criminal law punishes the corporate master on the ground that it acted through of its servants.

[4] See Wells, 2001: 88 citing Holdsworth, 1944: 46-47.

[5] Where the *pater familias* or head of an economic group was liable for the debt of a slave to the extent of an amount he had entrusted with the latter. See Johnston, 1995: 1515-1538; and Perrott, 1982: 81-121.

[6] In South African customary law for example, a *kraalhead* (a term used by the Dutch settlers to refer to the chief or head of a social unit) was vicariously liable for all the delictual/tortious acts of inhabitants of the kraal or chiefdom. See Bennett, 1991: 351; and Seymour, 1989: 82.

[7] See Fleming, 1998: 409.

[8] This was affirmed in *New York Central.* Although a majority of states have modelled their laws on the Model Penal Code, they nonetheless endorse vicarious liability as the mechanism for imputing acts and intents to corporations. See Gobert and Punch, 2003: 58-59.

[9] See section 332 of the South African Criminal Procedure Act 1977.

[10] After its independence, American law relied heavily on developments in England. See Friedman, 2005. Also, although the South African system is a mixed legal system, its company law was largely shaped by legal developments in the United Kingdom. Moreover, the Privy Council in the United Kingdom was the final court of appeal in South Africa until 1950.

[11] See for example, Law Commission, No 237, 1996: para. 7.28; and Law Commission Report No 300, 2006: 2.23, n. 27. See also Turner J in *P & O*

and in a fairly reasonable manner in the United Kingdom although it has been claimed that the operation of the doctrine of common employment (an employer could not liable for the negligence of one of her employees to another) checked its development,[12] especially as regards the employer's liability for the mode chosen by employees to carry out their work.[13]

Today, vicarious liability essentially operates to hold one person liable for the wrongful act of an intermediary employed by the former in spite of the fact that the former is not blameworthy in any respect.[14] The relationship between the former and the intermediary has invariably been described as a master-servant relationship or principal-agent relationship. The absence of blameworthiness on the part of the master or principal distinguishes vicarious liability from other forms of liability that require proof of the master's negligence or criminal intent although it does not make it synonymous to strict and absolute liability. In the latter case, the employer is held liable for her employee's act on the ground that the former had an absolute duty to prevent the latter's act and her failure to do

---

European Ferries; and Lord Woolf in *Attorney-General of Hong Kong v Lee Kwong-Kut* [1993] AC 951 at 969-970.

[12] See Simpson, 2000: 584. The doctrine of common employment was abolished in the United Kingdom by the Law Reform (Personal Injuries) Act 1948. Some important decisions discussing this doctrine include *Priestly v Fowler* (1837) 1 M & W 1 (Ex Ch); and *Woodhead v Gartness Mineral Company* (1877) 4 R 469.

[13] See *Wilson and Clyde Coal Company Ltd v English* (1937) 53 TLR 944 where the House of Lords sought to distinguish between the employer's liability for the conditions of safety under which work is carried out by the workers and the employer's liability for the negligence of one worker to another in carrying out the work. Due to the fact that the doctrine of common employment was still operational, their Lordships contended that the employer could not plead the doctrine of common employment in order to escape liability for the failure to provide safety measures because it was the employer's duty to provide a safe working environment. However, if one agrees that the House of Lords was right in limiting the operation of the doctrine of common employment one must nevertheless note that their argument showed a marked distinction between common employment and the personal or direct liability of the employer and not a distinction between common employment and vicarious liability. As such, the impact of common employment on vicarious liability may have been exaggerated given that the employer's vicarious liability was often (and is still sometimes) confused with her personal or direct liability.

[14] See Fleming, 1998: 409; and Clough and Mulhern, 2002: 79.

so constitutes a fault.[15] It is true that vicarious liability is sometimes imposed on the employer because she exercises control over the employee and can motivate or compel the latter to comply with the law. However, it is often imposed because the court deems it the right to impose liability on the employer in the circumstances.[16] As such, the primary rule of vicarious liability requires courts to compel corporations to substitute for their criminal agents in circumstances where the courts believe it is justified to hold the corporations liable.

This means that policy reasons constitute the "formal" or "first-order" reason for imposing vicarious liability. The facts that the negligent employee would most probably be insolvent or judgment proof and the employer who benefited from her labour often has the resources to pick up the burden of damages[17] have certainly spurred courts and legislators on to considering extending the employer's liability to include the risks of harm carried by the enterprise.[18] This is justified by the contention that if a person derives benefit from an act, it is only just that she should bear the risk of loss from the same act.[19] Equally, it has been submitted that where vicarious liability applies, a corporation is less likely to adopt measures to defeat the law such as decoupling policies and practices or delegating the control of criminogenic activities to middle-level or operational managers.[20]

---

[15] This is especially true in cases where the employer's duty is non-delegable. See Queensland Law Reform Commission Report 56, 2001: 5. However, it is not restricted to such cases. As stated in Chapter 3, strict liability and absolute liability are variants of direct or personal liability and not vicarious liability. *Cf* Ho and Papathanassiou, 2006: 19-20; and Lederman, 2000: 653.

[16] Queensland Law Reform Commission Report 56, 2001: 13.

[17] This argument also extends to the claim that the employer is in a better position to obtain insurance and can spread the risk across the network of persons connected to the negligent employee. See Fleming, 1998: 410. See also Queensland Law Reform Commission, Report 56, 2001: 13.

[18] Williams (1957) therefore quipped that vicarious liability was founded on the search for a solvent defendant. See also Simpson, 2000: 584. See also *Hamlyn v Houston & Co* [1903] 1 KB 81 at 85-86 per Collins MR; and *Nisbett v Dixon and Company* (1852) 14 D 973 at 979 per Lord Cunninghame who discusses *Richmond v Russell Mcnee and Company* (1849) 11 D 1035; and *Barwick v English Joint Stock Bank* (1867) LR 2 Ex 259.

[19] *New York Central* at 307.

[20] See Clark and Langsford, 2005: 33; and Burns PT, 1967: 702-703. These are some of the measures which corporations may adopt to circumvent the requirements of the identification doctrine and the senior management failure test.

It is however difficult to justify the imposition of vicarious liability in criminal law on the grounds stated above. The argument of the insolvency of the employee or agent does not hold much water because conviction and punishment ought to be mechanical processes that are invoked once the prosecutor establishes the defender's guilt beyond reasonable doubt.[21] Moreover, the correlation between the benefit conferred by the agent's work and the risk of harm created by the work does not always show vicarious liability to be reasonable. The correlation between both variables may sometimes be negative, such as where the worker's criminal act, although literarily in the course of employment, is unconnected to the purpose for which she was employed to such an extent that no benefit is conferred on the employer.[22] Equally, risk theories based on "risk assessment" and "enterprise risk" will not always provide sufficient justification for vicarious liability since a worker's sudden erratic conduct, such as rape, which is unconnected to the mode of performing his duties will seldom be within the ambit of the employer's assessment of risks created by the employee's work, lest employers are expected to become soothsayers.[23]

It is in this light that Williams described the abovementioned explanations as hollow[24] and the Australian Queensland Reform Commission contended that there is no single argument or explanation that is weighty enough to

[21] Also, this argument does not hold much water in civil law because there are laws governing situations where the defendant is insolvent. The argument that insolvent individuals are less likely to be deterred because they have nothing more to lose may explain why liability should be extended to the employer in certain circumstances but does not add much to the theory that underpins vicarious liability since the employer may also be insolvent sometimes. Equally, the law provides for the employer that has been held vicariously liable to seek indemnity from the worker that was at fault. See the Civil Liability (Contribution) Act 1978. Irrespective of the fact that employers seldom enforce this right (Ho and Papathanassiou, 2006: 19, footnote n. 12) its existence implies that vicarious liability could not have been founded on the worker's insolvency.

[22] If for example, a worker is hired to sell the employer's cars and in the course of selling a car forces the customer into making a purchase, holding the employer liable for duress on the ground that she benefited from the worker's sale is bluntly speaking absurd.

[23] However, where the employer is able to foresee the risk of the breach of the criminal law created by the worker's employment, it is logical that the employer should be held to have increased the risk of the commission of the crime by employing the worker.

[24] See Williams, 1957.

justify the imposition of vicarious liability.[25] The primary rule of this mechanism therefore fails to play the requisite linguistic or expressive role as it does not communicate what is required of courts in a clear manner. The Australian Queensland Law Reform Commission noted that vicarious liability is essentially a policy instrument[26] and recommended that emphasis be placed on the circumstances of each case and the nature of the relationship between the parties in order to determine whether vicarious liability should be invoked on policy grounds.[27] However, policy considerations have often determined the imposition of vicarious liability in civil cases and this has resulted in the broadening of vicarious liability, especially in tort cases where courts have deemed it fair and reasonable to hold employers liable for the wrongful acts of their employees that were closely connected to their employment.[28] Nonetheless, it may be fair and reasonable to impose vicarious liability in civil cases because court decisions are based on a balance of probabilities and it may be more probable that the employer could have prevented the breach by her worker or benefited from the latter's negligence where the bulk of the evidence shows that the employer exercised control over the negligent employee. However, in criminal cases decisions are based on the guilt or fault of the accused and this is a much more slippery ground for vicarious liability.

---

[25] The difficulty of justifying the use of vicarious liability in criminal law is exemplified by other explanations put forward by some commentators that endorse the practicality of the theory. Burns PT (1967) for example contended that vicarious criminal liability would be quite effective if it was based on the delegation test, although delegation implies personal liability of the person delegating her duties and logically excludes vicarious liability. Clark and Langford (2005) also suggest that vicarious liability that is based on due diligence is the most appropriate means of tackling corporate crime although due diligence also implies personal liability of the corporation (often used as a defence to strict liability offences) and logically excludes vicarious liability.

[26] See also the statements of McCarthy J in *Gifford v Police* [1965] NZLR 484 at 500; and Scarman LJ in *Rose v Plenty* [1976] 1 WLR 141 at 147. See also the contention by Gobert and Punch (2003: 56) that the decision in *New York Central* was based more on policy justifications than legislative intent.

[27] Queensland Law Reform Commission Report 56, 2001: 16. See also Brickey, 1981: 414; Clarkson, 1996: 565; and Clough and Mulhern, 2002: 80-85.

[28] See *Dubai Aluminium* at [23]; *Irving* at 290; and *Canadian Pacific Railway* at 599. However, these cases dealt with third parties seeking remedies from employers. Thus, they are not altogether analogous to situations where the state would seek to impose criminal sanctions on employers for crimes committed by their employees.

As such, the importation of the concept into the criminal law has been the subject of much controversy. In the United Kingdom, the common law position has been that the master is not criminally liable for the crime committed by her servant irrespective of the fact that the servant committed the crime within the course of her employment.[29] However, justifying the exclusion of the doctrine of vicarious liability from the criminal law may also prove to be a challenging task if one relies solely on the fact that the criminal law operates to punish only the morally blameworthy person that is shown to be responsible. As shown in Chapter 2, it is misguided to hold out the proof of blameworthiness of the accused (deontological facet of the criminal law) as the only concern of the criminal law. A person may also be held liable because of the need to meet a designated objective irrespective of the fact that she is not morally blameworthy (teleological facet of the criminal law). Also, it may be argued that ideas of morality and social interests sometimes overlap and it is important to show that even though the employer is not morally blameworthy she could have foreseen the risk of the worker committing the crime or that she provided the opportunity for the worker to commit the crime; and the policy objective of deterrence may be achieved if liability is imposed on the employer.[30] Nonetheless, it is difficult to predict when courts will impose vicarious liability. That notwithstanding, the mechanism's primary rule will be evaluated with reference to the substantive parameters set out in Chapter 4 in order to determine whether it may provide a better avenue for enforcing crimes against corporations despite the nebulousness of its primary rule.

---

[29] See *R v Hinggis* (1730) 2 Ld Raym 1574; and *Roberts v Woodward* (1890) 25 QBD 412. See also Welsh, 1946: 346, 348, 358; and Gillies, 1997: 111.

[30] See the reasons for imposing vicarious civil liability put forward in the United States case of *Commonwealth v Pulaski County Agric and Mech Association* 17 SW 442 (1891) and in the Canadian case of *Blackwater v Plint* 2005 SCC 58. The argument of deterrence is buttressed by the contention that imposing vicarious liability on corporations incites them to closely monitor and supervise all of their employees and reduces the probability of the latter breaching the law. However, reality may be more complicated than such a prediction as it has been suggested elsewhere that corporations may dispense with internal audits and thereby reduce the risk of detecting crimes for which they would be held liable. See Dana, 1996: 970. See also Chu and Qian, 1995: 306.

6.2.1 The congruity between the mechanism's primary rule and related legal principles

Vicarious liability is likely to conflict with a related legal principle such as separate corporate personality because it is based on the fact that the accused corporation was not in anyway personally responsible for the crime but is liable due to its relationship with the guilty agent.[31] Hence, talking of imposing direct liability on corporations via vicarious liability may logically be deemed oxymoronic given that direct or personal liability is essentially based on the personal fault of the accused. However, there are instances (in civil law) where vicarious liability may be used to target corporations directly.[32] In 1963, the House of Lords was held to have perforated the boundary between contract and tort at common law by ordaining that a claimant may sue in tort in situations where no action for breach of contract was available.[33] Such situations include where the defendant has assumed responsibility to such an extent that it may be said that there would have been a contract between the claimant and the defendant but for the absence of consideration.[34] The effect of this decision has been to expand the scope of the law of tort to include the intentions of the parties involved.[35] There is considerable literature on the practicality and importance of this position and how it ought to apply.[36] However, the fact that the reasoning is based on the intersection between contract law and tort law means that by default it cannot be applicable to

---

[31] It may then be posited that the argument put forward by Ho and Papathanassiou (2006: 20) that Bank of India was vicariously liable in *Bank of India v Morris* [2005] EWCA Civ 693 for the fraud committed by the general manager of its London branch is misguided. This is because the general manager had been vested with management functions with full discretion and acted as the company's "directing mind" and not merely as its agent. Thus, his fault was the fault of the company as held by the court. See *Bank of India v Morris* at [112].

[32] In establishing vicarious liability as the applicable mechanism, the Supreme Court of the United States in *New York Central* was clearly understood to imply that the corporate master is answerable for the criminal acts of its servants as it is in civil law. See also Vu, 2004: 466. However, the argument below is not based on the endorsement of such a brazen importation of the concept (as it applies in civil law) into the criminal law.

[33] See *Hedley Byrne & Co Ltd v Heller & Partners Ltd* [1964] AC 465, hereinafter referred to as *Hedley Byrne*.

[34] See O'Sullivan, 2007: 165. See also Whittaker, 1997: 169.

[35] See Barker, 1993: 464.

[36] See for example, Barker, 1993; Witting, 2005; Stanton, 2007; and O'Sullivan, 2007.

criminal law. This is because unlike some tort or delictual claims that may give rise to criminal prosecutions (negligence and gross negligence), contract law (agreement between parties) is not the criminal law's concern. Nonetheless, the mingling of tort (or delict) law and contract law may bridge criminal law and contract law and it is suggested here that vicarious liability may serve as the brick of such a bridge.

Normally, an employer is vicariously liable for the acts of her worker committed within the course or scope of the latter's employment, thus, the worker is personally responsible and the employer is vicariously liable.[37] As such, the worker's personal responsibility does not render her liable unless she also had a special relationship with the plaintiff, in which case the worker would not be able to escape liability on the ground that she was acting solely in the capacity as servant of the employer.[38] The person that is normally liable is the employer although such liability is vicarious. However, where the employer assumed responsibility for the acts of a client in circumstances where but for the absence of consideration there would have been a contract and the employer's worker (who was not in a special relationship with the client) breaches the duty of care owed to the client, the employer is vicariously liable for the worker's breach although her vicarious liability is treated as identical to personal liability. This is because the worker or agent who actually commits the tort or delict is not in a special relationship with the client and does not owe an incidental duty of care. Thus, the worker's act does not amount to a breach of the duty of care unless the act is imputed to the employer that owes the duty of care.

This may be deemed to be a classic example of the operation of the identification doctrine given that the worker is treated not as an agent of the company but as something more: the "embodiment" of the company.[39]

---

[37] Todd, 2003: 202.

[38] See *Standard Chartered Bank v Pakistan National Shipping Corporation* [2002] 3 WLR 1547, hereinafter referred to as *Standard Chartered Bank*.

[39] See *Williams v Natural Life Health Foods Ltd* [1998] 1 WLR 830 (hereinafter referred to as *Natural Life Health Foods*) at 838-839 where Lord Steyn held that the manager in such an instance is not a joint tortfeasor with the company but the embodiment of the company or an instrument which the company employed to perpetrate the act that resulted in the breach. See however Todd's (2003: 202) argument that the company is both vicariously liable and a joint tortfeasor. Vicarious and direct liability are fused here because in order to qualify as a joint tortfeasor, the company should be shown to be equally responsible for the breach,

However, the identification doctrine will be discounted on the ground that it requires the court to impute the agent's liability and not just her acts to the corporation and in this case the worker is responsible for the breach and not liable in law since her liability depends on whether she also assumed personal responsibility.[40] Thus, it is the corporate employer and not the agent that is liable because it was the former that was in a special relationship with the client and what is imputed to the corporation is simply the worker's act.

If this reasoning is imported into the criminal law, the imputation of the worker's wrongful act to the corporation would be indicative of vicarious criminal liability although the liability derives from the fact that the employer had assumed personal responsibility. A good example of such a conception is the South African case of *N K v Ministry of Safety and Security*[41] where a woman was raped by three policemen in a police van during night patrol. The Constitutional Court held the state vicariously liable because it contended amongst other things that the state had undertaken via the Constitution to ensure the safety and security of all citizens using its policemen. As such, even though the state was not responsible for the rape, it was vicariously liable due to the fact it had assumed personal responsibility for the victim's safety and was in a special relationship with her.[42]

It must however be noted that the operation of *Hedley Byrne* duty of care (and other duties of like design) in civil law is different from the plain and straightforward statutory and common law duties of care in criminal law. The *Hedley Byrne* duty of care arises not necessarily by the operation of the law and certainly not by contractual obligations but by virtue of a special relationship that exists between the employer and a third party. The

---

while in order to be vicariously liable, the company should not be responsible but should be liable simply because the breach was caused by an employee acting within the course or scope of her employment.

[40] Campbell and Armour (2003: 292-296) describe this approach as the "disattribution heresy" because the worker's acts are "disattributed" from her and attributed to the company. See also the New Zealand case they cite: *Natural Life Health Foods and Trevor Ivory Ltd v Anderson* [1992] 2 NZLR 517. See also Grantham and Rickett (1999: 133-139) focusing on directors' immunity.

[41] [2005] JOL 14864 (CC).

[42] Thus, given that the state cannot physically commit the offence of rape, its liability was essentially vicarious, although equally direct since it was in a special relationship with the victim. See Nana, 2008: 265-266.

employer may only be held (vicariously) liable if it had assumed personal responsibility for the acts carried out by its agents or employees that adversely affected a third party. As such, we may refer to this line of reasoning as an attempt to provide an aperture through which corporations may be targeted directly via the mechanism of vicarious liability and through which this mechanism may gain access into the criminal law (of the United Kingdom). Nonetheless, it may be argued that the fact that courts in such an instance would assume that the corporation's failure to perform its duty is sufficiently blameworthy (though not uncommon) implies that the corporation is personally and not vicariously liable. But given that the failure is not as a result of the corporation's act but that of an agent that would not be identified with the corporation in normal circumstances, the corporation is more likely to be vicariously liable.[43] Thus, the fact that vicarious liability may be imposed in this instance via the assumption of personal responsibility implies that vicarious liability can be used in criminal law to target corporations directly or personally.[44]

It is difficult to see another way in which the conception of the corporation within the context of vicarious criminal liability may be shown to correspond to the notion of corporate personality. As noted in Chapters 3 and 5, corporate psychology is much broader than the thoughts of an individual employee or manager and to reduce a corporation's knowledge to that of its individual employee or manager is tantamount to focusing on one aspect of the corporate psychology only. Vicarious liability applies to all employees of the corporation irrespective of their station and logically provides a wider view of the corporate psychology and a more holistic perspective to preventing and punishing crime in the corporate context when compared to the identification doctrine and the senior management failure test. Where the corporation benefits from the criminal or negligent act of any agent, whether a middle level manager (that does not exert substantial authority) or low-level employee, it cannot be prosecuted using the identification doctrine or senior management failure test. However,

---

[43] This line of reasoning is buttressed by the argument that where an act creating a legal relationship between the principal and a third party is most likely to be performed by an agent (such as selling alcohol in a licensed inn) the principal is more likely to be vicariously liable. See Clough and Mulhern, 2002: 85.

[44] This argument should not be discounted simply on the basis of the apparent sinuosity of the reasoning given that changes in the commercial world may lead to the criminal justice system confronting such situations in real life. It should not be forgotten that vicarious liability has been justified over the past centuries by social and economic changes. See Williams, 1957: 228.

vicarious liability (supported by policy considerations) would give courts good grounds to contend that it is fair to hold the corporation liable since it had control over the employee or manager. However, where the crime is the result of the sum of acts of several managers and junior employees, vicarious liability operates to acquit the accused corporation because the prosecution would not be able to pinpoint any guilty manager or employee whose place in the dock should be given to the corporation.[45] The prosecution may thus be tempted to identify the individual that had ultimate responsibility and knowledge of the consequences of the activities.[46] However, whether such responsibility and knowledge would be "sufficiently blameworthy" or meet the requirements of a crime (*mens rea* and *actus reus*) is another question. As noted in Chapter 5, *The Truculent* and *The Lady Gwendolen* provide hope that this may be possible although they constitute the exception and not the rule.

The use of vicarious liability to impose criminal liability may generally pose particular problems with regard to fulfilling the requirements of *mens rea* and *actus reus*. It must be noted that vicarious liability is a graft from the civil law, although in ancient societies (in its crudest form) such as those cited above it was also conceived to be applicable in criminal matters given that the head of a household was sometimes liable for the offences committed by members of his household. Moreover, the contemporary use of vicarious liability relates to situations where legislators or judges seek to protect social welfare by compelling employers to closely monitor their employees. Such situations logically include both civil wrongs and criminal offences committed by employees within the course of their employment. In line with the contention in Chapter 5 that credit should be given to the identification doctrine for providing the means of convicting corporations of offences requiring proof of *mens rea*,[47] it may equally be submitted here that credit should be given

---

[45] This is referred to by Png (2001) as the "problem of many hands." In as much as one may try to show that vicarious liability does not rely on individualism, the fact that it faces this problem implies that its reliance on individual fault is excessive and unfairly precludes the prosecution of corporations in a number of instances where the fault is collective.

[46] There is also the argument that where liability also depends on the policies and practices of the corporation, the prosecution may be tempted to avoid the difficult channel of identifying any guilty managers and simply focus on the corporation. See Fisse and Braithwaite, 1993: 1.

[47] In the United Kingdom or other commonwealth jurisdictions that began prosecuting corporations for crimes of intent employing the identification doctrine.

to vicarious liability for the same reason with regard to jurisdictions where it was the mechanism first employed.[48]

However, there is little evidence that vicarious liability was sufficiently modelled to suit the requirements of the criminal law. This mechanism involves compelling an employer that is free from guilt to substitute for an employee that is guilty and may have even acted contrary to instructions.[49] What is required as shown above is either evidence that the employee acted within the scope or course of her employment or that courts believe that the employer should be liable in the interest of the public. The idea of holding a person (the employer) criminally liable without proof of her culpability is incongruous with the fundamental principles of the criminal law and may even be said to be contrary to public policy itself.[50] That is why in some jurisdictions such as those of the United Kingdom, the criminal law is said to preclude vicarious liability. However, as noted above, it may be argued that given that vicarious liability is based on policy considerations it may be considered to part of the consequential or teleological facet of the criminal law as described in Chapter 2. It is true that legislators may decide to target a particular 'person' by imposing liability on her with no requirement of proof of culpability because it promises the most desirable of consequences. Nonetheless, these situations include strict and absolute liability and not vicarious liability.[51] Strict and absolute liability offences are governed by policy defined by legislation and sometimes courts[52] while vicarious liability is not based on any defined policy but considerations of the court in the circumstances.[53] Such

---

[48] Such as the United States and South Africa. See Coffee, 1983: 253-254; and Khanna, 1996: 182.

[49] It is however most unlikely that the employee acted contrary to instructions given that in theory an employer can only be vicariously liable where the employee acted within her scope of authority. An employee acting contrary to instructions may therefore be held to be acting outside this scope. Nonetheless, this is subject to debate since as noted in Chapter 4, the term 'scope of employment' is broadly interpreted by civil courts.

[50] Especially for crimes with high stigma. See Hippard's (1973: 1040) argument that criminal liability without fault (not *mens rea*) is inconsistent with the principles that underpin the American Constitution.

[51] It is the jumbling of these types of liability that has no doubt incited a backlash against strict and absolute liability in some quarters.

[52] For example liability for escape in *Rylands v Fletcher* [1868] UKHL 1.

[53] The different considerations by different courts in different circumstances cannot be said to amount to precedent (because there is nothing to bind subsequent or

considerations relate to reasoning about facts and do not fit the bill of the consequentialist or teleological criminal law facet which is concerned with rules of statutes or precedent. Hence, it would be absurd to seek to justify the use of vicarious liability to regulate corporate behaviour (especially as regards the enforcement *mens rea* offences) by referring to the mechanism's teleological or consequentialist basis.

As such, the absence of proof of the culpability of the accused, as well as looking past her personal or direct liability, is inconsistent with criminal liability. The accused corporation is expected to answer for the behaviour of its employee and treated as a criminal although it has not committed any crime and it is not in any way art and part in the employee's crime.[54] Moreover, a person's status as employer or employee is very relevant to the operation of vicarious liability unlike in criminal law where it is simply a question of whether such a person entertained the *mens rea* and performed or incited another person to perform the *actus reus* of the offence.[55] Thus, under vicarious liability an agent is logically not liable if she acted in her capacity as agent (on instructions from the principal). This is because her wrongful act is not legally attributable to her unless she assumed personal responsibility to the plaintiff or claimant.[56] As mentioned earlier, this has been described as the "disattribution heresy" and proponents of the approach contend that it is the result of the distinction between a corporation's personality and that of its agent.[57] Although the House of Lords in *Standard Chartered Bank* dismissed the

---

lower courts) unless all cases are deemed to be "cases of first impression." See Cross R and Harris, 1991: 186-187.

[54] It has been argued that this principle has sometimes been applied by criminal law courts in the United Kingdom as in the case of criminal libel prior to the Libel Act 1843 (section 7). See Welsh, 1946: 348-349. See also *R v Holbrook* (1878) 4 QBD 42 at 46-49. See also Brickey's (1981: 414) argument that corporations were vicariously liable for tortious or delictual acts of their employees that required proof of intent such as battery and assault. Thus, importing the concept into the criminal law is not altogether unusual.

[55] This is also open to argument because irrespective of the mechanism employed, the corporation can only be liable for the act or omission of its employee or agent. Thus, although the status of corporate employer/principal or employee/agent is not important to the criminal law, it is as important to corporate criminal liability as it is to vicarious liability.

[56] See *Natural Life Health Foods* and *Trevor Ivory Ltd v Anderson* [1992] 2 NZLR 517. See also the Canadian case of *Scotia McLeod Inc v Peoples Jewellers Ltd* (1995) 129 DLR (4th) 711.

[57] See Grantham and Rickett, 1999:138-139.

argument that agents are not personally liable where they had knowledge of the illegality of their acts, it is unclear whether the liability of such agents is secondary or primary where they were following instructions and whether their corporate employers would escape liability in spite of the instructions. This is closely related to the question of whether the agent through whom a company contracts with the plaintiff may be liable in case of breach of contract.[58] Notwithstanding, vicarious liability is simply unreasonably broad and the fact that it is imported into the criminal law with little or no modification implies that there is a major risk of intermingling civil law and criminal law concepts, something which may greatly impact upon the efficaciousness of criminal law sanctions.

As regards vicarious liability's compatibility with rules implied by the law of agency, it must be noted that both concepts of vicarious liability and agency are founded on the maxim *qui facit per alium facit per se*. Hence, they both operate to substitute the principal for her delinquent agent because the former was in a position of control and both parties consented to the power-liability relationship. Also, given that vicarious liability is largely governed by policy considerations and is not concerned with the agent's responsibility, the same reasons that provide judges with an incentive to invoke the rules of agency may be said to explain why vicarious liability is employed in certain instances.[59] Hence, the courts may decide to hold a corporate employer vicariously liable because its negligent agent acted within the scope of her employment or because the corporate employer is deemed to have had constructive knowledge of the agent's intent to commit an offence or the likelihood of that happening. However, unlike agency, the employer may only be vicariously liable where the agent was at fault. Thus, acts that do not amount to an offence cannot be imputed to a corporation in order to hold it vicariously liable in spite of the fact that they were performed by its agents in the course of the agency.

---

[58] See Campbell and Armour, 2003: 302.

[59] It is however challenging drawing a fine line between the two concepts as they sometimes overlap in both their legal and normative applications. Some commentators thus treat both concepts as synonyms. See for example, Lederman, 2000: 652.

6.2.2 The congruity between the mechanism's primary rule and other rules of recognition

Vicarious liability seems to be largely unconcerned with the essence or nature of the corporate person. Questions about its "brain" or "nerve centre" and "hands" and how these organs interact with each other in order to further the corporation's goals are largely ignored. A mechanism could not be further from the normative perspective of judges discussed in Chapter 4. Nonetheless, it may be argued that vicarious liability treats corporations as having no "souls" or "consciences" by not requiring proof of their blameworthiness. Also, it may be argued that the corporate employer's psychological autonomy is recognised by the requirement of proof of control over the employee's activities such as in cases where assumption of responsibility by the corporate employer is required. However, these arguments would have been valid if entertaining *mens rea* predicated the possession of a "soul" or "conscience" and if they applied to exonerate the corporate employer in a situation where it did not assume responsibility. *Mens rea* is related to the capacity of the accused and vicarious liability extends even to situations where the employer did not assume responsibility; it is sufficient that the negligent worker acted within the scope of her employment. As such, it may be advanced that the fact that vicarious liability is only at best remotely connected to the enforcement-generated metaphors implies that it is a mechanism that is out of touch with the reality of corporate criminal liability, at least in the United Kingdom.[60]

The mechanism's sweep however comprises some organisation theories (within the contingency approach discussed in Chapter 4) that identify the corporation with the decision-maker or the individual responsible for implementing policies or designated to perform any task. These theories include the Nominated Accountability Model, Mintzberg's Simple Structure Model, the *Noblese Oblige* Model, the Fault-based Individual Responsibility Model, and the Autopoiesis Model. Vicarious liability may also be said to include the Bureaucratic Politics Model that applies to senior managers because they exert more influence in bargaining processes, although it will be restricted to situations where one

---

[60] It is therefore unsurprising that it is reported that after the decision in *New York Central* importing vicarious liability into the criminal law of the United States, accused corporations entreated courts to consider their complex nature and the diligence that their board of directors or senior management had shown in preventing the crime. See Laufer, 2006: 17.

of the agents that constitute the senior management can be identified and shown to be at fault. An intriguing feature of vicarious liability is that it may be used to impose liability on any corporation irrespective of the structure it adopts in response to contingency factors. However, theories such as the Organisational Process Model and Machine Bureaucracy Model that place emphasis on established SOPs are not in consonance with vicarious liability except to the extent that they require liability to be imposed on the officer that formulated, implemented and monitored these SOPs. Since such an officer would normally formulate, implement and monitor these SOPs within the course of her employment, her corporate employers may naturally be held vicariously liable. Nonetheless, the formulation or implementation or monitoring of the SOPs must itself amount to an offence before vicarious liability may apply.

That notwithstanding, vicarious liability may be said to be more flexible than the two mechanisms evaluated in Chapter 5. There is no need, for example, to broadly interpret the statements of their Lordships in *Nattrass* in order to determine whether the mechanism is more flexible than envisaged or to seek to interpret the words of the CMCHA to such an extent as to indulge in sinuous dialectics. Whether it is a bureaucracy or an adhocracy the corporate employer is simply vicariously liable if the negligent employee acted within the course of her employment. This means that vicarious liability may be said to reflect the reality of contemporary complex corporations on the ground that it enables courts to hold corporations liable for the offences perpetrated by all employees. Given that some corporations employ thousands of employees and have hundreds of departments or branches, proving the guilt of a senior officer or the senior management may be an uphill task for the prosecution, especially where the corporation does not make use of central coordination. As such, vicarious criminal liability was adopted in the United States based on the contention that it may in several instances be the only available instrument.[61]

However, a number of commentators have contended that collective responsibility is the basis of corporate liability and the prosecution should be able to prove its case against the collective unit rather than strain to dissect the corporation's complex structure and identify a single manager or employee that is guilty.[62] This means that vicarious liability, as well as

[61] See Brickey, 1981: 413-414; and Khanna, 1996: 1483.

[62] See the discussion on the corporate culture mechanism below.

the identification doctrine (and to a certain extent the senior management failure test), is less sophisticated in dealing with crime committed by complex organic corporations. The prosecution is not required to examine the distribution of roles and responsibilities within the complex corporate structure or the corporation's policies and their implementation[63] and may only show that the act that breached the statutory provision was perpetrated by the corporation's agent within the course of her employment. The argument in favour of vicarious liability is that focussing on corporate policies and employment practices of large corporations invariably involves showing that they encouraged or tolerated the commission of the offence by one of the corporation's agents. However, where the employee that acted did not entertain the requisite intent, since she was simply obeying instructions from the hierarchy, vicarious liability may be precluded because the worker was not at fault. In this case, one agent entertained the *mens rea* and another performed the *actus reus* and the employer may not substitute for any of the agents since none of them is actually at fault.

Thus, in spite of attempts at justifying the use of vicarious liability it seems the mechanism sanctions only simple predictions. There is no doubt that holding corporations liable for the criminal acts of all of their employees is an oversimplified solution and may in some instances be as ludicrous as holding natural persons liable for every offence that is remotely connected to them.[64] A rigorous application of vicarious liability would no doubt be ruinous to business as corporations, especially the large ones with thousands of employees, would be subjected to routine sanctions. That notwithstanding, as stated in Chapter 2, no single theory captures the complexity of decision-making in the corporate context to such an extent that it may be held as a template for the enforcement of corporate criminal law. A mechanism may therefore be more efficacious in certain situations and less in others. However, the most appropriate mechanism ought to provide a fair means of modifying its structure in order to overcome the obstacles identified. As shown above, vicarious liability does not have such adaptability. It is largely based on consideration of policy rather than the reality of the defender's guilt implying that it places more emphasis on the end rather than the means. This makes it difficult to predict what the courts will do and such uncertainty does not augur well for business, as well as the coherent

[63] Lest it is to shown that the corporation had assumed responsibility over the employee's action that was not strictly within the scope of her employment.
[64] Gobert and Punch, 2003: 70.

development of corporate criminal law. It must however be noted that the principles underlying vicarious liability preceded the conception of corporate forms and they have been modified to suit social and legal changes on a continuous basis. Thus, this may also be the case with the prosecution of complex and large corporations.[65]

6.3 The Aggregation Doctrine

Due to the difficulty of identifying employees that could be shown to be responsible for the offence in order to hold their corporate employers vicariously liable, some American courts devised a mechanism by which corporations could be held liable for offences caused by a combination of the actions, omissions and intentions of some or all of their employees. Such a combination must amount to the requisite *mens rea* and *actus reus* of the offence to the effect that if it had been entertained and performed by an individual she would be liable in her personal capacity and/or her act and state of mind would have been imputed to her corporate employer in order to hold it vicariously liable. This mechanism is the aggregation doctrine and has invariably been referred to as the collective knowledge doctrine or collective *mens rea* standard.[66] It is based on the rationale that the aggregation of the acts, omissions and states of mind of a corporation's employees involved in a particular transaction is a more realistic reflection of the corporation's fault.[67] This is thought to provide even stronger motivation for the board of directors or senior management of a corporation to monitor its employees and ensure that they communicate with each other and the hierarchy.[68] Equally, the board or senior management would be less inclined to seek to defeat the course of justice by allocating criminogenic tasks in such a way that no single senior manager would have the full import.[69]

---

[65] In fact, in jurisdictions like those of the United States where vicarious liability is applicable it has often been modified to something similar to the identification doctrine or it is sometimes applied with the aggregation doctrine.

[66] See Clarkson, 1998: 6; and Khanna, 1999: 371.

[67] Gobert, 1994: 404. In other words, corporate activities that result in the breach of criminal law standards are almost always a combination of the acts and omissions of many individuals. See also Norrie, 2001: 95; and Gobert and Punch, 2003: 82.

[68] Khanna, 1999: 372.

[69] Clarkson, 1998: 6.

Two widely discussed American cases exemplify the application of the aggregation doctrine. The first is *Bank of New England*. In this case, a bank was convicted in a jury trial of thirty-one counts of infringing the Currency Transaction Report Act 1982. This Act required financial institutions to report transactions in excess of $10,000 and the court held that the bank had "wilfully" failed to report cash withdrawals by a customer that cumulatively exceeded the statutory limit although they were made using multiple cheques that were individually under $10,000. The bank's appeal was hinged upon the facts that no single cheque exceeded the statutory limit and the evidence adduced was not sufficient to justify the verdict that it had wilfully omitted to file reports on the said transactions.[70] Given that vicarious liability was the applicable mechanism, the trial judge instructed the jurors to first of all determine whether the employees involved in the transaction were acting within the course of their employment. He then advanced that the knowledge of the bank could be established by showing that one of these employees had the said knowledge of the reporting requirement and wilfully failed to file a report. He also stated that given that certain responsibilities accrue to the bank as an organisation, the jury should determine whether the evidence showed that the organisation as a whole was indifferent to the requirements of the applicable statute. Such evidence included the supervision and monitoring of employees and the establishment of effective communication channels at all levels.[71] The court then concluded that even if the teller that dealt with the customer was not aware of the reporting requirements, the corporation had knowledge because some employees had been shown to be aware of the obligations. The knowledge of these employees and the failure of the teller to file a report were thus aggregated and imputed to the corporation as *mens rea* and *actus reus* of the statutory offence.

The second case that exemplifies the application of the aggregation doctrine is *United States v TIME-DC, Inc.*[72] In this case, the defendant corporation was held liable for knowingly and wilfully violating section 322(a) of the Interstate Commerce Act which prohibited the operation of a motor vehicle by a driver whose attentiveness was impaired by exhaustion and illness, as well as the granting of permission to such a driver to operate a motor vehicle. The corporation had adopted a practice of exerting pressure on its drivers requiring them to continue working even

---

[70] The Act required evidence of the defendant's knowledge of the requirements and specific intention to commit the offence. See Brickey, 1995: 45.

[71] *Bank of New England* at 855-856.

[72] 381 F Supp 730 (1974), hereinafter referred to as *TIME-DC*.

when ill unless they could show a statement from a physician advising the contrary. The wife of a driver that had taken ill called the dispatcher and informed him of her husband's illness, the dispatcher referred her to the corporation's policy and the distressed husband later on called another dispatcher and asked to be placed on call. The court held that the corporation had the collective knowledge of both dispatchers and thus knew that the driver was ill and intended to work in spite of the illness.[73] As such, the information acquired by the employees was aggregated and imputed to the corporation as *mens rea* of the offence created by the Interstate Commerce Act.

These two cases elucidate the primary rule of the aggregation doctrine. This is to the effect that where no employee neither entertained the requisite *mens rea* nor performed the *actus reus* of the offence charged, the intent and knowledge of different employees may be combined together with the relevant deeds of other employees and the aggregate may be imputed to the corporation as *mens rea* and *actus reus* of the offence. In other words, the partial knowledge of one employee may be combined with the partial knowledge of another employee and the sum (full knowledge) may be imputed to the corporation. The logic is that the corporation's act and knowledge constitute the sum of the acts (within the scope of their authority) and knowledge of all of its employees or agents.[74]

This primary rule however invites several questions. It is true that the aggregation of the acts, omissions and states of mind of a corporation's employees involved in a transaction is a more realistic reflection of what was known and done within the corporation than what a single individual (senior manager) knew and did. However, determining the 'corporation's fault' using this theory begs the question of which employees should be considered in the aggregation process and why.[75] This is because some transactions involve a cross-section of employees and information may be obtained from different departments. Thus, if focus is limited to the acts and mental states of senior officers then we would be talking of a variant of the senior management failure test instituted by the CMCHA. If the aggregation should extend to all of the company's personnel regardless of status then we would be talking of a variant of vicarious liability.[76] Equally, if the aggregation should extend beyond the acts of junior

[73] *TIME-DC* at 738.
[74] See Brickey, 1995: 47.
[75] Gobert, 1994: 406. See also Clough and Mulhern, 2002: 107.
[76] See Bucy, 1991: 1157; and Gobert and Punch, 2003: 85.

employees and senior officers to include the organisational indifference as posited in *Bank of New England* then we would be talking yet again of a disguised form of the corporate culture mechanism.[77] The aggregation doctrine therefore brings nothing new to the judge's table and can hardly be said to be more reflective of corporate fault than the other mechanisms that it simply emulates and thereby gives credence to. This muddiness notwithstanding, it would be hasty to discard the aggregation doctrine given that it may nonetheless provide better solutions to some of the problems encountered by the use of the identification doctrine and the senior management failure test in the United Kingdom, as well as those revealed by the evaluation of vicarious liability.

6.3.1 The congruity between the mechanism's primary rule and related legal principles

The identification doctrine sometimes overlaps with vicarious liability in the imposition of liability on corporations for the acts and intentions of their agents. The reasoning underpinning these mechanisms is that the act and intention of a guilty agent (junior employee or senior manager) are a better reflection of the corporation's guilty act and intention. As mentioned in Chapter 5, this position has been criticised for failing to impose liability directly on the corporation by simply compelling it to substitute for its delinquent agent. This criticism is mostly levelled by proponents of the contention that corporate personality (although characteristic of a single entity) is founded on collective responsibility.[78] Hence, acts that are particular to a corporation are those that result from a confluence of acts of its employees or agents. Equally, knowledge particular to a corporation is an aggregate of the information obtained by its employees in their various compartments.[79] The aggregation mechanism may therefore be said to be a more appropriate tool for enforcing crimes against the corporate person given that it is focused on the collective unit and not on any individual who is simply a component element. Thus, where the aggregation doctrine is invoked the focus shifts from the individual employee or manager to the corporate person that is the person that is prosecuted, convicted and sanctioned.

---

[77] This mechanism is discussed below.

[78] See Chapter 2.

[79] Brickey, 1995: 47.

However, the selling point of the mechanism is not the claim that it focuses on the personal or direct liability of corporations[80] but that it focuses on a more realistic conception of the corporation's personality. As such, Gobert[81] posits that rather than proclaiming that an employee or senior officer is the company, it may be more appropriate to begin from the premise that the knowledge of the corporation is the aggregate of the knowledge of all of its employees (including senior managers) and then concluding that there are situations where the knowledge of one of them may be the knowledge of all of them. Nonetheless, in instances where the knowledge required to prove *mens rea* is located in the brain of a single individual, that individual will most probably be a senior manager or a middle-level manager that has been delegated senior management functions. This takes us back to the identification doctrine.[82] Also, Gobert's contention that the corporation's knowledge may in this vein be determined in line with a University Challenge quiz team makes the aggregation doctrine understandable. The University Challenge quiz team is said to know the answer to a question whenever any of its members has knowledge of the correct answer. However, such a team is deemed to know the correct answer whenever any of its members has knowledge of the correct answer because the members concert and agree to put forward an answer as 'their' answer. Where there is no consensus and several members of the team suggest different answers to the umpire, the team cannot be said to know the correct answer even if one of the answers suggested is the correct answer.[83] In the absence of consensus,[84] it is difficult to determine the team's position; it cannot be determined by referring to any one member's opinion because it will not suit the purpose of the enquiry, nor can it be determined by combining the opinions of all members, which may be contrasting.

---

[80] All mechanisms (except vicarious liability to a certain extent) lay claim to this assertion.

[81] 1994: 405.

[82] See Clough and Mulhern, 2002: 108. It is hard to see how an operational employee would apprehend the full import of information obtained by different departments and employees. She can hardly be the agent whose knowledge can be regarded as the knowledge of all.

[83] Lest the umpire decides to accept the answer given by the team leader that happens to be correct.

[84] Consensus certainly founds the agreement that brings the members together in the same light as the nexus of contracts brings employees and managers together.

This requires us to enquire about the process of aggregating the knowledge, acts and omissions of employees that form the corporate entity. What is the sum of employee A's knowledge of a faulty safety mechanism and employee B's lack of knowledge of the faulty safety mechanism?[85] If the sum ought to be the corporation's knowledge, is it possible to obtain such a sum by adding employee A's act that is contrary to corporate policy and employee B's act that was performed with due diligence and in accordance with corporate policy?[86] Looking at the cases where the aggregation doctrine has been applied one wonders how the sum approximated to the requisite *mens rea* and *actus reus* given that some or most of the employees did not entertain any intent to breach the statute or did not perform any act in violation of the statute. Thus, why is it that a wrongful act when added to a conforming act yields a bigger wrongful act (that is attributed to the corporation)? It seems the conforming act has no measurable or determinable value and so the corporation is simply liable because one or a number of its employees performed a wrongful act, in which case it may be concluded that this doctrine is just a fanciful restatement of vicariously liability.[87]

Even if it is accepted that a corporation may have knowledge of more than one thing through different agents, it is important to delineate the temporal context within which the knowledge and acts of the corporation's agents may be aggregated. In the Australian case of *Brambles Holdings Ltd v Carey*,[88] it was held that if employee A obtained information about X and employee B obtained information about Y, the company had knowledge of both X and Y. As such, it may be assumed that if employee A retired, the corporation should logically be held to have continuing knowledge of X.[89] Clough and Mulhern[90] discuss the *El Ajou* case and also cite the Australian case of *Fightvision Pty Ltd v Onisforou* where it was held that "[a] corporation cannot cause itself to shed knowledge by

---

[85] See Gobert, 1994: 406; and Clough and Mulhern, 2002: 109-110.

[86] Another interesting question is the importance of the employee's status on the measurement of her knowledge and acts given that an employee that exerts more influence would most probably impose her opinion on others and those that exert little or no influence can only act on instructions.

[87] See Bucy, 1991: 1157.

[88] (1976) 15 SASR 270 at 275-276 per Bray CJ.

[89] See *El Ajou* at 700 and 706 as per Rose LJ and Hoffmann LJ (as he then was) respectively.

[90] 2002: 111-112.

shedding people."[91] They however argue in line with the trial judge (Miller J) of *El Ajou* that where employee A obtained information about X and retired or left the company, the latter may be said to have "lost its memory" and thus did not possess information about X at the relevant time. However, their argument is based on the assumption that there is no proof that employee A communicated the information to another employee or officer that could be said to be the directing mind. Nonetheless, the importance of the information should be indicative of whether the company had continuing knowledge of it. Proof that at the time that the crime was committed a senior officer (or directing mind) had such knowledge may be implied in accordance with the constructive knowledge rule discussed in Chapter 4.[92] This is because if certain information still enables a corporation to obtain certain benefits, it is more likely that the senior management or board of directors still uses the information. However, where the policy is not criminogenic and the company is reasonably structured but employees A, B, C and D act contrary to corporate policy and by so doing breach the criminal law, they may be said to have acted outwith the scope of their authority and the corporation's liability may in no way be reflected by the combined acts of A, B, C and D.[93] Nonetheless, if an officer obtained information outside her scope of authority or from another agent who had since left the corporation and the information ought to have enabled the corporation to perform a statutory duty, in the event that it failed to perform the duty because the information was considered redundant at some point, the corporation should be liable for the consequences of its poor diligence. However, there is a danger here of extending corporate liability beyond acceptable limits in instances where the information obtained by agents over an unreasonably wide time span are aggregated. It will be unreasonably wide where such information was truly redundant to the current operation of the corporation's activities and its managers and employees could not be expected to still retain such information. Such aggregation that is carried out in an indefinite temporal

---

[91] (1999) 47 NSWLR 473 at 527.

[92] The question of the station of the agent that possessed the knowledge at the relevant time is not as important as the fact that the information was important and ought to have been communicated to the senior management of the corporation given that any reasonable senior management or board of directors would have ensured that such information was communicated to them.

[93] This is equally true of a scenario put forward by Khanna (1999: 375) where a corporation exercises due diligence in ensuring that its employees communicate and consolidate information but is held liable on the ground that the aggregation of the knowledge of its employees amounts to the requisite *mens rea*.

context may be referred to as 'anachronistic aggregation' and involves a major challenge to the process of aggregating the knowledge, acts and omissions of agents.

It may nevertheless be said that the aggregation doctrine reflects the legal principle of corporate personality in a more rational way although its rationale for establishing the corporation's separateness may be clogged by the sophistication required. The aggregation process explained above is also in consonance with other legal principles such as the constructive knowledge of the corporation of information obtained by its agents, as well as its responsibility for the acts of such agents that were intended to further its interests (within the scope of their employment). However, little regard is given to the fact that the individual that obtained the information or performed the requisite *actus reus* could have been acting to further her own selfish interests by defrauding the corporation. Just like the other mechanisms, the corporation will be liable for the act of such a maverick insofar as she acted within the scope of her employment.[94] Given that the courts are required to simply aggregate acts and knowledge of different employees, they may add the fraudulent act of one rogue employee to the information obtained by another employee and the corporation may be held liable for the sum.

The above notwithstanding, this mechanism may be lauded for providing the incentive for more oversight and overcoming the risk of making scapegoats or the disingenuous allocation of tasks susceptible to result in the breach of the law. Whether the method employed by the aggregation doctrine is legitimate from a criminal law perspective is another question. It has been argued that the mechanism operates to punish the corporation for its failure to maintain a proper and effective communication system and enabling its employees consolidate information rather than for intentionally perpetrating an offence.[95] This certainly does

---

[94] This shows that this mechanism equally relies on individualism a little bit more than is necessary.

[95] See Brickey, 1995: 46-47. It may be advanced that given that there is no obligation to obtain information on a particular issue, a corporation may escape liability if no employee has knowledge of what is required. See Khanna, 1999: 375. However, where obtaining such information is an obligation imposed by the law, a corporation would not escape liability on the ground that its employees had no knowledge of the law. Also, if obtaining such information is not a legal obligation but something that each employee in the industry is expected to do then

not prove that that the corporate defendant made a decision to violate the law.[96] Instead, it implies that using the aggregation doctrine for a *mens rea* offence is tantamount to creating a strict liability offence that nonetheless carries a mental element;[97] or worse, components that are not blameworthy are added up to get a blameworthy element of a crime. However, it may be posited that the doctrine provides the most appropriate way of punishing corporations for crimes caused by the acts of their agents/employees without punishing the employees themselves for the acts because no single agent/employee entertained the requisite *mens rea*. But this would certainly require a redefinition of *mens rea*, else one would hardly know what is actually imputed to a corporation and how the process of imputation converts employee A's knowledge of the statutory requirements and employee B's knowledge of a suspicious transaction into an intention to violate the statute (*mens rea*).[98] Apart from policy reasons, which are largely unsatisfactory in developing the theory, there is no cogent explanation of why and how this conversion takes place. Providing stronger motivation for the board of directors or senior management to closely monitor the employees and ensure that they communicate with each other and the hierarchy is a benefit to both the corporation and the society but it does not provide any justification for using the criminal law.

Also, following the reasoning underpinning the decision in *Bank of New England*, there is a possibility that the acts and intentions of employees A, B, C and D may not add up to the *mens rea* and *actus reus*

---

the corporation will not escape liability on the ground of its employees' omission to obtain the information.

[96] See Walsh and Pyrich, 1995: 641.

[97] See Khanna, 1999: 375 and 401-406. He suggests that *mens rea* could be considered an aggravating factor in the sanctioning of corporations for strict liability offences and elaborates on his proposal by putting forth a number of assumptions (some of which are numerical). In spite of the cogency of the proposal, it is worth mentioning that it is founded on the combination of contradictory concepts (strict liability and *mens rea*) and exemplifies a major problem with the aggregation doctrine, which is the undermining of principles of the criminal law, given that in practice courts would have to create *mens rea* by aggregating 'innocent' knowledge and omission even though there was no motive to commit the crime.

[98] Clough and Mulhern (2002: 108-109) warn that "knowledge will rarely fit together like a conceptual jigsaw to produce the desired mental state." They also cite the case of *Armstrong v Strain* [1952] 1 KB 232 at 246 where Birkett J reaffirmed the contention that it is not possible to add one innocent state of mind to another innocent state of mind to get a criminal state of mind.

of the offence charged. In such an instance, the courts may estimate the absence of an effective system to prevent A, B, C and D from breaching the law to be the quantity that may be added to the acts and intentions of these employees to finally get the sum that is the offence charged.[99] It would nonetheless be fair to ask who designed the system and whether such a person or persons did not know or could not foresee that the acts of A, B, C and D (if they were not properly instructed and controlled) would result in the breach of the relevant law. Such a person's poor judgement would be a better reflection of the corporation's fault than the cumulative acts of the employees who were simply submitting to the hierarchy.

It may therefore be said that although the objective intended to be achieved by the aggregation doctrine is commendable, the means indicated (aggregating the knowledge and acts of all or some of the employees) is beset by a number of flaws. These flaws are mainly in the process of aggregating the knowledge, acts and omissions of employees whereby some aspects of some legal principles (agency law and criminal law) are disregarded. Nonetheless, it may also be important to determine whether the primary rule of this mechanism is in consonance with other rules of recognition.

6.3.2 The congruity between the mechanism's primary rule and other rules of recognition

It was established in Chapter 4 that an appropriate mechanism of imputation ought to reflect the normative perspectives expressed by criminal law judges and some non-legal experts. Unfortunately, the aggregation doctrine as employed by courts in the United States hardly reflects the images of "body," "persons," "soul," "head," "alter ego," "brain," "nerve centre," "machine" and "hands." Proponents of aggregation conceive of the corporation as a substantive person that commits crimes by manipulating the individuals in its employment and little regard is given to the person's "head" or "nerve centre" that entertains the intention to manipulate the employees and directs the "body" accordingly. Nonetheless, the aggregation doctrine provides a good picture of how the corporate "machine" functions with several "cogs" or how the "body" functions with different units feeding information through designated

---

[99] *Cf* Clarkson, 1996: 6.

channels and impelling other units to act upon such information.[100] As such, the aggregation doctrine may be said to provide a more substantial justification for treating criminal corporations as defective "machines." However, given that no emphasis is placed on the department or person that acted as the corporation's "brain" or "nerve centre" or "head," the aggregation doctrine may be said to treat the corporation as an acephalous entity. This implies that questions of the management and control of corporate activities are ignored[101] and one may even wonder whether such a corporation has the capacity to commit a criminal offence. Nonetheless, it may be argued that as a distinct person a corporation ought not to be liable for the criminal intention and act of another distinct person (senior manager and employee) but for that which may be said to be particular to the corporation.[102] Thus, the corporation is not identifiable only with the criminal thought of one agent but with the synchronised thought processes of all agents. However, the judges and commentators that have applied this mechanism have proffered little evidence (theoretical or empirical) to support this postulate. It therefore seems that the aggregation doctrine was motivated by reasons of expediency rather than theory as American courts sought to overcome the difficulty of enforcing crimes of intent against corporations in situations where no guilty employee could be identified. That notwithstanding, if certain obstacles (such as delineating the process of aggregation and identifying the corporation's head) are overcome, the mechanism may be said to represent a more sophisticated approach to

---

[100] However, the activities of these units may not always reflect corporate policy and a corporation cannot always control them. See Walsh and Pyrich, 1995: 643-644. Also, in some instances the corporation's fault may be more than the sum of the activities of these units or departments, while in other instances (such as where there are maverick employees) it may be less. That notwithstanding, it may be more appropriate to hold a corporation accountable for the practices and policies of a dissident unit than for the acts and knowledge of a maverick employee.

[101] This may also be the reason why a corporation's liability under this doctrine is unlimited. Given that there is no ascertained way in which a corporation is expected to act and think (and thus no ascertained way of aggregating the acts and intentions of its agents), the knowledge and acts or omissions of all employees are held against the corporation. It is analogous to the situation of an umpire taking into consideration random answers suggested by all members of a rowdy University Challenge quiz team.

[102] In Chapter 8, the principle of "discursive dilemma" that describes how purposive bodies collectivise reason is shown to concur with the aggregation doctrine (and to a certain extent corporate culture) better than the other mechanisms that simply identify corporations with guilty or negligent individuals.

understanding corporations and holding them liable for crimes committed *qua* corporations and not *qua* agents.[103]

It is easier for the aggregation doctrine to come into adjustment with the perspective of non-legal categories because even if the corporate defender employed thousands of workers or had hundreds of branches and irrespective of whether it had adopted a mechanistic or an organic system, the relevant knowledge of any employee or employees and the acts of those that performed the *actus reus* of the crime may be aggregated and held against the corporation. However, the main problem as mentioned above is the unfairness of imputing the knowledge of any agent to the corporation. The knowledge of some agents (middle-level or senior managers) must surely be weightier than that of others (operational employees) given that the knowledge of the former is more likely to be communicated across the corporation or to the board of directors. It may therefore be advanced that the aggregation doctrine reflects the realities of contemporary corporate structures only to the extent that it is based on the assumption that the acts and knowledge of certain employees have more value than the acts and knowledge of others.[104] That notwithstanding, even if it is agreed that the knowledge and acts of agents can be given measurable or determinable values or their judgements may be aggregated into collective judgements, it is still important to show that the assumption or equation that underpins the mechanism approximates reality. In this context, reality connotes the different structural arrangements that may be made by corporations (elucidated by organisation theory).

As such, Mintzberg's Simple Structure Model, the *Noblese Oblige* Model, the Fault-based Individual Responsibility Model, the Nominated Accountability Model, the Autopoiesis Model and the Rational Actor Model[105] all fit within the aggregation paradigm because the knowledge

---

[103] It does not endorse the metonymic description of the human body by referring to its brain or mind only.

[104] The importance of such an assumption lies in the fact that decisions are often made in a corporation either by majority voting in board meetings or by senior managers or empowered middle-level managers. Thus, a corporation's collective judgment as regards a particular transaction is heavily influenced by the most senior agent involved in the transaction, lest the corporation's *modus operandi* is not consistent and businesspersons would seldom invest with such uncertainty.

[105] However, it must be noted that the Rational Actor Model endorses the idea of manipulating the corporation by punishing its responsible agents and agrees with other individualistic models such as the Dramaturgical Model that places emphasis

and acts of the operational employee and the responsible manager that furthered the interests of the corporation in a rational manner would be aggregated.[106] This is equally the case with theories that largely describe the functioning of large and organic structures such as the Organisational Process Model and Machine Bureaucracy Model. This is because the experiences that emerged from established SOPs or policies dictated by the CID would be aggregated with the knowledge of the officers that formulated, implemented and monitored these SOPs.[107] These policies and decisions do not reflect the choice of any particular individual but the collective preference of many individuals at different stations.

From the above, it may be contended that unlike the mechanisms evaluated previously, the aggregation doctrine does not rely on the fault of the corporation's agents as much as it relies on the construction of the corporation's conduct. However, policy considerations and the need to overcome the shortcomings of vicarious liability impelled courts in the United States to hastily employ the aggregation doctrine without setting the theoretical groundwork. As such, there are several theoretical loopholes that mar the logical and consistent use of the mechanism. The process of aggregating the acts, omissions and knowledge of agents (and in some cases the corporation's criminogenic policies) is obscure because these variables have not been given any kind of determinable or additive value. It also remains unclear why the conforming acts of other agents or corporate policies that are compliant with the law are not equally given determinable value and aggregated in order to determine whether the balance tilts towards collective non-compliance or collective diligence. Moreover, the temporal context within which the requisite knowledge, acts and omissions ought to be considered is not defined. Finally, the level of blameworthiness required for each of the individual acts and omissions or

---

on the agent's autonomy and responsibility. The aggregation doctrine is centred on the regulation of corporate behaviour by punishing the corporation itself although it does not preclude the punishment of both the agent and the corporation where only one agent is at fault.

[106] However, under the aggregation doctrine, the corporation will account for the actions and omissions of these individuals and the latter will seldom be held to account in their individual capacities, unless there is evidence that a manager's intention amounts to the requisite *mens rea* of the offence or her omission amounts to negligence as defined by the law.

[107] Nonetheless, as mentioned above, we must assume that the knowledge or act of one employee or manager has a higher measurable value than that of another, although this is not what obtains at present.

intents that are aggregated poses another challenge. In light of these shortcomings, it may be hasty to recommend the application of this doctrine without appropriate solutions.

6.4 The Corporate Culture Mechanism

The idea of holding corporations liable because of a causal link between an existing criminogenic culture and the offence charged was adumbrated by the Dutch Supreme Court in the *IJzerdraad* case,[108] the Australian Criminal Code of 1995 and the CMCHA. Commentators have developed a number of principles of attribution around this idea. Hence, the discussion below focuses on the provisions of the Australian Criminal Code,[109] the CMCHA and a number of cognate models devised by commentators, *viz.* the Self-Identity Model,[110] Corporate Ethos Model[111] and Corporate *Mens Rea* Model.[112] "Corporate culture" is therefore used in this book as a generic term encapsulating the ideas underpinning these principles of attribution, as well as the rules governing the interpretation and the application of the relevant provisions of the Australian Criminal Code 1995 and the CMCHA.[113]

With regard to the Australian Criminal Code 1995, corporate culture is captured by section 12.3(2)(c) and (d) and 12.6 and constitutes the response of the Australian Standing Committee of Attorneys-General from Federal, State and Territory Governments to what it perceived as the insular and rudimentary principle established in *Nattrass*.[114] This mechanism is therefore based on the contention that it is a much better

---

[108] Hoge Raad, February 23, 1954, NJ 378, hereinafter referred to as *IJzerdraad*. For discussion on this case, see Field and Jorg, 1991.

[109] Australian jurisprudence is founded on the common law developed in the United Kingdom. The Australian Courts Act 1828 provided that the laws in force in England would apply in New South Wales (including Victoria and Queensland) and Tasmania. The Interpretation Act 1918 and Interpretation Act 1919 provided the same for Western Australia and South Australia. Also, some Australian cases were referred to the Judicial Committee of the Privy Council before the coming into force of the Australia Act 1986.

[110] Lederman, 2000.

[111] Bucy, 1991.

[112] Clarkson, 1998.

[113] Reference is made to the Dutch Supreme Court's decision in *IJzerdraad* only for purposes of discussing the origin of the idea and understanding the contention by Field and Jorg (1991) that the Dutch position is more appropriate.

[114] See Rose, 1995: 129; and Hill, 2003: 17-18.

reflection of how contemporary corporate structures violate the law.[115] The argument is that mechanisms such as those evaluated above and in Chapter 5 are essentially derivative while this mechanism is based on organisational liability.[116] However, the description of the corporate culture mechanism as representative of organisational liability may be presumptuous given that other mechanisms are equally based on what is perceived as a guidebook for determining an organisation's blameworthiness.[117]

Emphasis is placed on the link between the requisite *mens rea* and the corporation's culture rather than the requisite *mens rea* and the knowledge and action of an agent.[118] This may be understood to imply that "corporate culture" is the corporate equivalent for the intention or mind of a natural person.[119] The Dutch Supreme Court held in *IJzerdraad* that the corporate employer will be liable for the acts of its employee if it exerted control over the employee and if the employee's act was in consonance with accepted practices within the corporation.[120] This bears a likeness to the provisions of section 12 of the Australian Criminal Code 1995 imposing liability on a corporation for amongst other things having a criminogenic

---

[115] See Laufer, 1994: 660; and Clarkson, 1998: 10.

[116] See Robinson, 2008: 68. Unfortunately, proponents of this approach do not distinguish between derivative liability and organisational liability in light of the fact that it is an individual that invariably acts or omits to act.

[117] This is even more so because the term 'corporation' is not defined in criminal law in light of how it should be structured unless one refers to the normative perspective of judges discussed in Chapter 4.

[118] See Colvin, 1995: 36; and Lederman, 2000: 680-681. As advanced by Gobert and Punch (2003: 86), a corporation's liability for gross negligence does not often depend on one agent's negligence or even the aggregated negligence of all agents but on the failure of the corporation to prevent the negligent actions or omissions of its agents.

[119] Hill, 2003: 18. However, it may be argued that the Australian Criminal Code does not adopt this view given that it provides for the examination of a corporation's culture only where there is no evidence that an agent entertained the relevant *mens rea*; and also even if there is no such evidence, the corporation may only be shown to be at fault if the culture was maintained by its board or senior management and it motivated the wrongdoing by the employees. See the Guide for Practitioners (2002: 309) published by the Australian Attorney-General's Department. It may nevertheless still be countered that since a corporation's failure to maintain a culture that prevents wrongdoing by its agents is the basis on which it is held liable (as per the abovementioned Australian Department's interpretation of the Criminal Code 1995), then a corporation's culture may be said to represent its intention or omission. These arguments will be considered below.

[120] See Field and Jorg, 1991: 163-164.

culture. Section 12.6 of the Code 1995 defines corporate culture as "an attitude, policy, rule, course of conduct or practice existing within the body corporate generally or in the part of the body corporate in which the relevant activities takes place." This also bears a likeness to section 8(3)(a) of the CMCHA (although no mention is made of corporate culture) which directs the jury to "consider the extent to which the evidence shows that there were attitudes, policies, systems or accepted practices within the organisation that were likely to have encouraged any…failure...or to have produced tolerance of it."

It is important to note that in both Australian and British systems corporate culture does not constitute the only basis on which the corporation's liability is established.[121] Section 12.2 of the Australian Code provides for the imputation of the physical element of any offence committed by an agent (while acting within the scope of her employment or authority) to the corporation, implying that the corporation is vicariously liable insofar as the offence committed by the agent does not have a mental element.[122] Section 12.3(1) and (2)(a) and (b) of this Code provide for the imputation of a mental element (intention, knowledge or recklessness) to the corporation only if the latter is shown to have authorised or permitted the commission of the offence charged via its board of directors or a high managerial agent or that the board of directors or a high managerial agent intentionally or recklessly perpetrated the offence. This section may therefore be said to predicate the adoption of three mechanisms: vicarious liability, identification and corporate culture.[123] The imposition of liability on the corporation based on the acts or omissions of a high managerial agent is in line with vicarious liability given that "high managerial agent" is defined as "an employee, agent or officer of the body corporate with duties of such responsibility that his or her conduct may fairly be assumed to represent the body corporate's policy."[124] Also, the imposition of liability on the corporation based on the acts or omissions of the board of directors is no doubt evocative of the

---

[121] It is shown in Chapter 5 that the CMCHA revolves around senior management failure and what can be described as a "corporate culture" is provided by the Act only as an indication to this state of affairs.

[122] Hill, 2003: 17.

[123] This is in line with the contention by Gobert and Punch (2003: 87) that an appropriate mechanism ought to provide a number of tools to the prosecutor to use against the accused corporation.

[124] Section 12.3(6). This may thus be any employee or agent, especially in organic structures.

identification doctrine, while evidence of a criminogenic corporate culture is only a third means of establishing the corporation's guilt by showing that the corporation authorised or permitted the commission of the offence. As such, the Australian Criminal Code may be said to provide a framework encapsulating different mechanisms and should be more appropriate in enforcing the criminal law against corporations.[125]

What is important to note is that a culture existing within a corporation is used in the Australian Criminal Code and the CMCHA only as an indicator of whether a corporation (or its senior management) permitted or authorised the commission of an offence. Thus, unlike the recommendations of some commentators cited above, these statutes do not employ corporate culture as a separate mechanism given that they do not direct the prosecution and court on how to locate a corporation's intention, knowledge or recklessness by referring to the corporation's culture but simply advise that in the absence of evidence showing the negligence or failure of specific agents, the existence of a criminogenic culture may be taken as an indicator of such an intention or failure.[126] This means that the approval of the position adopted in the Australian Criminal Code by many commentators is restricted to the introduction of the corporate culture mechanism within the pack.[127]

However, corporate culture may only exist as a separate mechanism if it can be shown to represent a corporation's criminal fault to such an extent that the corporation may be convicted or acquitted based on the fault. If courts have to refer to the intention, knowledge or recklessness of senior managers then they are simply invoking either the senior management failure test or the identification doctrine and have to confront the shortcomings of these mechanisms. Nonetheless, if courts have to

---

[125] Lederman, 2000: 699. Woolf (1995: 262) intimates that vicarious liability and identification may only be used to prosecute small and simple structures while corporate culture would be appropriate for large and complex structures.

[126] If the statutes had provided for the court to refer to the corporate culture in order to determine a corporation's liability irrespective of whether there is any evidence of negligence or failure of a high managerial agent or senior manager, then it could have been said that corporate culture is established as a separate mechanism. Courts in both systems therefore refer to the corporation's existing culture only to determine whether the corporation may be said to have authorised or permitted the commission of the offence charged. However, the absence of any clear outline of such a culture further compromises its use as a mechanism.

[127] See Hill, 2003: 18; and Lederman, 2000: 681.

convict solely on the attitudes, policies, systems or accepted practices existing within the corporation (at all levels) then the need for aggregation may also arise and the challenges facing the aggregation doctrine may have to be overcome. It may therefore be advanced that the corporate culture mechanism is based on the objective of targeting the corporation directly, but in the process of ascertaining the mental state and acts that are particular to the corporation the mechanism overlaps with other mechanisms. It then becomes fair to ask whether it is reasonable to develop a mechanism along the lines of the corporation's culture when it seems to be not a hybrid but an ordered set of other mechanisms.[128] However, Lederman[129] contends that the corporate culture mechanism (he calls it the self-identity doctrine) expands the scope of application of the other mechanisms and completes the development of the theoretical link that courts have sought to establish between the offence charged and the corporation and its agents.[130] Thus, the provisions of the abovementioned statutes foreshadow a more sophisticated mechanism. This means that there is a clearly defined primary rule requiring courts to impose liability on corporations for creating or failing to uproot a culture that encouraged or tolerated non-compliance by agents. Whether the pattern embedded in this rule is more suitable for enforcing crimes against corporations than those evaluated above and in Chapter 5 would depend on how it accords with the rules of recognition.

6.4.1 The congruity between the mechanism's primary rule and related legal principles

As stated above, Lederman contends that this mechanism links the concept of corporate personality with the acts of the agents, the policies and practices that they adopted and the offence they perpetrated. Thus, it shows how an artificial legal entity exercises its volition in particular

---

[128] This does not imply that the provision of different mechanisms (ammunition) to the prosecution by the Australian Criminal Code 1995 or the CMCHA is necessarily flawed. The corporate culture mechanism is evaluated here independently of how it may be used with other mechanisms to regulate corporations. The question of a comprehensive approach capturing salient features of different mechanisms is addressed in Chapter 8.

[129] 2000: 682.

[130] Nonetheless, this is hardly the case with the Australian Criminal Code given that section 12.3(1) and (2)(a) and (b) stipulate that a corporation can be convicted for acts of its agents or employees without any consideration of the corporate culture.

situations and holds regard for its existence in such a way that its self-identity can be established and distinguished from the identity of its members and employees.[131] Lederman also posits that one of the factors that influenced the development of the mechanism was the trend towards theories of rights and obligations of groups or collectivities. Hence, the mechanism reflects realist theories of the corporation's separate existence and independent action and fault.[132] The idea of placing emphasis on the corporation's exercise of volition and its independent actions no doubt accords with the concept of corporation within criminal liability discourse.[133] However, in light of the discussion in the introduction to this section, it may be a little presumptuous to treat the corporate culture mechanism as synonymous to organisational liability. This seems to be more of the objective of the proponents of this mechanism than what obtains in practice and unfortunately the proof of the pudding is not the baker's objective; in as much as the objective may be noble. Unless it is shown that a culture consisting of attitudes, policies, systems or accepted practices existing within the corporation represents a corporation's intention or recklessness, it may be difficult to submit that courts may not look elsewhere to ascertain the corporation's intention or recklessness.[134] Even Lederman[135] concedes that there has been little attempt at formulating a cogent theory that could be used by courts to establish the corporation's mental state on a consistent basis. Also, Fisse and Braithwaite[136] who advance unequivocally that a corporation's policy of non-compliance and collective capacity to prevent the commission of a crime are indicative of its intentionality hardly provide any concise

---

[131] Lederman, 2000: 678.

[132] Lederman, 2000: 680, 684. See also Colvin, 1995: 36.

[133] See Chapter 2. Thus, contrary to mechanisms such as the identification doctrine, senior management failure test and vicarious liability, corporate culture does not (in theory) reduce the corporation's act and intent to those of a single individual or a particular group of individuals. It accords with the contentions of Donaldson (1982) and Gobert (1994) discussed in Chapter 5 that individuals within the corporation such as the senior managers or the collective of managers or directors constitute only one component of the corporation or one aspect of its character and corporate activities in breach of criminal law standards often result from the failure of more than one of such components.

[134] They may look towards the intention or recklessness of the senior officer that managed the relevant transaction or of any employee that was acting under instructions from the senior management.

[135] 2000: 700.

[136] 1993: 25.

explanation of terms such as "policy" and "collective capacity" in order to guide courts when determining the accused corporation's state of mind.[137]

In this light, it is difficult to explicate whether corporate culture is predicated on the liability of the corporate person. It may only be liable if one implies that its liability is vicarious given that the existence of the criminogenic culture only shows that the negligent agent acted within the scope of her authority. However, if the corporation is accused to have been an accessory to the negligent agent then it may escape liability if it shows that its senior management and other agents exercised all due diligence (the culture was not criminogenic) and the negligent agent was a maverick. Conversely, if the senior management exercised all due diligence at their level, the corporation may still be liable for having a criminogenic culture at the operational level that encouraged or tolerated the commission of an offence by middle or operational level employees.[138] In the second instance, although the frontline employees are not acting in accordance with the direct instructions from the senior management, they are still acting within the scope of their employment (and are not rogue employees) because their actions are sanctioned by an existing culture. As such, the corporate culture mechanism does not only reflect the legal principles of maverick agent and scope of employment but also justifies the imposition of liability in cases where junior employees disobey instructions. Equally, a corporation may be said to have had constructive knowledge of the acts of the rogue agents on the ground that the existence of a criminogenic culture indicates failure by the senior management to

---

[137] It may nonetheless be contended that although the concept of "policy" is a nebulous one, it sometimes refers to the directions given by one person (senior manager) or group of persons (board of directors or senior management) responsible for formulating and/or implementing a plan of action. Thus, where it is accepted that policy emanates from these sources only, it would be natural to consider any plan of action drafted and/or adopted by the board of directors or senior management or senior manager as corporate "policy." This would imply that the term 'policy" underpinning the "corporate culture" as used in the Australian Criminal Code is the same as the term "policy" used by the US Model Penal Code (section 2.07(1)) whereby a corporation is liable if "the commission of the offence was authorized, requested, commanded, or performed by the board of directors, or by an agent having responsibility for formation of corporate policy."

[138] Gobert and Punch, 2003: 74. The corporation in such an instance may be said to have two sets of intentions.

foresee that frontline employees would breach the law in circumstances where a hypothetical reasonable senior management would.[139]

It is interesting that corporate culture accords with some important legal principles of agency law although it is not a graft of the civil law. However, the fact that it was specifically devised to hold corporations liable in circumstances where there was no identifiable agent that entertained the relevant *mens rea* or even committed the *actus reus*[140] means that courts may eventually be called upon to impose liability where there may be no proof of *mens rea* and *actus reus* per se. The argument in favour of this approach is that although a corporation is capable of malice and motive there is no evidence (both theoretically and practically) of an ascertained way in which this may be established and any rule describing the mental process of the corporate entity either by referring to one agent or a collective of agents is at best conceptional. Nonetheless, given that corporations invariably act through natural persons and *mens rea* can only be established with regard to the intentions of natural persons, those mechanisms that provide for a form of derivative (not vicarious) liability are more in keeping with the criminal law than mechanisms such as corporate culture that require courts to establish a special form of corporate *mens rea*.[141] On the face of this, the corporate culture mechanism may be said to fall outside the regulatory framework of the criminal law as regards the enforcement of crimes of intent. However, it may then be posited that this mechanism may enable a court to distinguish between acts and intentions particular to the corporate entity and those particular to its agents and thereby focus on corporate *mens rea*[142] and corporate *actus reus*.[143] That notwithstanding, given that the proponents of

---

[139] It must be noted that it is difficult to establish the existence of a criminogenic culture without recourse to senior management failure and it is difficult to establish the latter without recourse to the identification of the directing mind.

[140] Difficulties that mar other mechanisms such as the identification doctrine and vicarious liability.

[141] As such, Clarkson (1998) describes this mechanism or an outline of its attributes as the corporate *mens rea* model.

[142] The development of the concept of corporate *mens rea* may lower the level of blameworthiness required, make the prosecution of corporations easier and lessen the impact of the entire criminal process.

[143] It may be argued here that it provides an opportunity for these collective theories to develop the criminal law in light of the knowledge of new kinds of offenders (corporations) and novel ways of transgression (collective offending). However, if this were the case, the idea of corporate culture would have been expressed as a secondary rule and not as a primary rule (statute or precedent).

this approach have not shown how the accused corporation may entertain the specific intent and perform the specific act (required by the law), it may be said that the corporation may only be guilty for being an accessory by maintaining a defective compliance programme and not for personally committing the offence as charged.[144]

6.4.2 The congruity between the mechanism's primary rule and other rules of recognition

This mechanism may to be said to provide (to a certain extent) a channel for applying the criminal law to corporations in light of the characteristic features of corporate entities that may be abstracted from the outlook of criminal law judges. Even though it is difficult to pinpoint any equivalent for images such as "body," "head," "soul," "brain," "nerve centre," "hands" and "directing mind and will," what is important is that criminal law judges cited in Chapter 4 intimated that the prosecution of a corporation is analogous to that of a "person" who is psychologically autonomous. Thus, the corporate culture mechanism effectively shows how this can be done, albeit with a few modifications. The identification doctrine that was built around these metaphors has been enmeshed by their literal definitions to the extent that the mechanism shows little flexibility as regards moving beyond what has been seen as an attempt at anthropomorphism.[145] However, the corporate culture mechanism may be said to be based on the figurative meaning of the terms mentioned above (which is in consonance with their use as metaphors) and focuses on what may constitute a corporation's "brain" or "nerve centre" and why and how its "brain" is separate from its "body." Thus, the attitudes, practices and policies existing within a corporation are held to be indicative of its reasoning.

Equally, other mechanisms such as the identification doctrine, vicarious liability and the senior management failure test were shown to identify an

---

[144] Given that accessorial liability also requires specific intent it may be ruled out and only the failure to maintain an effective compliance programme (low level of culpability) may be plausible. However, it is uncertain whether this may be held to be a criminogenic culture and the question whether a court should employ an objective test or a subjective test in this regard remains to be answered.

[145] This is because this mechanism is based on the contention that such images represent natural persons that make up the corporation and the job of the prosecutor is to find the individual that was empowered to control the corporate body (under all circumstances) like the "brain" controls the "body."

individual manager or employee or a collective of managers as the "brain" or "nerve centre" although there are instances where the breach of the law is related to the corporation's activities and not the fault of an individual or a restricted group of individuals. Moreover, given that the acts of different individuals may at different times reflect different attitudes and practices, the corporation's reasoning may not be inferred from one source only. Its nerve centre may be manager A and employee B in one instance and manager C and employee B in another instance. The corporate culture mechanism (and to a certain extent the aggregation doctrine)[146] provides the opportunity for the courts to consider the effects of the confluence of actions of different individuals. The contention that the "brain" or "nerve centre" may not necessarily be an individual but the collective attitudes, policies and practices that motivate employees or managers to act on behalf of the corporation is therefore more characteristic of an entity that exists as a collective unit. Thus, it may be contended that judges employed metaphors such as "brain" and "directing mind" to make a comparison between an organism with distinct units or organs and a corporation with distinct units and persons. However, the judges may not be deemed to have insinuated that the corporation's "brain" or "directing mind" represents a wide range of persons and units, which may be disparate. As such, it is very unlikely that they sought to establish that corporations could be held accountable for the attitudes of frontline employees irrespective of the policies formulated by the hierarchy. This shows that the primary rule of the corporate culture mechanism ought to be modified to take into consideration the acts of the corporation's "directing mind" when determining its culture.

In Chapter 4, rules of recognition were also shown to emanate from non-legal categories and stress was laid on a framework (the contingency approach) within which a number of theories describing the functioning of organisations were fitted. It was noted that an appropriate mechanism for imputing acts and intents to corporations ought to reflect these theories because courts entertain cases of corporations that are not similarly structured. The ways in which corporations could be structured (in response to contingencies) were grouped under mechanistic and organic systems. The mechanisms evaluated above (except the aggregation

---

[146] As noted above, the aggregation doctrine simply describes (albeit unconvincingly) the process by which such collective attitudes and practices may be ascertained but does not provide any justification for finding recourse in such a process. Thus, the fact that the corporate culture mechanism is not founded on the delineation of such a process is also a flaw that needs to be addressed.

doctrine) are shown to be largely focused on mechanistic systems. However, the corporate culture mechanism provides an option of holding corporations accountable for crimes that are caused or aided by the synthesis of the activities of different agents at different stations. As such, it does not accord with organisation theories that largely describe mechanistic systems such as the Rational Actor Model, Mintzberg's Simple Structure Model, the *Noblese Oblige* Model, the Fault-based Individual Responsibility Model and the Autopoiesis Model. This implies that it would be difficult to use the corporate culture mechanism to target a corporation with a simple hierarchical structure in a situation where the offence is perpetrated by a senior officer although there was no existing culture that motivated or tolerated her action.[147] Equally, theories such as the Organisational Process Model and Machine Bureaucracy Model that favour the imposition of liability on agents that formulate, implement and monitor SOPs and control the bargaining processes do not reflect the logic that underpins corporate culture given that these models are geared towards targeting the individuals that formulated or implemented the SOPs and not the SOPs themselves.[148]

The corporate culture mechanism may however be held to be more adaptable to the enforcement of the criminal law against organic structures. Where the management of different activities has been delegated to separate departments, it may be difficult to hold the corporation liable by referring only to the acts of a particular senior manager or the senior management. As such, where a criminogenic practice was adopted in one department the corporation may be liable if

---

[147] This takes us back to the definition of "culture" and related concepts such as "corporate policy" and "accepted practices." This is because it may be argued that if the senior officer sought to further the interests of the corporation, then she may be said to have been motivated by an existing culture (of making profits). However, such a culture was not criminogenic. Just as in the case of the aggregation doctrine, proponents of the corporate culture mechanism have not provided guidelines on how relevant values and experiences may be sifted from irrelevant ones in order to determine whether the accused corporation had a criminogenic culture or not.

[148] However, corporate liability may be established by evidence showing that the SOPs (and to a certain extent the bargaining processes) motivated non-compliance. See Gobert and Punch, 2003: 88; and Field and Jorg, 1991: 164.
Nonetheless, in light of compliance programmes they may seldom be criminogenic and the culture that motivated non-compliance may often be ascertained by looking beyond the SOPs and considering the attitudes and practices existing unofficially.

such a practice encouraged employees within that department to breach the law. Equally, where loosely related experts are brought on ad hoc projects and left to work without guidelines and control, their actions if motivated by the lack of control would be imputed to the corporation. This means that the corporate culture mechanism is congruent with theories such as Adhocracy and Dramaturgical Model. However, other theories such as the Divisionalised Form and the Nominated Accountability Model (that are discussed as organic conceptions in Chapter 4) may only be congruent with the corporate culture mechanism if the criminogenic culture is ascertained by referring to the activities of the heads of the relevant units.[149]

However, in both instances (mechanistic and organic), courts would have to overcome the difficulty of ascertaining what constitute 'quantities' such as policies, practices and attitudes that are used to define corporate culture in order to determine whether a criminogenic culture existed in each instance. It may also be important to determine whether the fact that the culture existed within one branch or department may be understood to imply that it existed within the entire corporation in order to hold it liable, even though other departments or branches exercised all due diligence.[150] It seems courts would have to first of all aggregate the acts and knowledge of the employees and managers in each department in order to determine whether a criminogenic culture existed within each department; and then aggregate the cultures existing within all departments in order to determine whether there was a criminogenic corporate culture; and then decide whether the act that breached the law was encouraged or tolerated by that corporate culture. Thus, corporate culture as a separate mechanism faces the same problems as the aggregation doctrine, which includes *inter alia* giving determinable values to the acts and knowledge of the corporation's agents, as well as to the practices and policies that existed within each department.[151]

---

[149]Once again, this shows that the primary rule of this mechanism ought to be modified to take into consideration the acts of the corporation's "directing mind" when determining its culture. However, in this case the "directing mind" is the person that had control over the relevant activities.

[150] Following *Nattrass*, it seems the corporation will not be liable if the department or branch was only one of several. However, *Nattrass* did not consider the question of corporate culture.

[151] This may even involve a more tortuous computation than is required by the aggregation doctrine given that large corporations have thousands of employees

It may be concluded that the emphasis on collective failure provides impetus for claims that the corporate culture mechanism is a better reflection of organisational liability. It is an attempt to improve upon the shortcomings of other mechanisms. However, to claim that it is more appropriate than other mechanisms is presumptuous given the uncertainty of what constitutes 'corporate culture' and the lack of clarity as regards how the prosecution may show that such a culture existed within a corporation and motivated or tolerated non-compliance. There is no doubt a strong possibility that this mechanism, if properly developed, may provide a suitable means of enforcing crimes committed by a corporation *qua* corporation.[152] Nonetheless, corporations would most likely be held liable as accessories and not as principal offenders since the existence of a criminogenic culture presupposes the corporation aiding and abetting the commission of an offence by another person (its agent). As suggested in Chapter 3, this may be the appropriate form of liability to impose on corporations in cases where the offence may be proved against one of its agents.

6.5 Conclusion

In Chapter 5, the mechanisms of imputation applicable in the United Kingdom were evaluated and a number of loopholes were identified. In this Chapter, I have evaluated some alternative mechanisms applicable in other jurisdictions and/or proposed by some commentators and have shown that they are equally flawed and require modifications. The evaluations in both Chapters therefore support the statement that no single theory can effectively capture the realities of the functioning of contemporary corporate structures in order to serve as a template for the regulation of the activities of corporations. Nonetheless, some mechanisms are more suited to deal with certain issues than others. As such, the most appropriate mechanism is logically that which can be modified to suit issues that it does not effectively address.[153] Such a modified mechanism would provide the prosecution with an arsenal consisting of diverse

---

and hundreds of departments. The daunting prospect of such an endeavour may no doubt push the prosecution into looking for more expeditious channels.

[152] Although this may equally be said of the other mechanisms.

[153] Given that each mechanism is confronted with specific problems it is important to determine which one has the most potential of being modified to such an extent that it may be used by courts in a consistent and coherent manner.

weapons in order to deal with the diverse forms of corporate entities and corporate offending under justifiable circumstances.[154]

The alternative mechanisms were evaluated above on the basis of how they accord with rules described in Chapter 4 as rules of recognition. As regards the first set of rules of recognitions (rules deduced from related legal principles), separate corporate personality was shown to be reflected in the primary rules of the three mechanisms, although the channel for establishing the corporation's personal liability using vicarious liability is undoubtedly sinuous. The aggregation doctrine provides a more logical approach whereby the act and knowledge of a corporate person are ascertained by combining the knowledge and acts of all or some of its employees. The corporate culture mechanism on its part focuses on the corporation's policies and its collective capacity (including accepted practices, attitudes and systems) to prevent the commission of an offence by its agents. However, given that the acts and knowledge of agents have to be aggregated in order to determine what is a collective attitude or practice, it may be contended that aggregation (although not as elucidated via the aggregation doctrine) provides a justifiable medium of grappling with the sophistication required in criminal law to prosecute, convict and sanction corporate persons.[155] However, as mentioned above, the process

---

[154] As shown above, Australian and British legislators (and to a certain extent the Dutch Supreme Court) have attempted to provide their prosecution services with such an arsenal. However, their attempts leave much to be desired because what they have done is simply stuff one wrapping with a number of mechanisms and this runs the risk of creating a situation where the corporation's liability becomes over inclusive. If for example, the prosecution cannot prove the guilt of the accused corporation because it cannot identify a grossly negligent "high managerial agent" or "senior management" it can then establish the corporation's guilt by adducing evidence of the existence of a criminogenic culture that encouraged or tolerated non-compliance. This is no doubt unfair to the accused corporation as its liability is almost absolute in spite of the fact that most of its managers and employees may have exercised all due diligence and complied with the law in both instances. Equally, in spite of the fact that the attempt at providing the prosecution with such an arsenal is laudable, the Australian Criminal Code 1995 and the CMCHA fall short of delineating the process by which an incriminating element such as the existence of a criminogenic culture may be established.

[155]The prosecution would have to aggregate policies, practices and systems (corporate culture), as well as the acts of those that were involved in the relevant transactions. Where the corporation's act and knowledge are the same as those of its sole agent then the aggregation would involve combining her acts and

of aggregating may be marred by a daunting complexity since the intent, knowledge, acts and omissions of agents, as well as the policies, practices and systems existing within the corporation would have to be given additive or determinable values. Also, it may be important to determine whether there was a balance between the conforming and non-conforming acts.[156]

With regard to the rules deduced from agency law (maverick agent, scope of employment and constructive knowledge), the alternative mechanisms were shown to be congruent. As such, if the notion of aggregation is upheld as the most realistic conception of corporate personality then it may be submitted that courts should aggregate only those acts that were performed by agents within their scope of employment. These exclude acts performed by maverick agents but include those that the corporation knew or ought to have known. In order to determine whether the corporation had constructive knowledge, aggregation would equally be required although the knowledge or omission of some agents would be given a higher value than those of others. These are the agents that were responsible for obtaining such information and/or controlling the relevant transactions. The importance of identifying such agents is demonstrated by the fact that the uncertainty as regards the pattern and scope of aggregation will be reduced. Hence, the act or omission of the agent that had control is an indication of what was known or ought to have been known by a cross-section of the corporation's agents given that she ought to have apprehended the full import by virtue of her position.[157]

It may then be argued that the *actus reus* and *mens rea* of the offence in question has been proved against the corporation itself and not its agents. Nonetheless, this assertion has no basis in criminal law as there is no thing as corporate *mens rea* or corporate *actus reus*. Thus, although there is no undue focus on the fault of one of the agents (vicarious liability), the emphasis placed on the corporation's fault (organisational

---

knowledge and the policies she formulated as the corporation's sole member and imputing the sum to the corporation.

[156] An attempt is made to delineate the process of aggregation in Chapter 8.

[157] This may also modify the aggregation doctrine to suit the "internal point of view" of judges that is to the effect that a corporation is analogous to a body with a head and limbs.

liability) is not legitimate.[158] Equally, although courts may convict large and organic corporate structures following this means, the question of the sophistication required to deal with such corporations should not be allowed to trump the question of fairness. As shown above, the most sophisticated mechanisms may facilitate the prosecution and conviction of corporations while undermining some fundamental principles of the criminal law and the rights of the accused corporation.[159] On the other hand, the identification doctrine and vicarious liability are based on the proof of fault of an agent and the senior management failure test is also based on the proof of gross negligence of the senior management.[160] These simple mechanisms reflect the fairness of convicting the corporation of a *mens rea* offence where the requisite *mens rea* is established *simpliciter*. However, the aggregation and the corporate culture mechanisms seem to change the rules as regards what amounts to *mens rea* in order to hold the corporation liable. The conviction of the corporation for a number of 'innocent' acts and intents is no doubt unfair to the corporate person and may lead to the conclusion that these mechanisms are lopsided towards the policy goal of sanctioning the corporation and should not be used to enforce crimes of intent.

Also important is the fact that none of the alternative mechanisms evaluated above may be said to reflect the normative perspective of judges described through metaphors. They may only be modified to suit this perspective if one agent is identified as the directing mind. However, as regards the secondary rules deduced from non-legal categories, all of the mechanisms were shown to accord with the theories in one way or another and the question seems to be one of interpretation.

The above notwithstanding, there are other secondary rules that may equally be important to the evaluation of the primary rules of all

---

[158] It is therefore important to determine whether a criminogenic culture may be said to constitute *mens rea*.

[159] In spite of the complexity of mechanisms such as aggregation and corporate culture, their application may nevertheless simply facilitate the prosecution of the accused corporations by converting crimes of intent into absolute liability offences. This ironically reflects the easy way out of vicarious liability and policy considerations adopted by courts to circumvent the rigidity of the identification doctrine.

[160] However, as shown in the Chapter 5, the senior management failure test relies heavily on the civil law concept of "reasonable standard" which is not always compatible with the stigma of criminal liability.

mechanisms of imputation. In accordance with Hart's conception of rules, these other rules may be termed "rules of adjudication." These are rules that govern the proof and deliberation stages of the criminal justice process. As such, convincing the jury or judge would require more than a viable mechanism based on substantive law. An appropriate mechanism of imputation should equally enable the prosecution to establish that there is sufficient admissible evidence to convict the accused corporation. Also, the mechanism ought to inform the court about the most appropriate sanction to impose on the corporation. In the next Chapter, I will seek to determine which of the five mechanisms of imputation evaluated is the most suitable as regards prosecuting and sanctioning corporations or whether features of these mechanisms may be captured to build a comprehensive mechanism.

CHAPTER SEVEN

EVALUATING THE MECHANISMS WITH REFERENCE TO THE RULES OF ADJUDICATION

7.1 Introduction

> "Procedural justice must not be sacrificed on the altar of substantive justice."[1]

The criminal justice process involves three major stages namely the discovery, proof and deliberation stages.[2] The discovery stage involves the investigation that precedes the trial and in the case of a corporation, the examination of the link between the corporation and the offence in accordance with the applicable mechanism of imputation. As such, it may be said that the evaluations of the mechanisms in Chapters 5 and 6 were geared towards determining which mechanism (or which aspects of the mechanisms) is most appropriate for the discovery stage. It follows that it is also important to determine which mechanism is most appropriate for the proof and deliberation stages which comprise the trial (adduction of evidence) and the deliberation on whether to convict and which sanction should be imposed. In line with Hart's conception of legal rules, the proof and deliberation stages may be said to be governed by rules of adjudication.[3] Questions about such rules are important because in light of the above-captioned statement by Fisse and Braithwaite, it would be counterproductive for the criminal law if procedural justice is expediently forfeited for the validation of substantive rules.

The corporate maze presents a unique challenge to investigators and prosecutors who are required to adduce sufficient evidence of key elements

---

[1] Fisse and Braithwaite, 1993: 136.
[2] See Schum, 1986; and Jackson, 2004.
[3] See Hart, 1994: 97-99.

of crimes in order to establish the corporation's guilt. It is uncertain whether the corporate defender should be treated like an accused natural person or whether it is advisable to formulate rules of evidence and procedure that are tailored to the corporate entity[4] in the same way as rules are tailored to minors and the mentally deficient. Also, as shown in Chapter 3, there are offences that are enforced against duty-holders in circumstances where Parliament has ordained that some of the rights of these duty-holders may be disregarded.[5] However, the enactment of tailor-made rules should not be motivated by the desire to circumvent procedural difficulties and make conviction easier. It would be wanton and foolhardy to ignore the fact that as a legal person a corporation has rights that must be protected and regard for these rights go a long way towards safeguarding the integrity of the criminal justice system. Without a cogent argument positing the contrary it may therefore be advanced that courts are required to treat corporations in the same way as natural persons despite the nature of corporations.[6] This means that the prosecution must adduce evidence before a jury of an accused corporation's peers showing beyond reasonable doubt that the corporation perpetrated the offence charged or was art and part in its commission.

Thus, this Chapter is focussed on the challenges of prosecuting and sanctioning corporations using the mechanisms of imputation evaluated in Chapters 5 and 6. The first part will consider rules of adjudication that govern the prosecutorial decision-making process and the second part will look into the rules of adjudication guiding the court and/or criminal justice agency through the deliberation stage involving the decision to convict and the choice of sanction to be imposed. The objective is to determine which mechanism (or aspects of which mechanisms) reflects these rules and guides the prosecution and the court and/or the criminal justice agency efficaciously.

---

[4] See Gobert and Punch, 2003: 179-182.

[5] For example, the enforcement of absolute and strict liability offences requires the disregard of the right to be presumed innocent. Equally, the trial of cases in the Magistrate's Court by a single magistrate or in the District Court by a single Justice of the Peace implies that the right to be tried by a jury of one's peers is disregarded. However, it is difficult to argue that the same should apply to indictable crimes of intent or solemn cases.

[6] See section 46 of the Magistrate's Court Act 1980.

7.2 Rules governing the prosecutorial decision-making process

The Codes for prosecutors in Scotland and England[7] provide for a twofold process for assessing cases before prosecution. This comprises the evidential test and the public interest test.[8] They require the prosecutor to determine on the one hand whether the accused committed the offence and there is a reasonable prospect of conviction and on the other hand, whether it is in the interest of the public to bring an action against the accused.[9] This section is concerned with the congruity between the mechanisms of imputation evaluated in Chapters 5 and 6 and these tests. I will attempt to determine which mechanism provides the most cogent basis for the prosecutor to establish that an accused corporation ought to be prosecuted.

7.2.1 The evidential test

If evidence adduced by the prosecutor is not admissible before a criminal law court the case will be dismissed or the accused acquitted irrespective of how persuasive and incriminating the evidence seems to be. As such, the evidential test does not rest actually on the question of sufficient evidence but on sufficient admissible evidence. This means that the prosecutor is required to examine the evidence available and decide whether such evidence is both admissible and sufficient.[10] This may be quite problematic in cases involving corporations. As regards the sufficiency of evidence, the prosecutor is faced with the challenge of establishing key elements of the offence that point clearly to the corporate defender as the 'person' that committed the offence. Given that a corporation may only entertain the *mens rea* or perform the *actus reus* of an offence via the agency of natural persons, such evidence must show that the natural persons that entertained the *mens rea* or performed the *actus reus* are identifiable with the corporation. This implies that the evidence must not only establish the key elements of the offence against

[7] Prosecution Code, 2001 and Code for Crown Prosecutors, 2004 respectively.

[8] The tests may also be used by criminal justice agencies that prosecute specific offences. Although there is no requirement that the tests must be applied to bring private prosecution (see Jackson, 2007: 777) their application may considerably enhance the chances of success and also help avert situations where the DPP requests the court to stop the prosecution because it is "vexatious."

[9] The objective of elaborating these tests is to foster efficiency and consistency in prosecutorial decision-making. See Crisp and Moxon, 1994: 1.

[10] See Crisp and Moxon, 1994: 1-2; and Rogers, 2006: 777.

such natural persons but also point to the relationship between the natural persons and the accused corporation warranting the imputation of the former's intents and acts to the latter. Where the identification doctrine or vicarious liability applies, a case cannot pass the evidential test if the evidence does not establish the key elements of the offence against a single senior officer or single employee of the corporation. The focus on individual actions is deplored in Chapters 5 and 6 on the ground that in most cases the *actus reus* is the result of the combination of the acts of several agents while the *mens rea* is often reflected in the policies and practices adopted within the corporation. However, it is also unclear how a case will pass the evidential test where the applicable mechanism is based on collective liability (such as the senior management failure, aggregation and corporate culture mechanisms). This is because there is no defined pattern on how to combine the acts and knowledge of the agents and how to impute the combined acts (that constitute the *actus reus*) and combined knowledge and intentions (that constitute the *mens rea*) to the corporate defender.[11] This means that the case against a corporation may only pass the evidential test if the process of aggregation is delineated and standardised to such an extent that the prosecutor may adduce evidence showing that the sum of the acts and knowledge of certain agents (which are particular to the corporation) is equal to the *actus reus* and the *mens rea* of the offence charged. Thus, on the one hand, the simple mechanisms (identification doctrine and vicarious liability) pass the evidential test in straightforward cases (where the guilty agent may be identified) but are ineffective in complex cases (where the guilt is collective). On the other hand, the complex mechanisms (senior management failure, aggregation and corporate culture) are ineffective in both straightforward and complex cases although they may be modified to establish the corporate person's guilt in both instances.

The discussion below is focussed on the question of admissibility of evidence and the challenge faced by prosecutors and courts as regards giving careful consideration to the rights enjoyed by the accused corporation. The rights examined below may render evidence inadmissible if they are violated. Hence, an appropriate mechanism of imputation ought to enable prosecutors and courts to adduce sufficient evidence without encroaching upon these rights.

---

[11] As noted in Chapter 5, the collective knowledge of senior managers may not necessarily represent the collective knowledge of all the agents of the corporation.

7.2.1.1 The corporation's right to silence[12]

An accused in both England and Scotland is protected from incriminating herself by producing documents or providing answers that would make her accessible to a criminal charge. This is enshrined in Article 6 of the European Convention on Human Rights.[13] In *Triplex Safety Glass Co Ltd v Lancegaye Safety Glass Ltd*,[14] the court held that a corporation is entitled to such protection.[15] However, where a corporation is on trial the bulk of the evidence comprises policy documents (usually from the hierarchy) as well as documents containing information on the division of labour, instructions from different departmental heads and reports of employees to their respective heads and from the latter to the hierarchy. If the corporation invokes the right to silence, it is difficult to see how the prosecutor may obtain any evidence whatsoever to sustain the charge;[16] and if the documents are obtained forcibly, the evidence will not be admissible.[17]

As such, the prosecution of a corporation may be more successful where the prosecutor does not rely on evidence that may be obtained from the corporation itself. This implies that where the corporation's liability

---

[12] This right is treated here as identical to the privilege against self-incrimination although they are not altogether the same rights. See Gobert and Punch, 2003: 196, footnote n. 17. It is also treated as related to the legal professional privilege or confidentiality of communications since the end result is that the corporation or its counsel cannot be compelled to disclose information.

[13] See *Saunders v United Kingdom* [1997] 23 EHRR 313.

[14] [1939] 2 KB 395.

[15] See also *Rio Tinto Zinc Corporation v Westinghouse Electric Corporation* [1978] 1 All ER 434. For arguments for and against the maintaining of such a privilege, see Queensland Law Reform Committee Report, 2004: 23-30. For a brief analysis of the logical underpinning of the privilege against self-incrimination with regard to how it has developed in the United States, see Fisse and Braithwaite, 1993: 148; and Gobert and Punch, 2003: 196-199. For arguments for and against the extension of the legal professional privilege to corporate entities, see Higgins, 2008.

[16] Although sections 34 and 35 of the Criminal Justice and Public Order Act 1994 (applicable in both England and Scotland) provide that the jury or judge may draw adverse inferences where the right is invoked or where the accused declines to testify in her own trial, what is important to note here is that the right is recognised and protected in the United Kingdom and may be invoked by a corporation.

[17] See for example, section 20(7) of the HSWA and section 69 of the Environmental Protection Act 1990 (EPA).

can be established by showing that the offence was perpetrated by one of its agents while acting within the scope of her employment, the case is likely to pass the evidential test since there is little need for evidence showing that the corporation's hierarchy authorised or encouraged the act.[18] Thus, if vicarious liability is the applicable mechanism, there is a higher probability of adducing sufficient admissible evidence. This may also be said to be the case with the identification doctrine although the prosecutor would be required to set out the corporation's organigramme in order to show that the person guilty is of sufficient station to be identified with the corporation or the persons whom the senior officer directed acted within the scope of their authority.[19] However, as stated above, there are several instances where no responsible agent may be identified although a causal link may be established between the offence and the corporation's activities. In such cases, the corporation's guilt may only be proved by evidence of the knowledge of certain agents of the risks of the activities or their indifference to such risks. The prosecutor would then have to obtain documents that attest to the negligence of these agents and it is uncertain how this may be done if the corporation asserts its privilege against self-incrimination.

The Office of Fair Trading (OFT), Serious Fraud Office (SFO) and the Health and Safety Executive (HSE) have the power to compel witnesses to provide information, but in the case of HSE investigations, such information cannot be used against the person that provided them.[20] This is no doubt a grey area as it is uncertain whether the HSE would use the information against a corporation where the evidence was provided by an agent that cannot be identified with it. Thus, where a corporation invokes the privilege against self-incrimination it is uncertain whether it may be understood to mean that all senior officers are barred from providing evidence or that the prosecutor may not obtain evidence from any agent whatsoever. According to the identification doctrine, the corporation may only be identified with a single senior officer and the senior management failure test extends the frame to the collective of senior managers. Where both mechanisms apply (such as in the United Kingdom) it may be difficult to state that any information obtained from junior managers and operational staff was provided by the corporation. However, no mechanism has been applied with such consistency. *Belmont* established that where the corporation was the targeted victim the fraudulent senior

[18] It will be incumbent on the corporation to show that the agent was a maverick.

[19] See *Edwards v Brooks (Milk Ltd)* [1963] 3 All ER 62.

[20] See section 20(2)(j) of the HSWA.

manager is not the corporation and *British Steel* held the corporation liable for the acts of junior employees in breach of an absolute duty. As such, if it is posited that the identification doctrine applies for crimes committed by corporations (except absolute liability offences, corporate manslaughter or corporate homicide and instances where it was the targeted victim) then where a senior officer makes a statement against her corporate employer, such a statement may not be used against the corporation since the senior officer, for the purposes of the criminal law, is the corporation.[21] Nonetheless, courts have conveniently ignored the identification doctrine in cases where corporations invoked the right to silence. They have maintained that only the person (senior officer) that makes the statement may be protected against self-incrimination and the information provided may be used to prosecute the corporation (as a separate person) for the commission of an offence.[22]

These decisions are indicative of policy considerations and are quite innocent of principle. It is also unfortunate that the identification doctrine is still held out as the applicable mechanism in spite of its disregard in numerous instances. An officer cannot be treated as a person distinct from the corporation for the purpose of obtaining information from her and then identified with the same corporation for the purpose of imposing criminal liability on it. It is both unfair and incoherent. If this exception is added to that of absolute liability offences and instances where the corporation was the targeted victim then what is left for the observer is a patchwork of fitful applications of the law in the name of corporate criminal liability.

It may nevertheless be argued that an individual may qualify as a corporation's directing mind in one instance and not in another, the determining factor being whether the individual had plenary authority over the transaction under consideration.[23] This would imply that where manager A does not exercise authority over the transaction under

---

[21] It must be noted that in *Saunders v United Kingdom*, statements provided by Saunders, former chief executive officer of Guinness, under compulsion but in accordance with section 432(2) of the Companies Act 1985 were used against him in a subsequent trial. He complained to the European Court of Human Rights and this Court held that his complaint was well founded.
[22] See *Tate Access Floors Inc v Boswell* [1990] 3 All ER 303; *Walkers Snack Foods Ltd v Coventry City Council* [1998] 3 All ER 164; and *R v Hertfordshire County Council ex parte Green Environmental Industries Ltd and another* [2000] 1 All ER 773.
[23] See Chapter 5.

consideration but manager B does, a statement made by manager A incriminating both the company and manager B may be used against the latter two, the company being liable because it can only be identified in the circumstances with manager B. This means that the identification doctrine may only be effective where the manager or employee that provides the information is not the directing mind for the purpose of the offence that will be charged subsequently. Thus, the prosecution may compel junior managers or operational staff to make statements that may incriminate the senior managers and the corporation. However, where the evidence required are policy documents, minutes of board meetings and deliberations at the senior management level, it is seldom that junior managers and operational employees would be privy to such information. Moreover, the argument of manager A and manager B does not always hold water because a decision to dispose of waste in violation of the law may be made by members of the board of directors with none of them in particular having plenary authority over waste disposal. Any statement made by any of the members would automatically incriminate both herself and the company and should not be admissible if the corporation invokes the right to silence. This shows that the identification doctrine breaks down when confronted with the corporation's right to silence.

Nonetheless, it is uncertain whether there is a better alternative. The senior management failure test is confronted with the same obstacles as the identification doctrine given that it is equally focused on the acts of senior managers. On the other hand, where vicarious liability, aggregation and corporate culture are applied the corporation may be liable for the acts of any of its employees. Thus, if the corporation invokes the privilege against self-incrimination the investigators would naturally be prevented from obtaining information from any employee. If we agree that the argument that information incriminating a corporation may be obtained from any employee insofar as it does not incriminate the employee herself is not tenable in a court of logic then it may be difficult to find a defensible way of permitting the prosecutor to obtain information that may be crucial to its case where a corporation defiantly invokes the privilege against self-incrimination. This is because the privilege against self-incrimination ought to impose a code of silence on all of its agents.

However, the imposition of a code of silence on all agents may only be true with respect to vicarious liability. Under the aggregation and corporate culture mechanisms, a corporation is often the sum of the acts and knowledge of only some of its agents. This implies that in one instance the acts of manager A and the knowledge of manager B may be aggregated and imputed to the corporation while in another instance, the directives from manager A and the act of employee C may be aggregated and imputed to the corporation.[24] Also, where no single manager had plenary authority over the transaction under consideration, the acts of all agents (members of the board of directors for example) that had plenary authority may be aggregated. The sum should also include the policies and practices and the attitudes that motivated the actions of managers A and B and employee C. Thus, where a corporation invokes the privilege against self-incrimination, the prosecution or other investigator may obtain information from as many employees and managers but not from the managers and employees whose acts, knowledge and attitudes would be imputed subsequently to the corporation for the purpose of enforcing the offence charged against it. In other words, if the HSE is investigating a work-related death in the furniture department of a corporation, it may compel manager A and employee C from another department to disclose information in spite of the fact that the corporation has invoked the privilege against self-incrimination. However, this implies that the Crown Prosecution Service (CPS) or Crown Office and Procurator Fiscal Service (COPFS) may not subsequently impute the acts and knowledge of manager A and employee C to the corporation. This is because the corporation would successfully object to the use of the information disclosed by them given that for the purpose of the enforcement of that crime the corporation is manager A and employee C. However, if the CPS or COPFS imputes only the acts of manager B and employee D to the corporation, then the latter cannot object to the use of the information disclosed by manager A and employee C.[25]

---

[24] As submitted in Chapter 6, it is logical that the court should aggregate only the acts and knowledge of employees and managers concerned with the transaction under consideration.

[25] It is important to reiterate the point made in Chapter 6 that the prosecutor cannot arbitrarily aggregate the acts of employees in a manner that should make conviction inevitable. This is how acts and knowledge were aggregated in the American cases cited in Chapter 6 and this was criticised as being tantamount to changing a *mens rea* offence into an absolute liability offence. The corporation should therefore be liable for the aggregated acts of its agents only where it is shown that their acts were motivated by a collective reason and they were consistently treated as the corporation through out the process of enforcing the offence charged. This is discussed further in Chapter 8.

In spite of the complexity of the above stance, it may be shown to accord not only with the principle of separate personality[26] but also with the contention that a corporation as a legal person ought to be treated as a natural person while on trial. The corporation is not denied the right to silence in spite of its entitlement. Thus, it may be submitted that the aggregation and corporate culture mechanisms (as modified in this book) may provide a more logical alternative. This involves the corporation invoking the right to prevent the use of information only where such information was provided by the very agents whose acts and knowledge are aggregated and imputed to it.

7.2.1.2 The observance of hearsay and bad character rules

Even where compelled statements by employees or managers or documents begrudgingly disclosed are allowed, there are other factors that may affect the admissibility of such evidence. Where a corporation is on trial it is common that both oral evidence and physical evidence may overlap due to the fact that some employees or managers may be required to explicate what is written in some of the documents. Given that most of the documents may have been drafted by some person other than the manager or employee testifying or the latter may not have been present at the meetings which the documents describe, the bulk of evidence adduced against corporations may have to fall under the exceptions to the hearsay rule in order to be allowed by the court. However, where the documentary evidence is allowed as an exception to the hearsay rule, they may still be inadmissible if they constitute evidence of the corporation's bad character adduced outside the framework set by the Criminal Justice Act 2003 (CJA) for England and the Criminal Justice (Scotland) Act 1995 (CJSA).

The admissibility of hearsay evidence is governed by Chapter 2 of the CJA and sections 17, 18, 19 and 20 of the CJSA. Although there are still some misgivings about documentary evidence,[27] as mentioned above, such evidence make up a large part of the proof adduced to support cases against corporations. Documents detailing transactions entered into by a

---

[26] Contrary to the abovementioned position adopted by courts in order to expeditiously circumvent the difficulty of prosecuting and convicting a corporation that has invoked the right to silence.

[27] Gobert and Punch (2003: 191-192) contend that this is due to the fact that the jury as trier of fact in erstwhile courts was largely composed of illiterates. However, they cite Morgan EM (1956) and McEwan (1998) as positing that these misgivings are a consequence of employing an adversarial system of trial.

corporation (normally by agents acting on its behalf) are more reliable than oral evidence especially in cases where the transactions spanned over a considerable period of time and even prior to the employment of the person giving testimony.[28] Nonetheless, it is difficult to ascertain whether a corporation would be liable if material incriminating it is contained in a document drafted by a middle-level manager. The identification doctrine operates to the effect that the middle-level manager in spite of her knowledge cannot be identified with the corporation and is another person altogether. Thus, one agent cannot be said to have heard the corporation say something since the middle-level manager does not speak as the corporation. This is also true of the senior management failure test that restricts the corporation's knowledge and activities to the actions of the senior managers. However, section 117 of the CJA and section 17(1)(d)(ii) of the CJSA are to the effect that documentary evidence will be allowed provided that the person that supplied the information comprised in the document had or is reasonably expected to have had personal knowledge of the material discussed in the document and drafted the document or the part containing the relevant information while acting within the scope of her authority.[29] This means that information supplied by a middle-level or junior manager ought not to be hearsay if she had or was reasonably expected to have had personal knowledge of the material contained in the document. Just as in the case of the right to silence, this shows that the restrictive mechanisms that are applicable in the United Kingdom and the procedural rules are on a collision course, which unfortunately often results in the disregard of the corporate person's right for the sake of expediency. The provisions of the CJA and the CJSA are however in accord with the dicta in *Meridian* and *El Ajou* (modifying the identification doctrine) that a corporation should be identified with any agent that was concerned with the transaction under consideration. This is because such an agent is likely to have had personal knowledge of documents or statements made by other agents (especially the hierarchy)

---

[28] There are also instances where the drafters of incriminating documentary evidence are unavailable. See Gobert and Punch (2003: 192-193), especially their discussion of *Myers v DPP* [1965] AC 1001, as well as the lifting of restrictions by the Criminal Evidence Act 1965 (for England) and the recommendations of the Roskill Committee's Report.

[29] Nevertheless, section 117(7) of the CJA may be said to give discretionary power to the court to exclude such evidence on the grounds of the dubiousness of the content, the source and the way in which it was obtained or the document drafted. Section 114(2) also empowers courts to consider the probative value and the likelihood of prejudice before admitting statements not made in oral evidence.

in relation to the transaction. Nonetheless, the alternative mechanisms assessed in Chapter 6 (vicarious liability, aggregation and corporate culture) are more progressive in this regard as they provide for the identification of any agent with the corporation depending on the circumstances.

Information may still be inadmissible if it constitutes evidence of bad character. Evidence of a person's bad character is defined as evidence that is not related to the offence charged or the investigation and prosecution of the offence and shows a disposition towards misconduct on the person's part.[30] Given that a corporation is a legal person that is entitled to the same rights as natural persons it may be said to have a "bad character" that may not be revealed except in circumstances provided for by the law. However, given its amorphousness, the question of a corporation's bad character may only be resolved by giving regard to how courts ascribe criminal liability to it (mechanism of imputation). Thus, showing that the acts of certain employees constitute the corporation's character in accordance with the applicable mechanism ought to be a prerequisite for showing that the corporation was disposed towards misconduct ("bad character"). Following the evaluations in Chapters 5 and 6, it is fair to say that the identification doctrine and vicarious liability provide clearer propositions of what may constitute a corporation's "character" and "bad character." The moral action of a senior officer or any employee acting within the course of her employment represents the characteristic property that defines the corporation. However, bar the clarity and also the simplicity, these mechanisms do not reflect the factual accuracy of what may be considered a corporation's character, which ought to be distinct from that of its agent. The mechanisms based on collective liability (senior management failure, aggregation and corporate culture) represent a fair attempt at conceptualising the character of the corporation as a collective unit although they are largely unfixed as regards the essential notions of such a character. As shown in the Chapters 5 and 6, they are prone to pushing courts to grope among nebulous issues towards conclusions that are largely indefensible.

[30] Section 98 of the CJA. See also section 141 of the Criminal Procedure (Scotland) Act 1975 as amended by section 24 of the CJSA.

7.2.1.3 The question of burden of proof

This question may also determine whether there is a reasonable prospect of conviction. The prosecutor is required to prove criminal indictment beyond reasonable doubt. However, as mentioned in Chapter 5, where the accused is a corporation the offence may be the result of a number of actions and omissions spanning over a period of time. The prosecutor is therefore required to adduce evidence of these actions and omissions proving beyond reasonable doubt that they were connected to such an extent that the corporation through one of the agents had or ought to have had knowledge of the full import of the nexus and foresaw or ought to have foreseen the result which was the offence charged. Although all corporate offences are not complicated,[31] the task of establishing the elements of the offence charged beyond reasonable doubt is in contradiction with some of the underlying reasons for placing the burden of proof on the prosecutor, *viz.* to control and limit the power of the government to forcefully intervene in the lives of citizens using the criminal law[32] and to avoid compelling the accused to prove her innocence. The prosecution often lacks the requisite expertise and resources to process complex crimes such as fraud committed by large and organic corporate entities[33] and it has been argued that although it would be unfair to reverse the onus of proof, the standard of proof which is "beyond reasonable doubt" ought to be abandoned in favour of a less stringent standard of "clear and convincing evidence."[34] It is however difficult to distinguish between the "intermediate" standard of "clear and convincing evidence" recommended by Gobert and Punch and the applicable standard of proof beyond reasonable doubt. This is because if a reasonable doubt is that which would prevent a reasonable person from

---

[31] There are small and medium-sized corporations that commit offences that are perpetrated only by the general manager or a couple of agents at the general manager's direction.

[32] See Gobert and Punch, 2003: 201-202.

[33] The prosecution's task may be further complicated by the successful invocation of the privilege against self-incrimination or undue restrictions on the adduction of evidence of the corporation's "bad character" and hearsay evidence. See Gobert and Punch, 2003: 201-202.

[34] Gobert and Punch (2003: 202-204) discuss exceptions to the rule placing the burden on the prosecution, such as where the defendant raises the common law defence of insanity and where the statute specifically reverses the onus. They then assert that the defendant in such cases is not required to discharge the burden beyond reasonable doubt but by a balance of probabilities.

arriving at a particular conclusion[35] then it may be said that the reasonable person refrained from arriving at such a conclusion because the evidence was not "clear and convincing." This demonstrates a pervasive dilemma in corporate criminal law as regards either facilitating the prosecution of corporations[36] or maintaining the integrity of the criminal law by protecting the rights of the accused (whether a natural or an artificial person). It is submitted here that the latter option should have priority else procedural justice would be sacrificed on the altar of expediency. This may be achieved by ascertaining the nature of the accused corporation, as well as the type of evidence required to establish its guilt. As shown in Chapters 2 and 4, there is a vast amount of literature on the nature and functioning of corporations and no particular paradigm can be held out as a tenet. Thus, for the purposes of the criminal law, it may be better to refer to mechanisms of imputation and enquire about how they enable the prosecution to successfully discharge this burden.

If we refer to the mechanisms assessed in Chapters 5 and 6, it may be fair to say that those that are largely based on individualism (identification doctrine and vicarious liability) are less ambiguous and may be used consistently. It is easier to prove a corporation's bad character by adducing evidence of the general manager's disposition to commit crime while acting to further the interests of the corporation and it is also easier for the prosecutor to lay hands on such specific evidence and prove beyond reasonable doubt that the general manager committed the offence charged and consequently the corporation should be liable. However, where the crime was the result of a combination of several actions and omissions and/or a pervasive attitude existing within the corporation, the prosecution would terminate the case if the identification doctrine or vicarious liability was the applicable mechanism. The mechanisms based on collective liability (senior management failure, aggregation and corporate culture) require the prosecution to adduce evidence showing the confluence of actions and/or omissions that resulted in the offence. It may be an uphill task to present and explain documents to the effect that the senior management or a group of departmental heads encouraged or tolerated non-compliance if none of them was negligent in an individual capacity. However, as shown above, many criminal justice agencies such as the OFT, SFO and HSE have the power to compel agents to provide information

---

[35] See Denning LJ (as he then was) in *Bater v Bater* [1950] 2 All ER 458 at 459. See also *R v Summers* [1952] 1 All ER 1059 at 1060.

[36] Due to the fact that they can be very powerful and hold and control most of the evidence of the commission of the offence.

which they can use to prosecute a corporation.[37] The prosecutor may also rely solely on documentary evidence irrespective of whether the drafters of the documents give oral evidence. These powers which would no doubt be described as unfettered if natural persons were at the receiving end (and the offences prosecuted were not serious offences) certainly provide a reciprocal balance to the prosecution's lack of sufficient resources and the corporation's possession of the bulk of evidence.[38] The major challenge thus remains how to prosecute the corporation in light of a delineated mechanism of imputation. From the discussion above, the solution seems to lie in a mechanism that is based on collective liability but with the clarity and consistency of the mechanisms based on individual liability.

7.2.1.4 The question of using a jury

A jury is comprised of the defender's fellow citizens randomly selected. This follows from the right of the accused to be tried by a jury of her peers founded on a provision in Chapter 29 of the English *Magna Carta Libertatum* or Great Charter of Freedoms.[39] However, where a corporation is on trial, it may be difficult to determine who constitutes its "peers" or "fellow citizens." It is uncertain whether this should be taken to mean other managers of other corporations or other employees of other corporations or simply other natural persons who are citizens. The uncertainty is exacerbated by the fact that the concept of corporation is not amenable to any precise definition[40] in order to enable courts to determine whether the persons seated on the panel are of equal standing with the accused corporation.[41] As mentioned above, courts may consider the applicable mechanism of imputation in such a manner as to decide whether the corporation is a senior officer (directing mind), in which case the jury would be composed of senior officers that are directing minds of other corporations. However, where the corporation is the combination of different agents at different levels, as well as their attitudes and the practices they have adopted, it may be difficult to have other corporations

---

[37] And the corporation cannot invoke the privilege against self-incrimination.

[38] As such, the idea of reversing the onus of proof is largely unfounded.

[39] The practice of trial by jury is equally one of the oldest in Scotland. See Carruthers, 2001.

[40] The definition proposed in this book is intended to apply only as regards the enforcement of the offence charged and is largely based on the understanding that a corporation is foremost an abstract entity.

[41] Admitting only artificial persons as jurors would beg the question of whether they can swear or take an oath.

seated as the jury.[42] That notwithstanding, the courts use natural persons selected randomly as jurors in cases where corporations are on trial.[43] Thus, there is apparently no difference between a jury of an artificial person's peers and a jury of a natural person's peers.

Over the past four decades the practice of trial by jury underwent a critical appraisal.[44] The focus was on the rationale of resting the credibility of the trial institution on the shoulders of laymen who were more susceptible to emotional judgements. The disquiet is especially strong in complex cases where the jurors are expected to process a chunk of information and establish the truth in a just and economical manner.[45] The Roskill Committee[46] noted that a randomly selected jury would struggle to understand difficult and complex fraud cases and recommended the institution of a judicial assembly with the requisite skill, the Fraud Trial Tribunal. Some sixteen years later, the Auld Committee echoed similar concerns.[47] However, during the period between these publications, several commentators pointed out that empirical research does not support this stance.[48] That notwithstanding, in 1983 the British Government created the Fraud Trial Committee which was tasked with finding more effective means of tackling fraud using the criminal justice system. Equally, the Criminal Justice Act 1987 (as amended) created the SFO which investigates and prosecutes serious and complex fraud.[49] To facilitate the prosecution, sections 43 and 44 of the CJA entitles the prosecution in England to apply for fraud cases to be conducted without a jury. Section 43(5) of this statute is particularly pertinent because it relates

---

[42] This further demonstrates the clarity and consistency of mechanisms based on individual liability although it also betrays their simplicity.

[43] The argument about whether such juries are legitimately constituted has received very little attention compared to concerns about the competence of lay jurors.

[44] See the Thomson and Roskill Committees' Reports of 1975 and 1986 and the Auld Review of 2001.

[45] There is a substantial amount of literature on the desirability of the jury system. See particularly, Frank, 1930 and 1973; Findlay and Duff, 1988; Darbyshire, Maughan, and Stewart, 2002; and Honess, Levi and Charman, 2003. Questions about the use of the jury have sometimes been linked with questions about the efficiency of the common law systems. See for example, Murphy P, 2008.

[46] 1985: para 1.6.

[47] 2001: Chapter 11.

[48] See for example, Harding, 1988: 74-93; Levi, 1988: 95-111; Darbyshire, Maughan, and Stewart, 2002: 62; and Honess, Levi and Charman, 2003: 12-27.

[49] However, SFO's jurisdiction does not extend to Scotland where frauds are prosecuted by the COPFS which has a Fraud and Specialist Services unit.

to trials that are protracted and may require the juror to sacrifice much time and carry out an intensive examination of several documents in order to arrive at a fair and balanced conclusion.[50] However, after discussing these English sections, Lord MacLean maintained that "in Scotland there is no empirical evidence that juries are unable to absorb and understand complex issues, whether or not they arise in long trials."[51]

As shown in Chapters 5 and 6, the enforcement of the criminal law against corporations is especially problematic where corporations are large and complex. These are almost always complex cases because they involve the adduction of thousands of documents, the calling of hundreds of witnesses to make statements in oral evidence and convoluted arguments about issues such as whether the agent that acted or obtained information was acting within the scope of her authority and is of sufficient station to be identified with the corporation.[52] Thus, even where the offence charged is not fraud or does not involve complicated forensic evidence, it may very well be complex due to the difficulty of pinning blame on an artificial entity whose structure is labyrinthine.[53] It may then be said that the problem of complex fraud cases is symptomatic of corporate cases and it is advisable that the right of the accused corporation to be tried by a jury of its peers is left to the discretion of the court.[54]

Nonetheless, the argument of overlooking the jury in some cases is not made here on the basis of the jury's incompetence[55] but on the

---

[50] Section 43 is not for the time being in force as amendments to this section will be made by the Fraud (Trial Without a Jury) Bill which is presently in the House of Lords.

[51] *Transco* at [5].

[52] In *Transco* for example, the prosecution provided a list of 262 witnesses and submitted about 1450 documentary productions.

[53] See Gobert and Punch, 2003: 185.

[54] Some commentators that advance that the theory of jury incompetence is unfounded do however agree on the difficulty of maintaining a jury system for prolonged cases. See for example, Honess, Levi and Charman, 2003: 26.

[55] Some commentators have equally proffered evidence of the difficulty of criminal justice officials to present and control complex forensic evidence. Masters (2008: 116-117) for example says he visited the website of the Cambridgeshire Police and found out that formal education was not required to become a constable. He therefore wondered how individuals with little formal education would trace assets and evidence through a maze of bank accounts. He however notes that there has been remarkable improvement in the enforcement of white collar crime with the enactment of more appropriate laws, the increase in government funding for

inappropriateness of maintaining a jury system for trials that are relatively long in duration. Proving that a corporation is liable for an offence may involve the presentation of thousands of documents and the examination and cross-examination of hundreds of witnesses. If the applicable mechanism is based on individual liability (such as the identification doctrine or vicarious liability), the duration of the trial may be shorter (and less complex) given that the prosecution's job would largely be restricted to showing that an agent of the corporation committed the offence while acting within the course of her employment, and she is of sufficient station to be identified with the corporation.[56] However, evidence of the guilt of such agents may be hard to come by in large and complex corporations where they make decisions in committees and are often remote from operational staff. As shown in Chapter 5, the mechanisms that deal (or have the potential to deal) effectively with such cases are those based on collective liability.[57] If they become applicable then the prosecution would be required to show that the actions and omissions of a number of agents together with practices, policies, systems and attitudes that prevailed within the corporation combined in different degrees to cause the result that completed the offence. This is no doubt an arduous task that requires not only a substantial amount of information but also a considerable period of time. In this light, a trial without a jury may be preferable although that would imply that the right of the accused to be tried by a jury of its peers would be disregarded due to the weakness of the criminal justice system.[58] The question of whether the disregard of this right is tantamount to a denial of the right to a fair criminal trial is open to debate.[59] It may therefore be concluded that just like the right to silence and the rules against the adduction of hearsay evidence and evidence of bad character, the right to a trial by jury has been deemed incompatible with the ability of the prosecution to present a fair case against many corporations. This has

---

the activities of specialist agencies and units and the use of more skilled investigators.

[56] The prosecutor may even be reluctant to initiate proceedings if she is not satisfied that she has sufficient evidence against such a senior officer.

[57] Aggregation and corporate culture in particular since senior management failure would only require evidence of gross negligence by the senior managers.

[58] If proponents of trial by jury can find a way around the time factor then there is no reason to suggest that the corporation should not be tried by a jury although the question of its "peers" would also have to be resolved. From the discussion above, it seems the latter question may hardly be resolved where the applicable mechanisms of imputation are based on collective liability.

[59] See for example, Carruthers' (2001: 217-221) contention that both rights mean the same thing.

led to the simplification of the prosecution of corporations. However, the consequence is that any incriminating evidence against the corporation almost automatically passes the evidential test. As such, the low incidence of convictions may only be blamed on the process of collecting the evidence and the use of such evidence in accordance with the rules governing the applicable mechanisms of imputation namely, the identification doctrine and the senior management failure test.

7.2.2 The public interest test

Prosecutorial decision-making is not only governed by questions of whether evidence obtained is admissible and founds a reasonable prospect of conviction. The question of whether the prosecution is in the interest of the public is just as important.[60] The Codes for both Scotland and England[61] set out a number of factors that may be taken into account in the public interest assessment. These factors include the seriousness or gravity of the offence, the impact on the victim and the circumstances of the accused. With regard to the seriousness or gravity of the offence, the prosecution is expected to consider whether initiating a proceeding is a proportionate response to the action of the accused.[62] Where the accused is a corporation, the prosecutor may be concerned with the impact of the prosecution (and subsequent punishment) on the confidence of the community. Since corporations especially the large ones may cause widespread damage the institution of proceedings against them is almost always a strong message both to other corporations and the affected communities that corporate criminality will not be tolerated and public authorities are keeping watch.[63] Concerning the impact on the victim, although the prosecutor does not represent the former like an advocate would, it is important for the prosecutor to consider issues such as the injury suffered by the victim and the consequence of the prosecution on

---

[60] Proceedings may be discontinued if this test is not passed. See for example, section 23 of the Prosecution of Offences Act 1985.

[61] Prosecution Code, 2001: 06-08; Code for Crown Prosecutors, 2004: paras. 5.6-5.13.

[62] The prosecution will be indicated by things like the accused using violence to perpetrate the offence; whether she was in a position of trust vis-à-vis the victim; if the offence was preconceived; and whether the accused has previous convictions which are relevant to the offence considered, amongst other things.

[63] This is not tantamount to the idea that the criminal law is the most appropriate instrument for regulating the activities of corporations. See Clough and Mulhern, 2000.

her. The victim's views would therefore be important. Where the accused is a corporation it is more likely that the victim may have suffered great loss (financial, physical, psychological or otherwise) and would be eager to see punishment meted out to the corporation that is proportionate to the loss.[64]

Nonetheless, the prosecutor ought to initiate proceedings because of the unshakable belief that the accused justly deserves to be punished. The guidance by the Codes mentioned above has been described as ambiguous because the considerations set out (especially as regards the "seriousness" of the offence) do not provide any clear directions as to why a particular course of action has to be adopted.[65] Thus, Rogers notes that the prosecutor should limit her reflection to three things: the cost of the prosecution, the harms of the punishment and the harms that are ineluctably wrapped around the criminal trial, which he calls the "harms of prosecution."[66] The cost of the prosecution and the harms of the punishment are incidental to any trial and are not as important as the harms of prosecution. This is especially true as regards corporate defenders. The institution of criminal proceedings often carries a stigma that may seldom be blotted out even by an acquittal and the publication of

---

[64] A good example of the disappointment of victims and members of affected communities following the exoneration of the accused corporation is *Ex parte Spooner* where some victims and their families argued that the restriction of the scope of inquest greatly reduced the prospect of convicting the corporation (Townsend Thoresen and later on P&O European Ferries) that was investigated.

[65] See Rogers' (2006: 775-803) criticisms of the English Code for Crown Prosecutors. He wonders which of these factors may justify the prosecution of a petty shoplifter and suggests that the factors should have been set out as guidance towards seeking to obtain a particular result via punishment. Thus, there may be a pressing need to prosecute a corporation that has committed an offence although the crime is not necessarily "serious" and the corporation is a first-time offender and there is no victim. He also deplores the Code's silence on the question of cost-benefit analysis even though this constitutes a strong influence on the prosecutor when considering why she ought to seek the punishment of the accused.

[66] Rogers, 2006: 787-793. He was certainly inspired by Feeley's (1979) assertion that the process of going through the criminal justice system actually constitutes the punishment. Feeley (1979: 201) calls this punishment the "price tag." It must however be noted that his argument was based on the fact that most of the convicted persons he observed were not as concerned about the stigma of criminal sanction as they were about the cost of the process.

the judgment.[67] As such, it is imperative for the prosecutor to consider whether the harms of prosecution that may be inflicted upon the accused corporation are part and parcel of the just deserts. However, if just deserts consist of the effects of the perpetration of an offence then including harms of prosecution suffered by a person whose guilt has not been proved (and is apparently innocent) would be incompatible with the moral philosophy of justice that underpins the criminal justice systems of both England and Scotland. The fact that the Codes are silent in the face of such unfairness is rightly a cause for concern.[68] There may be claims in damages but these are severely restricted to cases where the harm of prosecution relates to the defendant's repute and the prosecution was malicious.[69] Nonetheless, what is important to note is that where the defendant is a corporation the prosecutor's consideration of the harms of prosecution that would be visited on it may logically be based on the prosecutor's perception of the nature of the corporation.

For example, if the prosecutor is required to conceive of the senior management as the embodiment of the corporation, then she would be less likely to think that the corporation would suffer from the prosecution of an offence allegedly committed by junior employees that acted in disregard of instructions from the diligent senior management.[70] On the other hand, where the offence was allegedly committed by senior managers the prosecutor is more likely to think that the trial process would harm the corporation since the message conferred would be that the corporation is prosecuted as a result of pervasive negligence. Conversely, where the aggregation and corporate culture mechanisms apply, the prosecutor (and the public) is more likely to perceive the trial as that of the corporation

---

[67] It may be difficult to argue that a fine of a few thousand pounds is a harsher penalty than the loss of reputation and customers due to the negative publicity of the prosecution. In his review of Feeley (1979), Atkins (1980: 822) noted that the latter failed to show evidence of the defendants' perceptions in order to buttress his argument that the process is the punishment.

[68] The consideration of the time the convicted person spent in custody during sentencing (as per sections 240-243 of the CJA) is an example of efforts to minimise the unfairness of the process. See Rogers (2006: 788, n. 65).

[69] For discussions on malicious prosecutions, see *Glinski v McIver* [1962] AC 726.

[70] In the United Kingdom this will most probably be a strict liability offence because corporations can only be prosecuted and sanctioned for crimes of intent (including corporate manslaughter or corporate homicide) where a senior manager or the senior management is guilty or grossly negligent.

rather than that of a handful of greedy senior officers.[71] Nonetheless, this implies that there is a feeling of just desert as regards whether there is reasonable ground for visiting the harms of the prosecution either on the greedy senior manager or on the accused corporation. As noted above, this runs counter to the moral philosophy of justice that underpins the criminal justice system. Rogers[72] posits that the Scottish Code is more progressive on the issue because it directs the prosecutor to consider whether the effect of the prosecution may be disproportionate to the gravity or seriousness of the offence.[73]

Finding an effective solution to this problem may prove impractical due to the fact that it is only incidental to the use of society's most effective weapon to regulate the activities of its subjects. That notwithstanding, a noteworthy distinction between the harms of punishment and the harms of prosecution is that unlike the former the latter should not be intended.[74] As such, the prosecutor should not label and discredit a corporation for the sake of making the whole process a deterrent, especially where the maximum penalty is a small fine or where there is little prospect of conviction.[75] It is imperative that the effects of the prosecution are mitigated. Mechanisms that compel corporations to substitute for delinquent senior officers (identification doctrine and senior management failure test) seem to provide lesser prospects for mitigating these harms. This is because the target is often thought to be the senior

---

[71]This is reflected in the empirical study carried out by Zemba, Young and Morris (2006) that shows that observers tend to blame senior managers for corporate failures.

[72] 2006: 790, n. 73.

[73] Prosecution Code, 2001: 08. This implies that the more serious the offence the more it is justifiable to tug the accused through the process. However, this does not only take us back to the problem of the ambiguity of the words "gravity" and "serious" (which Rogers deplores) but also to what may be seen as an 'innocent' person being harmed by the criminal process on the ground that she is likely to have a committed a "serious" offence.

[74] Rogers, 2006: 792.

[75] *P & O European Ferries* and *Transco* are examples of prosecutors continuing proceedings in spite of the absence of evidence incriminating any senior officer (and consequently the corporation). The decisions to prosecute were popular since there were clamant calls to bring these corporations and their controllers to justice. However, the prosecutors were neither "fair, independent and objective" (as required by section 2.2 of the Code for Crown Prosecutors, 2004) nor did they exercise their duty without "fear, favour, or prejudice" (as required by the Prosecution Code, 2001: 01).

officer or senior management that the prosecutor (as well as the public) believes is responsible for the perpetration of the offence. In other words, it is thought that blaming the corporation is a convenient way of attributing the blame to the individuals that make up the group.[76]

This implies that in addition to the disregard of some fundamental rights of the accused corporation (right to silence, privilege against hearsay evidence and evidence of bad character, right to be presumed innocent and right of trial by jury) the trial process is further undermined by the unfair punishment inflicted upon it. The rules of adjudication are therefore largely ignored and this provides a strong motive to consider fairer means of regulating the corporation's activities and reconciling the community with the corporation. It has been suggested that civil law and specialised criminal justice agencies may provide such an alternative.[77] This takes us to the question of restorative justice[78] and a comprehensive model of restorative justice in corporate liability designed by Fisse and Braithwaite. It is called the "Accountability Model" and has been presented as a more effective approach to solving procedural problems of enforcing corporate crime in most commonwealth jurisdictions. In light of the difficulties noted above, it is important to consider whether there is good reason to reduce the frequency of or dispense away with initiating criminal proceedings via the CPS and COPFS in favour of the process suggested by the Accountability Model. This is important because if that is the case then this model may be deemed to comprise more effective rules of adjudication than the judicial process discussed above.

7.2.3 The Accountability Model or a silver bullet

This model subscribes to three theoretical approaches of the nature and functioning of corporations, *viz.* individualism, collectivism and organisation theory. However, the legal focus is largely on individualism given that the architects of the model address the question of collectivism strictly from an economic standpoint (enterprise liability) while their

---

[76] See the discussion in Chapter 2 on the bracket theory.

[77] The argument is that disciplinary and remedial sanctions imposed by regulatory agencies have less stigma than both the prosecution and the subsequent imposition of criminal sanctions on corporations. See Masters' (2008: 112) argument that supermarkets successfully minimise theft in their stores without initiating proceedings and that could be the same for the criminal justice system and corporations.

[78] Although the focus here is on procedural justice.

analysis of organisation theory perspectives draws mostly from management. Nevertheless, the goal is to devise a means of using the corporation as an instrument for ensuring compliance. This involves exploiting the corporation's internal justice system to ensure that its members and agents comply with the law.[79] Thus, this model favours the transfer of enforcement costs to the corporation and the use of civil law at the early stages of enforcement.

Fisse and Braithwaite[80] state the desiderata which they believe emerged from the attribution of responsibility to corporations for the purposes of enforcing the criminal law against them. They then proceed to show how the Accountability Model meets the objectives of these desiderata through a regulatory framework described as "pyramidal enforcement."[81] The pyramid comprises a series of disciplinary, remedial and punitive interventions that the criminal justice system may make against a corporation that is guilty of an offence. These interventions include the use of warnings and persuasion at the base of the pyramid; civil fines and voluntary accountability agreements (between the regulator and/or prosecutor and the corporation); accountability or remedial orders or punitive injunctions; and at the apex of the pyramid are criminal sanctions which include revoking the corporation's licence. These interventions therefore equally involve a number of proposed sanctions that may be imposed on the convicted corporation. However, the focus here is on the use of the model to overcome the procedural obstacles that have been shown to be impregnable to the mechanisms of imputation (in their present forms).[82] Thus, I will seek to determine whether in a case where the evidence at the disposal of the prosecutor provides a realistic prospect of conviction and there are also good public interests grounds to prosecute the prosecutor may avoid going through a trial by adopting the measures of intervention discussed above.

---

[79] Fisse and Braithwaite, 1993: 15-16. This was inspired by Coffee's (1981: 431) proposal that probation and presentence reports could be used to incite corporations to use their internal disciplinary systems to sanction non-compliance. Earlier work on the model was done by Ayres and Braithwaite (1992). The underlying assumption is that a corporation has a greater capacity to ensure its agents' compliance than the criminal justice system.

[80] 1993: 135-138.

[81] For a description of the pyramid, see Fisse and Braithwaite, 1993: 141-153.

[82] These sanctions and a host of other sanctions proposed by other commentators, as well as the applicable sanctions in the United Kingdom are discussed below.

To begin with, it seems that the notion of the corporation as a legal person with rights that must be protected and respected is circumvented in favour of the notion of the corporation as simply a resourceful institution with the capacity to effectively sanction and prevent crime.[83] This is because the criminal justice agency is less concerned about how the law operates with regard to the accused corporation's procedural rights than about its presence behind the corporation with an "axe that ultimately can deliver the sanction of corporate capital punishment."[84] It must be noted that the seminal work of Fisse and Braithwaite has been cited by several commentators and has provided much impetus to the position that corporate compliance programmes ought to be used as a measure of a corporation's guilt.[85] It is also reflected in the operation of specific enforcement agencies created in the United Kingdom to regulate activities in certain industries.[86]

However, the fact that the model may only be used where the corporation has committed the *actus reus* of an offence implies that it is only suitable for strict and absolute liability offences. This is because crimes of intent require more than just evidence of the commission of the *actus reus* before action can be taken against the defendant. They also require evidence of the intention to cause the result that completed the offence or reckless action in disregard of the consequences of the commission of the *actus reus*.[87] Moreover, this model is based on the assumption that it is possible to identify all the responsible actors within the corporate body.[88] This is erroneous because as noted in Chapters 5 and 6, there are numerous occasions where the offence is the culmination of the confluence of different innocuous acts and omissions of different agents who sought to further the interests of the corporation. Not even an

[83] The idea is that if a corporation can harness its own resources to ensure responsibility the problem of the economic inefficiency of the enforcement of corporate crime will be solved.
[84] Fisse and Braithwaite, 1993: 15.
[85] See for example Ashworth, 2000: 247-248.
[86] Many enforcement agencies can advise corporations, as well as impose fines and prosecute them (in England) for specific offences if they believe the offences are of sufficient gravity.
[87] The adduction of evidence of an effective compliance programme which is similar to a credible remedial investigation and accountability report may only mitigate a corporation's liability for such crimes. The argument that it should be an absolute defence defeats the purpose of justice because a crime was committed by the corporation after all and it is deserves to be punished.
[88] See Fisse and Braithwaite, 1993: 135 and 140.

internal investigation by the corporation itself would identify a responsible individual. Also, given the emphasis on individual responsibility, corporations may feel compelled to appoint a senior officer that should be responsible for detecting and reporting non-compliance; and Fisse and Braithwaite[89] admit that this would no doubt motivate scapegoating or the recruitment of "vice-presidents in charge of going to jail."[90] Thus, the argument that individual responsibility is the bedrock of social control does not always justify the enforcement of corporate (collective) crime by targeting individuals.

The starting point of the pyramidal enforcement is therefore problematic. It is unclear whether the first interventions should be made where a corporation's guilt (for the commission of the *actus reus*) has been proved or where the prosecutor or regulator simply has sufficient evidence which in her opinion provides a realistic prospect of conviction. In the former case, it is unclear how such guilt (for the commission of the *actus reus*) may be established. It is difficult to see how this may be done without reference to the applicable mechanism of imputation since to say that a corporation has committed the *actus reus* of an offence implies that a senior officer has committed the *actus reus* or directed its commission (where the identification doctrine applies) or that the way the senior management organised or managed the corporation's activities was below acceptable standards and motivated the commission of the *actus reus*.[91] Equally, it is unclear whether the commission of the *actus reus* will be established in a court and following a trial. This is because if it is not established in this manner, it cannot be said that the corporation has committed the *actus reus* of the offence but only that the prosecution believes it has sufficient evidence required to prove that the corporation has committed the *actus reus*. As such, the objective of circumventing the procedural obstacles is not met.

That notwithstanding, as mentioned above, the model is reflected in the operation of many criminal justice agencies created to help prevent the commission of certain offences. The HSE for example can make a number of interventions to ensure that a corporation complies with the relevant

[89] 1993: 132.

[90] This may be one of the reasons why the CMCHA cannot be enforced against individual senior managers.

[91] Unless we are not concerned with corporate crime but crime within the corporate context. It seems the Accountability Model is geared towards finding ways of preventing the latter and not the former.

health and safety legislation. An HSE inspector may provide advice to a corporation and issue a warning in a situation where she believes there is a high propensity to breach the legislation.[92] The HSE may also (in England and Wales) issue simple cautions,[93] improvement and prohibition notices and it may vary and withdraw licences or other authorisations.[94] The Financial Service Authority (FSA) may also impose financial penalties and prosecute corporations that carry out regulated activities without prior authorisation amongst other disciplinary and remedial interventions.[95] The OFT may impose fines and disqualification orders and initiate criminal proceedings against corporations allegedly involved in anti-competitive activities or that breach consumer protection laws.[96]

These are examples of criminal justice agencies that may enforce certain offences without necessarily going through the 'tortuous' channel of the trial. They no doubt provide credence to the Accountability Model. As such, a number of offences which are commonly committed in certain industries may be effectively checked without the impression of the overbearing arm of the intervening prosecutor. That notwithstanding, if this were to become the norm in corporate criminal law there would be a specialised agency for each offence or set of related offences that can be committed by a corporation. Given that a corporation is a legal person that can commit all possible offences either directly or as an accessory, such a proposition hovers on fantasy. It is an alluring illusion that the law can be used in such a manner. It is evocative of the Austinian contention that the

---

[92] The policy statement (HSE, 2008: para. 3) however uses the words "that in the opinion of the inspector, they are failing to comply with the law." Although this is not as problematic as saying that "a corporation having committed the actus reus," it still leaves much uncertainty as regards what should motivate the issuing of a warning or providing of advice. It seems the HSE inspector should decide based on whether she has sufficient evidence which in her opinion provides a realistic prospect of conviction for breach of the statute. Then in a bid to avoid prosecution (because of some of the difficulties discussed above) and prevent other breaches she would make the necessary disciplinary and remedial interventions.

[93] A simple caution follows an admission of guilt and although it is not synonymous to a conviction it is included the offender's criminal record. Even the police issues cautions to about 38 percent of offenders. See Ashworth, 2000: 247.

[94] It is important to note that at the apex of the HSE pyramid is the power to prosecute in England and Wales or to refer a prosecution to the COFPS in Scotland. See the Legislative and Regulatory Reform Act 2006 and also the Regulators' Compliance Code 2008.

[95] See the Financial Services and Markets Act 2000 (FSMA).

[96] See the Fair Trading Act 1973; Competition Act 1998; and Enterprise Act 2002.

law is a command of a sovereign that becomes effective because of the threat of the sanction accompanying the command.[97] It is trite knowledge that the law owes its effectiveness to more reasons than envisaged by proponents of legal positivism.[98] Even for the purposes of regulating the activities of corporations that may cause widespread damage it is not appropriate to expunge ideas of justice from the literature of enforcement.[99] As such, the objective of reforming all corporations by ensuring that they have effective internal audit and disciplinary teams is just as achievable as reforming all humans by ensuring that they have disciplinary consciences.[100] It may be less costly to the state in certain instances[101] but justice (whether restorative or not) cannot rest on the sole question of the economic efficiency of enforcement.[102] Thus, although it is cheaper to rely on the internal disciplinary system of the corporation,[103] the

---

[97] Although they would rather that the system instills a sense of responsibility and not fear, Fisse and Braithwaite (1993: 143) advance that the model is based on the theory that "actors, individual or corporate, are most likely to comply if they know that enforcement is backed by sanctions which can be escalated in response to any given level of non-compliance." They (1993: 173-174) also cite with approval the consequentialist republican theory of "maximizing" the "dominion" put forward by Braithwaite and Pettit (1990) to justify the imposition of criminal sanctions even where there is no evidence of moral blameworthiness. However, it is shown in Chapter 2 that consequentialist or teleological enforcement is justifiable only for certain offences and seldom for crimes of intent which constitute the crux of the problem of corporate criminal liability.

[98] In fact one of the reasons for Hart's (1994) exposition of primary rules and secondary rules was to free legal positivism from the insularity of the Austinian model. However, MacCormick (2008: 194-200) did not believe Hart achieved the objective.

[99] Ironically, justice (or natural justice) once a subject of apprehension to lawyers seeking to protect industry and commerce (Cohen MR, 1927: 237) may now become the pith of their argument. See Nijman, 2004. However, it must be reiterated that it is important to protect the civil liberties of corporate persons and safeguard the integrity of the criminal law. See the concerns expressed by Fisse and Braithwaite, 1993: 169-177. See also Ashworth, 2000: 249-250.

[100] The argument that no legislation no matter how well drafted and implemented can stop corporate misconduct (Coburn, 2006: 366) is also true for human misconduct.

[101] See the ironic remark by Masters (2008: 118) that "[c]rime does pay! But not for the criminals" made because of huge financial returns registered by police forces after seizure and confiscation of assets.

[102] *Cf* Bayles 1990: 139 cited in Fisse and Braithwaite, 1993: 173. See also Masters, 2008: 112.

[103] See Masters, 1998: 118-119; and Coburn, 2006: 349.

monitoring and imposition of different sanctions and (may be) subsequent prosecution may amount to a heavy financial burden on the different agencies and consequently the state[104] and sometimes even the regulated.[105] Moreover, the change brought about by the use of these criminal justice agencies may be questioned when one considers statistics showing that 41 percent of corporate frauds were detected by pure chance in 2007.[106] Many corporations remain far too complex even for these specialist units or agencies and sometimes also for the corporations' senior management.[107]

What is important to note here is that even though criminal justice agencies are given such wide ranges of disciplinary and remedial power, in many cases they eventually prosecute or ask the COPFS or CPS to prosecute. These cases cannot be ignored for good measure. Thus, if questions of procedural rights have to be addressed invariably then the issue of the application of a mechanism of imputation would eventually resurface. Equally, a good number of the interventions within the framework of the Accountability Model constitute sanctions for the corporate offenders[108] and in light of the foregoing discussion the effectiveness of any sanction or a combination of sanctions[109] would depend on the mechanism of imputation adopted. This is because the sanction may only be effective if it achieves the most desirable result (compliance) given the circumstances; and it will only achieve such a result if it consists of a method of compelling the corporation to comply

---

[104] It is important to determine for example whether the Jubilee fraud trial (*R v Rayment and Others* Central Criminal Court, 24 March 2005, Unreported) that collapsed after 18 months and more than £25 million spent would have been handled in more cost effective manner by the Fraud Prosecution Service (FPS) of the CPS than the Casework Directorate that initially prosecuted serious fraud cases. The HMCPSI Report of June 2006 states that it is still early days.

[105] For example, corporations regulated by the FSA are required to pay fees or levies.

[106] See PriceWaterhouseCoopers, 2007: 10. See also Coburn (2006: 349) who notes that luck is the commonest "fraud detection tool."

[107] One cannot be surprised that WorldCom's senior management was bewildered by the pervasive fraudulent activities in the company. See Coburn, 2006: 349 and 364-365.

[108] These include conventional criminal sanctions and civil or "administrative" penalties that are thought to be suitable ways of achieving optimal compliance. See Ogus and Abbot, 2002.

[109] In this case the combination involves a coordinated sequence of different sanctions whereby one is imposed accompanied by the threat of another.

that is a function of the corporation's nature.[110] It may therefore be important to determine whether the types of sanctions pertaining to the operation of the Accountability Model, as well as other sanctions are appropriate and effective for the convicted corporation (as defined in this book) and which mechanisms or aspects of which mechanisms of imputation reflect these. This will complete the evaluation of the mechanisms of imputation. In Chapters 5 and 6 and the first part of this Chapter, they are evaluated in light of the substantive and procedural rules. They will be evaluated below in light of the sanctions that may be visited upon convicted corporations.

7.3 Sanctioning the corporate offender

It was argued in Chapter 2 that a corporation can be punished because it can be deterred, incapacitated and rehabilitated. However, the question that follows is how to punish a corporation in order to achieve one or all of these goals. This question is often addressed from two perspectives: the economic and the purely legal. As mentioned above, given the limited supply of resources, the actual goal of these sanctions (from an economic perspective) is optimal compliance. Hence, the criminal justice system seeks to maximise the social benefits of compliance and minimise the social costs of both non-compliance and enforcing compliance.[111] However, beyond this outlook of cost/benefit calculus it is futile to talk of punishment if it cannot be served and if it does not (or is purported to) have the stigma of a criminal sanction. As such, an imprisonment term cannot be imposed on a corporation which by its nature cannot be incarcerated; and it is in my opinion oxymoronic to impose a civil or "administrative" penalty for a criminal offence. This implies that the legal question necessarily takes precedence over the economic one since the sanction's legitimacy depends on whether it is conformable with legal principles and standards and not necessarily on whether it is economically efficient.[112] Equally, Coffee[113] approves of Stone's[114] criticism of the "black box" (economic) approach treating corporations as morally neutral entities. Coffee[115] distinguished between the economic approach and what

---

[110] Thus, the best guidance as regards how the prosecution should conceive of the corporation is the mechanism of imputation.
[111] See Stigler, 1970: 526-536; Coffee, 1981: 411; and Ogus and Abbot, 2002: 289.
[112] *Cf* Byam, 1982.
[113] 1981: 393.
[114] 1975: 35-37.
[115] 1981: 394.

he called the "behavioral perspective"[116] and advanced that although an actor (in this case the corporate actor) cannot have perfect knowledge[117] and cannot work out a perfect cost/benefit analysis (of all of the actions of its agents), what is important is whether the actor was a "risk preferrer" or a "risk averter."[118] Although it is improbable that many agents (acting on behalf of the corporation) may be so rational that they would commit an offence either individually or collectively only after balancing the probability of being apprehended against the benefit to be obtained from a particular activity,[119] it is certain that the propensity to take risks may increase with the collectivisation of decisions.[120]

Given that this book is concerned primarily with the theoretical underpinning of the criminal law rules applying to corporations, focus will naturally be on the legal perspective of sanctions.[121] This implies that more emphasis will be placed on the subjective perception of the punishment by the corporation than on the objective standards of imposing sanctions.[122] Thus, the corporation is sanctioned on the basis that the aggregate of its agents may relate to the expression of disapproval embedded in the sanction. As mentioned above, this ought to be a function of the mechanism of imputation adopted. A mechanism of imputation ought to enable the court to ascertain how the sanction to be imposed will discourage the adoption of the same course of action that resulted in the commission of the offence by the corporation and other corporations in

---

[116] In this book this is referred to as the purely legal perspective because it is (or ought to be) based on how the law defines a corporation and circumscribes its actions and knowledge.

[117] In this case perfect knowledge of the activities of all of its agents. See also Schlegel, 1990: 24-25. Some senior managers and middle-level or operational managers may have selfish and concealed agendas.

[118] This follows from Breit and Elzinger, 1973: 693-713.

[119] See Schlegel, 1990: 24.

[120] This assertion is certainly not backed by any empirical study that I can cite here. However, Laufer (2006) provides a good picture of the distinction between what senior managers think on individual bases and what they do while acting to further the interests of the corporation. This also accords with the assertion by Breit and Elzinger (1973: 704) that the average manager is averse to taking risks when acting on an individual basis.

[121] However, episodic references to the economic perspective will be appropriate to discuss the functional value of sanctions.

[122] However, more emphasis may be placed on objective standards where corporations are sanctioned to further the interests of the public (teleological facet of the criminal law).

similar circumstances. In this light, the discussion below is geared towards colligating sanctions[123] and the mechanisms of imputation evaluated above.

7.3.1 Fine

The traditional penalty for convicted corporations in the United Kingdom is the fine. This follows from the idea that the single most important motivation of corporate activity is either to make profit[124] or break-even.[125] However, the use of fines as an instrument of manipulation has hardly achieved the desired goal because of a number of reasons, prominent amongst which is the fact that the fines are often too low.[126] The expedient solution would be to impose much higher fines in order to make the offence less desirable since the anticipated cost of the punishment would be higher than the anticipated gain of non-compliance.[127] However, the imposition of high fines is confronted by what Coffee described as the "deterrence trap."[128] He proposed a way of imposing fines for serious offences that exploits the fears and interests of agents of the convicted corporation.[129] This was based on some empirical data that showed two things: firstly, managers are scared of a hostile takeover of their corporation, the loss of their autonomy and the communication of their misconduct to the public; and secondly, the interests of managers and stockholders and the value of the corporation's stock overlap. He then contended that the convenient way of imposing fines would be by appropriating part of the corporation's common stock

---

[123] Applicable in the United Kingdom and those applicable in other jurisdictions and/or proposed by some commentators such as those listed above pertaining to the Accountability Model.

[124] See Braithwaite, 1984: 331; and Schlegel, 1990: 22.

[125] This may also be related to the happiness of the stakeholders. See McConvill, 2005: 44.

[126] See *R v Howe and Sons (Engineers)* Ltd [1999] 2 All ER 249. See also Wells, 2001: 33-34.

[127] This utilitarian approach founds the economic perspective. See Posner (2001) extolling the virtues of the movement from Bentham to Becker. See also Becker, 1968; and Posner, 2003.

[128] 1981: 389-393. This was inspired by the "liquidity trap" and is to the effect that a corporation can only be deterred by a fine that it can pay. For the operation of this "deterrence trap" in the United States where the Sentencing Guidelines provide for the reduction of fines for corporations that have effective compliance programmes, see Bodapati, 1999.

[129] Coffee, 1981: 413-424.

(in any form of equity security or debenture) and called this the "equity fine."[130]

His argument was that the "equity fine" would hardly affect interest groups other than the stockholders[131] and managers. As such, given that the "equity fine" would certainly materialise the fears of these two groups they would be spurred into putting in place better systems of control and exerting pressure on their subordinates to comply with the law. In spite of the fact that this is a synecdochical representation of stockholders and managers,[132] Coffee's "equity fine" tells us two things:[133] firstly, a corporation is essentially a device employed by senior managers to make profits for themselves and the stockholders; and secondly, the court or agency that imposes the sanction is less concerned with why the offence was committed by the convicted corporation than the way in which the latter ought to be chastised as a just desert.[134] Concerning the first point, if the corporation is a device employed by senior managers then it may only be identified with the senior managers. This implies that the "equity fine" accords only with the identification doctrine and the senior management failure test. However, corporate crime may be the result of the acts of several operational and middle-level employees and the senior management may even be unaware of these acts. In such cases, targeting the fears and interests of the senior managers and stockholders would be as good as administering migraine medication to a patient suffering from diarrhoea. With regard to the second point, the sanction of "equity fine" is

---

[130] It must however be noted that Coffee sought amongst other things to overcome the problem of externalities whereby the imposition of a fine on a corporation adversely affects employees and creditors.

[131] The justification for targeting stockholders is that since they benefit from the fall out of the crime they should naturally suffer from the impact of the sanction (Coffee, 1981: 417). By this same token it may be suggested that if the community benefits from lower prices of goods because after committing a cost-effective offence the corporation reduced its prices, a suitable fine or sanction would be one that extends the burden to the community.

[132] As stated in the previous Chapters, corporations come in different shapes and sizes and their constituent members have different motivations and dispositions.

[133] With regard to criticisms of the practical difficulty of valuing the stocks and determining their deterrent effect, see Schlegel, 1990: 32-33. And as regards criticism of the difficulty of influencing the conduct of senior managers, see Fisse, 1983: 1235-1236.

[134] The idea being that if corporate criminals are punished appropriately then future non-compliance would be checked. However, this is akin to the preposterous idea of punishing a convict by breaking her will and intimidating her and others.

not imposed on a corporation because the evidence adduced by the prosecutor shows that the senior management failed to install an effective internal control system that discouraged non-compliance but because it is contended that the fine may incite the senior management to install such a system.[135] As such, the punishment is not actually imposed because the corporation failed to meet the requisite subjective standard in a particular case but because the corporation (and other corporations) will supposedly be impelled to meet an objective standard in future.

The deterrent objective of a fine, whether cash or equity, is the multiplier effect that it is expected to have at the different levels and in turn on the collective unit. Shareholders and the senior management would exert pressure on the middle-level staff who would in turn exert pressure on the operational staff. However, it has been shown that while the senior managers of some corporations would fight to avoid the most basic of fines, the senior managers and shareholders of other corporations would remain aloof.[136] That is why Coffee's representation is described above as synecdochical. Also, that is why it may be submitted that providing standard pecuniary penalties for different corporations committing different offences is ill-conceived. Corporations have different objectives and act on different impulses and cannot be similarly influenced by a standard amount or standard range of amounts. The criticisms of the use of fines have been that they are either too low or too high. However, what these commentators and judges actually decry is the fact that these fines fail to deter neither the sanctioned corporations from recidivating nor other corporations in the industry. They either constitute a toll for indulging in crime[137] or a blank cartridge because of the "deterrent-trap." It may thus be advanced that the level of the fine to be imposed must be a function of the evidence showing how the offence was committed in light of the corporation's structure and mode of operation. We may look at some examples. Sections 66 and 123 of the FSMA empower the FSA to impose

---

[135] The evidence may show that the crime was caused by other failures such as the negligence of a few operational employees even though there was no control system in place. Forcing the corporation to install such a system may be a good thing for its governance but it is totally unrelated to the offence in question especially where the negligence of the few operational employees would still have gone undetected.

[136] This is because they are protected by limited liability and from bankruptcy. See Stone, 1977: 58.

[137] Schlegel, 1990: 22.

financial penalties on corporations guilty of market abuse.[138] The FSA however determines the appropriate level of the fine following a number of criteria set out in its Decision Procedure and Penalties Manual (DEPP),[139] which include whether the fine would "promote high standards of regulatory and/or market conduct" by deterring the guilty corporation and other corporations in the same industry and demonstrate "the benefits of compliance business;" whether there were failures in the management and control systems within the corporation that affected the market and consumers; whether the evidence shows that the breach was deliberate in relation to the corporate person's knowledge of the risk and indifference to the consequences of its action; the corporation's ability to pay; the benefit derived by the breach; the difficulty of detecting such a breach; the corporation's conduct following the breach; and the corporation's compliance history.

What is important to note here is that although the FSA looks at failures of the management and control system, it neither seeks to dissect the system and locate the site of the problem nor impose a sanction that both punishes the corporation and fixes or eliminates the defective component.[140] It is very unlikely that the drafters of the FSMA and the DEPP considered that corporations have different objectives and act on different impulses. The fact that the corporation is consistently referred to as the "person" and defined as "a body corporate constituted under the law of a country or territory outside the United Kingdom"[141] implies that the way in which the breach of the FSMA ought to be imputed to the corporation would naturally be in accordance with the applicable mechanism of imputation in the United Kingdom or other jurisdiction in which the corporation is registered. This implies that the financial penalty imposed by the FSA on corporations in the United Kingdom is actually intended to impel the senior management (and possibly the shareholders) to exert pressure on the middle-level and operational staff to comply with the FSMA. As stated above, this would hardly have the desired effect because some senior managers and stockholders may be aloof for a

---

[138] That is failure of a corporation to meet reasonable standards of behaviour in relation to the market as prescribed by section 118 of the same Act.
[139] However, these criteria are not exhaustive.
[140] Given the labyrinthine nature of many corporations and the cerebral approach of many corporate criminals it was probably thought that there may be great difficulty in detecting such offences and thus it is important to increase the level of the fine where the breach seems more difficult to detect.
[141] Section 417(1) of the FSMA.

number of reasons. The bone of contention here is that no link is made between the sanction, the offence and the nature of the guilty corporation (and the mechanism of imputation). Moreover, given that the applicable mechanism of imputation for such offences relates only to mechanistic structures, it is highly unlikely that the level of the fine deemed appropriate would deter or rehabilitate an organic corporation with a complex structure and devolved decision-making.[142] A heavier fine may then simply be a much higher toll for indulging in an offence.

There is no denying that there are instances where a low fine may be appropriate and instances where a heavy fine may effectively deter the corporation. Equally, there are instances where an equity fine may be appropriate and instances where a charge against the corporation's turnover would be an effective deterrent. What I underscore is the importance of taking the structure of the corporate offender and the mechanism of imputation into consideration when determining the appropriate level and nature of the fine. If the corporate offender had diversified from manufacturing furniture to manufacturing cosmetic products and was less inclined to use central coordination because no synergies would be derived, where operational employees in the cosmetic department conjointly breached the law and the supervision within that department was sloppy as compared to the furniture department, an appropriate fine should target the cosmetic department and its criminogenic culture. Thus, if the applicable mechanism of imputation is corporate culture or aggregation, a fine may be imposed on the turnover of the cosmetic department with an order that any spillover (whether the reduction of salaries or other benefits or loss of jobs) must be limited to that department.[143] The above notwithstanding, it is difficult not to admit that calculating the appropriate financial penalty will always prove to be a daunting task irrespective of the nature of the fine and the reason why it is

---

[142] This demonstrates the importance of a suitable mechanism of imputation. For another example of how enforcement agencies determine the appropriate amount of penalties, see the OFT's Guidelines (2004).

[143] An example is the financial penalty of up to 10 percent of "relevant turnover" imposed by the OFT. "Relevant turnover" is defined in the Guidelines as "turnover of the undertaking in the relevant product market and relevant geographic market affected by the infringement in the undertaking's last business year." The fine is therefore restricted to the benefits derived from buying or selling the specific group of products that constituted the focus of the enquiry. In the same light, a fine may be restricted to a specific department or group of employees that was the focus of investigation.

imposed. Given that it may or may not prove to be an effective deterrent, it is important to consider other sanctions.

7.3.2 Orders and injunctions

The prosecution services as well as some criminal justice agencies may apply to a court to make a remedial order requiring the corporation to rectify any defects in its system or amend its policies and practices.[144] A community order can also be made requiring the guilty corporation to carry out some activity that is beneficial to society.[145] The rationale for making these orders or injunctions is that the corporation has the resources and the capacity to rectify the deficiency within its system and avoid future breach and these actions will improve relations between the corporation and the society.[146] This implies that the use of fines in such situations would be futile since it is uncertain what level of fine would influence a corporation to the extent that it rectifies deficiencies within its systems and participates in activities that are beneficial to society.[147] However, it is unfortunate that where the corporation fails to comply with these orders or injunctions the criminal justice system finds recourse in financial sanctions to punish the failure or contempt.[148] This implies that the threat of a fine (although larger) is the criminal justice system's ultimate weapon to spur corporations into reforming their management and control systems or to simply comply with the law. As such, the same

---

[144] See for example section 9 of the CMCHA and section 42 of the HSWA.

[145] See for example Part 12 of the CJA. A corporation may also be placed on "probation" if it fails to rectify the deficiency or perform the community service. See also Note, Yale Law Journal, 1980: 513; and Parker, 2002: 262. This is similar to a punitive injunction that requires the corporation to adopt proactive policies and develop new methods of detecting and sanctioning non-compliance. See Fisse and Braithwaite, 1993: 42-44. However, unlike in the United States, these options are seldom used in the United Kingdom.

[146] See Fisse, 1983: 1226; and Parker, 2002: 262. See also discussions on remedial investigations and accountability agreements within the pyramidal regulatory framework in Fisse and Braithwaite, 1993: 149-151.

[147] The problems of overspill and individual accountability encountered by the use of fines may also be overcome. See Note, Yale Law Journal, 1980: 537; and Fisse and Braithwaite, 1993: 43. Also, unlike the fine, there is a higher likelihood that these orders or injunctions will be related to the actual cause of the breach and may actually deter the action or actions that caused the breach.

[148] See for example, section 33(2A) of the HSWA. The fact that the failure to comply with the order is a separate offence (Section 33(1) of the HSWA) is of little importance since the sanction that is imposed ultimately is a fine.

problems faced by the use of fines discussed above will eventually resurface. Interestingly, Schlegel[149] warns that probative injunctions or orders[150] are unlikely to be successful unless those implementing them have a thorough understanding of how the corporate offender functions as a business entity. This is in line with the conclusion of the previous subsection that the imposition of a fine must be based on the systematic knowledge of how the corporate offender functions. Hence, it is hard to see how the court or agency would influence the corporation's practices and policies by the use of orders or injunctions or fines if the applicable mechanism of imputation does not give them the requisite flexibility to amend the orders to suit each corporate offender's *modus operandi*. A restrictive mechanism such as the identification doctrine or the senior management failure test limits their oversight to the acts that the senior management can reasonably perform given the circumstances.[151] The above notwithstanding, since the same problems faced by courts or agencies when imposing financial sanctions will resurface, it is important that they apply sanctions that are not in anyway related to the use of pecuniary penalties. A good number of such sanctions have been devised and are implemented in a number of jurisdictions including those of the United Kingdom.

7.3.3 Incapacitation and capital punishment

Ayres and Braithwaite[152] contend that where fines cannot reform the corporation it may be necessary to restrict or suspend or revoke its licence. There are several instances where agencies in the United Kingdom are empowered to impose such sanctions. The HSE/Asbestos Licensing Unit (ALU) is for example empowered to amend or revoke the licence of a corporation working with asbestos[153] where there is evidence of sustained poor performance following enforcement or breach of licensing conditions or a very serious incident even though isolated.[154] The Scottish

---

[149] 1990: 37.

[150] See for example, section 183 of the CJSA.

[151] This is because the corporation is the senior management for the purposes of these restrictive mechanisms. Thus, even though there may still be deficiencies in the system that may eventually cause a breach, the corporation cannot be liable for failing to comply with the order or injunction if its senior management has done all what may be reasonably expected of a senior management in the circumstances.

[152] 1992: 35.

[153] See Control of Asbestos Regulation 2006.

[154] See para. B55 of Asbestos License Assessment Guide 2007 Revision 3.

Environmental Protection Agency (SEPA) is also empowered to revoke the licence of a corporation where it deems that the latter's activities in relation to the licence will cause pollution or endanger public health.[155] An analogy may be made between the amendment and revocation of licences and the incapacitation and capital punishment of natural persons. The suspension of a licence or the restriction of a corporation's activities may be said to be incapacitation.[156] Equally, where the licence is revoked the corporation's right to engage in the activities is simply terminated. If the corporation was created with the sole or main objective of performing such activities then the corporation will simply be dissolved. This no doubt is akin to capital punishment.

The incapacitation and capital punishment of corporations, unlike the sanctions discussed in the previous subsection, are in no way related to the use of fines. Hence, the criminal justice system is unlikely to be caught in the "deterrence trap" if these forms of sanctions are used.[157] The deterrence factor plays a very important role in the imposition of these sanctions given that the threat of removing the corporation from society (temporally or permanently) may likely prompt the senior management and middle-level and operational employees to refrain from engaging in parlous activities and to report non-compliant colleagues.[158] However, Braithwaite[159] posits that the deterrence factor hangs on the questions of certainty and harshness of the sanction. If the question of harshness is adequately addressed by incapacitation and capital punishment,[160] the question of certainty remains very much open. This is especially true with

---

155 See section 7(4) of the Control of Pollution Act 1974.

156 See Ogus and Abbot, 2002: 294.

157 Ogus and Abbot, 2002: 294.

158 Although it is stated above that some senior managers and shareholders may be aloof due to the fact that they are protected from bankruptcy and the corporation's limited liability, it must be noted that managers may be disqualified from acting as director or manager or taking part in the management of a corporation for up to 15 years if they are deemed "unfit." They may be "unfit" where they fail to ensure compliance to the extent that they may be deemed to have been grossly negligent. See section 6 of the Company Directors Disqualification Act 1986 as amended by the Insolvency Act 2000 and the Enterprise Act 2002. See also Dillon J in *Re Sevenoaks Stationers (Retail) Ltd* [1990] BCC 765 at 780. Thus, the fear of this sanction (that affects them directly) may prompt managers to ensure that the corporation is compliant.

159 1984: 329.

160 Owing to the fact that the suspension and termination of licences will impact on the economic and social life of the corporation and its members and employees.

large corporations that have the resources to challenge the prosecution or agency and are less likely to suffer from such sanctions. Thus, they are less likely to be deterred since they know that punishment is far from certain.[161] Also, although I have placed emphasis on the legal perspective of corporate sanctioning, (economic) questions of spillover cannot be overlooked. They are certainly going to influence the court or enforcement agency because one of the main reasons why a corporation's licence is amended or revoked is the detrimental effect of its activities on society.[162] Thus, it would be counterproductive to impose a sanction that will achieve exactly what is being avoided: society suffering from indirect side-effects of the sanction through the loss of jobs and development opportunities.[163]

Ogus and Abbot[164] however state that even if these sanctions are seldom used, the fact that they remain an option on the table implies that they may still threaten corporations to the extent that they may effectively deter them. Nonetheless, they also agree with the contention that the uncertainty blunts the threat. As such, if the suspension and revocation of licences may be counterproductive, it has been suggested that nationalisation of the corporation should be considered.[165] However, although it is certainly a way of positively restraining the corporation, it is quite similar to the sanction of "equity fines" proposed by Coffee. This implies that the same shortcomings of "equity fines" discussed above are also true for nationalisation. That notwithstanding, in this year of the credit crunch the use of nationalisation has become an expedient tool for governments of certain afflicted countries including the United States and the United Kingdom. Rather than sanction the corporations and their managers and employees for high risk investments and speculative financial schemes these governments have favoured intervening and averting situations where the entire system suffers from the consequences of the actions of these corporations. What this tells us is that different

[161] See Braithwaite, 1984: 329; and Ayres and Braithwaite, 1992: 35.

[162] See Shavell, 1993: 261-262.

[163] This is evocative of Pope Innocent's criticism of the excommunication of corporations which although premised on the argument that corporations have no souls is interpreted by Weismann and Newman (2007: 419, footnote n. 14) as motivated by the fact that the excommunicated corporation had to move its assets outwith the Church's jurisdiction. However, as noted in Chapter 2, Weismann and Newman provide no justification (apart from a reference to Coffee, 1980: 3) for the plausible but cynical interpretation.

[164] 2002: 295.

[165] See Braithwaite, 1984: 328.

types of sanctions are appropriate for different corporations in different circumstances. As stated above, legislating on a standard sanction for corporate offenders irrespective of the circumstances is ill-advised. Hence, questions about the incapacitation and "execution" of corporations must be addressed with that of the functioning of the corporate offender and the circumstances in which it breached the law. As mentioned above, the applicable mechanism of imputation ought to enable courts and enforcement agencies to link the sanction to the corporate offender in order to ensure that the objective of imposing the sanction is achieved.

Thus, the identification doctrine restricts the suspension or revocation of a corporation's licence to cases where a senior manager authorised or was indifferent to the sustained negligent or dangerous activities of junior employees.[166] On the other hand, vicarious liability leads to the sanctioning of corporations for offences that may in no way be related to the way in which its activities were organised or managed. This includes where a maverick employee or manager takes upon herself to dispose of the corporation's waste and pollutes a river and the SEPA decides to suspend or restrict the corporation's licence although there is little evidence that the sanction may prevent similar maverick actions in the future and deter other corporations. As such, the mechanisms based on collective liability seem more appropriate for the use of these sanctions. Where for example the breach was caused by a criminogenic culture existing within a department or by the confluence of the acts of the employees within that department, a sanction preventing the corporation from performing activities assigned to that department certainly incapacitates the corporation with regard to the dangerous activities. As regards the revocation of licences and nationalisation, the question of the mechanism of imputation is less important although it certainly directs the investigation and enables the court or agency to determine whether the problem is so pervasive that the corporation's continuous existence or method of functioning poses a serious threat to society.[167]

---

[166] This is equally the case with the senior management failure test although given that this mechanism applies only for the enforcement of corporate manslaughter or corporate homicide and also that the governing statute, the CMCHA, does not provide for the suspension or revocation of licences or the nationalisation of guilty corporations, it is only meet that the mechanism is not be considered here.

[167] It must however be noted that the sanctions of suspension and revocation of licences are often used by agencies such as those cited above to enforce strict and absolute liability offences. Thus, the breach caused by any employee within the course of her employment automatically renders the corporation liable lest it shows

A common problem with incapacitation and capital punishment is the uncertainty as regards the extent to which certain corporations will be deterred. The shortcomings of the mechanisms of imputation assessed in this book may seriously impede the ability of courts and agencies to determine the prospective impact of the sanctions. Nonetheless, it must be pointed out that there are sanctions that may impact upon a corporation irrespective of the way it is structured and functions. Public censure is a good example.

7.3.4 Public censure

The interesting thing with the sanction of public censure is that it facilitates the deliberation process as courts or agencies do not have to consider how the sanction will coerce the corporate offender into altering its structure and functioning in order to be compliant. They only consider whether the stigmatisation and loss of prestige are painful to such an extent that they may be satisfied that the message has been hammered home. As such, discussion on the link between the use of public censure and the suitable mechanism of imputation is restricted to the question of whether the guilty corporation deserves such a sanction.

Public censure in the form of adverse publicity order or other form is frequently employed in the United Kingdom. Section 10 of the CMCHA for example empowers the court to order a corporation convicted of corporate manslaughter or corporate homicide to publish a statement about its conviction, particulars of the offence and the amount of any fine if such a sanction has also been imposed. Sections 66, 89, 123 and 205 of the FSMA also empower the FSA to publish statements about the contravention by corporations and/or individuals. These public statements impact upon the image of the corporate offender and unlike the fine they do not only target the corporation's financial interests but also its prestige and influence.[168] However, given that there is nothing in statutes such as the CMCHA proscribing counter publicity by the convicted corporation, the latter may simply engage in a sustained publicity campaign to reverse

---

that it exercised all due diligence (for strict liability). Courts in such cases are not concerned about whether and how the acts of the employees should be attributed to the corporation and this makes room for uncertainty since the pattern of attribution is distinct from cases where courts are enforcing crimes of intent.

[168] Schlegel, 1990: 38.

the effect of the sanction.[169] Moreover, there is little evidence that the public would not interpret the adverse publicity as the same hackneyed criticisms of corporations and the censure would hardly actually hurt the image of the convicted corporation. And even when they do impact upon the corporation's reputation they may also adversely affect 'innocent' stakeholders like employees, creditors and consumers in the same way as heavy fines.[170] As such, the use of public censure may only have an advantage if it is shown to minimise externalities better than the other sanctions.[171]

Nonetheless, the impact of an adverse publicity order cannot be measured easily. As mentioned earlier, public reaction can be very unpredictable and the court may be unable to determine whether the consumers will shun both the producer and the product.[172] The court or enforcement agency thus uses this sanction primarily to inflict pain upon the corporate offender as a just desert for the commission of the offence. This means that if it is assumed that a corporation will suffer from loss of prestige as a result of an adverse publicity order, then the most important question facing the court would be whether the convicted corporation deserves such a penalty.[173] As mentioned above, the court or agency should be guided through the deliberation by the applicable mechanism of imputation.

As shown in Chapter 3, in the United Kingdom if the offence is not a strict or absolute liability offence or statute does not provide otherwise and

---

[169]Coffee (1981: 426) even noted that a corporation has a constitutional right to comment on public issues. See also Schlegel, 1990: 39.

[170] Since the corporation may lose customers and be forced to cut production and manpower. See Coffee, 1981: 426-428. However, it seems that 'innocent' stakeholders may be adversely affected irrespective of the sanction imposed. Williams (1983) thus notes that third parties (such as families or creditors) are equally affected when natural persons are fined.

[171] It must be noted that this must be limited to the circumstances of each case. Hence, it must be a question of evidence adduced before the court or enforcement agency and not of an empirical study of a number of corporations in a given region. This is because corporations come in different sizes and shapes and react differently to contingencies. Thus, after a survey on environmental regulatory sectors, Prez (2000: 11) advances that the naming and shaming of corporate offenders is successful in some cases and otiose in others.

[172] See Coffee, 1981: 429.

[173] It must be noted that the corporation already suffers from some degree of loss of prestige due to the harms of the indictment and prosecution.

the corporation was not the targeted victim, the applicable mechanism is the identification doctrine. However, if the offence committed is corporate manslaughter or corporate homicide then the senior management failure test applies. The fact that these mechanisms fail to distinguish between instances where a maverick senior manager or a mercenary board of directors decides to further her/its own selfish interests and instances where agents simply further the corporation's interests implies that the corporation may suffer unjustly from the penalty (intended to visit pain directly on it) in a number of cases.[174] Vicarious liability bodes even worse for the corporation because it may suffer the loss of its reputation due to the non-compliant action of any agent acting within the literal course of her employment. The application of the mechanisms based on collective liability (aggregation and corporate culture) hardly provides better prospects although this may be due to the poor (or lack of) delineation of these mechanisms. In their present forms, courts may hold corporations liable for the actions or omissions and knowledge of a couple of employees although the majority were compliant. As such, in these cases the punishment certainly does not fit the crime.[175] Thus, given the ambiguity surrounding the use of public censure, it may be advised that the sanction be used sparingly and only where the court is satisfied that the corporation as a distinct entity perpetrated the offence and deserves to be punished. As shown above, the mechanisms of imputation assessed in this book do not provide the requisite flashlight to enable the courts to plod through this mire towards a cogent conclusion.

7.4 Conclusion

The applicable and alternative mechanisms of imputation were evaluated above with reference to another set of secondary rules called the rules of adjudication. These are rules that guide the court and criminal justice agency through the proof and deliberation stages of the criminal justice process. Focus was on the procedural rules observed during the criminal trial and it was shown that although the legal personality of the accused corporation is recognised, the rights that are incidental to such a status are not easily accommodated. This is largely due to the difficulty of grasping the nature of the corporation that is prosecuted, convicted (or

---

[174] This problem also stems from the nebulousness of the concept of 'course of employment' or 'scope of authority.'

[175] If the corporation (as a distinct person) may even be said to have "committed" the crime.

acquitted) and sanctioned. It is submitted here that the most suitable compass is the mechanism of imputation. The mechanism ought to enable the prosecutor or enforcement agency to determine whether on the strength of the evidence it would be fair to hold an accused corporate entity liable for perpetrating the offence. However, the mechanisms evaluated above are not sufficiently developed to enable the criminal justice system to protect and enforce the rights of the accused corporation during the proof and deliberation stages.

Prior to initiating the proceeding, the prosecutor or enforcement agency ought to make a decision as regards whether the evidence collected passes both evidential and public interests tests. The evidence test requires the prosecutor to examine the evidence available and decide whether it is admissible and sufficient. Questions of admissibility and sufficiency were shown to be quite problematic in cases involving corporate defenders in the United Kingdom due to the nebulous nature of the corporation. The mechanisms that ought to provide clarity have consistently failed to do so. A number of rights normally enjoyed by accused persons including the right to silence, the right not be incriminated by hearsay evidence and evidence of bad character (where the exceptions do not apply), the right to a trial by jury and the right to be presumed innocent appear incompatible with the ability of the prosecution to present a fair case against the corporate defender. This is largely due to the fact that the applicable mechanisms (identification doctrine and senior management failure test) seriously restrict the prosecutor's scope of search and the likelihood of finding incriminating evidence. Where the prosecutor cannot find documents with incriminating information about senior officers the corporation will be acquitted. On the other hand, vicarious liability as an alternative mechanism is too elastic as it operates to hold a corporation liable even in circumstances where the evidence shows that a maverick employee committed the offence within the course of her employment. The mechanisms based on collective liability (aggregation and corporate culture) are shown to be closer to the reality of how corporations act and why they should be liable in certain instances and acquitted in others. However, they are largely undelineated and operate in practice to hold corporations vicariously liable for the aggregated acts and omissions of any employees. Apprehensive courts and Parliament have thus opted for the simplification of the prosecution of corporations with the consequence that any incriminating evidence against the corporate defendant almost automatically passes the evidential test.[176]

With regard to the public interest test, it was noted that the prosecutor's major concern is the "gravity" or "seriousness" of the offence allegedly perpetrated by the corporation. However, since these words are ambiguous it was suggested that emphasis should be placed on the question of whether the prosecution is an appropriate response to the harm allegedly caused by the corporation. Thus, the prosecutor ought to consider the impact of the prosecution on the victims and their families and on the community as a whole. Nonetheless, given that the prosecutor is equally accountable to the accused it was noted that she is required to consider the undue harm that the prosecution may visit on the accused irrespective of the outcome of the trial. This is especially true with corporate defendants whose image or prestige is often tarnished by indictment and prosecution. It was shown that the mechanism of imputation employed may determine the extent to which a corporation is harmed by the prosecution. Where such a mechanism restricts corporate crime to the acts of senior managers (such as the identification doctrine and the senior management failure test) the likelihood of the corporation being adversely affected by the prosecution is low because of the understanding of the public that it is the greedy senior managers behind the corporation that are actually being targeted.[177] Equally, where the mechanism of imputation is based on collective liability (such as aggregation and corporate culture) the prosecution would likely harm the corporation due to the thought that there was pervasive negligence.

Due to the difficulties of using procedural rules of the criminal trial as rules of adjudication it was suggested that it may be better to use the rules governing other means of assigning punishments to corporations. In other words, if procedural justice cannot be achieved it may be better to focus on another theory of criminal justice such as restorative justice. As mentioned above, one way of achieving restorative justice is the use of civil and

---

[176] Procedural justice is thus forfeited for the validation of substantive corporate criminal law.

[177] This is especially true where the corporation is jointly prosecuted with the senior managers. It is for example difficult to hear people say Enron was cruel although such is often the view when describing Kenneth Lay's actions. Also, AIG, Freddie Mac and Fannie Mae and Citi Bank have been in the news for a few months now although it is the senior managers of these corporations that are subjected to the contempt and wrath of the media.

administrative penalties and threats of sanctions by enforcement agencies. Hence, focus was placed on a comprehensive model of restorative justice designed by Fisse and Braithwaite called the Accountability Model. The opportunity provided by this model to minimise the use of the criminal trial in regulating the activities of corporations is no doubt commendable. A number of examples of enforcement agencies based on a similar model were discussed. However, it was shown that not only is the model designed to avoid attribution (individuals are targeted) but also it is difficult to see how the criminal law can be enforced via this model without referring ultimately to the procedural rules of the criminal trial. This is because even though enforcement agencies are given wide ranges of disciplinary and remedial power, in many cases they eventually prosecute or ask the COPFS or CPS to prosecute. This implies that questions of procedural rights may have to be addressed ultimately. As such, it is submitted that it is better to consider how the (primary) rules of mechanisms of imputation conform to procedural rules. From the discussion above, the primary rules of mechanisms focussed on collective liability are more adaptable to the procedural rules although they lack the clarity of the primary rules of mechanisms based on individual liability. Thus, an appropriate mechanism of imputation ought to be based on collective liability although it ought to be as clearly delineated as mechanisms based on individual liability.

Where the indictment has been proven beyond reasonable doubt and the accused corporation convicted the court has to impose an appropriate sanction. The court is then faced with the knotty problem of which sanction or set of related sanctions to impose in order to effectively deter the corporate offender and other corporations in the same industry. Fines may be too low or too high or may simply constitute a toll for indulging in crime. The equity fine proposed by Coffee and nationalisation are based on the fears and interests of managers and stockholders and may seldom influence a corporation that commits offences via the agency of middle-level and junior employees. Remedial orders and punitive injunctions may produce good results but their effectiveness is hinged upon the threat of a fine if the corporate offender fails to comply. Suspension and revocation of licences may deter corporations in certain instances but they may have very severe consequences on the community that may have to deal with the loss of jobs and development opportunities. Public censure may also result in a similar spillover and the extent to which the corporation's image may be adversely affected by the censure is unknown.

It must be noted that these sanctions are not necessarily ineffective or worse, otiose. They may effectively be employed to deter, incapacitate and rehabilitate corporate offenders. However, the sanctioning authority ought to have a good grasp of how the corporate offender functions[178] and ought to be able to yoke this knowledge and that of the nature of the prescribed sanction together.[179] It is therefore submitted here that a satisfactory mechanism of imputation should be able to direct the courts or agencies in this regard. The notion that the corporate offender may only be deterred or rehabilitated if the interests of senior managers and stockholders are threatened should be discarded. This may be attributed to the fact that the identification doctrine and vicarious liability previously directed the thought processes of criminal law courts in both the United Kingdom and the United States.[180] If due regard is given to the alternative mechanisms of imputation, courts and enforcement agencies may easily dissect the corporate offender and ascertain where the defective component lies and impose a sanction with the goal of rectifying or eliminating the defective component. As noted above, if operational employees in one department were to conjointly breach the law because of poor supervision within that department, an appropriate penalty, whether a fine or punitive order or suspension of licence, should target that department. However, this may only be possible if two things are accepted. The first is that a corporation is a changeable entity that may be identified with manager A and employee B in one instance and manager A and employee C in another instance. Secondly, the applicable mechanism of imputation ought to provide the court or agency with the opportunity to combine the acts, knowledge and attitudes of employees involved in the transaction under consideration for the enforcement of an offence caused by such a transaction.[181]

---

[178] See Schlegel, 1990: 37.

[179] See Wells, 2001: 32.

[180] May be that is why Coffee (1981: 399-400) advanced that corporations that have decoupled decision-making and implementation (including supervision) are "essentially undeterrable."

[181] This follows from the same argument that where the corporation invokes the privilege against self-incrimination in the discovery and proof stages, the prosecutor should be able to obtain information from any agents whose acts or knowledge would not be aggregated subsequently. This is because for the purpose of enforcing that offence the agents whose acts and knowledge are aggregated are the embodiment of the corporation.

This completes the evaluation of the mechanisms of imputation. Five mechanisms have been evaluated in light of the substantive and procedural rules and the sanctions that may be visited upon convicted corporations. In the next Chapter, I will show which of these mechanisms is the most appropriate. This mechanism should collate the different related rules and enable courts to interpret and implement statutes and precedent in a consistent and coherent manner. Thus, it will be proposed as an effective means of harmonising the ways in which criminal law courts impute acts and intents to corporations for the purposes of imposing liability and sanctions on them. However, given that no mechanism is shown above and in Chapters 5 and 6 to be fully appropriate, what I will actually propose is the least inadequate mechanism or the mechanism that is most conformable to the secondary rules and has the potential of being modified into a model mechanism.

CHAPTER EIGHT

CONCLUSION

8.1 Introduction

This book set out to achieve coherence and integrity in the way in which courts in the United Kingdom impute acts and intents (or causal relationships) to corporations for the purposes of imposing criminal liability and sanctions on them. The idea that was tested was that the use of an appropriate mechanism of imputation is a viable prospect for this to happen. This followed from the contention that the ambiguity of the concept of corporation and the unsuitability of criminal law rules to deal with this singularity are the major causes of the incoherence of courts' decisions and lack of integrity of corporate criminal liability. The methodology adopted was the internal approach or "interpretive legal theory." However, due to the fact that it would be fallacious to prescribe novel measures based on an examination of legal edicts only, some non-legal knowledge was incorporated in the exposition but on the basis that they may be deemed to be pedigreed.

Hence, it was suggested in Chapter 1 that the first step towards achieving coherence and integrity is ascertaining the meaning of the concept of 'corporation.' Nonetheless, given that the concept is not amenable to a precise definition an attempt was made in Chapter 2 to depict the profile of the corporate offender by abstracting from principles and theories used by criminal law courts, legislators and some commentators. Equally, the adaptability of the criminal law in dealing with corporate defenders was examined in Chapter 3. I was then able to build a framework of rules to guide courts in the process of imputing acts and intents of agents to corporations. A number of substantive parameters were generated to this effect and the applicable mechanisms of imputation in the United Kingdom and some alternative mechanisms were evaluated with reference to these parameters in Chapters 5 and 6. The mechanisms were evaluated further with reference to adjectival rules guiding the proof and deliberation stages of the criminal justice process in Chapter 7. These evaluations have shown that just as no single theory best describes the structure and functioning of corporations, no single mechanism of imputation may enable courts to impute acts and intents of different agents to different types of corporations acting in different circumstances on a coherent and consistent basis. However, it was also noted that the panacea is not what has been done in some jurisdictions such as Australia whereby the prosecutor has been provided with a chest of different mechanisms. Such a system may only exacerbate the lack of coherence and integrity because it allows courts to arbitrarily establish the corporation's guilt negating the extension of the privilege of legal personality to corporations and the rights incidental thereto. Thus, at the end of Chapter 7, it was submitted that given that no mechanism is fully appropriate, the goal of this book will be achieved by using a single mechanism that is identified as the least inadequate mechanism and modifying such a mechanism into a model mechanism.

This Chapter is focused on showing which mechanism may be deemed to be the least inadequate and how it may be modified. It begins by highlighting the shortcomings of the mechanisms evaluated and suggests ways in which they may be overcome. Then it identifies the least inadequate mechanism and proposes steps which courts may follow in order to establish the corporate defender's guilt when using this mechanism. Hence, the rules of this mechanism may serve as common principles guiding courts and prosecutors. However, due to the fact that corporate criminal liability cuts across a number of legal disciplines, internal incoherence may not be completely eliminated (the principles of some disciplines may naturally conflict), although it may be minimised. Finally, I will discuss the implication of the study and put forward recommendations.

8.2 Determining the least inadequate mechanism

The evaluations of the mechanisms of imputation in Chapters 5, 6 and 7 were based on the description of the corporation in Chapter 2, the explanation of how the criminal law ought to be used against such an entity in Chapter 3 and the parameters set out in Chapter 4. Thus, it was established that a corporation is a changeable entity recognised by a court or Parliament as a corporation due to its independence of thought and action and criminal liability may be imposed upon it either directly or as an accessory. The parameters generated from the operation of corporate criminal law include substantive secondary rules (corporate personality, agency and culpability and responsibility) and adjectival secondary rules (that govern the deliberation and proof stages of the criminal justice process). As such, it was submitted that the mechanism that courts ought to use to impose criminal liability and sanctions on corporations should have a primary rule of attribution that accords with these secondary rules. Given that all the five mechanisms evaluated were shown to have shortcomings in this regard, I will actually seek to ascertain the least inadequate mechanism and show how its loopholes may be filled with properties abstracted from the other mechanisms where necessary.

8.2.1 Least inadequate mechanism from a substantive perspective (rules of recognition)

In Chapter 5, following the substantive evaluation of the applicable mechanisms of imputation (identification doctrine and senior management failure test) it was advanced that both mechanisms are conformable (to a certain extent) to related legal principles such as scope of employment and constructive knowledge and the criminal law component of *mens rea*. Equally, they were shown to be concordant with the normative outlook of judges. However, they were not conformable to the principle of corporate personality and the external viewpoint of some non-legal commentators. Hence, they are not suited for the imposition of liability directly on corporations and the enforcement of crimes against organic and complex corporate structures. Nonetheless, it was noted that the identification doctrine has been modified by some courts[1] and this leaves a door ajar for the effective use of the mechanism in cases where the accused corporation had adopted an organic management system and/or the agents that acted were sufficiently empowered middle-level or operational managers.[2] This notwithstanding, even if the identification doctrine is modified in this light, the corporation would still be compelled to substitute for a guilty agent. Thus, the facts that only the acts of a senior officer and the senior management are imputable to the corporation under both regimes and the corporation cannot be liable where such an agent or the collective of such agents is not shown to be liable or grossly negligent raise the question of whether the courts actually distinguish the corporation's independence of thought and action from that of its senior officer or senior management. As

[1] *Meridian* and *El Ajou.* See also Png, 2001: 156-157; and Wells, 2001: 155-156.
[2] It is uncertain whether the senior management failure test may be modified in this light since the CMCHA's definition of "senior management" is quite concise and restrictive.

such, these mechanisms may rightly be described as restrictive forms of vicarious liability.

Disparaging the applicable mechanisms because they are variants of vicarious liability may no doubt be deemed to be a dyslogistic stance given that vicarious liability is the applicable mechanism in some influential jurisdictions such as the United States and South Africa. However, as shown in Chapter 6, this mechanism is largely based on policy considerations rather than the reality of the corporate defender's guilt. The corporation is compelled to substitute for any of its agents that breached the law while acting within the scope of her employment irrespective of whether the corporation as a separate entity entertained the *mens rea* of the offence or performed the *actus reus* or aided the guilty agent.[3] Unlike the applicable mechanisms that are unnecessarily restrictive, vicarious liability is unnecessarily broad. Nonetheless, it may be argued that it provides a more holistic perspective to preventing and punishing crime in the corporate context given that the corporation may be held to account for all crimes committed to further its interests. This is important because corporations are amorphous and may change their structures to suit contingencies and may therefore act through agent X in one instance and agent Y or both agents in another instance. Thus, it is important to give courts the flexibility to impute the acts of either or both agents to the corporation in different circumstances. However, it was submitted that for the purposes of coherence and integrity such imputation ought to be governed by the obligation of courts to distinguish between instances where the independent corporation used 'innocent' agent X or Y to perpetrate the offence or encouraged guilty agent X or Y and instances where agent X and Y acted on their own accord.[4] Vicarious liability does not provide any cogent basis to achieve this. The fact that policy considerations determine the rationality of courts' decisions implies that coherence may seldom be the objective of any law providing for vicarious criminal liability. Likewise the identification doctrine, vicarious liability requires the court to impute the agent's act to the corporation only where

---

[3] However, it was shown that vicarious liability may be used to target the corporation directly in instances where the corporation was in a special relationship with the victim and harm was inflicted on the latter by the former's agent. Nonetheless, this pattern is sinuous in its present form and requires further development.

[4] The invocation of innocent agency also solves the "problem of many hands" where the prosecution or court is unable to identify any guilty agent.

the act amounts to the offence charged. Little regard is given to the corporation's culpability and responsibility *per se*.

The aggregation and corporate culture mechanisms are attempts to focus on the corporation's culpability and responsibility. The aggregation doctrine operates to hold a corporation liable for the sum of the acts and/or intents of its agents that amount to the *mens rea* and *actus reus* of the offence charged and the corporate culture mechanism operates to hold a corporation liable for the existence of a culture (policies, practices, attitudes and systems) that encouraged or tolerated non-compliance by its agents. Both mechanisms may enable the court to impose liability on a corporation for the acts of its 'innocent' agents that amount to collective fault and also on the basis of the corporation being art and part in the commission of the offence by its agents. Nonetheless, although these mechanisms were shown to be in consonance with (to a certain extent) related legal principles of company law and agency law, this is not actually the case with the criminal law principles of culpability and responsibility. This is because it is uncertain whether the sum of innocent acts may be said to be equal to a guilty act and whether the existence of a culture that may motivate some agents to breach the law is sufficiently culpable to be deserving of criminal punishment. It must be noted that the aggregation doctrine was rejected outright by Bingham J (as he then was) on the ground that "[a] case against a personal defendant cannot be fortified by evidence against another defendant. The case against a corporation can only be made by evidence properly addressed to showing guilt on the part of the corporation as such."[5] However, Bingham J surprisingly agreed with the coroner that the identification doctrine was the appropriate way of making a case against a corporation even though this doctrine simply identifies the corporation with a named senior officer that is culpable, while the aggregation doctrine seeks to distinguish acts that are particular to the culpable corporation from those that are particular to its innocent agents.[6]

The blameworthiness of the existence of a criminogenic culture may also constitute a good ground to reject the corporate culture mechanism,

---

[5] *Ex parte Spooner* at 16-17.

[6] See Gobert and Punch, 2003: 82-83. Subsequent judges did not seek to justify the rejection of aggregation. In *Great Western Trains*, Scott-Baker J rejected the doctrine on the ground that it was not a pedigreed rule and he was not persuaded by the logic. Similarly, Lord Osborne in *Transco* at 51 described it as "illegitimate" because of the lack of precedent.

especially where the offence charged requires proof of subjective intent or malice. The offence of corporate manslaughter or corporate homicide created by the CMCHA that relies in part on corporate culture is based on an objective test of the way the senior management organised or managed the activities of the corporation in light of the test established in *Prentice* and *Adomako*. It is unlikely that such a test may be used satisfactorily in cases where the offence charged requires proof of subjective intent.[7] It is difficult to show how both the aggregation and corporate culture mechanisms may be used to prove the corporation's subjective intent. There is no clear pattern by which the acts and intents of agents or the existing policies and practices ought to be combined in order to establish the *mens rea* and *actus reus* against the corporation. Equally, no distinction is made between the acts and knowledge of agents whose province is analogical to that of the "brain" and the acts and knowledge of those agents whose province is analogical to that of the "hands."[8]

Nevertheless, these mechanisms were shown to be conformable to related legal principles of company law such as corporate personality (the personal liability of the corporation is addressed) and agency law such as scope of employment (the acts of all but maverick agents are imputable). Unlike the applicable mechanisms, aggregation and corporate culture were also shown to be conformable to the external viewpoint of non-legal commentators as both mechanistic and organic corporations may be convicted using both mechanisms. It was however noted that these mechanisms are not a fair reflection of the internal viewpoint or normative outlook of judges as expressed through the framework of enforcement-generated metaphors. This is because, as noted above, the mechanisms do not lay stress on the agent that acted as the corporation's "brain" or "nerve centre" or "head." The corporation is treated as a body with no "soul" but also with no "head" although judges have made an analogy between the corporation and the human body in order to underscore the fact that a corporation comprises agents that control it as the "brain" controls the human body and agents that merely follow instructions from above as the "hands" of the human body. As such, when determining what constitutes a corporation's knowledge, it is important to consider the knowledge possessed by the agent that represents its "brain" because her knowledge is

---

[7] See Wells (1993: 553-558) on the inappropriateness of such an objective test in *P &O European Ferries*.

[8] It was noted in Chapter 6 that although the acts of all agents ought to be imputable to the corporation, some ought to carry more weight than others due to the responsibilities of the actors.

a reflection of the corporation's practical and theoretical understanding of facts. This does not mean that the corporation ought to be liable because the "brain" is liable (identification doctrine) but that the corporation ought to be liable because the "brain" formulated the intention or encouraged another agent to commit the offence or failed to assess the risk of the actions of other agents.[9]

Hence, it may be posited that the aggregation and corporate culture mechanisms are less inadequate than the other mechanisms, namely the identification doctrine, the senior management failure test and vicarious liability. This is because they provide more logical avenues of achieving coherence in the way in which the criminal liability of corporations is established. They do so by targeting the corporation and not its agents and they give criminal law courts the flexibility to impute the acts and intents of different agents to corporations of different sizes and shapes in different circumstances. As such, the aggregation and corporate culture mechanisms may be used consistently to impose liability on corporations in such a way that where the agent is innocent the corporation's liability may be established via the doctrine of innocent agency and where the agent is guilty the corporation's liability may be accessorial.

A major flaw common to both mechanisms is the risk that such flexibility may translate into arbitrariness to the point where the corporation's liability for all criminal offences would be absolute. This is because the court would be able to aggregate the act of one agent and the knowledge of any other agent (even though their actions and knowledge are not related) in order to get the requisite *actus reus* and *mens rea* of the offence charged. Nonetheless, if the process of aggregating acts and intents or policies and practices is sufficiently delineated, the absolutism of the criminal law may be avoided.

It may then be submitted that although all five mechanisms assessed have serious shortcomings from a substantive perspective, the aggregation and corporate culture mechanisms have the most potential of being able to meet the standards of the appropriate mechanism of imputation. This means that if modified they may be fully conformable to the rules of

---

[9] Equally, unlike the identification doctrine (as modified in *Meridian* and *El Ajou*) the "brain" may not be a single agent but a collective of agents (board of directors or committee of managers) and unlike the senior management failure test, the corporation is not identified only with the "brain" (senior management) but with both the "brain" and the "hands" (middle and low-level employees).

recognition. However, corporate culture falls within the scope of aggregation given that if corporate culture has to subsist on its own as an independent mechanism,[10] courts would have to aggregate several acts of different agents in order to determine whether there was a policy or practice adopted at a given level that encouraged or tolerated non-compliance. As such, the aggregation doctrine may be deemed to be the least inadequate mechanism from a substantive perspective. I will now seek to determine the least inadequate mechanism as regards applying adjectival law.

8.2.2 Least inadequate from an adjectival perspective (rules of adjudication)

In Chapter 7, emphasis was placed on how the primary rules of the mechanisms of imputation conform to the rules of adjudication. These rules were deemed to be the procedural rules governing the proof and deliberation stages of the criminal justice process. However, a brief examination of the procedural rules showed that the nature of the accused corporation poses a formidable obstacle to their enforcement and Parliament and courts have in many instances introduced tailor-made rules that disregard the accused corporation's rights and facilitate the prosecution and conviction of corporations. Hence, the ability of the prosecutor to adduce sufficient admissible evidence is hampered by the accused corporation's right to silence or privilege against self-incrimination (as well as legal professional privilege or confidentiality of communications). This is because the right may translate into an impermeable firewall when invoked by the accused corporation since the prosecutor often relies on evidence (documentary and oral) obtained from the corporation itself.[11] Nonetheless, courts have held that only the agent that provides the information may be protected against self-incrimination and the information may be used to prosecute the corporation (as a separate person) for the commission of an offence. As such, a senior officer may be treated as a person distinct from the corporation for the purpose of obtaining information from her and then identified with the same corporation for the purpose of imposing criminal liability on it. Equally, Parliament has ordained that the right cannot be invoked during

---

[10] In Australia and under the CMCHA it applies together with the identification doctrine and vicarious liability and the senior management failure test respectively.

[11] This will be far more than the proponents of the human rights conventions bargained for and with human beings in mind.

the investigations by some criminal justice agencies. These no doubt impact on the integrity of the criminal law. It was suggested that a fair and just solution lies in requiring the court to seek guidance from the applicable mechanism of imputation. Thus, the extent to which a mechanism enables the court to apply the rules of adjudication bespeaks its appropriateness.

As such, an appropriate mechanism may compel courts to recognise the accused corporation's right to silence and consider as admissible any incriminating statement provided by an agent that will not be identified with the corporation subsequently. This is because for the purpose of imposing liability on a corporation the agent that is identified with it is the corporation. Thus, given that a corporation will be identified with agents involved in the relevant transaction, where the corporation invokes the right to silence, any statement provided by an agent that was not involved in the transaction may be admissible because it cannot be said that the corporation provided the information since for the purposes of enforcing the offence charged the corporation will not be the agent that provided the information. The identification doctrine and the senior management failure test do not provide the opportunity for courts to recognise the corporation's right to silence in this light given that a corporation is identified with an agent because of her station or position and a corporation would be untouched behind the firewall if its right to silence is recognised by the court.[12] Vicarious liability, aggregation and corporate culture have the potential to be modified to direct the prosecutor in such a manner as to obtain incriminating information from agents that will not be identified with the corporation subsequently.[13]

It was also noted that where the documents may have been drafted by some agent other than the one that testified or supplied the information, the evidence may have to fall under the exceptions to the hearsay rule in order to be allowed by the court. Parliament (section 117 of the CJA and section 17 of the CJSA) has however ordained that the information supplied will be allowed where the person that supplied it had or was reasonably expected to have had personal knowledge of the material contained in the document. It is difficult to ascertain whether in the United Kingdom this exception may even be considered if the relevant document

[12] The constraint imposed by the identification doctrine may have impelled courts and Parliament to disregard the right.

[13] However, where vicarious liability applies, the corporation may only be identified with the agent that is guilty of the offence charged.

was drafted by a front line or middle-level manager. This is because the corporation may only speak through senior managers (identification doctrine and senior management failure test) and where the document was drafted by a junior manager, the hearsay testimony cannot be said to be based on what the witness heard the corporation say. Once again, the alternative mechanisms assessed in Chapter 6 (vicarious liability, aggregation and corporate culture) are more progressive as they provide for the attribution of the act of any agent to the corporation depending on the circumstance. However, where the evidence is that of the corporation's bad character, these alternative mechanisms (excepting vicarious liability) do not provide a clear proposition of how the acts of agents would be aggregated in order to show that a corporation had a bad character, unlike the applicable mechanisms that direct courts towards the disposition of a senior officer or the senior management. Nonetheless, it was noted in Chapter 7 that considering only the disposition of a senior officer or the senior management is tantamount to vicarious liability as the corporation substitutes for a delinquent agent or unit. Thus, it was advanced that an appropriate mechanism ought to exhibit the clarity (though not the simplicity) of the applicable mechanisms (and vicarious liability) and the flexibility of the aggregation and corporate culture mechanisms. However, it may be difficult to change the patterns embedded in the applicable mechanisms to such an extent that the essential notions of the corporation's character are ascertained by referring to the acts of all agents involved in the relevant transaction.

Emphasis was also placed on the accused corporation's right to be tried by a jury of its peers. It was noted that although unjustified, there is no difference between a jury of a corporate person's peers and a jury of a natural person's peers. However, if a distinction were to be made, regard would be had only to mechanisms based on individual liability such as the identification doctrine and vicarious liability since it would be impossible to sit an aggregate of corporate agents or policies and practices on the panel. Also, proving that a corporation is liable may involve the presentation of thousands of documents and the examination and cross-examination of hundreds of witnesses and the mechanisms based on individual liability may help shorten the duration of the trial and make it less complex since the prosecutor's job would be restricted to showing that an agent of the corporation committed the offence while acting within the course of her employment and she was of sufficient station to be identified with the corporation. Nevertheless, since corporate cases are often protracted and complex, it was suggested that a trial without jury (in light of sections of 43 and 44 of the CJA) may be preferable although this would imply that the right of the accused to be tried by a jury of its peers would be disregarded.[14]

It is important to note that criminal proceedings are not only initiated because the evidence is sufficient and admissible. The prosecutor must also be satisfied that the proceeding is in the interest of the public. Hence, the prosecutor ought to consider the impact of the prosecution on the victims, their families, the community and the accused. The latter's interest is also considered because it may be harmed by the prosecution such as where the accused corporation losses prestige due to the publicity of the indictment and prosecution. It was shown in Chapter 7 that the mechanism employed in the jurisdiction may either increase or reduce the prospect of the accused corporation being harmed. Where the corporation may only be identified with senior officers (identification doctrine, senior management failure test and to a certain extent vicarious liability) the understanding of the public would be that it is the greedy senior officers behind the corporation that are actually being targeted;[15] and where the corporation may be identified with an aggregate of agents or defective control systems or practices (aggregation and corporate culture) the understanding of the public would be that it is the corporation and not any individual that is targeted.

In light of the above, it may be said that none of the five mechanisms assessed fits the bill to such an extent that it may be said to be the appropriate option. However, the aggregation and corporate culture mechanisms are closest to what is required given that they are based on collective liability and have the property of being adaptable. Thus, they may be modified to such an extent that they may be used consistently by prosecutors and criminal law courts in a clear manner. As noted above, given that the corporate culture mechanism may be considered an abstract part of the aggregation doctrine, the least inadequate mechanism with the potential of being modified to suit the nature of the corporation and principles of the criminal law and other related legal rules is the aggregation doctrine.

---

[14] As noted in Chapter 7, this right is already disregarded where the trial is brought in a Magistrates Court (England) or District Court where only one Justice of the Peace sits and sometimes in the Sherriff Court (Scotland) where only one Sherriff sits.

[15] See Zemba, Young and Morris, 2006.

8.3 Modifying the least inadequate mechanism

The aggregation doctrine is based on the computation of innocent acts and states of mind of different agents to produce a criminal act and state of mind in situations where no single agent could have understood the full import of the acts and states of mind in order to foresee and prevent the perpetration of the offence. The rationale is that the corporation represents the collective identity that emanates from the actions of these agents.[16] As such, many people may perform innocent acts in order to achieve a set objective and in the process collectively breach the criminal law. The sum of their innocent acts is no doubt a criminal act although none of them may be shown to have intentionally perpetrated the offence. Thus, the aggregation doctrine enables the court to distinguish between the individual acts and the collective act. The appeal of this mechanism is that it targets the corporate entity directly and may be used justifiably to enforce different crimes against different types of corporations on a consistent basis.

As shown above and in Chapters 6 and 7, this mechanism has a number of flaws both from the substantive and adjectival perspectives. The absence of a delineated pattern of imputation creates a state of absolutism whereby any corporation prosecuted will be convicted. Also, the fact that the aggregate of innocent intents and acts of agents is deemed to amount to the requisite *mens rea* and *actus reus* may lead to the conclusion that aggregation is not a credible criminal law tool and may bring the subject into disrepute. An expedient solution to this problem may be to distinguish between the *mens rea* of natural persons and that of corporate entities and describe the latter as the aggregated knowledge and intentions of agents, as well as policies existing with the corporation.[17] The unfairness of this solution is conspicuous owing to the fact that there was no intention whatsoever to perpetrate the offence. However, the CMCHA operates to hold corporations liable for corporate manslaughter or corporate homicide on the ground that the way in which their activities were managed or organised by the senior management was below acceptable standards. As mentioned above, this is an objective assessment of the corporation's fault and this statute may be said to provide that the grossly negligent act of the collective of senior managers is (objectively) blameworthy. As such, it may also be said that the aggregate of acts and

[16] See Bottomley, 1997: 288; and Orts, 1993: 1576.

[17] See Clarkson, 1998. However, he equally wondered if such "corporate *mens rea*" may be sufficiently blameworthy.

intentions of many agents may be grossly negligent and (objectively) blameworthy. Whether such an aggregate may be subjectively blameworthy is very much open to debate.[18] It is submitted here that this may be possible given the porous boundaries between subjective and objective tests in some instances.[19]

This means that the court may aggregate the act of one agent and the knowledge of any other agent (where their actions and knowledge are related) to get the requisite *actus reus* and *mens rea* of the offence charged. However, it was noted in Chapter 6 that Gobert's contention that a corporation's knowledge may be determined in line with a University Challenge quiz team demonstrates the practical application of the aggregation doctrine. This is because where there is no consensus several members of the team may suggest different answers to the umpire and the team may not be said to know the correct answer even though one of the answers suggested is the correct answer. Thus, in the absence of consensus it is impossible to determine the team's position. Referring to any one member's opinion would be a metonymic description of the team and combining the opinions of all members may be not be feasible given that some opinions may conflict. This shows the difficulty of aggregating acts and intents of agents where there is no delineated pattern. Where employee A had knowledge of a faulty safety mechanism but employee B was unaware of the faulty safety mechanism it is uncertain whether the corporation may be said to have been aware of the fact that the safety mechanism was faulty and why. However, if the knowledge of agents are given measurable or determinable values then the knowledge possessed by employee A may be said to be more representative of the corporation's

---

[18] Many of the commentators cited in Chapter 6 that propound principles of attribution that are cognate with the corporate culture mechanism advance that corporations require separate criminal law rules since conventional criminal law was not configured to deal with artificial legal persons. However, given that it was noted in Chapter 1 that the criminal law was not configured to deal with natural persons only, this line of argument may be abandoned.

[19] Scottish criminal courts for example sometimes employ objective standards to establish subjective *mens rea* and subjective tests to establish objective standards. See Gough, 2000: 730-731. See also Schedule 3, para. 3 of the Criminal Procedure (Scotland) Act 1995 that provides that it is not necessary to show that an offence was committed "maliciously" and "wilfully" as they will be implied. For an analysis of the overlap between objective and subjective tests in corporate criminal law, see Wells, 1993.

knowledge than that possessed by employee B; where the latter's knowledge had a lower measurable value.[20]

As such, it is important that courts give measurable or determinable values to the intention, knowledge, acts and omissions of agents and determine whether there is a balance between conforming acts and non-conforming acts and which way the balance tilts.[21] Hence, where manager A was responsible for the relevant transaction and employee B was under manager A's supervision, it is only natural that manager A's knowledge would be weightier than employee B's.[22] It may then be said that manager A is the brain or directing mind and employee B is the hand. Thus, the scope of the aggregation doctrine is modified to enable it cover the ambit of the identification doctrine.[23] Nonetheless, it may be difficult to avoid the problem of 'anachronistic aggregation' as some prosecutors may include information obtained by manager A's predecessors several years before the offence was perpetrated. It is submitted here that the question of

---

[20] The measurable value is a function of the agreements and management system adopted by the corporation. Thus, where A is given more powers than B, the former's act will have a higher measurable value than B's. This reflects the idea of consensus in the quiz team: where the members of the group accept that the team will deliberate and A will act as spokesperson and give the answer then the umpire will consider A's answer as representing the team's position. However, given that a judge has more time and resources than the umpire of a quiz, it is important that the judge examines the deliberations in order to determine whether A's answer truly represents the collective position. The judge will be satisfied if the ideas of all members are aggregated and the balance tilts towards A's answer.

[21] The idea of determining whether there is a balance is based on the fact that there is an interdependent relationship between the acts, omissions, knowledge and intents of agents and no dimension of one agent's action, omission, knowledge and intent (within the scope of her employment) may be understood in isolation. This is also consonant with the contention that it is the causal relationship between the acts and intents of agents and the offence that is actually imputed to the corporation and not the acts and intents *per se*.

[22] This is because other agents are more likely to act upon manager A's knowledge. However, as noted in Chapter 4, the court ought to consider the management system adopted by the corporation. Thus, if on the one hand it was a mechanistic system, a manager may be said to be the directing mind (with weightier knowledge) if she was sufficiently high in the hierarchy (as in *Nattrass*). On the other hand, if it was an organic structure, the manager may be the directing mind if she was in charge of the transaction (as in *El Ajou* and *Meridian*).

[23] However, it is not the guilt of the directing mind that is imputed to the corporation but her act or actually, what her act caused.

the relevance of such evidence should be one of fact to be decided by the jury or judge.

However, where the action of the directing mind causes the balance to tilt towards liability, it may be difficult to say that the corporation is liable if the directing mind was a rogue agent furthering her own selfish interests or defrauding the corporation. The offence would be deemed to be a product of collectivisation although the agent whose act has the highest measurable value was not furthering the corporation's interests. *Belmont* directs courts to refrain from imputing fraudulent acts to the corporate victim due to the apparent unfairness. Thus, in the process of aggregation the court ought not only give measurable values to the actions of agents according to their relative positions and responsibilities but also consider whether the actions were geared towards furthering the interests of the corporation.[24] In other words, the actions of agents that are aggregated ought to represent the collective position. However, the question of whether there was an intention to further the interests of the corporation is itself problematic. This is because it ought to include tasks that were performed in compliance with instructions or policies, as well as modes of performing such tasks adopted by agents.[25]

From the above, it may be contended that the collectivised action that was intended to further the corporation's interest is the hypothetical distinct action of the corporate person. The court may ascertain such a collectivised action by aggregating the acts and intentions of all agents involved in the relevant transaction. The aggregation will involve a number of steps. Firstly, the court will give measurable values to the acts of these agents according to their responsibilities and the management system adopted by the corporation. Secondly, the court will determine whether the acts that are compliant carry more weight than those that are not. Finally, the court will consider the deliberation or decision-making process that preceded the performance of the relevant activities in order to determine whether the acts that are aggregated (especially the directing

[24] Under the French *Code Pénal* of 1992 for example, the act of the senior management cannot be imputed to the corporation if such an act was not performed with the intention to further the interests of the corporation. The same may be said to obtain in the United Kingdom given that the concept of scope of employment has been widely interpreted to include the furtherance of the principal's interests.

[25] The use of the concept of scope of employment in vicarious liability case law (see Chapter 6) may help in this regard.

mind's act) were within the scope of the agents' authority and truly represent the corporation's position.[26] The aggregation doctrine may thus be modified in light of the above steps in order to ensure that courts impute acts and intents to corporations on a consistent basis.

8.4 The modified aggregation doctrine as the appropriate mechanism

The modified aggregation doctrine may stand out as a guide to criminal justice institutions if we refer to the description of the term 'corporation' in Chapter 2, the proposal of how the criminal law may be employed to regulate corporations in Chapter 3 and the parameters for evaluation established in Chapters 4 and 7. The corporation was described in Chapter 2 as a changeable entity that is recognised by the court or Parliament as a corporation because of its independence of thought and action and ability to relate to the consequences of such thought and action. The fact that it is changeable implies that in one instance it may be identified with the aggregated acts of manager A and employee B while in another instance it may be identified with the aggregated acts of manager C and employee D. In both instances, the collective act (aggregated acts) is distinct from the act of any individual manager or employee and the fact that criminal sanctions may incite these agents to make changes to the way they work may be said to imply that the corporation relates to the consequences of its actions. In Chapter 3, it was submitted that courts may on the one hand employ the doctrine of innocent agency to target corporations directly where no agent is guilty and on the other hand use the principle of secondary or accessorial liability to hold a corporation liable as an accessory to an agent shown to be guilty. In the first instance, the aggregation doctrine operates to hold corporations liable for the acts of agents that collectively resulted in the breach of criminal law standards. Hence, the agents may be 'innocent' and the collective unit (the corporation) guilty. In the second instance, the aggregation doctrine may be modified to such an extent that the acts, omissions, knowledge and intents of agents are aggregated in order to show that there was an existing

---

[26] As mentioned above, where there is consensus in a quiz team that A will be the captain and provide answers to the umpire, the latter (if in a court of law) ought to give priority to A's answer but also consider whether it truly reflects the deliberations that preceded A giving the answer. This is because A could be a maverick that disregarded the collective position and sought to further her own interests.

criminogenic corporate culture (policies, practices, systems and attitudes) that encouraged or tolerated (assisted) an agent shown to be guilty.

As regards the parameters for evaluation, the modified aggregation doctrine has a clear primary rule which compels courts to impose liability directly on the corporation where the 'innocent' acts and states of mind of its agents collectively amount to a criminal act and state of mind. This primary rule may be shown to be conformable to relevant secondary rules (rules of recognition and rules of adjudication). As regards the rules of recognition, it is conformable to the principle of corporate personality because the corporation is targeted directly and not forced to substitute for its delinquent agent. It is also conformable to the principles of scope of employment/maverick agent and constructive knowledge because all the acts of all agents performed within the scope of their employment are imputable to the corporation. However, in order to avoid the unfairness of vicarious criminal liability, only the acts of agents that were involved in the relevant transaction may be imputed to the corporation. This modified version of the mechanism also accords with the normative outlook of judges as the corporation is treated as an artificial body that is analogous to the human body. There is a "head" or "brain" (agent responsible for the relevant transaction) that directs the "hands" or "cogs" (other agents involved in the relevant transaction) to perform the wrongful act. Equally, this mechanism accords with the external viewpoint of some non-legal categories (contingency approach) given that the corporation may be prosecuted and convicted justifiably irrespective of the management system (mechanistic or organic) adopted.

As regards the adjectival rules, the court may recognise the corporation's right to silence if it is invoked because the court would refrain from admitting incriminating evidence provided by any of the agents with whom the corporation may be identified subsequently. These agents include those concerned with the relevant transactions. Equally, the testimony given by one agent may fall under the exceptions to hearsay if the person quoted is an agent that may be identified subsequently with the corporation. Also, it is unnecessary to consider reversing the onus of proof and disregarding the corporation's right to be presumed innocent because the prosecutor may compel agents that may not be identified subsequently with the corporation to provide information. Concerning the corporation's right to be tried by a jury of the corporation's peers, it was noted that since many cases against corporations are protracted and complex it may be convenient to have no-jury trials. However, there could be a possibility of using persons of the same station in society as those that may be identified with the accused corporation as jurors. Thus, if the accused corporation had adopted a mechanistic system the jury would comprise senior managers of other mechanistic structures and if the accused corporation had adopted an organic structure the jury would comprise persons that manage transactions similar to the relevant transactions in the case.

The modified aggregation doctrine may also provide a good opportunity for enhancing the effectiveness of sanctions. If courts direct their attention to the individuals or departments that were concerned with the relevant transaction, the chances of deterring the convicted corporation (preventing it from committing the same offence) would be higher. The courts would focus on these individuals and departments because for the purposes of enforcing the offence charged they represent the corporation. Thus, if the sanction targets them they are more likely to be discouraged from indulging in wrongful acts or motivated to exercise due diligence. However, this does not imply that a fine may for example be imposed on the individuals and not the corporation.[27] The court may simply ensure that any spillover affects only the individuals that collectively violated the law or the department that sustained the criminogenic culture. In the same light, the court may make a remedial order requiring the corporation to rectify any defects in the department concerned or amend its criminogenic policies and practices.[28] Equally, the amendment or revocation of a licence ought to be directed at the department concerned unless it was a pervasive problem in a mechanistic structure.[29] As noted in Chapter 7, the publicity generated by the imposition of these sanctions, as well the imposition of public censure is a just desert for the corporate offender that perpetrated the offence *qua* corporation and not *qua* agent.[30]

---

[27] As shown in Chapter 7, there are laws that already impose sanctions on such individuals. An example is section 6 of Company Directors Disqualification Act 1986 as amended by the Insolvency Act 2000 and the Enterprise Act 2002.

[28] This is consonant with Schlegel's (1990: 37) statement that prohibitive injunctions or orders may only be effective if the court understands how the accused corporation functions.

[29] Focusing on the relevant department may mitigate the harshness of the sanction of suspension or revocation of a licence.

[30] However, it may be difficult to justify the harms of prosecution suffered by the corporation. The fact that it is prosecuted for the aggregated acts of its agents (collective failure) may be interpreted as implying that the corporation is generally corrupt.

Despite the fact that the modified aggregation doctrine stands out as the appropriate mechanism of imputation the uncertainty of how it may actually be employed by courts remains. It is mentioned above that courts may ascertain the accused corporation's distinct act by aggregating the acts of all agents involved in the relevant transaction; and the aggregation involves giving measurable values to the acts of these agents and determining whether the acts that are compliant carry more weight than those that are not. The practicality of such a proposition may be questioned owing to the fact that acts and intentions are not interchangeable variables that may be readily quantified. The thought of assigning values to the acts and intentions of hundreds of agents involved in a relevant transaction may also dissuade many jurists due to the cumbersomeness of the task. However, although further research is required there may be few better avenues for establishing a link between the conception of a corporation as a distinct but changeable entity and the principles of agency requiring the acts of all agents to be imputable to the corporation and the rules of the criminal law requiring the elements of the offence to proved against the accused and not her representative or *alter ego*. As regards the practicality of the proposition, it was noted that courts ought to consider the decision-making process that preceded the performance of the relevant activities in order to determine whether the acts that are given highest measurable values or acts that cause the balance to tilt to one side truly represent the corporation's position or the collective rationality that guided the decision-making process within the corporation. It is submitted here that courts may establish a link between the preceding deliberations and the acts and intentions given highest measurable values by using the theory of the "discursive dilemma"[31] that has been developed as a means of (amongst other things) establishing the distinct personality of organisations.[32]

---

[31] See Pettit, 2003; and 2007. See also List and Pettit, 2005.

[32] The discursive dilemma was also used by Rock (2005) to explain how the collective rationality of corporate actions prevents the dilemma. Several other commentators have also developed the theory to explain a large number of problems as regards choices made by groups.

8.4.1 Using the discursive dilemma to establish a link between acts given highest measurable values and the corporation's position

The discursive dilemma is a modification of the "doctrinal paradox" first identified by Kornhauser and Sager[33] as a conflict between two procedures facing a panel of more than two judges in the deliberation stage of the judicial process. The procedures are the conclusion-centred procedure and the premise-centred procedure. Thus, where three judges are for example required to make a decision by aggregating their views on the conclusions (conclusion-centred procedure) the decision may often be different from that made where they aggregate their views on the individual premises (premise-centred procedure). Pettit generalises this analysis beyond the panel of more than three judges to all instances where groups are required to make decisions via competing procedures. He prefers to talk of discursive dilemma because the views of some individuals would have to be disregarded irrespective of the procedure adopted. As such, the collective goal or interest is prioritised eventually and not the goal or interest of any individual.[34] According to Pettit, the furtherance of the collective interest is guided by collective reasoning which demonstrates a faculty of reason or mind belonging to the group and not to any individual member.[35] Rock also contends that the corporation epitomises what Pettit describes as "groups with minds of their own" or "social integrates" and the corporation's response to the discursive dilemma helps us understand two things: firstly, that the corporation is not reducible to an aggregation of choices of shareholders or members of the board of directors; and secondly, that certain actions are guided by collective rationality and these actions are particular to the group and not to the members of the group.[36]

An attempt was made in Chapter 2 to endorse these propositions in order to provide content to the corporation's legal personality. They may also be used to guide criminal law courts towards ascertaining the corporation's distinct action on a consistent basis. However, it must be noted that the concept of discursive dilemma has been subjected to varied criticisms due to its expansiveness; and an account of the theory requires a

[33] 1986 and 1993.

[34] Nonetheless, there are instances where the collective interests and individual interests may overlap.

[35] See Pettit, 2007: 192. See also Pekka, 2007: 458.

[36] Rock, 2005: 8 and 24-25.

lot more space than is allowed here. Thus, the discussion here is limited to a basic description of the theory and how its underpinning logic may serve the criminal law courts. As such, this theory can be used to show how criminal law courts may refer to deliberations prior to the commission of an offence in order to ascertain the corporation's position. The theory may be used to this effect because it advises that the process of a corporation's reasoning may be captured by the reaction of its members or agents to the discursive dilemma that arises when they have to make a decision collectively. This means that when confronted with a discursive dilemma the members or agents would seek to further the interests of the corporation by referring to the collective intentionality or rationality.[37] The collective intentionality or rationality represents the corporation's independent thought process. We may consider the example of an instance where a corporation was prosecuted and convicted in order to determine how the court could have used the discursive dilemma and the aggregation doctrine as modified above.

In *Gateway Foodmarkets,* a corporation[38] employed a firm of lift contractors to provide maintenance to all its stores on a regular basis. However, contrary to instructions and without the knowledge of the senior management, the managers of one of its stores refrained from calling out the lift contractors to repair the persistent jamming of its lift and made it a regular practice to rectify the problem manually. This resulted in a section manager (taking his turn as the duty manager in the absence of the store manager) falling to his death in the lift shaft. The corporation was charged under section 2(1) of the HSWA which provides for strict liability because the prosecution is not required to show the corporation's proof of intent to commit the offence and the latter bears the onus of showing that it had taken all reasonable steps to ensure the health and safety of its workers. The court was thus required to establish whether the corporation exercised the requisite level of due diligence and the store manager and duty manager of one of its branches could not be identified with the corporation. If the aggregation doctrine as modified above was employed, the court would have examined the acts and knowledge of the agents involved in the relevant transaction in order to determine whether their acts and intents could be aggregated and imputed to the corporation. The

[37] Although it is important to give concise definitions to terms such as rationality and intentionality, it may be pragmatic to refer to their literal meanings at this point because an attempt to define such terms would no doubt shove one into an ideological and metaphysical battle that is unwarranted here.

[38] Later on became known as Somerfield Stores.

agents involved were the duty manager, the store manager and officers that constituted the senior management.

In a first instance, the court would have identified the directing mind in order to give the highest measurable value to her acts and knowledge. As mentioned above, this ought to be a function of the responsibilities of the agents and the management system adopted by the corporation. Proponents of the discursive dilemma talk of hierarchical collectivities[39] and summative collectivities.[40] Thus, if the corporation was a hierarchical collectivity the acts of the senior management would have been given the highest measurable value and the balance would have tilted towards due diligence given that the senior management had hired lift contractors and given clear instructions that all the stores should call out the lift contractors when the need arose.[41] On the other hand, if the corporation was a summative collectivity or had adopted an organic management system the store manager and the duty manger would have been considered the directing minds. The acts and knowledge of the store manager would have been given a higher measurable value than those of the senior management and duty manager. However, the court would have had to ensure that the criminogenic practice adopted by the store manager (and duty manager) represented the corporation's position.[42] As suggested

---

[39] These are similar to mechanistic structures discussed in Chapter 4.

[40] These are similar to organic structures discussed in Chapter 4. See Goldman, 2004.

[41] Unless there was evidence that the senior management had constructive knowledge of the criminogenic practice adopted in one of its stores.

[42] If no link is established between the acts that are most likely to cause the balance to tilt and the distinct interests of the corporation then the latter's liability would be said to be absolute. Khanna (1999: 375, footnote n. 120) for example discusses the case of *United States v Twentieth Century Fox Film Corp* 882 F2d 656 (2d Cir 1989) where it was held that the existence of a compliance programme cannot exculpate a corporation from the wrongful act (even contrary to the programme) performed by an agent within the course of his duty. Although this equally points to vicarious liability, the court held that once the amount of information obtained by a corporation's agent is equal to the requisite knowledge or *mens rea* of the offence, the corporation's liability becomes strict. As said earlier, strict liability and *mens rea* are not bedfellows. Thus, this is tantamount to jumbling different types of offences and criminal law components (strict liability implies the absence of *mens rea*). It cannot be said that there is no need to show *mens rea* where the agents hold a sufficient amount of information (including that of the illegality of an omission) given that the process of showing that the agents held a sufficient

above, the question of whether the aggregated acts and knowledge represent the corporation's position may be addressed by referring to the collective rationality that guided the decision-making process that preceded the performance of the *actus reus*. In other words, the court would have looked at the way in which the senior management (in a hierarchical collectivity) or the store manager and duty manager (in a summative collectivity) responded to the discursive dilemma that arose each time they had to make a decision about the maintenance and repairs of the lifts.

In order to show how the principle of discursive dilemma may have been employed to examine the process through which the decision to hire the lift contractors was taken, a number of assumptions may be made. Firstly, the corporation had adopted a mechanistic system or was a hierarchical collectivity and three officers at the level of the senior management, A, B and C, deliberated on the question of hiring lift contractors. Secondly, these officers deliberated on a number of related questions, namely, whether the corporation should allocate £5000 to the maintenance and repairs of the lifts of its stores, whether it should do so by hiring a specialist company and whether it should hire company X. If each of the managers expressed a view with the objective of furthering the interests of the corporation[43] and their views were consistent over a period of time during which three meetings were held, then it may have been shown that a discursive dilemma arose in the following instance:[44]

	Allocate £5000 to lift maintenance	**Hire a specialist company**	**Hire company X**
A	No	Yes	No
B	Yes	No	No
C	Yes	Yes	Yes

In the first meeting the question of allocating £5000 to the maintenance and repairs of the corporation's lifts was posed and a majority answered in the affirmative. In the second meeting a year later, the question was asked whether a specialist company should be hired to provide maintenance and repair lifts and a majority answered in the affirmative. However, in the

---

amount of information is tantamount to the prosecution discharging its onus of proving *mens rea*.

[43] In other words, they had homogenous interests. See Rock, 2005:11.

[44] This follows from the expositions of Kornhauser and Sager (1992) and Pettit (2003) on the origin of the "doctrinal paradox" and the "discursive dilemma."

third meeting the question was asked whether the corporation should hire company X and a majority objected. If the panel customarily made decisions using a conclusion-based rule, the corporation would not have hired company X. On the other hand, if the panel made decisions using a premise-based rule, company X would have been hired since the majority accepted both premises. As such, the panel would have been confronted with a conflict between the previous endorsements of two similar issues by a majority (premise-based procedure) and the rejection of the ensuing decision by another majority (conclusion-based procedure). Pettit advances that for the purposes of coherence and credibility the corporation would adopt the majority view on the premises (premise-centred procedure).[45] This is because a corporation that behaves coherently is more credible in business.[46] As such, a corporation tends to respond to discursive dilemmas in a manner that enables its actions to be coherent and predictable to investors and the response is often the adoption of the majority view on the premises. Thus, it would have been established that the corporation favoured hiring a specialist company.

Given that the corporation was a hierarchical collectivity, the court would have assigned a higher measurable value to the acts or decisions of the senior management than the acts or decisions of the store manager and duty manager. If for example, the court assigned a value of 20 to the senior management and a value of 5 to both the store manager and the duty manager, the balance would have tilted towards the exercise of due diligence by the senior management that had hired a specialist company and instructed all the stores to call out this specialist company when the need arose.[47] What is important is that the deliberations prior to the senior management's decision (shown in the table above) attest to the fact that the decision represented the collective rationality that customarily governed the decision-making processes within the corporation and thus represented the corporation's position. As such, the corporation would have been acquitted. However, if the senior management was shown to have had constructive knowledge of the practice adopted in one of its stores,[48] the court would have had to consider other prior deliberations,

[45] 2003: 173.

[46] See Rock, 2005: 9-10.

[47] However, the senior managers could have been furthering their own selfish interests by recommending the hiring of a friend's company when none was actually needed.

[48] The prosecution could have shown that the senior management's omission to make an enquiry was reckless. See Lord Denning in *Compania Maritima* at 68.

such as discussions on the need for the senior management to make enquiries, in order to ensure that the senior management's failure to proscribe the criminogenic practice represented the corporation's position.

If on the other hand the corporation was a summative collectivity or had adopted an organic management structure, the court would have given the acts of the store manager and duty manager a higher measurable value than those of the senior management. However, if the deliberations shown in the table above were conducted by the store manager, the duty manager and other managers of the store, the court would have held that the criminogenic practice adopted by the store manager and duty manager did not represent the corporation's position, despite the fact that the balance would have tilted towards the criminogenic practice (given that the latter would have been the directing mind). The corporation would have been acquitted because the practice did not represent the collective rationality that governed decision-making within the corporation. The majority view on the premises favoured hiring a specialist company and the store manager and the duty manager were rogue agents, lest they had unfettered powers. However, it must be noted that there are instances where the prosecution or the court may be unable to find evidence of such prior deliberations.[49] It is submitted here that in such instances the court should assume that the way the balance tilts represents the corporation's position.

I have thus attempted to show how courts may aggregate the acts of agents and practices existing within corporations and believe that this is a more cogent approach than that adopted by the Court of Appeal in *Gateway Foodmarkets*. Evans LJ first of all raised the concept of vicarious liability and sought to establish that section 2(1) of the HSWA imposes vicarious liability on the employer for the criminal acts of all of its employees owing to the fact that both concepts of strict liability and vicarious liability overlap. However, referring to Lord Hoffmann's statement in *Associated Octel*, he dismissed the relevance of vicarious liability on the ground that section 2(1) of the HSWA imposed a duty directly on the corporate employer and not on the individual employees. The only available option was thus the mechanism for imposing liability directly on corporations in the United Kingdom, the identification doctrine. Counsel for the appellant company had submitted that the

[49] However, the prosecution has the power to compel agents to provide information. Also, in cases where the offence charged is a strict liability offence, the onus of proof is on the corporation and it is less likely that the corporation will withhold information that may exculpate it.

company could not be liable because neither the duty manager nor the store manager were of sufficient standing to be identified with the company and the facts of the case showed that the head office or senior management had conducted their undertakings in such a way as to ensure the safety of workers and did not know of the practice (contrary to their instructions) adopted in that store, which was only one of the company's many stores.

Evans LJ however turned to the purpose of the legislation and posited that it was axiomatic that Parliament intended to impose liability on the employer whenever the event, in this case failure to ensure the health and safety of employees, occurred.[50] He cited *British Steel* and concluded that the question of whether an employer should be liable for the criminal acts of even a maverick junior employee would depend on the construction of the applicable statutory provision. He further contended that the statutory defence of due diligence is available to the employer only when reasonable precautions have been taken at all levels and the failure was due to the act of a maverick employee. It is no doubt splitting hairs arguing that there is a distinction between vicarious criminal liability and Evans LJ's interpretation of section 2(1) of the HSWA. Although he dismissed vicarious liability, he eventually admitted that its principles may apply in certain circumstances given that Lord Hoffmann in *Associated Octel* had interpreted section 3(1) of the HSWA as extending the employer's liability to include work performed by an independent contractor that forms part of the employer's undertaking.[51] Evans LJ's decision is therefore illustrative of the lack of coherence in the way judges impose criminal liability on corporations. Although it is important to consider the equity or spirit of the statute, where the judge clearly disregarded express provisions, it is difficult to say that the objective of the statute was achieved. The statute clearly provides for a defence of due diligence and the precedent (*Nattrass*) dictates that a corporation would successfully invoke this defence if the negligent agent was not of sufficient station to be identified with the corporation. Thus, like Lord Hoffmann in *Meridian*, Evans LJ simply avoided the unduly restricted form of the rule in *Nattrass* and the unfair consequences of rigorously applying it. So he equally fashioned a "special rule" that should apply only when interpreting that particular statutory provision in the circumstances of that case. As such, although he dismissed the relevance of vicarious

[50] *Gateway Foodmarkets* at 83.
[51] See *Associated Octel* at 850.

liability he applied it anyway because it gave him the result Parliament supposedly intended to achieve.[52]

As shown in this book, coherence and integrity may be achieved by giving regard to a cogent theory linking the conception of the corporation as a distinct but changeable entity to the principles of agency requiring the acts of all agents to be imputable to the corporation and the rules of the criminal law requiring the elements of the offence to be proved against the accused and not her representative or *alter ego*. The modified aggregation doctrine described above provides a good opportunity. Internal incoherence will be avoided as the related legal rules are harmonised. It is true that there are instances where the equity of the relevant statute may provide "second-order reasons" that may discount the "first-order reason" of the primary rule of a mechanism.[53] However, where Parliament's intention is clearly stated as in the cases cited above, an apprehensive judge may neither discount such clear provisions nor disregard the primary rule that ought to apply.

8.5 Concluding Thoughts

This book proposes an approach to harmonise the imputation of acts and intents (or causal relationships) to corporations by criminal law courts. Such harmonisation requires establishing common ways of interpreting rules of statutes and precedent through a mechanism designed to collate relevant rules. This mechanism comprises a number of rules that direct courts to aggregate the acts, omissions, intents and knowledge of all agents involved in a relevant transaction in order to determine whether the aggregate is consistent with the collective rationality that governed the decision-making processes in the corporation prior to the performance of the *actus reus* of the offence charged. It is submitted that if courts seek direction from this mechanism when enforcing criminal laws against corporations their decisions will be fairly coherent and predictable.

---

[52] See also *Alphacell* where the House of Lords relied on the literal meaning of the words used in the provision and what they inferred as the purpose of the legislation; and also *Alfred McAlpine*, where Simon Brown LJ understood their Lordships' statements in *Alphacell* as implying vicarious liability (because nothing else could make legal sense) and so held the corporate defendant vicariously liable.

[53] See Perry (1989) on the weighting of decisions according to "second-order reasons."

In the process of explaining this approach a number of propositions were offered. Given the current uncertainty as regards what criminal law courts mean when they talk of a 'corporation,' this term was defined as any changeable entity (existing in the legal world) that is recognised either by the legislator or the court as a corporation because of its independence of thought and action and ability to relate to the consequences of such thought and action. The independence of thought and action and ability to relate to their consequences justify the ascription of responsibility and the imposition of punishments on corporations whether for deontological or teleological purposes. However, since criminal responsibility and punishability do not presuppose amenability to the criminal law it was also noted that the rules of the criminal law ought to be adaptable to deal with the peculiarity of the corporate defender.[54] It was therefore submitted that a corporation's liability ought to be either direct (non-derivative) where its agents are 'innocent' or accessorial (derivative) where one or many of its agents are shown to be guilty. This may resolve the quandary created by the facts that where the offence requires proof of intent, criminal law courts compel corporations to substitute for guilty senior managers (a restrictive form of vicarious liability); where the offence is a strict or absolute liability offence, criminal law courts hold corporations liable for the act of any agent;[55] and where the corporation was the targeted victim of the agent's fraud, some criminal law courts have declined to impute the fraud to the corporation in spite of the agent's station.[56]

Hence, coherence and integrity may be achieved if the imputation of acts and intents to corporations for the purposes of imposing criminal liability and sanctions on them are guided by the truth of the corporations' nature. In other words, if a corporation is agent X acting within the scope of her employment, whenever an offence is perpetrated by agent X within such a scope the court ought to say that the offence was perpetrated by the

---

[54] This is especially true in the United Kingdom where vicarious liability is shunned and the defendant may only be directly or personally liable in criminal law.

[55] The enforcement of strict and absolute liability offences is consonant with the principle of innocent agency because no agent may be guilty of such offences given that the corporation as the duty holder is the only person that can be liable in the event of the breach of the duty.

[56] Treating the corporation as an accessory in cases where one or many agents are shown to be guilty automatically discounts the imputation of fraud to the corporation if it was the targeted victim. This is because it may not be said that the corporation encouraged or assisted an agent in swindling its assets.

corporation. However, there are several patterns that a corporation may employ to act through an agent. In some instances, both the corporation and the agent may be guilty, while in others only the agent may be innocent. Thus, the conception of a corporation as an agent acting within the scope of her employment is only partially true and may be false sometimes because the corporate defender may comprise the innocent acts of agent X and the innocent knowledge of agent Y. Also, the corporation may comprise the innocent act of agent X and the guilty act of agent Y, where agent Y would not have been able to commit the offence without the opportunity provided by the corporation for agent Y to work with agent X. This shows that the corporation and its agent are two separate persons with distinct impulses.[57] As such, there are instances where the agent may use the corporation as a front to perpetrate an offence[58] and there are instances where the corporation may use the agent to perpetrate an offence.[59] In the first instance, the agent ought to be liable in her personal capacity and if there is any evidence that the corporation aided or abetted the guilty agent either acting through another agent or because of the existence of a criminogenic culture, then the guilty agent ought to be liable as the principal offender while the corporation ought to be liable as an accessory.[60] This is a more predictable and cogent basis for the imposition of criminal liability on corporations. However, such coherence may be maintained only if courts are guided by a set of rules directing the imputation of the acts and intents of certain agents to corporations in certain circumstances. The consistent relation of the rules that courts invoke to impute acts and intents to corporations is described as a mechanism of imputation.

---

[57] It also shows that what is actually imputed to the corporation is not agent Y's act but the causal relationship between agent Y's act (and may be agent X's knowledge) and the offence. In other words, the prosecutor's job is to show that the corporation used either agent X or both agents X and Y to cause the result that completed the offence.

[58] Thus, the corporation has been described as the agent's *ego*. See Note, Harvard Law Review, 1982: 853-871. See also *Gencor v Dalby* [2000] 2 BCLC 734. This may be a good ground for the court to lift the corporate veil in order to punish the agent behind the veil. See *Gilford Motor Co Ltd v Home*.

[59] It is submitted here that such instances should be governed by the principle of innocent agency which is related to the defence of "employee necessity" and the concept of "member-responsibility."

[60] However, the acts of the other agent that aids and abets the principal offender, as well as the culture must represent the collective rationality that governed decision-making prior to the commission of the offence.

It is submitted that the rules of an appropriate mechanism of imputation ought to provide patterns of attribution that are both predictable and legally acceptable. The conditions of predictability and legal acceptability require an observer to anticipate (within the specified bounds of the criminal law) what the courts will do. However, given that the understanding of the conception of rules of attribution is confounded by a confused usage of terminologies (primary rules, secondary rules, general rules), I believe that for the purposes of orderly continuity (and therefore predictability) it may be better to adopt the usage of terminologies by Hart and to a certain extent Dworkin.[61] As such, the rules of attribution that emanate from statute or precedent may be referred to as the primary rules.[62] Equally, since corporations may act (via their agents) in more ways than can possibly be envisaged by legislators and judges, the application of these primary rules ought to be directed by other rules that include related legal principles and factual considerations or explanations of the corporate phenomena. These other rules enable the courts to arrive at the "best constructive interpretation" of the primary rule and may be called secondary rules.[63] Factual considerations were deemed to be governed by common sense because secondary rules that are strictly legal ("pedigree-based test") do not always explain the meaning of a word used in expressing the primary rule. Such common sense may therefore involve the use of a "content-based test" with "non-pedigreed" rules including prescriptions by non-legal commentators. However, given that from a positivist perspective, courts will not give regard to non-pedigreed rules (they are not legally binding), it was suggested that reference to non-legal prescriptions ought to be restricted to theories invoked in the *obiter dicta* of criminal law judgements. This will limit the scope of interpretation of primary rules, avoid judicial activism and enhance predictability and integrity.

---

[61] The probability of achieving the goal of predictability is increased by the shift from Lord Hoffmann's conception to Hart's because unlike the former, the latter does not seek to further judicial activism (the making of "special rules" by judges), which is a source of incoherence.

[62] This is because the rules of attribution embedded in a statutory provision or precedent constitute the "first-order" or "formal" reason why courts impute the acts of certain agents to corporations in given circumstances.

[63] As noted in Chapter 4, the secondary rules are restricted to the rules of recognition (governing the discovery stage of the criminal justice process) and the rules of adjudication (governing the proof and deliberation stages). Rules of change are not discussed because they do not direct courts on how to interpret and apply primary rules but on how to change them.

Thus, the primary rule of a mechanism of imputation ought to emanate from a statute or precedent (*rationes decidendi*) but it ought to be consonant with secondary rules that set standards which are essential for the use of the criminal law against corporations. The first types of secondary rules, rules of recognition (substantive corporate criminal liability) include related legal principles deduced from company law such as corporate personality; principles of scope of employment/maverick employee and constructive knowledge deduced from agency law; and principles of responsibility and culpability deduced from the criminal law. The rules of recognition also include the patterns of attribution that may be deduced from the outlook of judges (internal point of view) expressed in the *obiter dicta* of their judgements and the factual propositions of non-participants in legal practice equally alluded to by judges in the *obiter dicta* of their judgements but described here as the external point of view.

The internal point of view is restricted further to the metaphors (enforcement-generated metaphors) employed by judges to describe how acts and intents ought to be imputed to corporations. The external point of view is also limited to organisation theories on the restructuring of corporations to suit contingencies in light of allusions by judges to the fact that courts should consider the systems of management and control adopted by accused corporations. The external viewpoint is restricted further to two major theories of management systems regularly used in contingency thinking: the mechanistic and organic theories. These theories are said to explain the agent's commitment to the corporation with regard to her function and responsibility and the mode she adopts to perform her function or further the corporation's interests. As such, if emphasis is placed on the transaction that allegedly breached the law and the motivations or objectives of the various agents that were involved, where the evidence shows that the corporation had adopted a mechanistic system, the act (and not necessarily the guilty act) of any senior manager involved ought to be assigned a higher measurable value when combining the acts of all the agents involved.[64] Equally, where the evidence shows that the corporation had adopted an organic system, the act of any agent that had control over the transaction under consideration would be assigned a higher measurable value.

---

[64] Thus, if the senior manager of a mechanistic system was reckless, there is a high probability that the corporation would also be deemed to have been reckless.

It was also noted that the existence of so many constructs is indicative of the diverseness of corporations and the different ways in which they use their agents to perform defined actions and breach the law. As such, where the constructs have been standardised and developed as a set of legal rules (mechanism of imputation), it has been difficult to use the same set of rules to regulate corporations that are different in terms of structure and functioning from those previously envisaged. As shown in Chapters 3, 5 and 7, the identification doctrine and senior management failure test were premised on the assumption that corporations are mechanistic structures and so it is difficult to prosecute organic structures successfully using these mechanisms. Thus, an appropriate mechanism ought to be flexible to such an extent that it could be used to impute the acts and omissions of different agents to different corporations in different circumstances. Equally, the mechanism ought to enable the court to distinguish between transgressions that may be blamed on the corporate person and those that cannot be blamed on it due to the fact that they fall outside the scope of its legal responsibility. In other words, the mechanism ought to ensure that a corporation is punished only for crimes committed *qua* corporation. Although all five mechanisms evaluated are shown to have serious flaws, the aggregation doctrine is deemed to be the least inadequate mechanism because it is closest to the paradigm of what may be described as the appropriate mechanism of imputation. It is shown above how it may be modified to suit this paradigm.

There is no doubt that there is still more work to be done than has been achieved so far. This book discusses the major points of a comprehensive approach to achieve coherence and integrity in the way courts impose criminal liability on corporations. In Chapter 1, it was noted that previous commentators have deplored corporate criminal law's lack of a cogent theoretical base. Hence, the analysis carried out here was geared towards finding that common thread in the different interpretations and explanations of statutes and precedent which, in light of Allan's logic,[65] would demonstrate that there is some coherence after all. Thus, although I started with a bias that the subject was marred by incoherence, my analysis confirms this bias. However, it seems courts and legislators that have adjudicated and legislated on criminal cases involving corporations must not be the only ones to bear the brunt of the blame.

[65] The common thread would justify the way in which judges have interpreted and applied the law. See Allan, 2004: 709-711.

There is hardly any clear legal methodology and some commentators even contend that there is none truly.[66] This may be blamed on an ambient fear that incorporating non-legal concepts (including moral constructs) into legal doctrinal analysis dilutes legal scholarship and seriously impacts upon its practical utility.[67] Thus, in order to minimise incoherence, corporate criminal law was examined in this book using the "internal approach" or "interpretive legal theory," whereby the analysis was restricted to the features of the law. This typifies the standard positivist view. However, "inclusive" positivists argue that some non-legal norms (non-pedigreed) may also be relevant in such an analysis.[68] Also, logic surmises that explaining legal edicts and recommending changes following an analysis based solely on legal rules would be fallacious and may create an is-ought problem. Nonetheless, the different interpretations and explanations of statutes and precedent discussed in this book do not show how non-legal knowledge and non-pedigreed rules may be used without increasing the number of contradictions. As such, it is not only the "messy work product of judges and legislators" that requires tidying up[69] but also that of commentators. In order to import non-legal knowledge and yet avoid a deluge, I submit that the use of non-legal knowledge should be restricted to instances where it has been alluded to by judges in their *obiter dicta*. This is because *obiter dicta* by their very nature guide other courts on how to enforce certain laws in peculiar instances and their relevance cannot be readily dismissed. Moreover, there are instances where it may be difficult to distinguish between the *ratio decidendi* and a very persuasive *obiter dictum*.[70] It is however important to carry out further research on the means of allowing a controlled use of non-legal and non-pedigreed rules. Equally, research on this proposal would be incidental to that geared towards distinguishing the *ratio decidendi* from the *obiter dictum* in clear and practical terms.

In a bid to achieve coherence and integrity, I therefore circumscribed the nature of the corporation within criminal law discourse. The definition

---

[66] See generally, Cheffins, 1997; Greeen, 2005; McCrudden, 2006; and Siems, 2008.
[67] See Edwards, 1997; and Cheffins, 1999.
[68] For the "exclusivist" positivist view, see Raz, 1979; Shapiro, 2000; and Marmor, 2001. For the "inclusivist" positivist view, see Waluchow, 1994; and Coleman, 2001.
[69] Posner, 2007: 437.
[70] See Cross R and Harris, 1991: 77.

provided here may be deemed too broad, neutral and even superfluous.[71] However, the different ways in which the term has been used by courts and commentators throw light on an independence of thought and action and the ability to relate to the consequences of such thought and action. This implies that there is on the one hand, consensus on the need to distinguish between collective (corporate) and individual actions and objectives, and on the other hand, the idea that the collective may be held to account has substantial appeal. Nonetheless, the debate about whether collectivisation within purposive groups is a standard for identity will continue for a long time,[72] even though I believe that (irrespective of the position endorsed) this is no cogent reason for refraining from attempting to define the term 'corporation.'[73] It is important that everyone understands what a judge means when she talks of a 'corporation' because this certainly facilitates the understanding of why she thinks the (corporate) defendant could not have committed the offence charged or cannot be sanctioned with the penalty required by the law.[74] Further research may therefore be carried out on the essence of the corporation within criminal law discourse, analysing more cases and statutes than I have in this book.

Equally, the idea of invoking the doctrine of innocent agency (employee necessity or member-responsibility) in cases where the offence was caused by collective failure and to use secondary or accessorial liability where one or many agents are guilty also requires further research. However, note must be taken of the fact that both innocent agency and (especially) accessorial liability are complex and problematic[75] and to use these as the bases for establishing a corporation's criminal liability may leave jurors perplexed. Nonetheless, given that corporations always act through their agents, the mandatory use of mechanisms of imputation in defined circumstances may reduce such complexity. This is also a solution to the problem of the lack of coherence and integrity. Thus, an appropriate mechanism of imputation (with a prescribed pattern as its primary rule)

---

[71] See Hart (1983: 24-25) on the futility of premising such a study with a definition of the term 'corporation.'

[72] See Hart, 1983; French, 1984 and 1995; and Pettit, 1997 and 2007.

[73] *Cf* Orts, 1993: 1574.

[74] That is why Coke in *Sutton's Hospital*, Lord Reid in *Nattrass* and Lord Hoffmann in *Meridian* premised their decisions on assertions about the fictitious nature of corporations.

[75] See Law Commission No 300, 2006; and Law Commission No 305, 2007. See also Wilson, 2008.

may be identified by an observer as a common thread linking the different decisions of different judges addressing different facts involving corporate defendants.

However, it would be presumptuous to claim that the proposition of using the aggregation doctrine as modified above eliminates incoherence as regards the imputation of acts and intents to corporations by criminal law courts. This is because there is truly no outer limit to legal rules that may be invoked as secondary rules. This may engender conflict as principles of other legal branches such as agency and contract and tort may contradict those of the criminal law. For example, a corporate principal may not be criminally liable for all the wrongs committed by all of its agents within the scope of the agency. Equally, criminal law courts may not be prepared to enforce principles such as *ex turpi causa non oritur actio* and *volenti non fit injuria*.[76] Nonetheless, I have used the term 'related legal principles' suggesting that the legal rule invoked as a secondary rule must have a bearing on the case before the court. It is however important that further research be carried out to clearly distinguish between primary rules and secondary rules in the light of Hart's use of these terminologies. Equally, the outlook of judges and the perspectives of non-legal theorists ought to be developed further in light of the ever-expanding case law and literature on organisational theory. Given that the integrity of the criminal law is threatened by the inclination to circumvent the procedural rules in order to facilitate the prosecution and/or conviction of corporations, it is important to ensure that a corporation's rights are not simply disregarded. This book has undertaken to show how these rights may be recognised. However, there is need for further research into the implications of recognising these rights and how they may be enforced.

Given that the aggregation doctrine as modified above may fit well within the theoretical framework built here for evaluating mechanisms of imputation and yet have little practical utility, I have proposed that courts may use the theory of the discursive dilemma. Despite some strong criticisms, this theory has maintained its appeal and some commentators like Pettit and Rock have used it to explain how the distinct identity of corporations may be established.[77] I have sought on a previous occasion to demonstrate how this theory may be used to establish a link between the

[76] See for example, section 2(6)(a) and (b) of the CMCHA.

[77] See especially, Rock, 2005; and Pettit, 2007.

accused corporation and a criminogenic practice.[78] As such, it is submitted here that the use of this theory may be the last step in the process of aggregation, whereby the court seeks to determine whether the combined acts reflect the collective rationality that governed deliberations prior to the commission of the offence. The discursive dilemma is a certainly a very rich and complex theory that may offer a lot to corporate criminal law scholarship.

[78] See Nana, 2009. This paper was described by Pettit as developing a "terrifically interesting idea."

REFERENCES

Abell, P. (2006), *Organisation Theory: An Interdisciplinary Approach* (London: University of London Press).

Allan, T. R. S. (2004), 'Legislative Supremacy and Legislative Intention: Interpretation, Meaning, and Authority', *Cambridge Law Journal*, 63(3): 685-711.

Archbald, T., Jull, K., and Roach, K. (2004), 'The Changed Face of Corporate Criminal Liability', *Criminal Law Quarterly*, 48(3): 367-396.

Arthur, B. (1940), *English Saga 1840-1940* (London: Collins).

Ashworth, A. (1989), 'Towards a Theory of Criminal Legislation', *Criminal Law Forum*, 1(1): 41-63.

—. (2000), 'Is the Criminal Law a Lost Cause?' *Law Quarterly Review*, 116: 225-256.

Atkins, B. M. (1980), 'The Process is the Punishment: Handling Criminal Cases in a Lower Criminal Court by Malcolm M. Feeley', *The American Political Science Review*, 74(3): 820-822.

Atiyah, P. S. (1967), *Vicarious Liability in the Law of Torts* (London: Butterworths).

—. (1987), *Pragmatism and Theory in English Law* (London: Stevens and Sons).

Atiyah, P. S., and Summers, R. S. (1987), *Form and Substance in Anglo-American Law: A Comparative Study of Legal Reasoning, Legal Theory, and Legal Institutions* (Oxford: Clarendon Press).

Attorney-General's Department, (2002), *Commonwealth Criminal Code: A Guide for Practitioners* (Melbourne: Australian Institute of Judicial Administration).

Aubrey, D. L. (1982), 'Corporate Personality and Limited Liability' in *Limited Liability and the Firm*, Orhnial, T. (ed) (London: Methuen).

Austin, J. (1885) *Lectures on Jurisprudence: Or The Philosophy of Positive Law* Campbell, R. (ed) 5th edn (London: John Murray).

Ayres, I., and Braithwaite, J. (1992), *Responsive Regulation: Transcending the Deregulation Debate* (New York: Oxford University Press).

Barker, K. (1993), 'Unreliable Assumptions in the Modern Law of Negligence', *Law Quarterly Review* 109: 461- 484.

Bartlett, A. (1998), 'Attribution of Contributory Negligence – Agents, Company Directors and Fraudsters', *Law Quarterly Review* 114: 460-478.

Bateman, R. S., and Snell, S. A. (2007), *Management: Leading & collaborating in a competitive world*, 7th edn (New York: McGraw Hill/Irwin).

Baty, T. (1919), 'The Rights of Ideas: And of Corporations', *Harvard Law Review* 33(3): 358-375.

Bayles, M. D. (1990), *Procedural Justice: Allocating to Individuals* (Dordrecht: Kluwer Academic Publishers).

Beattie, J. (1986), *Crime and the Courts in England, 1660-1800* (Oxford: Clarendon Press).

Becker, G. S. (1968), 'Crime and Punishment: An Economic Approach', *Journal of Political Economy*, 76(2): 169-217.

Beever, A., and Rickett, C. (2005), 'Interpretive Legal Theory and the Academic Lawyer, Review of Waddams, Dimensions of Private Law', *Modern Law Review* 68(2): 320-337.

Behrens, G. (1999), 'Equity in the Commentaries of Edmund Plowden', *Journal of Legal History*, 20(3): 25-50.

Bennett, A. (1991), *A sourcebook of African Customary Law for Southern Africa* (Cape Town: Juta).

Berger, B. L. (2002), 'Trial by Metaphor: Rhetoric, Innovation and the Juridical Context', *Journal of the American Judges Association*, 39(1): 30-38.

Berle, A. A., and Means G. C. (1968), *The Modern Corporation and Private Property*, Revised edn (New York: Harcourt, Brace and World).

Black, M. (1964), 'The Gap Between 'Is' and 'Should'', *Philosophical Review*, 73(2): 165-181.

Black, B. S. (1992), 'Agents Watching Agents: The Promise of Institutional Investor Voice', *University of California Law Review*, 39: 811-895. Available at: http://papers.ssrn.com/sol3/papers.cfm?abstract_id=1132082 [Accessed on 20/07/2009].

Blackstone, W. *Commentaries on the Laws of England* (1765-1769).Available at: http://www.lonang.com/exlibris/blackstone/ [Accessed on 15/07/2009].

Blair, M. M. (1995), 'Corporate 'Ownership': A Misleading Word Muddies the Corporate Governance Debate', *Brookings Review*, 13(1): 16-19.

Blair, M. M., and Stout, L. A. (1999), 'A Team Production Theory of Corporate Law', *Virginia Law Review*, 85(2): 247-328.

Blair, M. M., and Stout, L. A. (2001), 'Corporate Accountability: Director Accountability and the Mediating Role of the Corporate Board', *Washington University Law Quarterly*, 79(2): 403-447.

Blecker, R. (1990), 'Haven or Hell? Inside London Central Prison: Experiences of Punishment Justified', *Stanford Law Review*, 42(5): 1149-1249.

Blumberg, P. I. (1993), *The Multinational Challenge To Corporation Law: The Search For A New Corporate Personality* (New York: Oxford University Press).

Binavince, E. S. (1964), 'The Ethical Foundations of Criminal Liability', *Fordham Law Review*, 33(1): 1-38.

Bodapati, M. (1999), 'The 'Deterrence Trap' in the Federal Fining of Organizations: A Research Note', *Criminal Justice Policy Review*, 10(4): 547-559.

Bolodeoku, O. I. (2002), 'Economic Theories of the Corporation and Corporate Governance: A Critique', *Journal of Business Law*: 411-438.

Bottomley, S. (1990), 'Taking Corporations Seriously: Some Considerations for Corporate Regulation', *Federal Law Review*, 19(3): 203-213.

—. (1997), 'From Contractualism to Constitutionalism: A Framework for Corporate Governance', *Sydney Law Review*, 19, Available at: http://www.austlii.edu.au/au/journals/SydLRev/1997/17.html (Accessed on17/07/2009).

Bouzat, P., and Pinatel, J. (1970), *Traite de Droit Pénal et de Criminologie*, 2nd edn (Paris : Dalloz).

Box, S. (1983), *Power, Crime and Mystification* (London: Tavistock).

Braithwaite, J. (1984), *Corporate Crime in the Pharmaceutical Industry* (London: Routledge and Kegan Paul).

Braithwaite, J., and Pettit, P. (1990), *Not Just Deserts: A Republican Theory of Criminal Justice* (Oxford: Oxford Clarendon Press).

Bratman, M. (1999), *Faces of Intention: Selected Essays on Intention and Agency* (Cambridge: Cambridge University Press).

Bratton, W. W. (1989), 'The 'Nexus of Contracts' corporation: A Critical Appraisal', *Cornell Law Review*, 74(2): 407-465.

Braucher, J. (1990), 'Contract Versus Contractarianism: The Regulatory Role of Contract Law', *Washington and Lee Law Review*, 47: 697-739.

Breit, W., and Elzinger, K. (1973), 'Antitrust penalties and attitudes toward risk: an economic analysis,' *Harvard Law Review*, 86(4): 693-713.

Brickey, K. F. (1981), 'Corporate criminal accountability: a brief history and an observation', *Washington University Law Quarterly*, 60(2): 393-423.

—. (1988), 'Rethinking Corporate Liability Under the Model Penal Code', *Rutgers Law Journal*, 19: 593-631.

—. (1995), *Corporate and White Collar Crime: Cases and Materials*, 2nd edn (Toronto: Little, Brown).

Bucy, P. H. (1991), 'Corporate Ethos: A Standard for Imposing Corporate Criminal Liability', *Minnesota Law Review*, 75(4): 1095-1184.

Burns, P. T. (1967), 'The Test of Vicarious Criminal Liability', *Criminal Law Review*: 702-707.

Burns, T., and Stalker, G. M. (1990), 'Organic and Mechanistic Organizations' in Tosi, H. L. (ed) *Organizational Behavior and Management: A Contingency Approach* (Boston: PWS-Kent).

Burns, T., and Stalker, G. M. (1966), *The Management of Innovation*, 2nd edn, (London: Tavistock).

Butler, H. N. (1989), 'The Contractual Theory of the Corporation', *George Mason University Law Review*, 11(4): 99-123.

Byam, J. T. (1982), 'The Economic Inefficiency of Corporate Criminal Liability', *Journal of Criminal Law and Criminology*, 73(2): 582-603.

Campbell, N., and Armour, J. (2003), 'Demystifying the Civil Liability of Corporate Agents', *Cambridge Law Journal*, 62(2): 290-303.

Cane, P. (2002), *Responsibility in Law and Morality* (Oxford: Hart Publishing).

Capara, F. (1996), *The Web of Life* (London: Harper Collins).

Carr, C. T. (ed) (1913), *Select Charters of Trading Companies* (London: Selden Society).

Carruthers, J. (2001), 'Are Juries Safe?' *Scots Law Times*, 25: 217-221.

Carson, W. (1979), 'The Conventionalization of Early Factory Crime', *International Journal of Sociology of Law*, 7(1): 37-60.

—. (1982), *The Other Price of Britain's Oil* (Oxford: Martin Robertson).

Cheffins, B. R. (1997), *Company Law: Theory, Structure and Operation* (Oxford: Clarendon Press).

—. (1999), 'Using Theory to Study Law: A Company Law Perspective', *Cambridge law Journal*, 58(1): 197-221.

Christian, L. (2001), 'Rail Crash Litigation – Southall and Ladbroke Grove', *Journal of Personal Injury Law*, 4: 339-355.

Chu, C. Y. C., and Qian, Y. (1995), 'Vicarious Liability under a Negligence Rule', *International Review of Law and Economics*, 15(3): 305-322.

Clark, R. D. (1985), 'Agency Costs Versus Fiduciary Duties' in Pratt, J. W., and Zeckhauser, R. J. (eds) *Principals and Agents: The Structure of Business* (Boston: Harvard Business School Press).

Clark, B., and Langsford, H. (2005), 'A Re-Birth of Corporate Killing? Lessons from America in a New Law for Scotland', *International Company and Commercial Law Review*, 2005 16(1): 28-37.

Clarkson, C. M. V. (1996), 'Kicking Corporate Bodies and Damning Their Souls', *Modern Law Review*, 59(4): 557-572.

—. (1998), 'Corporate Culpability', *Web Journal of Current Legal Issues*, 2. Available at: http://webjcli.ncl.ac.uk/1998/issue2/clarkson2.html [accessed on 06-07-2009].

—. (2005), 'Corporate Manslaughter: Yet More Government Proposals', *Criminal Law Review*: 677-689.

Clough, J., and Mulhern, C. (2002), *The Prosecution of Corporations* (Melbourne: Oxford University Press).

Clive, E., Ferguson, P., Gane, C., and Smith, A. M. (2003) *A Draft Criminal Code for Scotland with Commentary* (Scottish Law Commission). Available at http://www.scotlawcom.gov.uk/downloads/cp_criminal_code.pdf [Accessed on 6/7/2009].

Coburn, N. F. (2006), 'Corporate investigations', *Journal of Financial Crime*, 13(3): 348-368

Coffee, J. C. (1981), 'No Soul to Damn: No Body to Kick': An Unscandalized Inquiry into the Problem of Corporate Punishment', *Michigan Law Review*, 79(3): 386-459.

—. (1983), 'Corporate Criminal responsibility' in Kadish, S. H. (ed), 1 *Encyclopaedia of Crime and Justice* (New York: Free Press).

Cohen, M. R. (1927), 'Positivism and the Limits of Legal Idealism in Law', *Columbia Law Review*, 27(3): 237-250.

Cohen, F. S. (1993), *Ethical Systems and Legal Ideals* (New York: Falcon Press).

Coleman, J. L. (1982), 'Negative and Positive Positivism', *Journal of Legal Studies*, 11(1): 139-164.

—. (2001), *The Practice Of Principle: In Defence Of A Pragmatist Approach To Legal Theory* (Oxford: Oxford University Press).

Colvin, E. (1995), 'Corporate Personality and Criminal Liability', *Criminal Law Forum*, 6(1): 8-25.

Corporate Homicide Expert Group, (2005), *Corporate Homicide: Expert Group Report* (Edinburgh: Scottish Executive).

Cownie, F. (2004), *Legal Academics: Cultures and Identities* (Oxford: Hart Publishing).

Coyle, S. (2006), 'Positivism, Idealism and the Rule of Law' *Oxford Journal of Legal Studies*, 26(2): 257-288.

Criminal Law Revision Committee (1980), 14th Report *on Offences Against the Person*, Cm. 7844 (London: HMSO).

Crisp, D., and Moxon, D. (1994), *Case Screening by the Crown Prosecution Service: How and Why Cases are Terminated* (London: HMSO).

Cross, F. B., and Emerson, H. T. (2006), 'What is Legal Doctrine', *Northwestern University Law Review*, 100(1): 517-533.

Cross, R., and Harris, J.W. (1991), *Precedent in English Law* 4th edn (Oxford: Clarendon Press).

Dahl, R. A. (1973), 'Governing the Giant Corporation', in Nader, R., and Green, M. J. (eds) *Corporate Power in America* (New York: Grossman).

Dana, D. A. (1996), 'The Perverse Incentives of Environmental Audit Immunity', *Iowa Law Review*, 81(4): 969-1006.

Dan-Cohen, M. (1986), *Rights, Persons, and Organisations: A Legal Theory for Bureaucratic Society* (Berkeley: University of California Press).

Darbyshire, P., Maughan, A., and Stewart, A. (2002), *What Can the English Legal System Learn from Jury Research Published up to 2001?* Available at: http://www.kingston.ac.uk/~ku00596/elsres01.pdf [Accessed on 06-07-2008].

Davis, J.P. (1905), *Corporations: A Study of the Origin and Development of Great Business Combinations and of their Relation to the Authority of the State* (New York: G. P. Putnam's Sons).

Deakin, S., and Hughes, A. (1997), 'Comparative Corporate Governance: An Interdisciplinary Agenda' in Deakin, S., and Hughes, A. (eds), *Enterprise and Community: New Directions in Corporate Governance*, (Oxford: Blackwell Publishers).

Demott, D. A. (2003), 'When is a principal charged with an agent's knowledge?' *Duke Journal of Comparative and International Law*, 13(3): 291-330.

Department of Environment, Transport and the Regions, (2000), *Revitalising Health and Safety: Strategy Statement*. Available at: http://www.corporateaccountability.org/dl/strategy.pdf [Accessed on 02/03/2009].

Derham, D. P. (1958), Theories of Legal Personality' in Webb, L. (ed) *Legal Personality and Political Pluralism* (Melbourne: Melbourne University Press).

Dewey, J. (1926), 'The Historic Background of Corporate Legal Personality', *Yale Law Journal*, 35(6): 655-673.

Dine, J. (2000), *The Governance of Corporate Groups* (Cambridge: Cambridge University Press).

Dodd, E. M. (1932), 'For Whom Are Corporate Managers Trustees?' *Harvard Law Review*, 45(7): 1145-1163.

Donaldson, T. (1982), *Corporations and Morality* (Englewood Cliffs: Prentice-Hall).

Donaldson, L. (1985), *In Defence of Organisation Theory: A Reply to the Critics* (Cambridge: Cambridge University Press).

Dresser, R. (1993), 'Culpability and Other Minds', *Southern California Interdisciplinary Law Journal*, 2(1): 41-88.

Drucker, P.F. (1968), *The Age of Discontinuity* (New York: Harper and Brothers).

Ducor, P. (1996), 'The Legal Status of Human Materials', *Drake Law Review*, 44(3): 195-259.

Duff, R. A. (2005), 'Theorizing Criminal Law: A 25th Anniversary Essay', Autumn Oxford Journal of Legal Studies, 25(3): 353-367.

—. (2007), *Answering for Crime – Responsibility and Liability in the Criminal Law* (Oxford: Hart Publishing).

Duxbury, N. (2004), 'Why English Jurisprudence is Analytical', *Current Legal Problems*, 57: 1-52.

Dworkin, R. (1986), *Law's Empire* (Oxford: Hart Publishing).

—. (2004), 'Hart's Postscript and the Character of Political Philosophy', *Oxford Journal of Legal Philosophy*, 24(1): 1-37.

—. (2006), *Justice in Robes* (Cambridge, Mass: Harvard University Press).

Easterbook, F. H., and Fishel, D. R., (1989), 'The Corporate Contract', *Columbia Law Review*, 89(7): 1416-1448.

Easterbrook, F. H., and Fishel, D. R. (1991), *The Economic Structure of Corporate Law* (Cambridge, Mass: Harvard University Press).

Edwards, H. T. (1992), 'The Growing Disjunction between Legal Education and the Legal Profession', *Michigan Law Review*, 91(1): 34-78.

Eisenberg, M. A. (1989), 'The Mandatory Structure of Corporation Law', *Columbia Law Review*, 89(7): 1461-1525.

Emberland, M. (2006), *The Human Rights of Companies: Exploring the Structure of ECHR Protection* (Oxford: Oxford University Press).

Explanatory Notes to the Corporate Manslaughter and Corporate Homicide Bill 220 - EN 54/1 2006 (London: HMSO).

Explanatory Notes to the Corporate Manslaughter and Corporate Homicide Act 2007 (London: HMSO).

Ezorsky, G. (1972), *Philosophical Perspectives on Punishment* (New York: State University of New York Press).

Farrow, S. (1998), 'Environmental Equity and Sustainability: Rejecting the Kaldor-Hicks Criteria November', *Environmental Economics*, 27(2): 183-186.

Feeley, M. M. (1979), *The Process is the Punishment: Handling Cases in a Lower Criminal Court* (New York: Russell Sage).

Feinberg, J. (1970), *Doing and Deserving* (Princeton: Princeton University Press).

—. (1986), *The Moral Limits of the Criminal Law: Harm to Self* (New York: Oxford University Press).

Ferguson, P. (2007), 'Corporate Manslaughter and Corporate Homicide Act 2007' *Scots Law Times*, 35: 251-260.

Field, S., and Jorg, N. (1991), 'Corporate Liability and Manslaughter: Should We Be Going Dutch?' *Criminal Law Review*: 156-171.

Financial Services Authority, (2007), *Decision Procedure and Penalties Manual Release* 070 October 2007. Available at: http://www.fsa.gov.uk/pubs/hb-releases/rel70/rel70depp.pdf [Accessed on 17/07/2009].

Finnis, J. (2000), 'The Priority of Persons' in Horder, J. (ed), *Oxford Essays on Jurisprudence* (Oxford: Oxford University Press).

—. (2003), 'On the Incoherence of Legal Positivism' in Patterson, D. M. (ed), *Philosophy of Law and Legal Theory: An Anthropology* (Malden, MA: Wiley-Blackwell).

Fischel, D. R. (1982), 'The Corporate Governance Movement', *Vanderbilt Law Review*, 35(6): 1259-1292.

Fisse, B. (1983), 'Reconstructing Corporate Criminal Law: Deterrence, Retribution, Fault, and Sanctions', *Southern California Law Review*, 56(6): 1141-1246.

Fisse, B., and Braithwaite, J. (1993), *Corporations, Crime and Accountability* (Cambridge: Cambridge University Press).

Fitzgerald, P. J. (1966), *Salmond on Jurisprudence* 12th edn (London: Sweet and Maxwell).

Fleming, J.G. (1998), *The Law of Torts* 9th edn, (North Ryde: Law Book).

Fort, T. L. (2001), *Ethics and Governance: Business as Mediating Institutions* (New York: Oxford University Press).

Frank, J. (1930), *Law and the Modern Mind* (New Jersey: Anchor).

—. (1973), *The Courts on Trial* (Princeton: Princeton University Press).

Fraud Trial Committee Report, (1986), HL Deb Volume 471 cc7-73 (London: HSMO).

Frazer, A. (1998), *Reinventing Aristocracy: The Constitutional Reformation of Corporate Governance* (Aldershot: Ashgate-Dartmouth).

French, P. (1975), 'Types of Collectivities and Blame', *The Personalist*, 56: 160-169.

—. (1984), *Collective and Corporate Responsibility* (New York: Columbia University).

—. (1995), *Corporate Ethics* (London: Harcourt Brace).

Freund, E. (1897), *The Legal Nature of Corporations* (Chicago: Chicago University Press).

Friedman, L. M. (2005), *History of American Law* 3rd edn (New York: Simon and Schuster).

Friedman, M. (1962), *Capitalism and Freedom* (Chicago: University of Chicago Press).

Fuller, L. L. (1967), *Legal Fictions* (Stanford: Stanford University Press).

—. (1969), *The Morality of Law* 2nd edn (New Haven: Yale University Press).

Gardner, S. (1995), 'Manslaughter by Gross Negligence: R v Adomako', *Law Quarterly Review*, 111: 22-27.

Geis, G. (1967), 'White Collar Crime: The Heavy Electrical Equipment Antitrust Cases of 1961' in Clinard, M. B., and Quinney, R. (eds) *Criminal Behavior Systems: A Typology* (New York: Holt, Reinhart and Winston).

Geldart, W. (1911), 'Legal Personality', *Law Quarterly Review*, 27: 90-108.

Gillies, P. (1997), *Criminal Law* 4th edn, (Sydney: LBC Information Services).

Glazebrook, P. R. (2002), 'A better way of convicting businesses', *Cambridge Law Journal*, 61(2): 405-422.

Gobert, J. (1994), 'Corporate Criminality: Four Models of Fault', *Legal Studies*, 14(3): 393-410.

—. (2008), 'Corporate Manslaughter and Corporate Homicide Act 2007 – Thirteen Years in the Making But was it Worth the Wait?' *Modern Law Review*, 71(3): 413-433.

Gobert, J., and Punch, M. (2003), *Rethinking Corporate Crime* (London: LexisNexis/Butterworths).

Goebel, J.W. (1946), *Cases and Materials on the Development of Legal Institutions* (Brattleboro: Vermont Publishing).

Gold, N., and Sugden, R. (2007), 'Collective Intentions and Team Agency' *Journal of Philosophy*, 104(3): 109-37.

Golding, M. P. (1981), 'Realism and Functionalism in the Legal Thought of Felix S. Cohen', *Cornell Law Review*, 66: 1032-1057.

Goldman, A. (2004), 'Group Knowledge versus Group Rationality: Two Approaches to Social Epistemology', *Episteme, A Journal of Social Epistemology*, 1: 11-22.

Goodrich, P. (1987), *Legal Discourse: Studies in Linguistics, Rhetoric, and Legal Analysis* (London: Macmillan).

Gough, S. (2000), 'Surviving without Majewski', *Criminal Law Review*: 719-733.

Gower, L. C. B. (1956), 'Some Contrasts Between British and American Corporation Law', *Harvard Law Review*, 69(8): 1369-1402.

—. (1992), *Gower's Principles of Modern Company Law* 5th edn (London: Sweet and Maxwell).

Grantham R., and Rickett, C. (1999), 'Directors' Tortious' Liability: Contract, Tort, or Company Law?' *Modern Law Review*, 62(1): 133-139.

Gray, J.C. (1921), *The Nature and Sources of the Law* 2nd edn (New York: Macmillan).

Green, L. (2005), 'General Jurisprudence: A 25th Anniversary Essay' *Oxford Journal of Legal Studies*, 25(4): 565-580.

Green, S. P. (2005), 'Six Senses of Strict Liability: A Plea for Formalism in Simester' in Simester, A. P. (ed), *Appraising Strict Liability* (Oxford: Oxford University Press).

Griffiths, M. (2005), *A Practical Guide to the Memorandum and Articles of Association* (London: ICSA).

Gross, H. (1979), *A Theory of Criminal Justice* (New York: Oxford University Press).

Hall, A., Johnstone, R., and Ridgway, A. (2004), *Reflection on Reforms: Developing Criminal Accountability for Industrial Deaths*, Working Paper No 26, National Research Centre for Occupational Health and Safety, 2004. Available at: http://ohs.anu.edu.au/publications/pdf/wp%2026%20-%20Hall,%20 Johnstone%20and%20Ridgeway.pdf [Accessed on 06/07/2009].

Hallis, F. (1930), *Corporate Personality: A Study in Jurisprudence* (London: Oxford University Press).

Hans, V.P. (2000), *Business on Trial: The Civil Jury and Corporate Responsibility* (New Haven: Yale University Press).

Hair, P E. H. (1971), 'Deaths from Violence in Britain: A Tentative Secular Survey', *Population Studies*, 25(1): 5-24.

Harding, R.W. (1988), 'Jury Performance in Complex Cases' in Findlay, M., and Duff, P. (eds) *The Jury Under Attack* (London: Butterworths).

Harris, J. (2001) 'Human Beings, Persons and Conjoined Twins: An Ethical Analysis of the Judgment in Re A', *Medical Law Review*, 9(3): 221-236.

Hart, H. L. A. (1968), *Punishment and Responsibility: Essays in the Philosophy of Law* (Oxford: Clarendon Press).

—. (1983), *Essays in Jurisprudence and Philosophy* (Oxford: Clarendon Press).

—. (1994), *The Concept of Law* 2nd edn (Oxford: Oxford University Press).

Hausman, D., and McPherson, M. (1996), *Economic Analysis and Moral Philosophy* (Cambridge: Cambridge University Press).

Hawke, N. (2000), *Corporate Liability* (London: Sweet and Maxwell).

Hayek, F. A. (1949), *Individualism and the Economic Order* (London: Routledge and Kegan Paul).

Hessen, R. (1979), *In Defense of the Corporation* (Stanford: Hoover Institution Press).

Heuston, R.F.V., and Buckley R.A. (1996), *Salmond and Heuston on the Law of Torts* 21st edn (London: Sweet and Maxwell).

Hickson, C. R., and Turner, J. D. (2005) 'Corporation Or Limited Liability Company' 2005 in McCusker, J. J., Engerman, S., Fischer, L. R., Hancock, D. J., Kenneth, L., and Pomeranz, L. (eds) *Encyclopaedia Of World Trade Since 1450*: Available at http://www.qub.ac.uk/mgt/efirg/Corporation.pdf [Accessed on 06/07/2009].

Higgins, J. M. (1994), *The Management Challenge* 2nd edn (Ontario: Macmillan).

Higgins, A. (2008), 'Corporate abuse of legal professional privilege', *Civil Justice Quarterly*, 27(3): 377-406.

Hill, J. (2000), 'Visions and Revisions of the Shareholder', *American Journal of Comparative Law*, 48(1): 39-79.

—. (2003), 'Corporate Criminal Liability in Australia: An Evolving Corporate Governance Technique', *Journal of Business Law*: 1-44.

Hippard, J. J. (1973), 'The Unconstitutionality of Criminal Liability Without Fault: An Argument for a Constitutional Doctrine of Mens Rea', *Houston Law Review*, 10: 1039-1058.

HM Crown Prosecution Service Inspectorate, (2006), *Review of the Investigation and Criminal Proceedings Relating to the Jubilee Line Case* (London: HMSO).

Ho, C.L., and Papathanassiou, C. (2006), 'Fraudulent Trading and Vicarious Liability: Bank of India v Morris', *Journal of International Banking Law and Regulation*, 21(1): 17-23.

Hofler, A. (2001), 'The Spiritual Problems of Crime and Punishment', *Justice of the Peace and Local Government*, 165(47): 922-924.

Hohfeld, W. N. (1923), 'Some Fundamental Conceptions as Applied in Judicial Reasoning' in Cook, W. W. (ed) *Fundamental Legal Conceptions as Applied in Judicial Reasoning and other Legal Essays by WN Hohfeld* (New Haven: Yale University Press).

Holmes, O. W. (1938), *The Common Law* (Boston: Little, Brown).

Holdsworth, W. (1944), *A History of English Law* 3rd edn (London: Sweet & Maxwell).

Home Affairs and Work and Pensions Committee, (2005), *Draft Corporate Manslaughter Bill* HC 540-I (London: HMSO).

Home Office, (2000), *Reforming the Law on Involuntary Manslaughter: The Government's Proposals* (London: HMSO).

Honess, T. M., Levi, M., Charman, E. A., (2003), 'Jury Competence in Serious Frauds since Roskill: A Research-Based Assessment', *Journal of Financial Crime*, 11(1): 12-27.

Honore, T. (2002), 'The Necessary Connection between Law and Morality' *Oxford Journal of Legal Studies*, 22(3): 489-495.

Horder, J. C. N. (1997), Two Histories and Four Hidden Principles of Mens Rea', *Law Quarterly Review*, 113: 95-119.

—. (2002), 'Strict Liability, Statutory Construction and the Spirit of Liberty', *Law Quarterly Review*, 118: 458-475.

Hunt, B. (2002), 'Plain Language in Legislative Drafting: Is It Really the Answer?' *Statute Law Review*, 23(1): 24-46

Husak, D. (2005), 'Strict Liability, Justice and Proportionality' in Simester, A.P. (ed) *Appraising Strict Liability* (Oxford: Oxford University Press).

Ibbetson, D. (2003), 'Historical Research in Law' in Cane, P., and Tushnet, M. (eds) Oxford Handbook of Legal Studies (Oxford: Oxford University Press).

Institute of Directors and the Health and Safety Commission (2007), *Leading Health and Safety at Work: Leadership Actions for Directors and Board Members*. Available at: http://www.hse.gov.uk/pubns/indg417.pdf [Accessed on 02/03/2009].

Jackson, J. D. (2004), 'Effects of Legal Culture and Proof in Decisions to Prosecute', *Law, Probability and Risk*, 3(2): 109-131.

Jensen, M. C., and Meckling, W. H. (1976), 'Theory of the Firm: Managerial Behaviour, Agency Costs and Ownership Structure', *Journal of Financial Economics*, 3(4): 305-360.

Johansson, P. (1993), *Cost-Benefit Analysis of Environmental Change* (Cambridge: Cambridge University Press).

Johnston, D. (1995), 'Limiting Liability: Roman Law and the Civil Law Tradition', *Chicago-Kent Law Review*, 70: 1515-1538.

Kadish, S. H., and Paulsen, M. G. (1975), *Criminal Law and its Processes* 3rd edn (Boston: Little Brown).

Kant, I. (1965), *The Metaphysical Elements of Justice*, Ladd J. (trans) (Indianapolis: Bobbs-Merrill).

Kelsen, H. (1945), *General Theory of Law and Statute* (New York: Russell and Russell).

Kerlin, M. J. (1997), 'Peter French, Corporate Ethics and the Wizard of Oz', *Journal of Business Ethics*, 16(12/13): 1431-1438.

Kester, C. M. (1994), 'Is there a Person in that Body?: An Argument for the Priority of Persons and the Need for a New Legal Paradigm' *The Georgetown Law Journal*, 82(4): 1643-1687.

Khanna, V. S. (1996), 'Corporate Criminal Liability: What Purpose Does It Serve?' *Harvard Law Review*, 109(7): 1477-1534.

—. (1999), 'Is The Notion of Corporate Fault A Faulty Notion?: The Case of Corporate Mens Rea' *Boston University Law Review*, 79(2): 355-415.

Kinley, D. (ed) (1998), *Human Rights in Australian Law: Principles, Practice and Potential* (Sydney: Federation Press).

Klein, W. A., and Coffee, J. C. (1990), *Business Organization and Finance: Legal and Economic Principles* (New York: Foundation Press).

Klein, W. A., and Coffee, J. C. (2007), *Business Organization and Finance, Legal and Economic Principles (Concepts and Insights)* 10th edn (New York: Foundation Press).

Kornhauser, L. A. (1989), 'The Nexus of Contracts Approach to Corporations: A Comment on Easterbrook and Fischel', *Columbia Law Review*, 89(7): 1449-1460.

Kornhauser, L., and Sager, L. (1986), 'Unpacking the Court', *Yale Law Journal* 96(1): 82-117.

Kornhauser, L., and Sager, L. (1993), 'The One and the Many: Adjudication in Collegial Courts', *California Law Review*, 81(1): 1-59.

Kramer, M. H. (1989), 'Rights Without Trimmings' in Kramer, M. H., Simmonds, N. E., and Steiner, H. (ed) *A Debate Over Rights: Philosophical Enquiries* (Oxford: Clarendon Press).

—. (2001), 'Do Animals and Dead People Have Legal Rights?' *Canadian Journal of Law and Jurisprudence*, 14(1): 29-54.

Kriesberg, S. M. (1976), 'Decisionmaking Models and the Control of Corporate Crime', *Yale Law Journal*, 85(8): 1091-1129.

Lacey, N. (1988), *State Punishment: Political Principles and Community Values* (London: Routledge).

—. (1998), 'Contingency, Coherence and Conceptualism: Reflections on the Encounter between 'Critique' and 'the Philosophy of the Criminal Law' in Duff, R. A. (ed) *Philosophy and the Criminal Law: Principle and Critique* (Cambridge: Cambridge University Press).

—. (2001), 'In Search of the Responsible Subject: History, Philosophy and Social Sciences in Criminal Law Theory', *Modern Law Review*, 64 (3): 350-371.

LaFave, W., and Scot, A. (1986), *Criminal Law* 2nd edn (St. Paul, Minnesota: West Group).

Lakoff, G., and Johnson, M. (1980), *Metaphors We Live By* (Chicago: University of Chicago Press).

Laski, H. J. (1916), 'The Personality of Associations', *Harvard Law Review*, 29(4): 404-426.

Laufer, W. S. (1994), 'Corporate Bodies and Guilty Minds', *Emroy Law Journal*, 43(2): 647-730.

—. (2006), *Corporate Bodies and Guilty Minds: The Failure of Corporate Criminal Liability* (Chicago: University of Chicago Press).

Law Commission No 413 (1985), *Codification of the Criminal Law: A Report to the Law Commission*, Cm 143 (London: HMSO).

Law Commission No 177 (1989), *A Criminal Code for England and Wales* HC Volume 156 cc1119-20 (London: HMSO).

Law Commission (1994), *Criminal* Law*: Involuntary Manslaughter* Consultation Paper No 135 (London: HMSO).

Law Commission No 237, (1996), *Legislating the Criminal Code: Involuntary Manslaughter*, HC 171 (London: HMSO).

Law Commission No 300, (2006), *Inchoate Liability for Assisting and Encouraging Crime* Cm 6878 (London: HMSO).

Law Commission No 305, (2007), *Participating in Crime* Cm 7084 (London: HMSO).

Lawley, J., and Tompkins, P. (2000), *Metaphors in Mind: Transformation through Symbolic Modelling* (London: Developing Company Press).

Lawson, F. H. (1957), 'The Creative Use of Legal Concepts', *New York University Law Review*, 32(5): 907-916.

Lederman, E. (2000), 'Models for Imposing Corporate Criminal Liability: From Adaptation and Imitation toward Aggregation and the Search for Self-Identity', *Buffalo Criminal Law Review*, 4(1): 641-708.

Legge, K. (1978), 'Power, Innovation and Problem-Solving in Personnel Management (London: McGraw-Hill).

Leigh, L. H. (1966), 'By Whom Does the Company Permit?' *Modern Law Review*, 29(5): 568-570.

—. (1969), *The Criminal Liability of Corporations in English Law* (London: Weidenfeld and Nicholson).

Legrand, P., and Munday, R. (eds) (2003), *Comparative Legal Studies: Traditions and Transitions* (Cambridge: Cambridge University Press).

Leiter, B. (1998), 'Realism, Hard Positivism, and Conceptual Analysis', *Legal Theory*, 4(4): 533-547.

—. (2003), 'Beyond the Hart/Dworkin Debate: The Methodology Problem in Jurisprudence', *American Journal of Jurisprudence*, 48(1): 17-51.

Leonard, G. (2003), 'Towards a Legal History of American Criminal Theory: Culture and Doctrine from Blackstone to the American Penal Code', *Buffalo Criminal Law Review*, 6(2): 691-832.

Levi, M. (1988), 'The Role of the Jury in Complex Cases' in Findlay, M., and Duff, P. (eds) *The Jury Under Attack* (London: Butterworths).

Lindley, N. (1863), 'On the Principles Which Govern the Criminal and Civil Responsibilities of Corporations (March 30, 1857) in 2 *Papers Read Before the Judicial Society* (London, William Maxwell).

List, C., and Pettit, P. (2005), 'On the Many as One', *Philosophy and Public Affairs*, 33(4): 377-390.

Lizee, M. (1996), 'De la Capacité Organique et des Responsabilités Délictuelle et Pénale des Personnes Morales', *McGill Law Journal*, 41(1): 131- 168.

Lord Justice Auld, (2001), *Review of the Criminal Courts of England and Wales* (London: HMSO).

MacCormick, N. (2005), *Rhetoric and the Rule of Law* (Oxford: Oxford University Press).

—. (2008a), 'Publication Review: Our Knowledge of the Law: Objectivity and Practice in Legal Theory', *Edinburgh Law Review*, 12(1): 150-153.

—. (2008b), *H.L.A. Hart* 2nd edn (Stanford: Stanford University Press).

Machen, A.W. (1911), 'Corporate Personality', *Harvard Law Review*, 24(4), 253-267.

Maitland, F.W. (1900a), 'Introduction,' to Gierke, O. *Political Theories of the Middle Ages* (Cambridge: Cambridge University Press)

—. (1900b), 'The Corporation Sole', *Law Quarterly Review* 16: 335-354.

—. (1911), 'Moral Philosophy and Legal Personality' in Fisher, H. A. L. (ed) *Collected Papers* Volume 3 (Cambridge: Cambridge University Press).

Malkiel, B.G. (1972), *The Debt-Equity Combination of the Firm and the Cost of Capital* (New York: General Learning Press).

Manchester, C. (2006), 'Knowledge, Due Diligence and Strict Liability in Regulatory Offences', *Criminal Law Review*: 213-228.

Mangham, I. (1978) *Interactions and Interventions in Organisations* (New York: Wiley).

Manning, B., and Hanks, J. J. (1990), *Legal Capital* 3rd edn (St. Paul: West Publishing Company).

Mark, G. (1987), 'The Personification of the Business Corporation in American Law', *University of Chicago Law Review*, 54(4): 1441-1483.

Marmor, A. (2001), *Positive Law and Objective Values* (Oxford: Clarendon Press).

—. (2006), 'Legal Positivism: Still Descriptive and Morally Neutral', *Oxford Journal of Legal Studies*, 26(4): 683-704.

Marshall, E.A. (1999), *General Principles of Scots Law* 7th Revised edn (Edinburgh: W. Green/Sweet and Maxwell).

Masters, J. L. (2008) 'Fraud and Money Laundering: The Evolving Criminalization of Corporate Non-Compliance', *Journal of Money Laundering Control*, 11(2): 103-122.

Mays, R. (2000), 'The Criminal Liability of Corporations and Scots Law: Learning the Lessons of Anglo-American Jurisprudence', *Edinburgh Law Review*, 4(1): 46-73.

McConvill, J. (2005), 'The Separation of Ownership and Control under a Happiness Based Theory of the Corporation', *Company Lawyer*, 26(2): 35-53.

McCrudden, C. (2006), 'Legal Research and the Social Sciences' *Law Quarterly Review*, 122: 632-650.

McEwan, J. (1998), *Evidence and the Adversarial Process: The Modern Law* 2nd edn (Oxford: Hart Publishing).

McHugh, J. T. (1992), 'What is the Difference Between a 'Person' and a 'Human Being' within the Law?' *Review of Politics*, 54(3): 445-462.

McVisk, W. (1978), 'Toward a Rational Theory of Criminal Liability for the Corporate Executive', *Journal of Criminal law and Criminology*, 69(1): 75-91.

Mestre, A. (1899), *Les Personnes Morales et le Problème de Leur Responsabilité Pénale* (Paris : Librairie Nouvelle de Droit et de Jurisprudence).

Miers, D. R. (1983), 'Compensation and Conception of Victims of Crime', *Victimology*, 8 (1-2): 204-212.

Miller, D. (2001), 'Distributing Responsibilities', *Journal of Political Philosophy*, 19(4): 453-471.

Millon, D. (1991), 'Redefining Corporate Law', *Indiana Law Review*, 24: 223-277.

—. (1993), Communitarians, Contractarians and the Crisis in Corporate Law, *Washington and Lee Law Review*, 50(4): 1373-1393.

Minkes, J. P., and Minkes, A. L. (2001), 'Mays on Corporate Crime: A Transdisciplinary Perspective', *Edinburgh Law Review*, 5(2): 242-247.

Mintzberg, H. (1979), *The Structure of Organisations* (Englewood Cliffs, New Jersey: Prentice-Hall).

Moore, M. (1984), *Law and Psychiatry: Rethinking the Relationship* (Cambridge: Cambridge University Press).

—. (1997), *Placing Blame: A General Theory of the Criminal Law* (Oxford: Oxford University Press).

Morgan, E. M. (1956), *Some Problems of Proof under the Anglo-American System of Litigation* (New York: Columbia University Press).

Morgan, G. (1986), *Images of Organization* (Beverly Hills: Sage).

Murphy, J. (1985), 'Retributivism and the State's Interest in Punishment' in Penncock, J. R., and Chapman, R. W. (eds) *Criminal Justice* (New York: New York University Press).

Murphy, P. (2008), 'Excluding Justice or Facilitating Justice? International Criminal Law Would Benefit from Rules of Evidence', *International Journal of Evidence and Proof*, 12(1): 1-31.

Nader, R., Green, M.J., and Seligman, J. (1976), *Taming the Giant Corporation* (New York: W.W. Norton).

Naffine, N. (2003), 'Who are the Law's Persons? From Cheshire Cats to Responsible Subjects', *Modern Law Review*, 66(3): 346-367.

Nana, C. N. (2008), 'Sexual Harassment in the Workplace in South Africa: The Unlimited Vicarious Liability of Employers?' *Journal of African Law*, 52(2): 245-267.

—. (2009) 'Do Criminogenic Employment Practices Truly Reflect a Company's Liability for Non-Compliance?' *Queen's Discussion Paper on Corporate Responsibility* Research no 7/2009. Belfast: Queen's University Management School. Available at: www.qub.ac.uk/mgt/sustainability/downloads/072009nana.pdf [Accessed on 01/10/2009].

Nekam, A. (1938), *The Personality Conception of the Legal Entity* (Cambridge, MA: Harvard University Press).

Nesteruk, J. (1990), 'Property and the Corporation: A Proposal for a New Paradigm', *DePaul Law Review*, 39: 453-565.

—. (2002) 'Conceptions of the Corporation and the Prospects of Sustainable Peace', *Vanderbilt Journal of Transnational Law,* 35: 438-456.

Nicholls, C.C. (2005) *Corporate Law* (Toronto: Edmond Montgomery).

Nobles, R., and Schiff, D. (2006), 'Communicating Moral Responsibility through Criminal Law', *Oxford Journal of Legal Studies*, 26(1): 207-217.

Norrie, A. (1999), 'After Wollin', *Criminal Law Review*: 532-544.

—. (1999), 'Michael Moore's Deviation', *Oxford Journal of Legal Studies*, 19(1): 111-132.

—. (2000), *Punishment, Responsibility and Justice: A Relational Critique* (Oxford: Oxford University Press).

—. (2001), *Crime, Reason and History* 2nd edn (London: Butterworths).

—. (2002), 'From Criminal Law to Legal Theory: The Mysterious Case of the Reasonable Glue Sniffer', *Modern Law Review*, 65(4): 538-555.

Note, (1979), 'Corporate Crime: Regulating Corporate Behaviour through Criminal Sanctions', *Harvard Law Review*, 92(5): 1227-1375.

—. (1980), 'Judicial Intervention and the Organizational Theory: Changing Bureaucratic Behavior and Policy', *Yale Law Journal*, 89(4): 513-537.

—. (1982), 'Piercing the Corporate Law Veil: The Alter Ego Doctrine under Federal Common Law', Harvard Law Review, 95(4): 853-871.

O'Connor, M. A. (1991), 'Restructuring the Corporation's Nexus of Contracts: Recognizing a Fiduciary Duty to Protect Displaced Workers', *North Carolina Law Review*, 69: 1189-1260.

Office of Fair Trading, (2004), *Guidelines* Available at: http://www.oft.gov.uk/ [Accessed on 20/07/2009].

O'Neil, P.M. (1983), 'Ayn Rand and the Is-Ought Problem', *Journal of Libertarian Studies*, 2(1): 81-99.

O'Neill, T. (1997), 'The Patriarchal Meaning of Contract: Feminist Reflections on the Corporate Governance Debate' in Patfield, F.M. (ed), *Perspectives on Company Law* Volume 2 (London: Kluwer Law International).

O'Sullivan, J. (2007) 'Suing in Tort where no Contractual Claim will Lie: A bird's eye view', *Professional Negligence*, 23(3):165-192.

Ogus, A., and Abbot, C. (2002), 'Sanctions for Pollution: Do We Have the Right Regime?' *Journal of Environmental Law*, 14(3):283-298.

Orgus, A. (1994), *Regulation: Legal Form and Economic Theory* (Oxford: Clarendon Press).

Orts, E. W. (1993), 'The Complexity and Legitimacy of Corporate Law', *Washington and Lee Law Review*, 50: 1565-1623.

Packer, H. L. (1968), *The Limits of Criminal Sanction* (Stanford: Stanford University Press).

Parker, C. (2002), *The Open Corporation: Effective Self-Regulation and Democracy* (Cambridge: Cambridge University Press).

Parkinson, J. (1995), *Corporate Power and Responsibility* (Oxford: Clarendon Press).

Paton, G.W. (1972), *A Textbook of Jurisprudence* 4th edn (Oxford: Clarendon Press).

Patry, W. (2008), 'Metaphors and Moral Panics in Copyright: The Stephen Stewart Memorial Lecture, November 13, 2007', *Intellectual Property Quarterly*, 1: 1-13.

Pekka, M. (2007), 'Collective Agents and Moral Responsibility', *Journal of Social Philosophy*, 38(3): 456-468.

Perelman, C. (1963), *The Idea of Justice and the Problem of Argument* (Petrie, J. trans.) (London: Routledge and Kegan Paul).

—. (1980) *Justice, Law, and Argument: Essays on Moral and Legal Reasoning* (Kluback, W. et. 8 al., trans.) (Boston: D. Reidel Publishing).

Perrott, D. L. (1982), 'Changes in Attitude to Limited Liability – the European Experience', in Orhnial, T. (ed) *Limited Liability and the Corporation* (London: Croom Helm).

Perry, S.R. (1987), 'Judicial Obligation, Precedent and the Common Law', *Oxford Journal of Legal Studies*, 7(2): 215-257.

—. (1989), 'Second-Order Reasons, Uncertainty, and Legal Theory', *Southern California Law Review*, 62(3/4): 913-994.

Pettit P. (1992), 'Groups with Minds of Their Own' in Schmitt, F. (ed) *Socializing Metaphysics* (Lanham: Rowan and Littlefield).

—. (2007), 'Responsibility Incorporated', *Ethics*, 117(2): 171-201.

Pinto, A., and Evans, M. (2003), *Corporate Criminal Liability* (London: Thomson/ Sweet and Maxwell).

Pinto, A., and Evans, M. (2008), *Corporate Criminal Liability* 2nd edn (London: Thomson/ Sweet and Maxwell).

Png, C. 'Corporate Liability: A Study in Principles of Attribution' (London: Kluwer Law International).

Poole, R. (1996), 'On Being a Person', *Australian Journal of Philosophy*, 74(1): 38-56.

Posner, R. A. (2001), *Frontiers of Legal Theory* (Cambridge: Harvard University Press).

—. (2003), 'Law, Pragmatism and Democracy', (Harvard: Harvard University Press).

—. (2007), 'In Memoriam: Bernard D. Meltzer (1914-2007)', *University of Chicago Law Review*, 74: 435-438.

Pound, R. (1959), *Jurisprudence* Volume IV, (St Paul: West Publishing).

Prez, P. (2000), 'Beyond Judicial Sanctions: The Negative Impact of Conviction for Environmental Offences', *Environmental Law Review*, 2(1): 11-23.

PriceWaterhouseCoopers (2007) 'Economic crime: people, culture and controls', *The 4th biennial Global Economic Crime Survey*. Available at: http://www.pwc.com/extweb/pwcpublications.nsf/docid/29FA0E335A 50687280257372003D70B3 [Accessed on 08/07/2009].

Queensland Law Reform Commission, (2001), *Vicarious Liability* Report No 56 (Brisbane: National Library of Australia).

Radin, M. (1932), 'The Endless Problem of Corporate Personality', *Columbia Law Review*, 32(4): 643-667.

Ragozino, A. (1995), 'Replacing the Collective Knowledge Doctrine with a Better Theory for Establishing Corporate Mens Rea: The Duty Stratification Approach', *Southwestern University Law Review*, 24(2): 423-449.

Rammeloo, S. (2001), 'Cross Border Mobility of Corporations and the European Union: Two Future Landmark Cases', *Maastricht Journal of European and Comparative Law*, 8(2): 117-120.

Rand, A. (1964), *The Virtue of Selfishness* (New York: New American Library).

Ray, A. (1984), *Cost-Benefit Analysis* (Baltimore: John Hopkins University Press).

Raz, J. (1972), 'Legal Principles and the Limits of the Law', *Yale Law Journal*, 81(5): 823-854.

—. (1975), *Practical Reason and Norms* (London, Hutchinson).

—. (1979), *The Authority of Law: Essays on Law and Morality* (Oxford: Clarendon Press).

Reed, R. (2006), 'Company Directors – Collective or Functional Responsibility', *Company Lawyer*, 27(6): 170-178.

Richards, I. A. (1936), *The Philosophy of Rhetoric* (New York: Oxford University Press).

Robinson, A. A. (2008), *Corporate Culture as a Basis for the Criminal Liability of Corporations*, Paper prepared for the use of the United Nations Special Representative of the Secretary General for Business and Human Rights (UNSRSG), Available at:

http://198.170.85.29/Allens-Arthur-Robinson-Corporate-Culture-paper-for-Ruggie-Feb-2008.pdf [Accessed on 21/07/2009].

Robinson, P. (1997), *Structure and Function in Criminal Law* (Oxford: Clarendon Press).

Rock, E. B. (2005), 'The Corporate Form as a Solution to the Discursive Dilemma' Research Paper No 05-20, University of Pennsylvania Law School. Available at: http://papers.ssrn.com/sol3/papers.cfm?abstract_id=803866 [Accessed on 24/07/2009].

Rogers, J. (2006), 'Restructuring the exercise of prosecutorial discretion in England', *Oxford Journal of Legal Studies*, 26(4): 775-803.

Rose, A. (1995), '1995 Australian Criminal Code Act: Corporate Criminal Provisions', *Criminal Law Forum*, 6(1): 129-142.

Saleem, S. (2007), 'Corporate Manslaughter and Corporate Homicide Bill: Part 1' *International Company and Commercial Law Review*, 18(8): 261-278.

Salmond, J. W. (1907), *Law of Torts* 1st edn (London: Steven and Hayes).

Samuels, W.J. (1987), 'The Idea of a Corporation as a Person: On the Normative Significance of Judicial Language' in Samuels, W.J., and Miller, A.S. (eds) *Corporations and Society: Power and Responsibility* (Westport: Greenwood Press).

Savigny, F. K. (1884), 'La Personnalité Juridique' Rattigan, W. H. (trans) in *Jural Relations* (London: Wildy and Sons).

Schauer, F. (1991), *Playing by the Rules: A Philosophical Examination of Rule-Based Decision-Making in Law and in Life* (Oxford: Clarendon Press).

Schlegel, K. (1990), *Just Deserts For Corporate Criminals* (Boston: Northeastern University Press).

Schum, D. (1986), 'Probability and the Processes of Discovery, Proof and Choice', *Boston University Law Review*, 66(3-4): 825-876.

Scruton, R., and Finnis, J. (1989), 'Corporate Persons', *Proceedings of the Aristotelian Society, Supplementary Volumes*, 63: 239-274.

Sealy, L. S. (1984), *Company Law and Commercial Reality* (London: Sweet And Maxwell).

—. (1992), *Cases and Materials in Company Law* (London: Butterworths).

Searle, J. (1964), 'How to Derive 'Ought' From 'Is'', *Philosophical Review* 73(1): 43-58.

—. (1990), 'Collective Intentions and Actions', in Cohen, P., Morgan, J. and Pollack, M. (eds.) *Intentions in Communication* (Cambridge: MIT Press).

Seymour, B. (1989), *Seymour's Customary Law in Southern Africa* (Cape Town: Juta).

Shapiro, S. (2000), 'Law, Morality, and the Guidance of Conduct', *Legal Theory*, 6(2): 127-170.

—. (2001), 'On Hart's way out' in Coleman, J. (ed) *Hart's Postscript: Essays on the Prescript to the Concept of Law* (Oxford: Oxford University Press).

Shavell, S. (1993), 'The Optimal Structure of Law Enforcement', *Journal of Law and Economics*, 36(1): 255-287.

Siems, M. M (2008), 'Legal Originality', *Oxford Journal of Legal Studies*, 28(1): 147-164.

Simester, A. P. (1999), 'Murder, Mens Rea and the House of Lords Again', *Law Quarterly Review*, 115: 17-21.

—. (2005) 'Is Strict Liability Always Wrong?' in Simester, A. P. (ed) *Appraising Strict Liability* (Oxford: Oxford University Press).

—. (2006), 'The Mental Element in Complicity', *Law Quarterly Review*, 122: 578-601.

Simpson, P. (2000), 'Vicarious Liability' in Reid, K. G. C., Reid, K., and Zimmerman, R. (eds) *A History of Private Law in Scotland: Obligations* Volume 2 (Oxford: Oxford University Press).

Singer, R. (1989), 'The Resurgence of Mens Rea: III – The Rise and Fall of Strict Criminal Liability', *Boston College Law Review*, 30(2): 337-408.

Singer, R., and Husak, D. (1999) 'Of Innocence and Innocents: The Supreme Court and Mens Rea since Herbert Packer', *Buffalo Criminal Law Review*, 2(2): 861-945.

Smith, B. (1928), 'Legal Personality', *Yale Law Review*, 37(3): 283-299.

Smith, J. C. (1995), 'R v British Steel', *Criminal Law Review*: 655.

Smith, K. J. M. (1991), *A Modern Treatise on the Law of Criminal Complicity* (New York, Oxford University Press).

Smith, P. J. (2007), 'New Legal Fictions', *Georgetown Law Journal*, 95(5): 1435- 1496.

Smith, T. A. (1999), 'The Efficient Norm for Corporate Law: A Neotraditional Interpretation of Fiduciary Duty', *Michigan Law Review*, 98(1): 214-268.

Spurgeon, W. A. and Fagan, T. P. (1981), 'Criminal Liability for Life-Endangering Corporate Conduct', *Journal of Criminal Law and Criminology*, 72(2): 400-433.

Stapledon, G. P. (1996), *Institutional Shareholders and Corporate Governance* (Oxford: Clarendon Press).

Stanton, K. M. (2007), 'Hedley Byrne v Heller: The Relationship Factor', *Professional Negligence*, 23(2): 94-107.
Stanton-Ife, J. (2007), 'Strict Liability: Stigma and Regret', *Oxford Journal of Legal Studies*, 27(1): 151-173.
Steiner, H. (1998), 'Working Rights' in Kramer, M.H., Simmonds, N.E., and Steiner, H. (eds) *A Debate Over Rights: Philosophical Enquiries* (Oxford: Clarendon Press).
Stern, Y. Z. (1987), 'Corporate Criminal Liability – Who is the Corporation?' *Journal of Corporate Law*, 13(1): 125-143.
Stevens, R.S., and Henn, H.G. (1965), *Cases and Materials on the Law of Corporations* (St. Paul: West Publishing).
Stigler, G. J. (1970), 'The Optimum Enforcement of Laws', *Journal of Political Economy*, 78(3): 526-536.
Stokes, M. (1986), 'Company Law and Legal Theory', in Twining, W. (ed) *Legal Theory and Common Law* (Oxford: Blackwell).
Stoljar S. J. (1973), *Groups and Entities: An Enquiry into Corporate Theory* (Canberra: Australian National University Press).
Stone, C. D. (1975), *Where the Law Ends: The Social Control of Corporate Behaviour* (New York: Harper and Row).
—. (1977), 'Controlling Corporate Misconduct', *Public Interest*, 48: 55-71.
—. (1982), 'Corporate Vices and Corporate Virtues: Do Public/Private Distinctions Matter?' *University of Pennsylvania Law Review*, 130(6): 1441-1509.
Strawson, P. F. (1974), *Freedom and Resentment and Other Essays* (London, Methuen).
Sullivan, G. R. (1995), 'Expressing Corporate Guilt', *Oxford Journal of Legal Studies*, 15(2): 281-293.
—. (2002), 'Is Criminal Law Possible?' *Oxford Journal of Legal Studies*, 22(4): 747- 758.
Taylor, I. (1983), *Crime, Capitalism and Community* (Toronto: Butterworths).
Teubner, G. (ed) (1988), *Autopoietic Law: A New Approach to Law and Society* (Berlin: Walter and Gruyter).
Thomson Committee, (1975), *Criminal Procedure in Scotland* 2nd Report, Cmnd 6218 (Edinburgh: HMSO).
Thurman, W. A. (1937), *The Folklore of Capitalism* (New Haven: Yale University Press).
Todarello, V. (2002), 'Corporations Don't Kill People – People Do: Exploring the Goals of the United Kingdom's Corporate Homicide Bill', *New York Law School Law Review*, 46(8): 851-865.

Todd, S. (2003), 'Assuming responsibility for torts', *Law Quarterly Review*, 119: 199-204.

Tosi, H. L. (1990), 'A Contingency Model of Organizational Behavior' in Tosi, H. L. (ed) *Organizational Behavior and Management: A Contingency Approach* (Boston: PWS-Kent Publishing).

Townsend, J. (2006), 'The Human Rights of Companies: Exploring the Structure of the ECHR Protection', (Publication Review) *Human Rights Law Review*, 6(3): 593-597.

Tuomela, R., and Miller, K. 1988: 'We-Intentions', *Philosophical Studies* 53(3): 367-389.

Tur, R. (1987), 'The 'Person' in Law' in Peacocke, A., and Gillett, G. (eds) *Persons and Personality: A Contemporary Inquiry* (Oxford: Basil Blackwell).

Valeur, R. (1931), *La Responsabilité Pénale des Personnes Morales dans les Droits Français et Anglo-américain*s (Paris : Marcel Giard).

van Eeghen, P. (2005), 'The Corporation at Issue, Part 1: The Clash with Classical Liberal Values and the Negative Consequences for Capitalist Practice', *Journal of Libertarian Studies*, 19(3): 49-70.

Vu, S. N. (2004), 'Corporate Criminal Liability: Patchwork Verdicts and the Problem of Locating a Guilty Agent', *Columbia Law Review* 104(2): 459-495.

Wallace, R. J. (1994), *Responsibility and the Moral Sentiments* (Cambridge, Mass: Harvard).

Waller, L. (1987), 'Any Reasonable Creature in Being', *Monash University Law Review*, 13(1): 31-55.

Walsh, C. J., and Pyrich, A. (1995), 'Corporate Compliance Programs as a Defense to Criminal Liability', *Rutgers Law Review* 74(1): 605-691.

Waluchow, W. (1994), *Inclusive legal positivism* (Oxford: Oxford University Press).

Watkins, J. (2006), 'Responsibility in Context', *Oxford Journal of Legal Studies*, 26(3): 593-608.

Watts, P. (2001), 'Imputed Knowledge in Agency Law – Excising The Fraud Exception', *Law Quarterly Review*, 117: 300-333.

Wedderburn, K (1985), 'The Social Responsibility of Companies', *Melbourne University Law Review*, 15(1): 4-30.

Welch, P. W., and Turezyn, A. J. (1993), Folk on the Delaware General Corporation Law: Fundamentals (New York: Aspen).

Welch, P. W., Turezyn, A. J., and Saunders, R. S. (2006), Folk on the Delaware General Corporation Law: Fundamentals 5th edn (New York: Aspen)

Wells, C. (1988), 'The Decline and Rise of English Murder', *Criminal Law Review*: 788-801.
—. (1993), 'Corporations: Culture, Risk and Criminal Liability', *Criminal Law Review*: 551-566.
—. (1995), 'Corporate liability for crime: the neglected question', *International Banking and Financial Law*, 14(4): 42-44.
—. (1999), 'The Millennium Bug and Corporate Criminal Liability', *Journal of Information, Law and Technology*. Available at: http://www2.warwick.ac.uk/fac/soc/law/elj/jilt/1999_2/wells/wells.rtf [Accessed 16/10/2007].
—. (2001), *Corporations and Criminal Responsibility* 2nd edn (Oxford: Oxford University Press).
Welsh, R. S. (1946), 'The Criminal Liability of Corporations', *Law Quarterly Review*, 62: 345-365.
Weismann, A., and Newman, D. (2007), 'Rethinking Criminal Corporate Liability' *Indiana Law Journal*, 82(2): 411-451.
Westen, P. (2008), 'Offences and defences again', Oxford Journal of Legal Studies, 28(3): 563-584
Whittaker, S. (1997), 'The Application of the 'Broad Principle of *Hedley Byrne*' as between Parties to a Contract', *Legal Studies*, 17(1): 169-191.
Williams, G. (1957), 'Vicarious Liability and the Master's Indemnity', *Modern Law Review*, 20(5): 437-446.
—. (1961), *Criminal Law (The General Part)* 2nd edn (London: Stevens and Sons).
—. (1983), *Textbook of Criminal Law* 2nd edn (London: Gordon, Stevens and Sons).
Wilson, W. (2003), *Central Issues in Criminal Law Theory* (Oxford: Hart Publishing).
—. (2008), 'A Rational Scheme of Liability for Participating in Crime', *Criminal Law Review*, 1: 3-18.
Winfield, P. H. (1950), *Pollock's Principles of Contract* 13th edn (London: Stevens and Sons).
Witting, C. (2005), 'Duty of Care: An Analytical Approach', *Oxford Journal of Legal Studies*, 25(1): 33-63.
Wolf, S., (1985), 'The Legal and Moral Responsibility of Organizations' in Penncock, J. R., and Chapman, R. W. (eds) *Criminal Justice* (New York: New York University Press).
Wolff, M. (1938), 'On the Nature of Legal Persons', *Law Quarterly Review*, 54: 494-451.

Wolgast, E. (1992), *Ethics of an Artificial Person: Lost Responsibility in Professions and Organizations* (Stanford: Stanford University Press).

Wood, S. (1979), 'A Reappraisal of the Contingency Approach to Organization', *Journal of Management Studies*, 16(3): 334-354.

Woolf, T. (1995), 'The Criminal Code Act 1995 (Cth): Towards a Realist Vision of Corporate Criminal Liability', *Criminal Law Journal*, 21(5): 257-272.

Zemba, Y., Young, M. J., and Morris, M. W. (2006), 'Blaming Leaders for Organizational Accidents: Proxy Logic in Collective- versus Individual-Agency Cultures', *Organizational Behavior and Human Decision Processes*, 101(1):36-51.

Zimring, F. E., and Hawkins, G. J. (1973), *Deterrence: The Legal Threat in Crime Control* (Chicago: University of Chicago Press).

Index

A

absolute liability, 8, 12, 63, 65, 66, 67, 72, 80, 95, 96, 112, 125, 145, 147, 169, 179, 180, 189, 223, 231, 233, 249, 265, 267, 302
accessory, 52, 72, 90, 91, 92, 95, 96, 117, 146, 175, 214, 216, 251, 276, 290, 302, 303
Accountability Model, 247
accountability report, 249
actus reus, 8, 9, 43, 45, 63, 65, 67, 70, 80, 82, 86, 95, 99, 112, 119, 145, 150, 168, 170, 188, 190, 194, 195, 196, 197, 200, 202, 203, 206, 215, 222, 227, 249, 250, 251, 278, 279, 280, 281, 286, 287, 297, 301
aggregation, 88, 93, 123, 139, 147, 150, 164, 195, 196, 197, 198, 200, 201, 202, 203, 204, 205, 206, 207, 212, 217, 218, 219, 221, 222, 223, 228, 232, 234, 236, 238, 245, 260, 268, 269, 270, 279, 280, 281, 283, 284, 285, 286, 288, 289, 290, 291, 292, 293, 294, 295, 301, 306, 309
alter ego, 119, 127, 144, 146, 204, 293, 301
Auld, 240, 325
autonomy, 24, 35, 64, 65, 192, 207, 256

B

bad character, 234, 236, 237, 238, 242, 247, 269, 284
bankruptcy, 22, 258, 263
Bingham, 82, 279

Blackstone, 6, 16, 70

C

Caldecote, 9, 75, 78, 126, 128
capital punishment, 262
causation, 105
Channell J, 69, 70, 71, 72, 75, 80
coherence, 2
collective rationality, 40, 293, 294, 297, 298, 299, 301, 303, 310
collectivisation, 41, 52, 255, 289, 308
collectivism, 147, 247
collectivities
    hierarchical, 296
    summative, 296
common employment, 74, 179
communitarian theory, 28, 29
compensation, 28
compliance programme, 57, 91, 117, 216, 249, 296
concession theory, 25, 27, 28, 29, 30, 101
confidentiality of communications, 229
consequentialism, 45, 48, 49, 54, 64, 67, 174, 190, 252
corporate culture, 91, 116, 135, 152, 163, 193, 198, 205, 208, 209, 210, 211, 212, 213, 214, 215, 216, 217, 218, 219, 220, 221, 223, 228, 232, 234, 236, 238, 242, 245, 260, 268, 269, 270, 279, 280, 281, 283, 284, 285, 287, 291
corporate homicide, 9, 12, 81, 87, 162, 168, 169, 175, 231, 266, 268, 280, 286
Corporate Internal Decision Structure - CID, 136, 155, 172, 207

corporate manslaughter, 9, 12, 81, 85, 87, 162, 168, 169, 175, 231, 266, 268, 280, 286
cost of the prosecution, 244
criminal justice agencies, 10, 13, 100, 227, 238, 247, 250, 251, 253, 261, 283
Crown Office and Procurator Fiscal Service - COPFS, 233, 240, 247, 253, 271
Crown Prosecution Service - CPS, 148, 233, 247, 253, 271
culpable homicide, 81, 84, 86, 87, 96, 152, 161, 167, 170, 171, 173, 175

D

decision-making, 13, 39, 40, 127, 133, 136, 148, 161, 162, 165, 172, 194, 226, 227, 243, 260, 272, 289, 293, 297, 298, 299, 301, 303
Denning, Lord, 74, 78, 86, 117, 118, 119, 126, 127, 129, 144, 146, 158, 238, 298
deontological theory, 44, 46, 48, 49, 51, 52, 53, 55, 64, 68, 72, 76, 79, 183, 302
deterrence, 53, 58, 183
 general, 54
 specific deterence, 54
 trap, 256, 263
Dilhorne, Viscount, 131, 154, 155
directors' disqualification, 57, 251, 263, 292
directors' liability, 37
disattribution heresy, 186, 190
discursive dilemma, 38, 293, 295, 297, 298, 309
doctrinal paradox, 38, 294, 297
documentary evidence, 10, 234, 235, 239
due diligence, 9, 68, 74, 78, 117, 154, 170, 172, 182, 200, 201, 214, 219, 221, 266, 292, 295, 296, 298, 300
duty of care, 62, 87, 162, 163, 165, 166, 167, 168, 169, 175, 185, 186
duty of care
 Hedley Byrne, 186

E

employee necessity, 94, 303, 308
enforcement
 objective/target driven, 50, 54, 71
 pyramid, 248

F

Fenton Atkinson LJ, 89, 90
fiction theory, 4, 16, 17, 20, 26, 29, 31, 101, 113, 128, 129, 168
Financial Service Authority, 10, 251, 253, 258, 259, 266
fine, 69, 75, 248, 251, 256, 258, 263, 266, 272, 292
 equity, 257, 260, 264, 271
 level of, 259, 260, 261, 271
Finlay J, 45, 75
first-order reasons, 107
foresight, 83
fraud, 93, 115, 184, 237, 240, 241, 253, 302
 exception, 115

G

Great Western Trains, 66, 84, 86, 87, 279
gross breach, 87, 162, 163, 170
gross negligence, 64, 82, 83, 84, 85, 86, 163, 164, 166, 169, 170, 175, 185, 209, 223, 242
 manslaughter, 85, 170, 175
groups, 2, 50, 213, 257, 308
 identity, 38, 39
 purposive, 38, 59
 social expressions, 25, 40, 294

H

Haldane, Viscount, 73, 74, 75, 76, 78, 125, 127, 128, 129, 130, 146
harm, 21, 49, 50, 106, 270
  principle, 53, 54, 63
  prosecution, 244, 245, 246, 267, 270, 285, 292
  risk of, 181
harms
  prosecution, 116
Health and Safety Executive - HSE, 10, 230, 233, 238, 250
  Asbestos Licensing Unit - ALU, 262
hearsay rule, 10, 234, 235, 237, 242, 247, 283, 291
Herald of Free Enterprise, 51, 82, 95
Hoffmann, Lord, 5, 7, 11, 15, 16, 37, 69, 71, 79, 80, 97, 100, 101, 102, 103, 104, 108, 109, 113, 118, 129, 130, 144, 145, 149, 162, 168, 200, 299, 300, 304, 308

I

identification doctrine, 73, 80, 81, 82, 86, 87, 88, 96, 119, 125, 128, 143, 230
imprisonment, 57, 69
individual liability, 37, 99, 139, 149, 164
individualism, 35, 152, 172, 188, 202, 206, 238, 247
  methodological, 46, 146, 174
injunctions, 261
innocent agency, 50, 63, 64, 94, 95, 99, 150, 223, 278, 279, 281, 286, 290, 302, 308
integrity, 2
interpretation, 5, 11, 102, 108

J

juries, 10, 226, 239
  Auld Committee, 240
  magna carta, 239
  Roskill Committee, 240
just desert theory, 52, 64, 245, 257
justice
  procedural, 225
  restorative, 247

K

Kaldor-Hicks, 28, 318
knowledge, 5, 65, 101, 118, 128, 160, 199, 206, 272
  collective, 195, 197, 228
  constructive, 92, 93, 111, 113, 117, 118, 119, 151, 152, 165, 191, 201, 202, 214, 222, 277, 291, 296, 298, 305
  external, 2, 105, 120, 130, 133, 139, 307
  imputed, 9, 67, 172, 187, 197, 198, 200, 201, 203, 228
  juristic, 34
  personal, 10, 118, 235, 283

L

legal personality, 1, 11, 16, 23, 26, 30, 31, 32, 33, 34, 35, 36, 37, 38, 40, 42, 59, 60, 124, 125, 146, 162, 268, 276, 294
limited liability, 1, 27, 41, 59, 258, 263

M

MacNaghten, Lord, 124
manslaughter
  gross negligence, 83, 85, 86, 166, 170
mens rea, 8, 9, 12, 43, 45, 48, 50, 63, 64, 65, 66, 67, 68, 69, 71, 72, 76, 77, 80, 82, 87, 96, 112, 119, 145, 150, 168, 170, 188, 189, 190, 192, 194, 195, 196, 197, 199, 200, 201, 203, 207, 208, 209, 215, 222, 223, 227, 233,

277, 278, 279, 280, 281, 286, 287, 296
moral blameworthiness, 47, 48, 51, 52, 173, 252
moral stigma, 71
morality, 6, 7, 31, 46, 48, 107, 245, 246
motive, 203, 215

N

nationalisation, 264, 265, 271
negative retributivism, 53
normative perspectives, 121
Nourse LJ, 81, 88, 113, 128, 129, 131, 144, 159

O

obiter dicta, 16, 17, 108, 109, 110, 120, 139, 141, 153, 304, 305, 307
Office of Fair Trading, 230, 238, 251
order
    community, 261
    remedial, 57, 261, 292
organisation theory, 132
organisational liability, 209, 213, 223
overcriminalisation, 92

P

Pareto efficiency, 21, 28
Pearson, Lord, 131, 155, 156
police, 70, 241, 251, 252
policy, 71, 96, 105, 144, 183, 188, 189, 191, 207, 223, 231, 278
precedent, 5, 10, 107, 120
presentence, 248
probation, 248, 261
prosecution
    malicious, 245
    vexatious, 227
prosecution
    private, 227
psychology, 147, 187
public censure, 266, 271

Q

quasi crime, 71

R

real entity theory, 58
realist theory, 4, 17, 168
recklessness, 67, 84, 88
regulatory crime, 71
rehabilitation, 53, 54, 58
right to silence, 9, 229
risk assessment, 170, 181
Rose LJ, 80, 86, 200
rule
    change, 104
    primary, 12, 104, 105, 106, 108, 109, 110, 111, 112, 113, 117, 119, 120, 121, 123, 127, 128, 129, 130, 131, 133, 134, 135, 139, 140, 141, 143, 144, 145, 150, 151, 152, 153, 154, 160, 162, 163, 165, 168, 169, 171, 180, 182, 183, 184, 192, 197, 198, 204, 212, 215, 216, 217, 219, 277, 291, 301, 304, 305, 308
    recognition, 6, 12, 104, 109, 119, 120, 140, 142, 143, 144, 145, 152, 153, 160, 162, 171, 176, 192, 204, 212, 216, 217, 221, 277, 282, 291, 304, 305
    secondary, 12, 110, 133, 215, 309
    adjudication, 12, 13, 104, 109, 140, 142, 224, 225, 226, 247, 268, 270, 282, 283, 291, 304

S

Serious Fraud Office, 10, 230, 238, 240
Stable J, 45, 62, 88, 129, 154

strict liability, 48, 62, 63, 65, 66, 68, 71, 88, 93, 95, 104, 169, 174, 180, 182, 203, 226, 245, 266, 295, 296, 299
substantive reason, 107, 108, 109

T

Thurlow, Baron, 172
Turner J, 82, 84, 129, 148, 179

V

vicarious liability, 9, 66, 115, 177